How the Millennium Comes Violently
From Jonestown to Heaven's Gate

Catherine Wessinger

Foreword by
Jayne Seminare Docherty

SEVEN BRIDGES PRESS
NEW YORK • LONDON

Seven Bridges Press, LLC
135 Fifth Avenue, New York, N.Y. 10010

Publisher: Ted Bolen
Project manager: Electronic Publishing Services Inc., N.Y.C.
Cover design: Stefan Killen Design
Printing and binding: Versa Press, Inc.

Library of Congress Cataloging-in-Publication Data

Wessinger, Catherine.
    How the millennium comes violently: from Jonestown to Heaven's Gate / Catherine Wessinger.
        p. cm.
    Includes bibliographical references and index.
    ISBN 1-889119-24-5
    1. Millennialism Case studies.   2. Violence—Religious aspects Case Studies.   I. Title
    BL503.2.W47   2000
    291.2'3—dc21
                                                                            99-39978
                                                                                CIP

Manufactured in the United States of America
10   9   8   7   6   5   4   3   2   1

Dedicated to my parents,
Bryson and Ellen Lowman
with love and gratitude

May all beings be happy and safe,
and may their hearts
be filled with joy.

May all beings live
in security and peace—

whether weak or strong
large or small,
near or far away,
visible or invisible,
already born
or yet to be born—

May all of them dwell
in perfect tranquility.

—Heart of the Metta Sutta
as utilized by the Blue Iris Sangha, New Orleans, Louisiana

Contents

Acknowledgments

SCHOLARS WHO HAVE READ portions of this book and have given me very helpful feedback include Phillip Lucas, Jean Rosenfeld, J. Phillip Arnold, Michael Barkun, Eugene V. Gallagher, James Tabor, Linda Collette, Timothy Miller, Allen Sapp, Jeffrey Kaplan, Mary McCormick Maaga, Rebecca Moore, John R. Hall, Thomas Robbins, Michael York, Jayne Seminare Docherty, Ian Reader, Robert Kisala, David G. Goodman, Manabu Watanabe, James T. Richardson, Massimo Introvigne, Robert Balch, Lonnie Kliever, Richard Gardner, Dale A. Stover, and Jean-François Mayer.

Eugene V. Gallagher, Rebecca Moore, and Eileen Barker read the manuscript in its entirety and provided me with insightful critiques as well as encouragement.

I thank persons who provided me with various types of information. Timothy Miller, James Tabor, and Phillip Lucas forwarded important resources, and Jean Rosenfeld has provided me with numerous sources of information. I am appreciative to Laurie Efrein Kahalas for sending me a copy of her book on Jonestown. Robert L. Uzzel kindly sent news articles from Waco concerning the Branch Davidians. I have benefited from Carol Moore's "Waco Updates," which she distributes by email. I appreciate receiving written works from Livingstone Fagan, a surviving Branch Davidian, who is in prison. I am grateful to Eugene V. Gallagher for forwarding me the Waco negotiation transcripts on disk, and to J. Phillip Arnold for sending key audiotapes of the Waco negotiations and the videotapes made by the Branch Davidians during the siege. Phillip Arnold also has sent me information relating to the Montana Freemen. I am grateful to the Telah Foundation for sending me the four videotapes prepared by Do and the students in Heaven's Gate before their exit. I am grateful to the late Chuck Humphrey, a Heaven's Gate believer, for making available the group's "Blue Book," *How and When "Heaven's Gate" (The Door to the Physical Kingdom Level Above Human) May Be Entered*, before he exited. I thank Christine Wicker, religion newswriter for the *Dallas Morning News*, for forwarding to me articles on Chen Tao that were not posted on the newspaper's web page. I am grateful to Massimo Introvigne and Forrest Jackson for sending the Chen Tao desktop-published book, *God's Descending in Clouds (Flying Saucers) on Earth to Save People*. All of these have been crucial sources of data.

I am grateful to David Estes and Leslie Parr of Loyola University, New Orleans, for including me in their faculty seminar on photography and America. I appreciate the collegiality and insights of the colleagues who participated in this seminar: Mark Fernandez, Rosalee McReynolds, David Moore, Mary McCay, Larry Lorenz, Alex Reichl, and Barbara Ewell. My participation in this NEH-funded seminar was an impetus to including photographs in this book.

I received help locating the photographs used in this volume from a number of people. Clair Johnson of the *Billings Gazette* located photographs of the Montana Freemen. Christine Wicker, religion newswriter of the *Dallas Morning News*, directed me to the correct person from whom to obtain photographs of Chen Tao. I am a big fan of the accurate and balanced reporting of both Clair Johnson and Christine Wicker. Their non-sensationalized and humane reporting contributed positively to the peaceful resolutions of the Freemen standoff and the Chen Tao episode in Garland, Texas. I thank Francis Hogan of Electronic Publishing Services, Inc., for his research of photographs. I am grateful to Lt. Rod Gregg of the Garland, Texas, police for providing his photographs of Chen Tao. I am grateful to Rebecca Moore and her parents John and Barbara Moore for giving me permission to use their photographs of family members in Jonestown. I have been touched and impressed by the sincere, intelligent, and self-reflective manner in which they have sought to understand the deaths of Carolyn, Annie, and Kimo. I am deeply appreciative of their trust in me.

I thank Brooks Ellis of Electronic Publishing Services, Inc., and Katharine Miller of Seven Bridges Press for their work on the manuscript. My appreciation goes to Ted Bolen of Seven Bridges Press for the vision and energy with which he has promoted this book.

I express my deep gratitude to Carol Cortazzo, the administrative assistant for the Religious Studies Dept. at Loyola University, New Orleans. Carol has kept me organized and efficient for thirteen years—no mean feat! The department and its faculty would not work as well without her compassionate and meticulous attention.

I am indebted to my aforementioned colleagues, who study new religious movements, for their numerous kindnesses and insights. They are excellent educators, researchers, and coworkers in trying to make the world a little better place. This is an exciting period in which to try to understand the varieties of millennialism as expressions of human nature, and I have benefited from the friendship of these many colleagues in the course of this adventure.

Catherine Wessinger

Loyola University, New Orleans

〈http://www.loyno.edu/~wessing〉

Foreword

WE ARE BLESSED, OR CURSED, to live in interesting times. As the new millennium fast approaches, rationalists among us pooh-pooh the significance of a date that happens to end in three zeroes. And, the rationalists are correct. The demarcation of a millennium—a period lasting one thousand years—is an arbitrary act of human categorization. In this respect, it is unlike temporal cycles associated with such natural phenomena as earthly rotations, or revolutions of the moon around the earth, or the earth around the sun.[1] But millennialism as a system of belief is not driven by dates on a calendar or the natural cycles of the cosmos. Millennialism is about human hope, the longing for a time when the limitations of the human condition will be transformed. In *Millennialism, Persecution, and Violence: Historical Cases*, Catherine Wessinger gathered accounts of millennial movements from around the world.[2] It is obvious from these case studies that the yearning for an end to illness, suffering, death, injustice, conflict, war, and other human travails transcends the bounds of culture and history. Indeed, a propensity toward millennial beliefs appears to be imprinted on the human psyche, awaiting the appropriate mix of collective anxiety, "signs" of social breakdown, and rhetorical themes to burst full-grown upon the stage of history.

Many millennial movements are associated with oppressed cultures. South Pacific Island communities, traumatized first by the imposition of a foreign culture by missionaries and then by occupying armies during World War II, eagerly anticipated a coming age of wealth and plenty. The Plains Indians of North America, defeated by the onslaught of white settlers, took up the Ghost Dance. They expected their ritual to bring a return of the buffalo, a restoration of Indian culture, and the disappearance of the White Man. Instead, it brought them Wounded Knee. But millennial beliefs are not the sole province of oppressed communities. Millennialism also has fueled large-scale political movements such as Nazism, the Taiping Revolution, the Khmer Rouge, and Mao's Great Leap Forward.[3] Today, millennial themes are evident in the rhetoric of nationalist and ethnic-identity movements around the world, including the Serbian nationalism espoused by Slobodan Milosevic.

In spite of the great variety of social and political movements organized around millennial beliefs, millennialism is most commonly associated in the popular press with groups that are pejoratively labeled "cults." The leaders of these unconventional religious groups are caricatured as manipulative madmen. Their followers are portrayed as brainwashed victims, and, collectively, they are treated with suspicion, fear, and ridicule. The result of ensuing interactions between millennial groups and the societies within which they emerge is, in all too many cases, violent. Why does this happen? How does it happen? And, more importantly, can violent confrontations between millennial groups and the larger society be prevented? These are the questions to which Wessinger directs her attention in this volume.

In a refreshing break from popular—and even scholarly—literature, Wessinger begins with the premise that violent confrontations cannot be explained solely by the defective character attributes of one party. Violence is not about "good guys" and "bad guys." And violence is not an inherent characteristic of millennial movements. The roots of any violent encounter are *interactive*. Millennial groups that become involved in violence do so as a consequence of factors specific to the group *combined with* the types of responses they evoke from "outsiders." If we want to understand the scenes of violence associated with Jonestown, the Branch Davidians, Aum Shinrikyo, Solar Temple, and Heaven's Gate, we must examine the internal characteristics of those groups *and* the responses they elicited from society. If we want to understand why violence did not occur in potentially volatile situations such as the FBI standoff with the Montana Freemen, or the failed prophecy in 1998 of the Chen Tao community, we must examine the same combination of internal and relational factors.

Juggling all of these internal and relational variables is no small feat. Just describing the internal factors that influence the actions of a millennial group requires a full array of analytical skills. One must be a student of sacred texts able to interpret even the most esoteric and obscure written documents or sermons. One must be an organizational expert cognizant of the internal structures and relational dynamics that occur in sectarian communities. One must be a rhetorician capable of explaining millennial themes and their impact on the actions of believers. Describing the relational factors that may embroil millennial groups and the representatives of mainstream society in violence requires additional expertise. One must be a public administration expert able to explain the actions and motivations of various organizations mandated to uphold the dominant social order. One must be a political scientist aware of the external pressures placed on social control organizations. One must be an expert in conflict studies able to identify and articulate cycles of conflict escalation and de-escalation. And, one must be an interpretive anthropologist capable of describing the meaning and belief systems of millennial groups, social control agents, and the society in which they both exist.

It is always easier to explain violence by detailing the evils of a single party. Saddam Hussein is another Hitler and the Iraqi people are being duped or coerced into following him. Iraq has no legitimate grievances against Kuwait. Hussein is a dangerous threat to the world order. Law-abiding nations have no choice but to wage a war against Iraq. David Koresh is a madman who is victimizing his followers. The Branch Davidians have no legitimate religious convictions. They are a threat to the peace of the community. Law enforcement agents have no choice but to raid Mount Carmel. The parallels in reasoning are obvious to anyone who cares to examine them.

Millennial groups, like "rogue nations," are particularly easy to demonize. They hold unusual beliefs. They see the world in ways that oppose a commonly accepted sense of reality. And, as a result of their beliefs, they engage in practices that outsiders consider deviant or dangerous. Because millennial groups view "mainstream" society with suspicion and distrust, they tend to live in relative isolation. If millennialists attempt to explain their beliefs and behaviors, they sound crazy to most people.

When members of millennial groups must interact with public agencies, such as a child welfare department or the police, the encounters often are tense. Officials may assume that group members are irrational, unpredictable, and possibly violent. Acting out of their own fear or suspicion, public officials may approach a millennial group in ways that feed further the suspicion and distrust of the group. The result can be an escalatory cycle of encounters that ends in violence. Only by better understanding millennial groups and the ways they are likely to respond to encounters with mainstream society can we hope to prevent tragedies such as Jonestown or Waco.

Unfortunately, understanding millennial groups usually has appeared impossible to most people outside of the academy. Wessinger is working to change that. She, with a handful of other scholars, has shouldered the task of making research on millennial movements readily available to non-academics, including law enforcement agents. Wessinger is motivated in part by a sense of her own "complicity in passively watching [the FBI/Branch Davidian standoff] unfold in the news." There is ample guilt to go around regarding Waco. And not all of the guilt belongs to Religious Studies scholars. Few members of my own field of conflict resolution made any effort to help the FBI find a nonviolent way out of their encounter with the Branch Davidians. Fewer still are now reaching out to public officials in preparation for future encounters with millennial groups. Thus, Wessinger's book is refreshing in two respects: It is academically substantial; and, it is an important contribution to the dialogue between Religious Studies scholars and nonacademics who need to understand millennial groups.

Wessinger demonstrates her own mastery of the many skills necessary for studying encounters between millennial groups and society. For this, she deserves the respect of her academic colleagues. Even more noteworthy than her case studies, however, are the conceptual tools Wessinger develops for categorizing, interpreting, and understanding millennial groups. For this, Wessinger no doubt will receive the ultimate praise in academe; others will appropriate and expand her conceptual framework. I fully expect concepts such as *fragile millennial groups*, *assaulted millennial groups*, and *revolutionary millennial movements* to enter the standard vocabulary of scholars who study new religious movements.

· But, more important than academic honors, Wessinger's work deserves the attention of all those public servants whose jobs may involve them in managing delicate diplomatic encounters between a millennial group and mainstream social institutions. For them, this book is a must read. Wessinger provides a commonsense, clear vocabulary for understanding millennial beliefs. She also develops usable, dynamic conceptual categories capable of describing the complex mix of internal characteristics and relational encounters that shape a millennial group's decision to embrace or reject violence. Finally, Wessinger demonstrates the power of her insights by applying them to the most dramatic and largely misunderstood recent incidences of violence involving millennial groups.

Throughout her analysis, Wessinger is fair-minded and even-handed. She refuses to replace a demonizing narrative about millennial groups with a demonizing narrative about public officials or law enforcement agents. She raises tough questions. She does not overstate her argument. Nor does she avoid identifying what we don't know about millennialism and violence. This blend of scholarship, practicality, integrity, and humility leads me to hope that Wessinger's conceptual framework and ideas will also infiltrate the practical realm.

Jayne Seminare Docherty
Assistant Professor of Conflict Resolution
Columbia College of South Carolina

Notes

1. Stephen Jay Gould, *Questioning the Millennium: A Rationalist's Guide to a Precisely Arbitrary Countdown* (New York: Harmony Books, 1997).
2. Catherine Wessinger, ed., *Millennialism, Persecution, and Violence: Historical Cases* (Syracuse: Syracuse University Press, 2000).
3. Wessinger, *Millennialism, Persecution, and Violence*.

CHAPTER ONE

Introduction

My Involvement

When Jonestown occurred in 1978, I was a graduate student at the University of Iowa focusing on the religions of India. Jonestown was shocking and tragic, but it was not something for which I had to account.

When the Branch Davidian tragedy occurred in 1993, I was a professor teaching Religious Studies at Loyola University in New Orleans, and I was the chair of the New Religious Movements Group, a program unit in the American Academy of Religion. After the ill-fated assault on the Mount Carmel Center, the Branch Davidian residence, on February 28, 1993, by agents of the Bureau of Alcohol, Tobacco, and Firearms (BATF or ATF), and all throughout the fifty-one-day siege, I checked the news daily. I wondered how the siege would be resolved. I naively believed the news reports that FBI agents were consulting experts, and I took comfort in the length of the siege. There was ample time for FBI agents to consult experts on unconventional religions and to develop a strategy that avoided the mistake of the ATF agents—excessive force used against an armed religious group that believed it was the godly community that would be attacked by satanic "Babylon."

I should have been tipped off, however, when the media reported that FBI agents were consulting "cult experts." *Bona fide* scholars who study new religious movements (NRMs) usually avoid the pejorative term, *cult*, but at that time, I thought reporters were utilizing the term for alternative religions with which they were most familiar. I should have been alerted also by the fact that no one I knew in the field of NRM studies was being consulted by the FBI.

On April 19, 1993, I was teaching a class in which I mentioned the Branch Davidians as an example of a millennial religion. One of my students raised his hand and informed me that after an assault by tanks, the

Branch Davidian residence was going up in flames, and "no one is coming out." I rushed home that afternoon to watch on television the horrifying inferno that killed fifty-one adults and twenty-three children. This was a tragedy that I needed to understand. I needed to account for my own complicity in passively watching it unfold in the news.

In order to understand the Branch Davidian tragedy, I found that I needed to understand Jonestown, and other millennial groups such as Aum Shinrikyo, whose members released nerve gas in Tokyo subway trains in 1995. My emerging understanding of potentially violent millennial groups was put to practical application when I and other scholars advised FBI agents during the Freemen standoff in Montana in 1996. At that time, I offered to the FBI a theory that a sense of persecution could prompt members of an armed millennial group to commit violence, especially if they were so pressured as to cause them to despair of achieving their *ultimate concern* (their religious goal). The low-key approach taken by FBI agents in the Freemen standoff successfully avoided persecution. Furthermore, FBI agents offered final terms to the Freemen that permitted them to remain faithful to their ultimate concern and be taken into custody (see chapter 6).

In March 1997, the American public was startled by the group suicide of thirty-nine members of Heaven's Gate in a mansion near San Diego. These people believed that by abandoning their earthly bodies, they would receive eternal extraterrestrial bodies on a mothership that was following the Hale-Bopp comet. This was their way of entering the Kingdom of Heaven. As I examined the documents posted on the Heaven's Gate web site, I found that feelings of persecution contributed to the decision of Marshall Herff Applewhite ("Do") and his followers to exit planet Earth. The Heaven's Gate group also possessed internal weaknesses caused by the leaders that called into question whether they would achieve their ultimate concern (see chapter 7). In the case of Heaven's Gate, the process involving internal stresses and a sense of persecution took about twenty-five years to culminate in the suicide of the thirty-nine. Group suicide was the strategy adopted to preserve their ultimate goal.

In my book published in 1988, *Annie Besant and Progressive Messianism*, I predicted that as we neared the year 2000, manifestations of millennialism would increase.[1] This was not a difficult prediction to make. The approach of the new millennium was bound to excite people's imaginations to hope that the limitations of the human condition would be transcended once and for all. Scholars have termed this hope for earthly salvation *millennialism* or *millenarianism,* because so often terrestrial perfection has been expected to last for one thousand years. In scholarly discourse, the term *millennium* has become divorced from its original reference to a period lasting one thousand years, and is used as a synonym for belief in a collective terrestrial salvation, "the kingdom of God on earth." Believers expect that in the millennial kingdom, limitations of the human condition such as illness, suffering, death, injustice, conflict, and war will be overcome. Many millennialists expect the millennial kingdom to be earthly, but Heaven's Gate is a reminder that millennialists also can expect the millennial kingdom to be heavenly or other-worldly. Often there will be ambiguity in the minds of millennialists about whether the millennial kingdom will be heavenly or earthly. This appears to have been the case with the Branch Davidians, and also with the early followers of Jesus of Nazareth.

What has surprised me is the number of millennial groups involved in violence that have erupted into the news as the year 2000 approached. In 1992, there was the conflict between federal law enforcement officers and the Weaver family at Ruby Ridge, Idaho. In 1993 the Branch Davidian tragedy occurred, again, involving conflict with federal law enforcement officers. In 1994, the first Solar Temple deaths took place involving French-speaking people in Quebec, France, and Switzerland in murders and group suicides. In 1995, members of Aum Shinrikyo released sarin gas on the Tokyo subway. In 1996, there was the 81-day standoff in Justus Township Montana between FBI agents and the Freemen, whose religious beliefs are known as Christian Identity. In 1997, the Heaven's Gate group suicide occurred.

It is my hope that this book will be helpful to potential converts and members of NRMs, concerned relatives of members, the neighbors of unconventional religious communities, law enforcement agents, news reporters, and scholars by illuminating the characteristics and dynamics that can contribute to the volatility of religious groups. The manner in which outsiders interact with a millennial group is an important factor in stimulating volatility. Still, scholars should refrain from predicting violence in some groups or giving a "clean bill of health" to other religious groups. There is always the factor of human free will that makes it impossible to predict such things reliably. We can never know in advance what actions individuals will choose, and there will always be new contributing factors to be identified in future studies.

Religions, Not "Cults"

The reader will have noticed that I have refrained from calling the religious groups studied in this book "cults." The word *cult* originally referred to an organized system of worship focused on an object of worship. According to this neutral and descriptive definition, the Roman Catholic Mass is a cult, as are other systems of worship. Since the 1970s, however, the word *cult* has taken on pejorative connotations. It is a term widely used to refer to religious groups regarded as aberrant and dangerous. It is a convenient four-letter word to put into headlines.

Today *cult* is a put-down, an insult conveying that a group is despised by the social mainstream. *Cult* has become a word that expresses prejudice against a religious group. It imposes on the group a simplistic stereotype that is assumed to be true. Most Americans are not yet aware of the bigoted stereotype conveyed in the word *cult*[2] as it is applied to religions that people don't understand and don't like. It expresses prejudice and antagonism just as much as racial slurs and insulting words for women and homosexuals. *Cult* represents an oversimplified and bigoted stereotype that is applied to numerous diverse religions.

It is important that people become aware of the bigotry conveyed by *cult*. The word *cult* dehumanizes the religion's members and their children. It strongly implies that these people are deviants; they are seen as crazy, brainwashed, duped by their leader. When we label people as subhuman, we create a context in which it is considered virtuous to kill them. For instance, in the nineteenth century, when Joseph Smith received his revelation and founded the Church of Jesus Christ of the Latter-day Saints, its members, the Mormons, were violently driven from New York, Ohio, Missouri, and Illinois. On October 27, 1838, the governor of Missouri issued an "Order of Extermination" stating, "The Mormons must be treated as enemies and must be exterminated or driven from the state for the public good." Eighteen Mormons were massacred by the state militia at Shoal Creek. Sardius Smith, who shot and killed a ten-year-old boy, explained, "Nits will make lice and if he had lived he would have become a Mormon."[3] The Mormons were fortunate that the American frontier provided space for them to move far away from their oppressors in mainstream society, and thus they were able to succeed in building a society in which *their* church was dominant. Mormons in the twentieth century are a respected part of the American mainstream. Today, however, members of NRMs do not have the space to flee their social opponents. Labeling people with dehumanizing names continues to be a means of justifying violence against members of new and unconventional religions. The label *cult* played a role in determining how ATF and FBI agents related to the Branch Davidians (see chapter 4).

When we label a group with the pejorative term *cult*, it makes us feel safe because the violence associated with religion is split off from conventional religions, projected onto others, and imagined to involve only aberrant groups. As we well know, however, child abuse, sexual abuse, financial extortion, torture, terrorism, murder, and warfare also have been committed by mainstream religious believers. The human desires, weaknesses, and evils that produce violence are expressed by members of mainstream religious institutions as well as of marginal groups, but the pejorative stereotype of the "cult" helps us avoid confronting this uncomfortable fact.

I study unconventional religions in the same manner that I study all religions. The comparative study of the world's religions shows that beliefs and practices that are regarded as strange in one religion are normative in another. For instance, Hindus and Buddhists believe in reincarnation, while reincarnation is viewed by most Christians as an unusual belief associated with "cults." Conversely, Christians believe that Jesus's resurrection from the dead is true, but this doctrine is viewed by members of other religions as fantastic and unbelievable.

The groups examined in this book that were involved in violence, the Peoples Temple (Jonestown), the Branch Davidians, Aum Shinrikyo, the Montana Freemen, the Solar Temple, and Heaven's Gate were *religions*. These were religions whose members became involved in violence, or as in the case of the Montana Freemen, had great potential for violence. In chapter 8, a final group is considered that did not become involved in violence. Chen Tao, a Taiwanese millennial group that had relocated to Garland, Texas, attracted media attention in 1998 as potentially violent. *How the Millennium Comes Violently* is a comparative study of these religious groups to determine the characteristics that contribute to volatile episodes.

A *religion* is a comprehensive worldview that makes sense of the universe and of human existence. Religion explains where we came from and where we are going. Religion teaches what is right and what is wrong. Religion is an expression of an *ultimate concern,* which is the most important thing in the world for an individual or group.[4] The ultimate concern is the religious goal people want to achieve, and this goal is about achieving a condition of permanent well-being (salvation). The ultimate concern may be heaven, the Kingdom of God on earth, escape from the cycle of rebirth (as in Hinduism and Buddhism), or perfect happiness in everyday life. The ultimate concern is determined by the religion's cosmology and understanding of human nature. A *cosmology* is a view of the universe and its source (for instance, God, multiple gods, extraterrestrials). The cosmology also pinpoints the source of evil (for example, Satan, demons, space aliens). A religion's view of human nature may involve beliefs about life after death and about how humans were created. The view of human nature will state whether humans are capable of achieving the ultimate goal through self-effort, or whether they must rely on divine assistance. The cosmology and understanding of human nature will determine the methods used to obtain the ultimate goal. These methods may consist of prayer, faith and worship, meditation, yogic disciplines, God's grace, the guru's grace, asceticism, community-building, or social reform.

The ultimate concerns studied in this book are related to *millennialism,* the belief in an imminent transition to a collective condition consisting of total well-being (salvation), which may be earthly or heavenly. Millennialism entails a "collective salvation," because it involves a group, not salvation for individuals only. In the following chapters' subheadings, the term I use to refer to the ultimate concern of a millennial religion is the *millennial goal*.

"Brainwashing" and the Charismatic Leader

The "cult" stereotype conveys the belief that members of unconventional religions are "brainwashed." The brainwashing theory provides a simplistic explanation of why people adopt strange beliefs that are unbelievable to members of mainstream society. The brainwashing theory overlooks the fact that mainstream social and religious institutions also indoctrinate and socialize people. Children are indoctrinated in Sunday and church schools, in catechism classes, and by homeschooling. Individuals attending military schools are socialized in brutal hazing processes.[5] Persons joining the military are indoctrinated and socialized in boot camp. We are all socialized by our parents, teachers, ministers, friends, spouses, and peers. Sometimes we choose to convert from one worldview to another when an alternative perspective is presented in a persuasive manner. Usually, however, the processes utilized by members of NRMs to attract and socialize converts are not different from those used in mainstream families and institutions.

Belief in brainwashing offers a simplistic explanation for why people adopt unconventional beliefs. It obscures the fact that people adopt alternative beliefs because those beliefs make sense to them, and that people join groups because those groups offer them benefits. Brainwashing is a handy excuse for the person who has defected from an unconventional religion. She or he can claim temporary loss of good judgment and free will. Theoretically, if a person is successfully brainwashed, she or he would be incapable of choosing to leave. In reality, most people who choose to join an NRM subsequently choose to leave it. NRMs typically have a high rate of turnover in membership.

In mainstream society, brainwashing is commonly assumed to be real, and the following chapters demonstrate that the leaders and members of Peoples Temple, Branch Davidians, Aum Shinrikyo, the Freemen, and Heaven's Gate also believed in brainwashing. They all regarded people in mainstream society as being brainwashed by television, the media, educational institutions, and by the values of materialistic society. They believed that their respective groups taught the truth as opposed to the delusions of the brainwashed people in external society. In most cases, the members willingly undertook the discipline and lifestyle of their unconventional religion, which they believed would lead to achieving salvation, their ultimate concern.

This is not to say that some of these groups did not resort to coercive measures to keep people from defecting. Some people in Jonestown were drugged and confined to keep them from voicing dissent or leaving. Prior to the mass suicide, a number of individuals and families did leave—either by walking away or by departing with the visiting delegation led by Congressman Leo Ryan. There is documentation[6] that Jonestown residents discussed group suicide as an option and came to a consensus that what they called "revolutionary suicide" was an honorable way to preserve their ultimate concern when under attack. Contrary to media assertions, there is no evidence that able-bodied persons in Jonestown were physically coerced into committing suicide (see chapter 3).

Prior to the 1993 Waco siege, Branch Davidians were free to defect. During the siege, people could come out of the Mount Carmel Center (their home and church) whenever they chose. This may not have been true of Koresh's young wives and their children, but we have no evidence that they wanted to come out (see chapter 4).

Aum Shinrikyo made extensive use of coercion, confinement, and drugs in attempting to program dissidents into compliant devotees. Aum's brutal indoctrination methods severely hurt numerous people and probably caused deaths. But there were people who, despite the severe indoctrination and torture, managed to escape Aum. Aum's attempts to brainwash forceably people were notably ineffective. People who rejected Aum's beliefs continued to reject them, despite being confined and coercively indoctrinated (see chapter 5). On the other hand, devotees who believed in Aum doctrines willingly subjected themselves to socialization procedures, such as listening to audiotaped affirmations for long periods of time. Because believers voluntarily participated in the socialization processes, their socialization was more successful than the coercive measures imposed on unbelievers.

Robert Balch's study of the group that became known as Heaven's Gate reveals that in 1975, when the two leaders were first gaining converts to their message, there was little socialization, little indoctrination, and little organization, and not surprisingly, many people left. In 1976, the leaders instituted monastic disciplines in which believers willingly participated. These social influence processes, which included periods of silence, celibacy, withdrawal from society, focusing on the present moment, daily work, special diets, and the cultivation of dependence on the two leaders as the means to enter the Kingdom of Heaven, are common in monastic institutions in the world's religions. That these disciplines were undertaken voluntarily made the socialization quite effective, so that even when members chose to leave the group, they usually remained believers.[7] Note, however, that the successful socialization of Heaven's Gate believers did not eliminate the free will of those who chose to leave.

The "cult" stereotype often alleges that the members of an NRM are under the mind control of the charismatic leader. *Charisma*, in the academic field of Religious Studies, refers to the quality of someone believed by a group to receive special revelation from an unseen source (such as God, angels, masters, extraterrestrials). An individual claiming charisma will have no impact unless others believe his or her claim to be true. If people believe a person's claim that he or she receives special revelation, a religious group will form around the charismatic leader. Acknowledged charisma certainly gives a leader the potential to exercise a great deal of power over peoples' lives, although the charismatic leader also will have to cope with other people in the group claiming that they, too, receive revelation. It is not easy to maintain the position of being the sole charismatic leader of a religious group. After one person receives revelation from an unseen source, probably other people in the movement will make the same claim.[8]

In a new religious group, a charismatic leader can exercise control over people only to the extent that followers permit and implement that control. The agency, free will, and judgment of the believers are crucial in determining whether a charismatic leader has the scope to develop totalitarian control over followers.

Aum Shinrikyo demonstrates that once coercive practices are implemented on a large scale, it can be very difficult to leave. We know this also from the example of Nazi Germany and other totalitarian governments. Aum Shinrikyo dissidents often were detained and coerced into staying. After his arrest, Yoshihiro Inoue, the former Aum Shinrikyo Minister of Intelligence, described the evolution of Asahara into a totalitarian leader, as well as Inoue's own motivations for carrying out criminal actions on behalf of Aum. Inoue reported, "At first, he [Asahara] was like a teacher. Then he became more of an absolute leader." Asahara could not have become an absolute leader without the agency and complicity of his followers. Why did Inoue continue to carry out Aum's criminal activities? "I was afraid that if I got out that I would be killed, but I also wanted enlightenment. I was fooling myself."[9] Inoue was motivated to achieve Aum's ultimate concern (enlightenment), but as he found out, once the charismatic leader acquired a critical mass of followers willing to kill to achieve the religious goal and to protect the charismatic leader and his organization, it was nearly impossible to extricate oneself. This is how totalitarian states are made, and we each have the responsibility not to facilitate the formation of such institutions.

A totalitarian group threatens imprisonment, torture, and/or death on dissidents who do not support its goal and methods. The extreme example of totalitarianism is related to the fact that members of NRMs may find it difficult to leave because these "exit costs" appear to outweigh the benefits of staying in the group.[10] Most of the people who chose to leave Jonestown, which was located in the jungles of Guyana, were Euro-Americans who had the financial and personal resources to make the transition back into American culture. The African-American residents of Jonestown lacked those resources. They literally had nowhere else to go; they did not want to return to the dehumanizing ghettos of racist America. They and the whites loyal to them chose to die together in Jonestown rather than return to unjust American society.

We should consider carefully the consequences of permitting our socialization into any group with which we are considering an affiliation. If we are attracted to a charismatic leader, we should weigh the possible consequences of giving so much authority to one person. We need to consider carefully the activities required by a religious commitment, especially the consequences of affiliation with a group that requires abandonment of one's former identity, family, and associations, and requires that one's entire income and assets be given to the group. In such a case, it will cost a great deal to leave if the situation turns out to be unsatisfactory.

Jonestown and Aum Shinrikyo are extreme cases of groups that resorted to coercion to detain members. More commonly, people join an unconventional religious group out of personal choice, because its worldview makes sense to them, and the religion offers a congenial social group, an alternative family. Usually, people leave a marginal religion due to personal choice; they no longer find its worldview plausible, or they have formed negative judgments about the leader, believers, or the organization.

The Montana Freemen offer an interesting case, because the Freemen are part of a diffuse millennial movement that, at present, has not developed a single charismatic leader. The Freemen's religious worldview, Christian Identity, teaches an understanding of human nature that many Americans find abhorrent (although many do not). According to Christian Identity, white Americans are the true Israelites of the Old Testament; they are Yahweh's chosen people who were given the promised land of America. Many Identity Christians also believe that Jews are the offspring of Satan, and that people of color are animals. This unconventional cosmology and understanding of human nature is not the product of a single charismatic leader. It is the product of an accumulated tradition of numerous individuals' thought that goes back at least to the nineteenth century.[11] Christian Identity is an example of a diffuse movement of people coming to a consensus about a shared worldview.[12] Christian Identity has many pastors and leaders, but there is no one charismatic leader to "brainwash" anyone. Christian Identity is a religion that has been the product of many people reading and interpreting the King James Version of the Bible. People become Identity Christians because the worldview makes sense to them and they find benefits in adopting the faith. People may choose to repudiate Christian Identity when it no longer makes sense to them and there are costs to remaining Identity Christians that they do not want to pay.

Many people are offended when Christian Identity is studied as a religion and its adherents are termed Christians. However, Christian Identity meets my criteria for a religion. It has an ultimate concern (which involves white supremacy), a cosmology, a view of human nature, and methods to achieve the ultimate concern. The King James Version of the Bible is an important scripture for Christian Identity. The believers consider themselves Christians; they regard Jesus as their savior, and Yahweh as God. Although I find the Christian Identity views of Jews and people of color abhorrent, I believe it is important to make a serious study of the religion, while refraining from demonizing Identity Christians. Although Identity Christians demonize and dehumanize groups of human beings, they will not be integrated into mainstream society by reciprocal demonization. Mutual demonization only results in coordinated warfare and/or random acts of terrorism. The Identity Christians who have repudiated their racist and anti-Semitic beliefs have done so because they experienced the humanity of the "other" through acts of kindness directed toward them and through mutually respectful dialogue.

The Case Studies

Each of the following chapters on Jonestown, the Branch Davidians, Aum Shinrikyo, and the Montana Freemen begins with a mystery. The same organization is followed in my treatment of the Solar Temple and Heaven's Gate in chapter 7. The mystery is the violence that occurred, or in the case of the Freemen, their potential for violence. In order to understand why violence did or did not occur, each chapter describes the characteristics of the leader (in the case of the Freemen, the cast of characters), the religious group, their millennial views, whether or not the group experienced persecution, whether the group's millennial goal (their ultimate concern) was failing, and how the group arrived at the decision to commit or to refrain from violence.

Chapter 8 provides a treatment of Chen Tao, a group that was not involved in violence when it became prominent in the news in 1998, but which shared numerous characteristics with the groups involved in violence studied in this book. I take a different approach in discussing Chen Tao, first listing Chen Tao's characteristics that could promote violence in a "minus column" and its positive characteristics in a "plus column," and then discussing the significance of each of these characteristics. This leads to the comparative conclusions drawn in chapter 9.

In the next chapter, I provide a general description of how the millennium comes violently.

Notes

1. Catherine Lowman Wessinger, *Annie Besant and Progressive Messianism* (Lewiston, N.Y.: Edwin Mellen Press, 1988).
2. In other languages, a version of the word *sect* is the pejorative term. The French word *secte,* the Spanish word *secta,* the German word *sekte,* and the Italian word *setta* would be best translated with the English word *cult* in its pejorative sense. Any formerly neutral word can be given pejorative connotations by society. I thank Massimo Introvigne for informing me of the pejorative words for *cult* in European languages.
3. Michael W. Homer, "Violence in Nineteenth-Century New Religion: The Mormon Case," paper presented at the Society for the Scientific Study of Religion, Nashville, November 10, 1996, 3.
4. Robert D. Baird, *Category Formation and the History of Religions* (The Hague: Mouton, 1971).
5. I think that when someone permits himself or herself to be brutally hazed to join a group, whether it is a military school, a fraternity or sorority, or a religious organization, that person is then motivated to recruit other people to the group to prove to self and others that he or she was not stupid to submit to such demeaning socialization.
6. Mary McCormick Maaga, "Triple Erasure: Women and Power in Peoples Temple," Ph.D. dissertation, Drew University, 1996. Maaga's dissertation has been published as *Hearing the Voices of Jonestown: Putting a Human Face on an American Tragedy* (Syracuse: Syracuse University Press, 1998).
7. Robert W. Balch, "Waiting for the Ships: Disillusionment and the Revitalization of Faith in Bo and Peep's UFO Cult," in *The Gods Have Landed: New Religions from Other Worlds*, ed. James R. Lewis (Albany: State University of New York Press, 1995), 137-66.
8. For examples, see Catherine Wessinger, "Democracy vs. Hierarchy: The Evolution of Authority in the Theosophical Society," 93-106; and Steven L. Shields, "The Latter-day Saint Movement: A Study in Survival," 59-77; both in *When Prophets Die: The Postcharismatic Fate of New Religious Movements*, ed. Timothy Miller (Albany: State University of New York Press, 1991). See also Scott Lowe's discussion of the Taiping Revolution in "Western Millennial Ideology Goes East: The Taiping Revolution and Mao's Great Leap Forward," in *Millennialism, Persecution, and Violence: Historical Cases*, ed. Catherine Wessinger (Syracuse: Syracuse University Press, 2000).
9. Eric Talmadge, Associated Press, "Disciple Rats Out Japan Guru," Reuters (AOL), September 20, 1996.
10. Benjamin Zablocki, "The Blacklisting of a Concept: The Strange History of the Brainwashing Conjecture in the Sociology of Religion," *Nova Religio: The Journal of Alternative and Emergent Religions* 1, no. 1 (October 1997): 96-121.
11. This is carefully traced out in Michael Barkun, *Religion and the Racist Right: The Origins of the Christian Identity Movement*, rev. ed. (Chapel Hill: University of North Carolina Press, 1997).
12. This is not to suggest that there are not different interpretations and variations of Christian Identity.

CHAPTER TWO

How the Millennium Comes Violently

Those who do not remember the past are condemned to repeat it.
—Sign at the Jonestown pavillion (George Santayana)

Recent Events

The year 2000 is stimulating religious imaginations to spin millennial dreams. The new millennium is stimulating hopes that the limitations of the human condition will be transcended finally and completely. Scholars have termed this *hope for collective earthly or heavenly salvation* "millennialism" or "millenarianism," because, so often, the terrestrial perfection has been expected to last one thousand years. Many millennialists believe the transition will take place catastrophically, and sometimes this conflict expectation and its accompanying radical dualistic perspective have contributed to episodes of violence.

In the last decade of the twentieth century, a number of millennial groups involved in violence burst into the news. In 1992, the family of Randy and Vicki Weaver, who had strong millennial beliefs and had taken refuge in the mountains at Ruby Ridge, Idaho, was caught up in a conflict with law enforcement agents that killed Sam Weaver (age 14), Vicki Weaver, and U.S. Marshal William Degan.[1] In 1993, the Branch Davidians were subjected to not one, but two assaults by federal officers, resulting in the deaths of four ATF agents and eighty Davidians. In October 1994, fifty-three members and former members of the Order of the Solar Temple (Ordre du Temple Solaire) were discovered dead in Quebec and Switzerland. Some were murdered and some committed suicide. At the winter solstice just before Christmas 1995, sixteen more members of the

Solar Temple died in a group murder/suicide near Grenoble, France. On March 20, 1995, members of Aum Shinrikyo released sarin gas on Tokyo subway trains, injuring over 5,000 people and killing twelve. Aum members previously had committed a variety of murders, and they attempted to commit more murders after the Tokyo subway attack. The 1996 eighty-one-day standoff between FBI agents and the Montana Freemen contained an armed group that was part of a revolutionary movement in the United States that aimed to overthrow the federal government. On March 22, 1997, when the Hale-Bopp comet was closest to the earth, five more members of the Solar Temple committed suicide in Quebec, and thirty-nine members of Heaven's Gate began their group suicide near San Diego. On May 6, 1997, two more Heaven's Gate believers attempted suicide, and one succeeded. The Heaven's Gate believer who was revived at that time, Chuck Humphrey, committed suicide in February 1998.

Members of all of these groups were millennialists, as were members of the Peoples Temple, who, in 1978, committed murder and "revolutionary suicide" in and near Jonestown, Guyana. Millennial hopes are perennial and are not necessarily tied to unusual dates on the calendar. On November 18, 1978, Peoples Temple members opened fire on the party of U.S. Congressman Leo Ryan, who had just completed an unwelcome visit to Jonestown and was leaving with some defectors. Five people were killed, including Congressman Ryan, and ten were wounded. Back in Jonestown, the community gathered to commit suicide by drinking Fla-Vor-Aid laced with tranquilizers and cyanide. Some people, including children, were injected with the deadly potion. Nine hundred and nine people died in Jonestown, including 294 children under age nineteen. A loyal member of Peoples Temple stationed in Georgetown, Guyana, slit the throats of her three children and then killed herself. Four months later, Mike Prokes, the church's public relations man, called a news conference in a Modesto, California, motel. Prokes said, "I can't disassociate myself from the people who died, nor do I want to. The people weren't brainwashed fanatics or cultists; the Temple was not a cult." Then he went to the bathroom and shot himself. [2]

Each one of these cases teaches us that well-meaning and ordinary people (lower class, middle class, and upper class, young and old, people of all races, nationalities, and educational levels) can become caught up in religious systems and social dynamics that can culminate in violence and death. Jim Jones's sign at the Jonestown pavillion, quoting Santayana, is pertinent. If we neglect to study these millennial movements, and do not understand the dynamics that produce tragic violence, then these scenarios will continue to occur.

When we learn of an episode of violence involving a religious group, we distance those people from us by considering them to be brainwashed cultists

Jim Jones's chair in the Jonestown pavilion with the sign overhead stating, "Those who do not remember the past are condemned to repeat it," surrounded by deceased members of Peoples Temple. (Corbis)

who have nothing in common with ordinary people like ourselves. We make them completely "other" from ourselves. But in fact, members of these religious groups *are* ordinary people, who are sincerely committed to their religious beliefs. We need to recall that millennial beliefs are at the core of a number of mainstream scriptures, especially the Bible, and that these scriptures, therefore, serve as resources upon which religious people can draw.

After the deaths at Jonestown, the members of Peoples Temple were dehumanized, because we saw them in the news only as corpses.[3] The news media did not characterize the residents of Jonestown as good people who were committed to an ideal of interracial harmony and human equality. Peoples Temple members were building a community based on "apostolic socialism," in which financial resources were held in common to serve the needs of all community members. The members of the community worked for each others' well-being.

The Branch Davidians also were dehumanized in the news media. Because the FBI controlled the flow of information about the Davidians, the Davidians were not permitted to tell their side of the story. They were obstructed from explaining their religious beliefs to the American public. All we saw in the media were depictions of a deranged-looking David Koresh. The invisibility of the other Davidians made them into nonentities and created a cultural situation in which it became acceptable to exterminate them. By this I mean that, because the news did not depict the Davidians as human beings, the media coverage produced a cultural consensus that their deaths did not warrant public outcry against the excessive force used against them.[4] Seventy-four Davidians died in the fire on April 19, 1993. Of these, twenty-three were children, including two infants who were born after the death of their mothers.[5]

It is my hope that my comparative study of Jonestown, the Branch Davidians, Aum Shinrikyo, the Montana Freemen, the Solar Temple, Heaven's Gate, and Chen Tao[6] will enable ordinary people—religious believers, potential converts, news reporters, law enforcement agents, and scholars—to deal constructively with the dynamics of millennial groups and to avoid violence.

Key Terms

In understanding violent millennial groups, I have found Robert D. Baird's definition of religion to be useful. Utilizing the phrase coined by theologian Paul Tillich, Baird defines religion as "ultimate concern," and he defines ultimate concern as "a concern which *is more important than anything else in the universe for the person [or the group] involved.*"[7] Many of us are pragmatic and will change our ultimate concerns if placed in life-threatening situations. However, groups such as Jonestown, the Branch Davidians, Aum Shinrikyo, the Montana Freemen, the Solar Temple, and Heaven's Gate show us that people can be willing to kill or die for their ultimate concerns.

The ultimate concern of the Jonestown residents was to preserve their communal solidarity, and, thus, be an example that would help establish a future society free of racism, sexism, classism, and ageism. Jim Jones taught that a period of turmoil, race war, and nuclear destruction would precede the establishment of the perfect society, which he believed would be communist. The ultimate concern of the Branch Davidians was to be obedient to God's will as revealed in the Bible in order to be included in God's salvation kingdom. The Davidians believed that Koresh would be killed in armageddon[8] and then he would return to establish God's kingdom. The ultimate concern for Aum Shinrikyo devotees was the creation of communities of enlightened individuals, who would survive armageddon and establish the Buddhist millennial kingdom called Shambhala. The ultimate concern of the Montana Freemen was to overthrow the illegitimate American government to establish true American republics obedient to Yahweh's laws revealed in the Bible. These are all millennial goals involving the expectation that salvation will be terrestrial.

In millennial religions, however, the expectation of an earthly salvation also involves belief in heaven or an otherworld. This permits shifting to an expectation of a heavenly salvation if historical conditions disprove the earthly salvation. When the Solar Temple adepts decided that the world's population was stubbornly refusing to transform to create the Age of Aquarius, they shifted their expectation of terrestrial salvation to an otherworldly realm, to which they made several group "transits" by murder and group suicide.

Heaven's Gate serves as a reminder to scholars that millennial groups are not always concerned with terrestrial salvation. The Heaven's Gate class members saw the terrestrial world, which they designated the Human Kingdom, as sorely lacking in perfection. In order to achieve the Kingdom of Heaven, or what they termed The Level Above Human (T.E.L.A.H.), each believer had to learn how to overcome human desires. Ultimately, they abandoned their human bodies, their terrestrial "vehicles," confident that their souls were transferring into divinized extraterrestrial bodies in T.E.L.A.H. They believed that as inhabitants of T.E.L.A.H., they would travel the universe with their teachers, Ti and Do, in a "mothership." As T.E.L.A.H. inhabitants, they would spend eternity in service by guiding the evolution of life on various planets regarded as "gardens" for the growth of souls. They exited Earth in 1997 (they did not regard this as suicide), because catastrophic destruction was imminent due to an overgrowth of evil here in this "garden."

We need to note that increasingly in new religions, extraterrestrials and space aliens are the superhuman agents that act in the roles previously filled by God, gods, angels, and devils. The religious outlook remains the same; there is continued belief that there are normally unseen superhuman agents that affect us in our earthly existence for good or ill.

There are two primary types of millennialism, which I call catastrophic millennialism and progressive millennialism.[9]

Catastrophic millennialism involves a pessimistic view of humanity and society. We are so corrupt and sinful that the world as we know it must be destroyed and then created anew. This will be accomplished by God (or by superhuman agents such as extraterrestrials), perhaps with the assistance of human beings. The millennial kingdom will be created only after the violent destruction of the old world.

Progressive millennialism involves an optimistic view of human nature that became prevalent in the nineteenth century. Humans engaging in social work in harmony with the divine will can effect changes that non-catastrophically and progressively create the millennial kingdom.[10]

Believers in both catastrophic millennialism and progressive millennialism are certain that there is a divine (or superhuman) plan to establish the millennial kingdom. Both types of millennialism possess an urgent sense of the imminence of the millennial kingdom. Catastrophic millennialism and progressive millennialism differ on whether humanity contains enough positive potential to make the transition noncatastrophically or is so depraved that violent destruction of the old world is necessary before the millennial kingdom can be established.

Both catastrophic millennialism and progressive millennialism may or may not involve messianism.[11] I use the Hebrew word *messiah* to refer to an individual believed to be empowered by God (or a superhuman agent) to create the millennial kingdom. A messiah is always a prophet, but a prophet is not necessarily a messiah.[12] A *prophet* is someone who is believed to receive revelation from a normally unseen source, such as God, angels, ascended masters, or extraterrestrials. Both messiahs and prophets have charismatic authority (see the discussion of charisma in chapter 1), but the messiah is the individual believed to be empowered to bring about the millennial kingdom. The prophet may announce the imminent arrival of the millennial kingdom, and perhaps even the imminent arrival of the messiah, but the prophet who is not a messiah is not regarded as having the power to create the millennial kingdom.

The Dynamics of Violence

Catastrophic millennialism inherently possesses a dualistic worldview.[13] The world is seen as a battleground between good and evil, God and Satan, us and them. This radical dualism expects, and often produces, conflict. It identifies particular groups and individuals as enemies. It is the embattled worldview of people engaging in warfare. Many religious people hold this dualistic worldview and wage their warfare spiritually with prayers, faith, and worship as their weapons. But if the warfare becomes physical, people are killed, they kill others, people are martyred and die for a cause. Jonestown, the Branch Davidians, Aum Shinrikyo, and the Montana Freemen were catastrophic millennial groups willing to fight the battle on the physical level.

Catastrophic millennialism and progressive millennialism are not mutually exclusive. If a group experiences some prosperity, some success at building its millennial kingdom, the expectations of catastrophe may wane and progressive expectations will come to the fore. But if the group experiences conflict with "cultural opponents,"[14] if it experiences persecution, then the group may be pushed to exaggerated expectations of catastrophe and a radical dualism that tends toward paranoia.

I suggest that if members of a catastrophic millennial group perceive themselves as being persecuted by outside cultural opponents, and furthermore perceive that they are failing to achieve their ultimate concern, this will be a group that is likely to commit violent acts in order to preserve its ultimate concern.[15] In attempting to deal with such a catastrophic millennial group, it is counterproductive to undertake actions that make the members feel persecuted, and the worst thing to do is to apply increased pressure that causes the members to despair about achieving their ultimate goal. Persecution just confirms the millennial group's dualism and perception of being locked in a conflict with powerful and demonic enemies. If the group members are pushed to the point of despair about the success of their goal, they will not abandon their ultimate concern, but instead they will be motivated to take desperate actions to preserve it.

If, due to internal weaknesses and the experience of cultural opposition, a catastrophic millennial community gives up on the possibility of including individuals in the outside world in salvation and turns inward to ensure the salvation of its members alone, then violent actions are more likely to be committed. This was the point reached by the Jonestown residents and Aum Shinrikyo devotees as well as by the Solar Temple adepts and Heaven's Gate students. The violence may be directed outwardly against enemies, or it may be directed inwardly to control dissidents or perhaps to commit suicide and remove the group from the hopelessly corrupt world. Jonestown, Aum Shinrikyo, and the Solar Temple indicate that it is likely that *both* inwardly-directed and outwardly-directed violent acts will be committed.

In studying catastrophic millennial groups involved in violence, we need to distinguish between fragile groups that initiate violence to preserve their ultimate concern, and groups that are assaulted because law enforcement agents regard them as dangerous. There are also revolutionary millennial movements that possess theologies or ideologies that prompt believers to commit violent acts against enemies perceived as demonic or subhuman.

Fragile Millennial Groups That Initiate Violence Due to Internal Weaknesses and Cultural Opposition

Jonestown and Aum Shinrikyo are examples of catastrophic millennial groups experiencing internal and external pressures that can produce violence.[16] Jonestown and Aum Shinrikyo are examples of fragile catastrophic millennial groups whose members commit violent acts because they feel persecuted and perceive their millennial goal (their ultimate concern) as failing.

Both Jim Jones and Shoko Asahara created stresses internal to the group that endangered the ultimate concern. Both leaders set goals for their groups that were impossible to achieve. Both Jones and Asahara were, by virtue of their own actions, in danger of failing to be the messiahs they claimed to be. Jones's descent into debilitating drug addiction after he moved to Jonestown intensified the pressure felt by the other leaders to keep Jonestown economically viable. Jonestown was in danger of failing as a communal experiment, and was suffering from Jones's erratic behavior when the unwanted visit by Congressman Leo Ryan, reporters, and concerned relatives—all perceived as enemies—pushed the community over the edge. Shoko Asahara styled himself as a perfect Buddha, a fully enlightened person with infallible powers of prophecy. He created stresses internal to Aum Shinrikyo by stipulating that an impossible number of individuals had to become renunciants (monastics). Once Asahara, as an infallible Buddha, predicted armageddon, then armageddon had to occur. Asahara's insistence that devotees perform violent acts of asceticism led to a devotee's death and subsequently the murder of an individual who wanted to defect. Aum Shinrikyo, therefore, possessed criminal secrets, and any investigation of the group endangered its ultimate concern of establishing the Buddhist millennial kingdom.[17]

The stresses internal to Jonestown and Aum Shinrikyo were exacerbated by the activities of outside opponents—concerned relatives, anticult activists, reporters, law enforcement agents, and government representatives—that caused members of both groups to feel persecuted. The response within both Jonestown and Aum Shinrikyo was to turn inward and give up on the outside society as being hopelessly corrupt and sinful. Jonestown residents opted to take revenge against their enemies by killing Congressman Ryan and attacking news reporters and defectors in Ryan's party, and then to preserve their communal solidarity by murdering their children and committing group suicide. Their revolutionary suicide in protest of corrupt capitalism was meant to prevent the further disruption of their community by defectors and outside opponents.[18] Aum Shinrikyo devotees committed a variety of murders to prevent defections and to silence outside opponents. They developed weapons of mass destruction for revolutionary purposes, but they utilized these weapons to wage war against their immediate enemies. The Tokyo subway gas attack had the short-term aim of preventing a massive police raid from being carried out against Aum communes. Fortunately, Japanese police were able to take the Aum leaders into custody before they became a full-fledged revolutionary millennial movement and initiated armageddon.

Both Jonestown residents and Aum Shinrikyo devotees possessed a radically dualistic worldview. The Jonestown leaders saw reality in terms of a conflict between communism and capitalism. Jim Jones used the biblical metaphor of "Babylon" to refer to evil capitalistic society.[19] The Aum guru and leaders saw reality in terms of a conflict between spirituality and materialism. Because Aum Shinrikyo concealed criminal secrets, its leaders saw every possibility of investigation as part of a conspiracy to destroy Aum. Residents of Jonestown and residents of the Aum communes felt persecuted and besieged by outside enemies. The integrity of their communes was threatened from within by potential and actual defectors.

Because of their fragility due to internal weaknesses, many of which were caused by their respective leaders and their experience of cultural opposition, Jonestown residents and Aum Shinrikyo devotees initiated violence to preserve their ultimate concerns. In both cases, violence was directed both inwardly against members and dissidents and outwardly against enemies.

The Solar Temple and Heaven's Gate, both treated in chapter 7, were also fragile millennial groups whose members committed violent acts to preserve their ultimate concerns. In the case of the Solar Temple, internal weaknesses, plus the experience of cultural opposition, caused the adepts to despair that the Age of Aquarius would be created on earth, so they opted to make a "transit" to a "heavenly" salvation on the star Sirius. Before leaving, they executed their enemies, and they murdered some less resolute Solar Temple members to assist them in making the transit. In the Heaven's Gate group, the two leaders, Ti and Do, had set impossible goals for their "class," and their dualistic catastrophic millennial worldview made the group's members extremely sensitive to any negative response to their message, which they interpreted as persecution. The Heaven's Gate class members committed suicide, which they regarded as an "exit" from Earth to enter the Kingdom of Heaven, to preserve their ultimate concern.

ASSAULTED MILLENNIAL GROUPS THAT ARE ATTACKED BY LAW ENFORCEMENT AGENTS BECAUSE THEY ARE PERCEIVED AS DANGEROUS

Although the Branch Davidians also saw themselves in conflict with sinful "Babylon," they differ from Jonestown and Aum Shinrikyo because they never doubted the achievement of their ultimate concern.[20] All of the actions taken by the ATF and FBI agents[21] against the Davidians had the effect of confirming David Koresh's prophecies about the violent events of the endtime and thereby enhanced his authority as the messiah. The Branch Davidians were catastrophic millennialists and they felt persecuted, but their persecution strengthened their faith in David Koresh and his prophecies. They had no reason to doubt that God would accomplish the millennial kingdom. The events of the ATF assault and the fifty-one-day siege conducted by FBI agents confirmed that everything was going according to God's plan, and that David Koresh had the divinely-inspired ability to interpret the Bible. I believe that this explains why the Davidians were able to withstand such an incredible amount of persecution by law enforcement agents. The Davidians never gave up their efforts to convert individuals in the outside world because their persecution made it appear more likely that the ultimate concern would be achieved. David Koresh attempted to get his message out during the siege, and when that was prevented, he and other Davidians attempted to convert the FBI negotiators.

The problem was that the FBI agents were unequipped to understand the Bible-based language spoken by Koresh and the Davidians. The transcripts of the negotiation tapes[22] show that the Davidians tried valiantly throughout the siege to communicate and negotiate with the FBI agents, and that clearly indicates that the Davidians did not want to die. They believed that God might will them to die at the hands of agents of Babylon to initiate the catastrophic endtime, and they were willing to die for their ultimate concern, but *the Branch Davidians did not want to die*. The Davidians attempted to communicate with FBI agents up until the very end.

During the siege, at least one Davidian (Livingstone Fagan) came out of Mount Carmel for the purpose of explaining the Davidians' faith. Other Davidians came out for personal reasons or they sent their children out. The persecution confirmed Koresh's prophecies, so the community was not endangered when people chose to come out. But many Davidians stayed inside Mount Carmel because they were waiting for a revelation of God's will, and because each time Davidians came out, FBI agents punished them by escalating the psychological warfare.[23]

The Branch Davidian tragedy illustrates how law enforcement agents *should not* deal with armed catastrophic millennial groups.[24] To avoid violence, law enforcement agents have to take seriously the group's religious views and avoid acting in ways that make them appear to be the agents of Satan. In the event of a siege, group members should be offered terms that permit them to remain true to their ultimate concern even while surrendering. This was not done with the Branch Davidians, to a great extent because of the advice being given to law enforcement agents by anticult activists.[25] Anticult activists possess their own radical dualistic worldview that perpetuates the prejudiced stereotype of the so-called cult.

After being ignored by the FBI when they offered their services, two Bible scholars, Dr. J. Phillip Arnold and Dr. James Tabor, pursued a plan to persuade the Davidians to surrender. Arnold and Tabor were concerned because the Davidians believed they were in the "Fifth Seal" of Revelation (Rev. 6: 9-11). The Davidians interpreted this Bible passage as a prediction that some of the members of the godly community would be killed by Babylon, and after a waiting period the rest of the community would be martyred.[26] Arnold and Tabor directed a radio broadcast to the Davidians in which they discussed the biblical prophecies. The Davidians were elated that *finally* someone was communicating with them who understood their Bible-based language.[27] Arnold and Tabor suggested that other prophecies in Revelation indicated that David Koresh should come out in order to present his interpretation of the Seven Seals to the world, even after being imprisoned. They argued that the waiting period described in the Fifth Seal would be longer than a few months. The Davidians should exit Mount Carmel because God did not intend them to be martyred there. Once out of Mount Carmel David Koresh would be able to spread his message of God's salvation to the rest of the world.

On April 14, 1993, Koresh sent out a letter in which he reported that he had received permission from God to write a "little book" [28] containing his interpretation of the Seven Seals. Koresh's letter said that once the manuscript was in safekeeping with Tabor and Arnold, he and the Davidians would come out.[29] The negotiation tapes reveal that the Davidians were heard cheering at the prospect of coming out.[30] On April 16, Koresh reported to the FBI that he had completed writing his interpretation of the First Seal.[31] When Attorney General Janet Reno asked if there were reasons to continue waiting and negotiating with the Davidians, FBI agents did not tell her about Koresh's promise to surrender. A woman who escaped the fire on April 19 carried out a disk that contained David Koresh's interpretation of the First Seal of Revelation, indicating that Koresh was sincere in his promise.[32]

J. Phillip Arnold and James Tabor succeeded in offering the Davidians a way they could remain true to their ultimate concern and still come out, but their successful efforts were nullified by the FBI gas and tank assault on April 19. During the assault, the Davidians probably concluded that the prophecies of Revelation were being fulfilled in their martyrdom at the hands of Babylon. Only nine Davidians escaped the fire.

REVOLUTIONARY MILLENNIAL MOVEMENTS POSSESSING THEOLOGIES OF VIOLENCE[33]

The eighty-one-day soft siege of the Montana Freemen in 1996 was handled correctly by the FBI. The standoff involved a group of armed people who aimed to spark "the second American revolution" to overthrow the federal government they identified as "Babylon" and to establish true American republics obedient to Yahweh and his laws. Revolutionary millennial movements have an inherent potential for violence because they aim to overthrow what they view as a persecuting government. The believers are convinced that they are participating in the divine plan to violently destroy the illicit government and then establish the millennial kingdom. They believe that violent revolution is necessary and divinely ordained in order to establish the millennial kingdom.

The Freemen indicate for us that there is no need to have a messiah or a guru in order to have a potentially violent religious movement. In 1996, the Freemen living in Justus Township were the most visible portion of an ongoing revolution against the American federal government. This revolutionary movement is a Euro-American nativist movement (see chapter 6). Extremist individuals associated with militias, white supremacist groups, and the religion known as Christian Identity are committing acts of domestic terrorism, and federal and local law enforcement agents are working to contain this revolution.

Unlike Jonestown, the Branch Davidians, Aum Shinrikyo, and the Solar Temple, anticult activists were not opposing the Montana Freemen. The national news coverage of the Freemen was mediocre, but they were not demonized. Instead we saw the Freemen and their children on television, and we saw that they were human beings. The news coverage in the *Billings Gazette* was exceptionally good. Relatives of the Freemen were interviewed, and the Freemen were depicted as being farmers, ranchers, and working people with concerns that other Americans had.

During the Freemen standoff, FBI agents consulted scholars knowledgeable about millennial and new religious movements, including Dr. Michael Barkun, Dr. J. Phillip Arnold, Dr. Jean Rosenfeld, and myself. The scholars advising the FBI agents urged them to keep the siege low-key and to avoid making the Freemen feel persecuted. We urged the FBI agents to utilize third-party intermediaries (worldview translators),[34] who could understand the Freemen's worldview and speak the Freemen's language, but also who had the cognitive distance from the Freemen worldview to analyze it. We urged the FBI agents not to pressure the Freemen or cause them to despair of achieving their religious goal. Finally, we urged the FBI agents to offer terms to the Freemen that permitted them to simultaneously remain true to their ultimate concern and come out of Justus Township.

Toward the end of the Freemen standoff, J. Phillip Arnold spent four days with the FBI negotiators in Montana, which contributed to the breakthrough involving the exit of a couple along with the woman's two young daughters (ages eight and ten). FBI agents offered final terms to the remaining Freemen that reassured the Freemen they could continue striving to achieve their ultimate concern while in federal custody.[35] According to the Freemen perspective, they did not surrender, but took their fight against Babylon into the federal courts.[36] The Freemen were not put into a position in which they felt their only options were either to kill or die for their ultimate concern.[37]

Conclusion

The categories highlighted here—fragile millennial groups, assaulted millennial groups, and revolutionary millennial movements—can be seen as distinct moments on a continuum involving millennial beliefs and the potential for violence. A particular millennial group may possess several of these features simultaneously—fragility, revolutionary ideology and activity, and being subjected to assault. A group may move from one of these categories to another as it develops.[38] I have assigned one of these categories to each millennial group treated in this book according to whether the members or outside opponents initiated the violence, and whether a revolutionary ideology, fragility, or self-defense was the primary motivation for violent acts committed by believers.

Aum Shinrikyo possessed a revolutionary ideology and was actively acquiring weapons of mass destruction in preparation for initiating armageddon, but in fact, the violent acts committed by devotees were related to the fragility of Aum Shinrikyo and its endangered ultimate concern. Hence, I conclude that at the times of the sarin gas attack on the Tokyo subway and earlier acts of violence, Aum Shinrikyo was a fragile millennial group.

The Branch Davidians had revolutionary potential in that David Koresh taught that they would go to Israel and fight on the side of the Israelis against the United States and the United Nations in armageddon in 1995. Initially, the Davidians were not expecting armageddon to take place in Texas. David Koresh and one of his followers supported the group financially by buying and selling arms at gun shows. No conclusive evidence has been produced that the Davidians' weapons were illegal, and in 1993 the Davidians were not preparing to fight armageddon against their Texas neighbors. ATF agents and FBI agents assaulted the Branch Davidians twice because they misunderstood their religious commitment and intention.

Jonestown, the Solar Temple, and Heaven's Gate were unambiguously fragile millennial groups, whose members committed violent acts to preserve their ultimate concerns. Each suffered from internal stresses that endangered their respective goals as well as from varying degrees of cultural opposition that members viewed as persecution.

The Montana Freemen were part of a diffuse revolutionary millennial movement in contemporary America, and the Freemen were prepared to commit violent acts, but if the Freemen, like similar Christian Identity communities in the United States, had experienced some success at building their millennial kingdom set apart from corrupt mainstream society, then the potential for violent acts committed by believers could have diminished over time.

It needs to be noted that catastrophic millennial beliefs do not necessarily cause violent episodes.[39] Numerous catastrophic millennial groups exist and have existed without getting caught up in violence.

On the other hand, every millennial movement is revolutionary in its hope for a radical transformation to a collective salvation.[40] A key issue in determining the potential for volatility is whether the believers expect that the transformation will be accomplished by divine intervention or by the active participation of the faithful in overthrowing the current sinful order. Under specific social conditions, otherwise peaceful catastrophic millennial groups may become assaulted or fragile.

The comparative study of Jonestown, the Branch Davidians, Aum Shinrikyo, the Montana Freemen, the Solar Temple, Heaven's Gate, and also of Chen Tao, reveals the persistent folly of a radical dualistic worldview, and shows that such "dichotomous thinking"[41] is found not only in members of catastrophic millennial groups, but also among defectors from new religious movements, anticult activists, law enforcement agents, and news reporters. It is all too human to see things in conflictual terms—us vs. the enemy, the good guys vs. the bad guys. The persistence of a radical dualistic view is seen in defectors from catastrophic millennial groups, who simply reverse those they define as the enemy. The religious group they have left and its leader are redefined as evil, and they work as passionately to destroy that group as they previously worked to promote it.[42] Law enforcement agents and members of the military are trained to see situations in terms of the good guys in conflict with the bad guys. Numerous retired police officers and former military personnel populate the continuing Euro-American nativist movement that includes the Freemen, constitution and Common Law study groups, and militias. They have merely redefined the federal government and its agents as evil, and they work passionately to destroy the government's dominance. Police officers and former military personnel were active in helping Aum Shinrikyo prepare to wage deadly armageddon against the population of Japan. In the cases of Jonestown, the Branch Davidians, and the Solar Temple, news reporters in search of sensationalized stories of conflict contributed to the tragic conclusions. The Heaven's Gate leader, Do, felt persecuted by the news media in the mid-1970s, and this contributed to his decision to lead his class to commit a group suicide more than twenty years later.

In order to deal constructively with members of unconventional religious groups, law enforcement agents, reporters, and scholars have to learn to regard the members as human beings possessing a sincere commitment to their ultimate concern. If people can regard each other as human beings, as persons like "us," and not as demonic and inhuman enemies, conflictual dualism on all sides will diminish. For law enforcement agents, this means it is necessary to meet with members of new religious groups, listen to them, and, whenever possible, enlist their cooperation in the investigation of their activities. News reporters can contribute to peaceful dialogue rather than violent conflict by respectfully permitting members of unconventional religions to articulate their views and to be seen as human beings. Scholars need to promote increased public understanding of religion by making their expertise available to reporters, law enforcement agents, and the wider community. However, as scholars attempt to humanize the members of new religious movements for the general public, they should not be in the business of giving "clean bills of health" to particular groups. Aum Shinrikyo stands as a warning that sometimes NRMs contain nasty surprises. Scholars also should be leary of labeling a group as potentially dangerous given the propensity of law enforcement agents, reporters, relatives, and anticult activists to step up cultural opposition to unconventional groups. How to utilize skillfully the lessons learned from this comparative study remains at issue.

Notes

1. Tom Morganthau, Michael Isikoff, and Bob Cohn, "The Echoes of Ruby Ridge," *Newsweek*, August 28, 1995, 25-28; Jess Walter, "'Every Knee Shall Bow': Exclusive Book Excerpt," *Newsweek*, August 28, 1995, 29-33; Jess Walter, *Every Knee Shall Bow: The Truth and Tragedy of Ruby Ridge and the Randy Weaver Family* (New York: Harper Paperbacks, 1995).
2. John R. Hall, *Gone From the Promised Land: Jonestown in American Cultural History* (New Brunswick, N.J.: Transaction Books, 1987), 291.
3. I thank Rebecca Moore for sharing this observation with me.
4. James T. Richardson, "Manufacturing Consent about Koresh: A Structural Analysis of the Role of Media in the Waco Tragedy," in *Armageddon in Waco: Critical Perspectives on the Branch Davidian Conflict*, ed. Stuart A. Wright (Chicago: University of Chicago Press, 1995), 153-76. Richardson does not use the word *exterminate* in his article, but he does point out that the news coverage of the Davidians made them into victims "unworthy" of the compassion of the general public.
5. James D. Tabor and Eugene V. Gallagher, *Why Waco? Cults and the Battle for Religious Freedom in America* (Berkeley: University of California Press, 1995), 3; Carol Moore, *The Davidian Massacre: Disturbing Questions about Waco Which Must Be Answered* (Franklin, Tenn., and Springfield, Va.: Legacy Communications and Gun Owners Foundation, 1995), xiii-xiv; Dick J. Reavis, *The Ashes of Waco: An Investigation* (New York: Simon & Schuster, 1995), 277.

    The two pregnant women were Aisha Gyarfas (17), who died of a gunshot wound, and Nicole Gent (23), who was killed by falling cement as she huddled with other women and the children in a room made of concrete blocks.

    In the ATF raid on Mount Carmel on Sunday, February 28, 1993, four ATF agents were killed, twenty ATF agents were wounded, five Davidians were killed, and four Davidians (including David Koresh) were wounded. That afternoon about 4:55 P.M., Michael Schroeder was shot and killed by ATF agents as he attempted to walk to Mount Carmel to rejoin his family.

6. The episode involving the Randy Weaver family is discussed in chapter 6.

7. Robert D. Baird, *Category Formation and the History of Religions* (The Hague: Mouton, 1971), 18. Baird's emphasis, my addition in brackets.

8. Armageddon in the book of Revelation refers to a place where the final battle between good and evil will occur. Throughout this book I use *armageddon* in its popular sense of the final battle that will destroy the world as we know it.

9. I offer these readily comprehensible terms as alternatives to the obscure and misleading terms used by historians, *pre-millennialism* and *post-millennialism*. See Catherine Wessinger, "Millennialism With and Without the Mayhem: Catastrophic and Progressive Expectations," in *Millennium, Messiahs, and Mayhem: Contemporary Apocalyptic Movements*, ed. Thomas Robbins and Susan J. Palmer (New York: Routledge, 1997), 47-59.

10. This is the type of millennialism I studied in *Annie Besant and Progressive Messianism* (Lewiston, N.Y.: Edwin Mellen Press, 1988).

     In *Millennialism, Persecution, and Violence: Historical Cases*, ed. Catherine Wessinger (Syracuse: Syracuse University Press, 2000), the chapters by Robert Ellwood on German Nazis, Scott Lowe on Mao Zedong's Great Leap Forward in the People's Republic of China, and Richard Salter on the Khmer Rouge in Cambodia indicate that progressive millennialism can motivate revolutionary violence. Revolutionary progressive millennial beliefs promote violence, but it appears that *noncatastrophic* progressive millennialism as defined in this chapter is unlikely to promote violence. See the discussion in my introduction to *Millennialism, Persecution, and Violence*, "The Interacting Dynamics of Millennial Beliefs, Persecution, and Violence," 3-39. None of the groups studied here are noncatastrophic progressive millennialists or revolutionary progressive millennialists.

11. This assertion is contrary to most scholarly assumptions about "post-millennialism." See the discussion in Wessinger, "Millennialism With and Without the Mayhem."

12. See my discussion in "Interacting Dynamics of Millennial Beliefs, Persecution, and Violence."

13. Revolutionary progressive millennialism possesses the dualistic view found in catastrophic millennialism.

14. John R. Hall, "Public Narratives and the Apocalyptic Sect: From Jonestown to Mt. Carmel" in Wright, *Armageddon in Waco*, 207.

15. I derived this thesis from reading simultaneously works of two scholars: Mary McCormick Maaga, "Triple Erasure: Women and Power in Peoples Temple," Ph.D. diss. Drew University, 1996; Ian Reader, *A Poisonous Cocktail? Aum Shinrikyo's Path to Violence* (Copenhagen: Nordic Institute of Asian Studies Books, 1996). I rely to a great extent on these works by Maaga and Reader in my description and analysis of events involving Jonestown and Aum Shinrikyo.

16. Millennial groups becoming involved in violence due to simultaneous endogenous and exogenous factors are also discussed in Thomas Robbins and Dick Anthony, "Sects and Violence: Factors Enhancing the Volatility of Marginal Religious Movements," in Wright, *Armageddon in Waco*, 236-59. In Wessinger, *Millennialism, Persecution, and Violence*, the fragile millennial groups discussed are Jonestown by Rebecca Moore, Solar Temple and Heaven's Gate by Massimo Introvigne, and Aum Shinrikyo by Ian Reader.

17. Ian Reader, "Imagined Persecution: Aum Shinrikyo, Millennialism, and the Legitimation of Violence," in Wessinger, *Millennialism, Persecution, and Violence*, 158-82.

18. The Jonestown residents felt they had no other place to go. They did not view returning to American society with its capitalism and inequality as an option.

They had explored relocating to Cuba or the U.S.S.R. with no result.
19. Hall, *Gone from the Promised Land*, 31, 145.
20. In Wessinger, *Millennialism, Persecution, and Violence*, other assaulted groups studied are the Mormons by Grant Underwood, the massacre of a Lakota Sioux band in 1890 at Wounded Knee by Michelene E. Pesantubbee, the Dreads in Dominica by Richard C. Salter, and the massacre of black Israelites at Bulhoek, South Africa, by Christine Steyn. Assaulted millennial groups are not rare.
21. These agencies are the Bureau of Alcohol, Tobacco, and Firearms, and the Federal Bureau of Investigation.
22. For studies of the Waco negotiations, see Eugene V. Gallagher, "'Theology Is Life and Death': David Koresh on Violence, Persecution, and the Millennium," in Wessinger, *Millennialism, Persecution, and Violence*, 82–100; Jayne Seminare Docherty, "When the Parties Bring Their Gods to the Table: Learning Lessons from Waco," Ph.D. diss., 1998, George Mason University; and the forthcoming dissertation by Cary R.W. Voss, Communications, University of Kansas.
23. James Tabor, "The Events at Waco: An Interpretive Log," at <http://home.maine.rr.com/waco/ww.html>.
24. See Catherine Wessinger, "Review Essay: Understanding the Branch Davidian Tragedy," *Nova Religio: The Journal of Alternative and Emergent Religions* 1 (October 1997): 122-38. Information on *Nova Religio* can be found at <http://www.novareligio.com>.
25. See John R. Hall, "Public Narratives and the Apocalyptic Sect," 205-35; Nancy T. Ammerman, "Waco, Federal Law Enforcement, and Scholars of Religion, 282-96; Stuart A. Wright, "Construction and Escalation of a Cult Threat," 75-94; all in Wright, *Armageddon in Waco*; see also Tabor and Gallagher, *Why Waco?*
26. The Fifth Seal described in Revelation 6:9-11 is given below. The following is quoted in J. Phillip Arnold, "The Davidian Dilemma—To Obey God or Man?" in *From the Ashes: Making Sense of Waco*, ed. James R. Lewis (Lanham, Md.: Rowman & Littlefield, 1994), 25.

> And when he had opened the fifth seal, I saw under the altar the souls of *them that were slain* for the word of God, and for the testimony which they held: And they cried with a loud voice, saying, *How long*, O Lord, holy and true, dost thou not judge and avenge our blood on them that dwell on the earth? And white robes were given unto every one of them; and it was said unto them, that they should *rest* yet for a little season, until their fellow servants also and their brethren, that should be *killed* as they were, should be fulfilled.

27. Negotiation tape no. 129, March 15, 1993, of Steve Schneider reporting the enthusiastic responses of Davidians to hearing on the radio Dr. J. Phillip Arnold discussing the Bible. Schneider asked that Dr. Arnold be permitted to discuss the biblical prophecies with David Koresh to see if Arnold could offer alternative interpretations. Schneider stated that if Arnold could prove by the biblical texts that the Davidians should come out, they would exit Mount Carmel regardless of whether or not David Koresh agreed with Arnold's interpretations.
　　Audiotape of discussion of James Tabor and J. Phillip Arnold on the Ron Engleman radio talk show station KGBS on April 1, 1993; audiotape of "The Last Recorded Words of David Koresh April 16-18, 1993," narrated by James Tabor.
　　On April 16, 1993, David Koresh enthusiastically discussed with a negotiator that when he had written his commentary on the Seven Seals, he and the Davidians would come out. Koresh explained that he would give the manuscript to James Tabor and Phillip Arnold for safekeeping, because they had expressed a

sincere interest in his biblical interpretations. Koresh wanted his teachings preserved and disseminated in writing because he believed that once he was taken into custody, he would be presented to the public as a monstrosity.

For the full story, see chapter 4.

28. This is a reference to a messenger with a "little book" in Revelation 10. See Tabor and Gallagher, *Why Waco?* 16.
29. Tabor and Gallagher, *Why Waco?* 15.
30. House of Representatives, *Investigation into the Activities of Federal Law Enforcement Agencies toward the Branch Davidians: Thirteenth Report by the Committee on Government Reform and Oversight Prepared in Conjunction with the Committee on the Judiciary together with Additional and Dissenting Views*, Report 104-749 (Washington, DC: U. S. Government Printing Office, 1996), 65.
31. "Last Recorded Words of David Koresh" audiotape.
32. For these events, see Tabor and Gallagher, *Why Waco?*; James D. Tabor, "Religious Discourse and Failed Negotiations: The Dynamics of Biblical Apocalypticism in Waco," in Wright, *Armageddon in Waco*, 263-81; James D. Tabor, "The Waco Tragedy: An Autobiographical Account of One Attempt to Prevent Disaster," in Lewis, *From the Ashes*, 13-21; Arnold, "Davidian Dilemma," 23-31.
33. In Wessinger, *Millennialism, Persecution, and Violence*, the revolutionary millennial groups studied are the Russian Old Believers by Thomas Robbins, the Taiping Revolution and Mao Zedong's Great Leap Forward by Scott Lowe, German Nazism by Robert Ellwood, the appropriation of *Lotus Sutra* millennialism by militant Japanese nationalists by Jacqueline Stone, the Khmer Rouge by Richard C. Salter, American Neo-Nazis by Jeffrey Kaplan, and the Montana Freemen by Jean E. Rosenfeld. Revolutionary millennial movements are very common and can cause massive suffering.
34. I thank Jayne Seminare Docherty for this term, *worldview translator*, which she uses in her dissertation. Docherty, "When the Parties Bring Their Gods to the Table." Docherty derived this phrase from Phillip Lucas, "How Future Wacos Might Be Avoided: Two Proposals," in Lewis, *From the Ashes*, 209-12.
35. The terms were reported in Clair Johnson, "Freemen deal includes 5: Negotiator spells out points in agreement," *Billings Gazette Online*, June 19, 1996.
36. Neill H. Payne, "Shades of Waco: CAUSE Negotiates Peaceful End to Siege of Justus Township Standoff," *The Balance: A Newsletter of Civil Rights and Current Events* 7, no. 2 (Summer 1996): 1-3.
37. The standoff was concluded peacefully because the Freemen were offered terms that permitted them to remain true to their ultimate concern. The peaceful resolution did *not* occur because their electricity was cut off although that may have been a contributing factor. Unlike their dealings with the Branch Davidians, FBI agents increased the pressure on the Freemen cautiously.
38. I thank Eugene V. Gallagher for stressing these points to me in personal communications.
39. I thank Lonnie Kliever and Grant Underwood for emphasizing this point to me in personal communications. See Grant Underwood, "Millennialism, Persecution, and Violence: The Mormons," in Wessinger, *Millennialism, Persecution, and Violence*, 43–61.
40. I thank Eugene V. Gallagher for emphasizing this to me in personal communications.
41. Linda E. Olds discusses the problematic features of dichotomous thinking in promoting patriarchy and sexism in *Fully Human: How Everyone Can Integrate the Benefits of Masculine and Feminine Sex Roles* (Englewood Cliffs, N.J.: Prentice-Hall, 1981).
42. For example, while a member of Peoples Temple, Tim Stoen idolized Jim Jones.

CHAPTER THREE

1978—Jonestown

We tried to find a new beginning. But it's too late. You can't separate yourself from your brother and sister. No way I'm going to do it. I refuse. I don't know who fired the shot. I don't know who killed the Congressman. But as far as I am concerned, I killed him. You understand what I'm saying? I killed him. He had no business coming. I told him not to come.
—Jim Jones at the final Jonestown gathering

And I just like to thank Dad for giving us life, and also death. And I appreciate the fact of the way our children are going. Because, like Dad said, when they come in, what they're gonna do to our children—they're gonna massacre our children. And also the ones that they take capture, they're gonna just let them grow up and be dummies like they want them to be. And not grow up to be a person like the one and only Jim Jones. So I'd like to thank Dad for the opportunity for letting Jonestown be not what it could be, but what Jonestown is. Thank you, Dad. [Applause]
—Man at the final Jonestown gathering[1]

The Violence

On Saturday, November 18, 1978, the communal settlement of the Peoples Temple in Guyana, South America, became the paradigmatic "destructive cult." A total of 918 persons died on that day as a result of the activities of Peoples Temple members. Prior to the mass suicide/murder, a group of Jonestown men shot and killed five persons and wounded ten in U.S. Congressman Leo Ryan's party, who were attempting to depart from a nearby airstrip. The five killed were Congressman Ryan, NBC reporter Don Harris, NBC cameraman Bob Brown, *San Francisco Examiner* photographer Greg Robinson, and Peoples Temple defector Patricia Parks.[2] The assassins then returned to Jonestown to commit suicide with their community. In Jonestown, residents carried out a group suicide/murder that they had discussed and planned for years. The Jonestown physician and nurses prepared a brew of tranquilizers and cyanide. People were either injected with the deadly mixture, or they drank Fla-Vor-Aid, which contained the poison. Nine hundred and nine people died at Jonestown including 294 children under the age of eighteen. The Peoples Temple minister, Jim Jones, age forty-seven, and a nurse, Annie Moore, age twenty-four, died of gunshot wounds. Because only seven autopsies were performed, it was never determined if any people died of causes other than poisoning.[3] There was no evidence that people were forced at gunpoint to commit suicide. After hearing about the suicides by shortwave radio, a loyal member of Peoples Temple stationed in Georgetown, Guyana, slit the throats of her three children and then killed herself. Four months later, the church's public relations man, Mike Prokes, a former television news bureau chief, called a news conference in a Modesto, California, motel. Prokes said, "I can't disassociate myself from the people who died, nor do I want to. The people weren't brainwashed fanatics or cultists; the Temple was not a cult." Then he went into the bathroom and shot himself in the head.[4]

Eighty-five members of Peoples Temple survived, including an elderly woman who slept through the group suicide/murder, an elderly man who hid in a ditch, people who escaped into the jungle, and members who were away from Jonestown. The latter included three sons of Jim Jones who were in Georgetown playing in a basketball tournament.[5]

Jim Jones

James Warren Jones was born on May 13, 1931, in a small farming town in Indiana. He was the only child of James T. Jones and Lynetta Putnam Jones. His father, a World War I veteran disabled by mustard gas, felt defeated by life and was emotionally distant. His mother, whose features revealed her Cherokee blood, worked hard to support the family during the Great Depression. Lynetta worked at a variety of jobs, including farm and factory labor. As a child, Jim Jones felt unloved and was an aggressive and angry boy. Lynetta Jones resented being poor, and she became a trade union organizer and agitator in the factories. Lynetta's son also resented having been born on the wrong side of the tracks. Being considered poor white trash, Jim Jones felt alienated from society.[6]

As a young man, Jim Jones worked in a hospital in Richmond, Indiana, attended college, and preached on the street corners in working-class and industrial neighborhoods. He preached a message of brotherhood to racially mixed audiences. In 1949, Jones married Marceline Baldwin, a young white woman from a Methodist family who subsequently completed her nurse's training. During this time, Jim Jones was associating with communists. These friends told him, "Don't become a member of the Party; work for the Party."[7]

In 1951 Jim and Marceline Jones moved to Indianapolis, where Jim attended communist meetings and rallies. He later reported that the harassment he experienced during the McCarthy era increased his commitment to communism. Jones was distraught at the execution of the Rosenbergs in 1953 for spying, because he believed that they were executed because they were communists. Jones asked himself, "How can I demonstrate my Marxism?" and concluded that the answer was to "infiltrate the church." Jones embarked on a project to use the church as a cover to preach that religion was "the opiate of the people."[8]

In 1952 in Indianapolis, Jones became a student pastor in a Methodist church. According to Marceline, he "was eager to awaken people to the humanity of Jesus and to let them know that what Jesus was, they could be also.... He said there must be no creed but the helping ministry of Christ and no law but the law of love."[9] Jones left that church, because those Methodists refused to permit him to integrate African Americans into the church.[10]

Jones attended a faith-healing service at the Seventh Day Baptist Church, and observed that healing attracted people and their money. Jones concluded that with financial resources he could do some good in society. At a Pentecostal convention, a Pentecostal/Holiness woman minister called Jones out and declared, "I perceive that you are a prophet that shall go around the world.... And tonight ye shall begin your ministry." Immediately Jones called out people by their names and Social Security numbers, identified their illnesses, and healed them. Jones became a popular revival preacher who healed, discerned people's thoughts and troubles, and prophesied. With the help of accomplices, he faked some healings because they found that the staged healings increased faith among people, which in turn produced healings.[11]

Jones's goal in healing and thus in attracting people and financial resources was to help the poor. He always preached the social gospel, but in his early revival days Jones did not reveal that his gospel was communism. By the late 1960s, Jones openly preached in the Peoples Temple his version of communism, which he called "apostolic socialism." Citing Acts 4:31-32, he taught that Christians should hold their financial resources in common, and, citing Acts 4:35 that distribution of resources should be according to need. Peoples Temple members held to the Marxist axiom: From each according to his ability, to each according to his need. Even after Jones openly preached socialism and derided religion, the Peoples Temple stationery continued to quote Matthew 25:35-40, in which Jesus asserts that the hungry, the thirsty, the sick, the naked, the imprisoned, and strangers should be served, and concludes, "Inasmuch as ye have done it unto one of the least of these, ye have done it unto me."[12]

Jones taught that he was a manifestation of the Christ Principle. Jones healed like Jesus did, and he even claimed to have raised the dead. Like Jesus, Jones preached the importance of right human relations and radical egalitarianism. He taught that all people had access to the Holy Spirit within themselves, but that his own healing power demonstrated that he was a special manifestation of "Christ the Revolution."[13] In a sermon in San Francisco, Jones preached,

> I have put on Christ, you see. I have followed after the example of Christ. When you see me it's no longer Jim Jones here. I'm crucified with Christ, nevertheless I live, yet not I, but Christ that lives here. Now Christ is in this body.
>
> You will not get Christ's blessing in Jim Jones' blessing until you walk like Jim Jones, until you talk like Jim Jones, until you act like Jim Jones, until you look like Jim Jones. How long will I be with you until you understand that *I* am no longer a man, but a Principle. I am the Way, the Truth, and the Light. No one can come to the Father but through me.[14]

Jones warned that a cataclysmic period of race war, genocide, and ultimately nuclear war was nearing. He taught that Nazi fascists and Ku Klux Klan white supremacists would put people of color in concentration camps. As the messiah, Jones offered a place of refuge in his church and ultimately the "promised land" in Jonestown. Utilizing a powerful metaphor from the book of Revelation in the New Testament, Jones taught that American capitalist culture was irredeemable "Babylon." There was no point in trying to reform its corrupt institutions. Instead, the elect had to withdraw to a place of safety to survive the destruction, after which they would emerge to establish the perfect communist society.[15]

Jim Jones sincerely preached a gospel of socialist redemption, and he did not personally enrich himself from the financial resources accumulated by the Peoples Temple.[16] Barton and Dorothy Hunter, Disciples of Christ members who knew Jones in the 1950s in Indianapolis reported that he "was not always evil; he became evil."[17] Jones became evil because the people around him permitted and assisted him in committing evil acts. Peoples Temple members' dualistic (us versus them) perspective, in which they saw Peoples Temple, the righteous remnant, as being attacked by evil capitalistic society, Babylon, led them to resort to violent acts to preserve their community. For the residents of Jonestown, the preservation of their community was the most important thing in the world—it was their ultimate concern—and any means could be employed to save that community.

Peoples Temple

After having to leave the Sommerset Southside Methodist Church for bringing black people to the services, Jones began a church called Community Unity in a rented building in Indianapolis. In 1955 a building was purchased, and the church was renamed Wings of Deliverance. Later in 1955 its name was changed to Peoples Temple Full Gospel Church.[18]

While living in Indianapolis, Jim Jones engaged in numerous activities to help the poor and to work for racial equality and justice. Jim and Marceline Jones turned their residence into a nursing home for the elderly, and they started their "rainbow family" by adopting children of several races. In the late 1950s Jim Jones visited Father Divine's Peace Mission in Philadelphia, and he subsequently borrowed some of Father Divine's themes and emulated his organizational structure. Jones became known to his congregation as "Father" or "Dad." Borrowing the rhetoric of Father Divine, Jones emphasized "the promised land" in his sermons. In 1959 Jones affiliated his congregation with the Christian Church (Disciples of Christ) naming it the Peoples Temple Christian Church Full Gospel. In 1961 Jones was hired as the executive director of the Indianapolis Human Rights Commission, and he successfully integrated churches, restaurants, the telephone company, the police department, a theater, an amusement park, and the Methodist Hospital.[19]

Jones's work for integration and his multiracial family attracted the ire of local racists. In response, Jones increasingly became preoccupied with finding a nonracist environment in which his family and congregation could thrive. In 1961 Jones visited British Guiana (after independence, known as Guyana).[20]

Jones read an article in the January 1962 issue of *Esquire* entitled "Nine Places in the World to Hide," which gave advice on locations that would be safe in the event of nuclear holocaust. Based on that article, Jones and his family moved to Belo Horizonte, Brazil, and lived there from 1962 to 1963. The Cuban missile crisis occurred in October 1962, and Brazilians made bitter remarks to Jones such as, "You goddamn Yankees, you're gonna blow up the world."[21]

After returning to the United States, Jones visited Redwood Valley, California, another safe place specified by the *Esquire* article. Upon his return to Indianapolis from Redwood Valley, Jones had a vision of a nuclear flash originating in Chicago. In 1965, Jones, his family, and about seventy members of Peoples Temple relocated to Redwood Valley. In California, the church was known as the Peoples Temple of the Disciples of Christ.[22]

Mary McCormick Maaga has identified three populations within the Peoples Temple: 1) people, predominantly whites, who joined primarily in family groups when Peoples Temple was a Christian sect in Indiana affiliated with the Disciples of Christ; 2) young, college-educated whites who joined Peoples Temple beginning in 1968 in California; and 3) blacks who joined in the early 1970s when the Peoples Temple began urban ministries in San Francisco and Los Angeles. Maaga terms these three Peoples Temple constituencies the white Indiana sect members, the white California new religious movement (NRM) members, and the black urban church members. The white Indiana sect members were loyal to Jones's ideal of apostolic socialism and maintained a personal loyalty to Marceline Jones after Jim Jones began his psychological decline into drug addiction. The white NRM members became church leaders. They were the administrators of the Peoples Temple, and later of Jonestown; they extended the Peoples Temple ministry to urban blacks in San Francisco and Los Angeles. The black urban church members constituted the majority of Peoples Temple's membership. They were the beneficiaries of a variety of social services organized by the Peoples Temple, including nine homes for the elderly, six homes for foster children, assistance in negotiating the American welfare system, and a ranch for the mentally retarded.[23]

Among the white California NRM members, commitment to the goals of the Peoples Temple often was expressed in sexual relations with Jim Jones. Jones had sexual relations with a number of young women and with some of the men. While undoubtedly personal pathologies and insecurities were being acted out in the inner circle in which Jim Jones was idealized as the sole virile male,[24] there was also a sociological aspect to the sexual relations with Jim Jones. The young adults' sexually expressed love for Jones empowered them as his delegates to perform administrative duties in their collective work for social justice and the establishment of their ideal socialist community.[25] Marceline Jones's acquiescence to this situation is puzzling, but her commitment to the ultimate concern and work of the Peoples Temple apparently outweighed her pain at having to share her husband.[26] Quite a few young white women were empowered by their relationship with Jones to challenging careers in the Peoples Temple in which they worked for the socialist transformation of society. Given the limited options for women to find meaningful work at that time in the United States, Maaga has stressed that "for the women, it wasn't until they met Jim Jones and joined Peoples Temple that their personal power and institutional influence matched their desire to make a difference in the world."[27]

In 1972 Temple member Grace Stoen gave birth to John Victor Stoen. Grace's husband, Timothy Stoen, signed an affidavit stating that John Victor was fathered by Jim Jones, "the most compassionate, honest, and courageous human being the world contains."[28] Tim Stoen stated in the affidavit:

> The child, John Victor Stoen, was born January 15, 1972. I am privileged beyond words to have the responsibility for caring for him, and I undertake this task humbly with the steadfast hope that said child will become a devoted follower of Jesus Christ and be instrumental in bringing God's kingdom here on earth, as has been his wonderful natural father.[29]

After Grace and Tim Stoen defected separately, leaving John Victor in Jonestown, this child became the focus of a bitter custody battle that was an important catalyst for the group suicide/murder.

Foremost among the women of Jones's inner circle was Carolyn Moore Layton, a high school political science teacher and a daughter of a United Methodist minister's family committed to working for social justice. In 1969 Carolyn Moore Layton functioned as Jim Jones's partner, and in 1975 she gave birth to a son fathered by Jones named James John (nicknamed Jim-Jon, and also Kimo). Jim Jones and Carolyn Moore Layton believed that they were the reincarnations of Lenin and his mistress.[30]

Pressures on Peoples Temple in California prompted preparations to relocate to Guyana. The first news stories to be critical of Jim Jones and the Peoples Temple began to appear in 1972, particularly in the *San Francisco Examiner*. In 1973, the Peoples Temple church building in San Francisco was set on fire, probably by white racists. The Peoples Temple board of directors decided on October 8, 1973, to establish an agricultural settlement in Guyana. After Jones was arrested for lewd conduct in a Los Angeles public bathroom, he visited Guyana to initiate the preparations for the move there. In 1974 Jones sent a small group of pioneers to Guyana to clear a portion of the 3,824 acres leased from the socialist Guyanese government and to begin the building of Jonestown. By 1975 there were about fifty residents in Jonestown. Peoples Temple moved from Redwood Valley to San Francisco, where the members' activities helped to elect George Moscone as mayor.[31] Jones's "populist and paranoid antigovernment stand"[32] attracted support from California Republicans, but the liberal success of electing Moscone mayor of San Francisco in 1975 moved Jones to the center of Democratic Party activities in California; Jones cultivated contacts with Rosalynn Carter and Walter Mondale. In 1976 Jones was appointed to the San Francisco Housing Authority and elected its chair. While Jonestown was being established as the new "promised land" and a refuge from persecution, Jones openly allied himself with leftist political figures and groups in California.[33]

The activities of Peoples Temple defectors in producing with reporters sensationalized news stories, sparking an investigation by the Treasury Department and the interest of the Internal Revenue Service, confirmed Jones's belief that Peoples Temple would be persecuted and that they needed to seek refuge in their separated promised land.[34] During the summer of 1977 over 1,000 Peoples Temple members, including Jim Jones, moved to Jonestown, their promised land in the Guyanese jungle.[35]

Catastrophic Millennialism

Jim Jones taught that the ultimate reality, the true God, was "Principle" or "Divine Principle." Principle was equated with "Love," and Love was equated with "Socialism." Jones derided traditional Christianity as "fly away religion," and rejected the Bible, particularly the influential King James Version, as being written by white men to justify the subordination of women and the oppression and enslavement of people of color. According to Jones, the Bible only contained beliefs about a "Sky God" or "Buzzard God," who was no God at all.[36]

Jones asserted that he was a savior or messiah sent by the true God, the Principle of Socialism, to rescue humans from their imprisonment in the evil earthly realm of suffering in which the Buzzard God was ignorantly believed to be the true God. Jones cited his psychic abilities, his powers to prophesy, to heal, and to raise the dead as demonstrating that he was the messiah sent by the true God, Socialism. Jones asserted that he had been immaculately conceived. His mother's desire to give birth to a savior had put her into mental attunement with a highly evolved planet outside the Sky God's realm of influence. Jones claimed that he was a highly evolved black soul incarnated in a white body, but whose black hair and dark eyes revealed his affinity with black people. Like Jesus, Jones was born into a poor family. Jones claimed that he was previously incarnated as Moses to lead the Hebrews out of slavery, as Jesus to preach the gospel of human dignity and equality to the socially oppressed, and as Lenin to establish communism in the U.S.S.R. Jones as savior was the person who most fully manifested the Principle of Socialism, and his mission was to teach others to become gods like himself, complete manifestations of Socialism. Jones's purpose was to liberate all, particularly people of color and women, who were oppressed, commodified, enslaved, and used in the capitalist economic system. Jones would save people from being classified as subhuman by sinful capitalism, and restore to them their dignity and full humanity.[37]

David Chidester has pointed out that Jim Jones's alienation from American culture was expressed in his orientation toward the communism of the U.S.S.R., the People's Republic of China, and Cuba, and also in his claim to be an extraterrestrial visiting this degraded and corrupt world on a rescue mission. Jones's doctrine of reincarnation relativized embodiedness; characteristics of sex and race were temporary and would, in all likelihood, change in the next incarnation.[38]

Jones taught that the world soon would be destroyed by nuclear holocaust, and that the surviving elect would then create a new socialist Eden on Earth. After he returned to Indiana from Brazil, Jones predicted that the nuclear catastrophe would occur on July 15, 1967. This prediction impelled the relocation of Peoples Temple to Redwood Valley. After his prophecy was disconfirmed, Jones claimed that "I know the day," but would not specify another date. This had the effect of maintaining the urgency generated by belief that the current world would be destroyed imminently.[39]

Jones taught that the United States would suffer the greatest destruction in the nuclear holocaust. Only communists, such as members of Peoples

In May 1978, Rev. John and Barbara Moore visited their two daughters and grandson in Jonestown. Barbara Moore, on the right, stands with Peoples Temple members relocating to Jonestown. The majority of Jonestown residents were African Americans seeking relief from racism and poverty in the United States. (Photo courtesy of Rebecca Moore)

Temple, the U.S.S.R., and China had made adequate preparations to survive. Nuclear destruction would be the means used by Divine Socialism to wipe away evil capitalism and open the way for the socialist millennial condition.[40]

Dualism characterized the catastrophic millennial worldview taught by Jim Jones. The United States was the Antichrist and capitalism was "the Antichrist system." The United States was "Babylon,"[41] and Jones would lead the elect to the promised land where they would build a new Eden.

The success of Jones's political and social service activities in California marked a period in which Peoples Temple had the potential to become a progressive millennial movement, achieving its millennial condition through social service. Instead, active opposition by the federal government, the anticult organization calling itself the Concerned Relatives, and the media convinced Peoples Temple members they were being systematically persecuted, which caused them to cling to their dualistic catastrophic millennial perspective and to see themselves as being on the righteous side in a pitched battle of good versus evil.

The Persecution

The racially integrated Peoples Temple was persecuted by white racists in California. After the San Francisco church building was fire-bombed and badly damaged in August 1973, the church's board of directors passed a resolution on October 8, 1973, to establish an agricultural mission in Guyana. Temple members believed local Neo-Nazis had burned their church. Members of the American Nazi Party threatened Peoples Temple members and their children in Redwood Valley and Ukiah, California. Neo-Nazis sent them hate mail, and slashed the tires of Temple members' cars.[42]

By 1977 Peoples Temple was under attack by ex-members, particularly Tim Stoen, and Al and Jeannie Mills (formerly named Elmer and Deanna Mertle), who initiated a campaign against Peoples Temple with multiple fronts. They enrolled reporters to produce highly negative news stories about Peoples Temple, they prompted several federal agencies to investigate Peoples Temple, and they lobbied congressmen to investigate Peoples Temple. The defectors and parents of Peoples Temple members coalesced into a group (of primarily whites) calling themselves Concerned Relatives.

Both the Concerned Relatives and Jonestown residents perceived their relation to each other in simplistic, dualistic terms. It was a battle of good versus evil, with each side convinced it was in the right and the other was evil. The dualism of Jim Jones and Peoples Temple members had long led them to act on their conviction that their ultimate goal of multiracial communal justice and brotherhood justified the use of any means including deception, illegal activities, coercion, and violence. The dualism of the Concerned Relatives also led them to conclude that their goal of their loved ones' liberation from Peoples Temple justified the use of any means, including telling exaggerated atrocity tales to the press and to government agents, kidnapping, and "deprogramming." Steve Katsaris made unsuccessful plans to kidnap and deprogram his daughter. Tim Stoen likewise claimed that he would kidnap John Victor Stoen. Concerned Relatives and Peoples Temple were opponents in a war.[43]

The mass exodus of Peoples Temple members to Jonestown before adequate facilities were constructed was in response to a negative article appearing in the August 1, 1977, issue of *New West*,[44] in which defectors made allegations of sexual, financial, and physical abuses. Tim Stoen and Grace Stoen (by that time divorced) initiated legal proceedings to wrest custody of John Victor from Jones.

In a manner typical of the anticult movement, Concerned Relatives demonized Jim Jones and Jonestown as a dangerous "cult" that had to be dismantled.[45] The defectors continued to see the world in dualistic terms, but now Jim Jones was evil incarnate and the Concerned Relatives were the good guys. It was still a war of good versus evil, and former Peoples Temple members worked just as eagerly to oppose Jim Jones as they earlier had worked to support Jones and his cause. The dualism of the defectors only fed the fears of distressed relatives, such as Steve Katsaris, the father of Maria Katsaris, a young woman in Jones's inner circle who had taken over the mothering of John Victor Stoen.

The aggressive mobilization of legal, media, and federal resources to attack Jonestown, which culminated in the investigative visit by Congressman Leo Ryan, increased the sense within Jonestown of being besieged by evil forces that aimed to destroy their precious community. John Victor Stoen, whom Jones was determined not to give up, became the symbol in Jonestown for the potential for dismemberment of their community by outside evil forces. The demonization of Jim Jones and Jonestown by the Concerned Relatives was matched by the demonization of the Concerned Relatives, the news media, the federal government, and American capitalism by the residents of Jonestown. For both sides it was "us versus them," us versus the alien, evil other.

Jim Jones, a professed communist, expected to be persecuted by the United States government, and the facts appeared to bear out his expectation. In California in November 1976, when Unita Blackwell Wright, an African American mayor of a small Mississippi town, spoke to the Peoples Temple about her trip in 1973 to the People's Republic of China, Peoples Temple security guards noticed a man with electronic equipment on church grounds. They traced his rental car and discovered that he was an air force electronics expert who investigated possible sources of interference with the

U.S. national defense radar system. In 1977, Jones learned through an informant and his people's intelligence work, that the allegations of defectors had stimulated a Treasury Department investigation of the Peoples Temple. Peoples Temple leaders were well aware of the harassment of another new religious movement, the Unification Church ("Moonies"), by the Internal Revenue Service. The Peoples Temple leaders believed it was better to leave the United States than risk loss of financial resources to the IRS.[46]

Rebecca Moore has argued that Jonestown residents were caught in a "vise," consisting of lawsuits filed by Tim Stoen and Concerned Relatives, investigations and actions by federal agencies that threatened the continued existence of Jonestown, dismay caused by internal dissension, highly negative press stories, and fears that their status in Guyana was precarious because of the Guyanese political situation. The Jonestown residents had no place to go to escape the multiple pressures. Jim Jones could not return to the United States, where lawsuits and a criminal complaint were pending against him.[47] African American residents of Jonestown did not see returning to racist America and ghetto life as a viable option. The white members did not want to be disloyal to the blacks and their shared ideal of multiracial justice and harmony.

In May 1978, Tim Stoen, an attorney, filed suit against Jones and Peoples Temple asking for damages of over $56 million. A detective, Joe Mazor, working for Concerned Relatives, hired a San Francisco public relations firm to coordinate a negative publicity campaign against Peoples Temple. Jeannie Mills made false allegations that Jonestown was stockpiling illegal weapons, and this prompted an investigation by the U.S. Customs Service beginning in February 1977.[48] The Customs Service sent reports containing the exaggerated allegations to the State Department and Interpol, the international police organization. An Interpol report based on the Customs Report was shown to Peoples Temple leaders by Guyanese police.[49] Carolyn Moore Layton wrote to her parents in December 1977 that the Interpol document confirmed for the Jonestown residents that there was a conspiracy against Jonestown.

> The media has advertised us in the most grotesque and unreal manner—due to this conspiracy which is indeed real, though I know you are not conspiracy-minded and tend to pooh-pooh the idea. I saw myself the Interpol [Customs] report which a high officer in government allowed a number of us to read firsthand. They are accusing us of the most absurd things—trafficking in weapons and currencies. This I saw with my own eyes....[50]

The negative news reports about Peoples Temple prompted a variety of investigations by American federal agencies. The Social Security Administration (SSA) asked the U.S. embassy in Guyana to send officials to Jonestown to interview Social Security recipients to make sure they were not being held against their will. Consul McCoy visited Jonestown a total of three times in 1977 and 1978, and none of the seventy-five people interviewed wanted to leave. McCoy later said, "Anyone who says it was a concentration camp is just being silly. For the old people, and the people coming from the ghetto, it was relatively better."[51] The Federal Communications Commission (FCC) began monitoring Jonestown shortwave radio communications beginning in April 1977. The FCC fined Jonestown ham operators for broadcasting messages out-of-band, and Jonestown residents feared that the FCC intended to cut off their sole source of communication with the outside world. In the summer of 1977, the U.S. Postal Service returned Social Security checks (totalling about $37,000 monthly for about 200 recipients) bound for people living in Jonestown to the U.S. Treasury Department. This continued until December 1977, but in spring 1978 more Social Security checks were misrouted. Since financial assets were held in common in the Peoples Temple, the loss of the monthly Social Security income threatened the economic survival of Jonestown. Another threat materialized in February 1978, when the Internal Revenue Service said it was investigating Peoples Temple to determine if any of its income was taxable.[52]

The residents of Jonestown were convinced that the Central Intelligence Agency (CIA) was working to destroy their community. After all, they were Americans espousing communism and living in a socialist country. To determine if the CIA actually had an interest in Jonestown, Fielding McGehee (whose two sisters-in-law died in Jonestown) filed a lawsuit in 1980 under the Freedom of Information Act to obtain the CIA's files on Peoples Temple and Jonestown. The heavily excised documents that were obtained from the CIA indicated that CIA agents were operating in Guyana. The CIA was the agency that first notified the U.S. Defense Department of the deaths by poisoning at Jonestown.[53] Subsequent to the 1978 Jonestown deaths, the House Foreign Affairs Committee produced a report on "The Assassination of Representative Leo Ryan and the Jonestown, Guyana Tragedy." The vast bulk of this twelve-volume report remains classified, including sections on whether there was a conspiracy against Jim Jones and Peoples Temple, whether the violence could have been foreseen, whether there was a conspiracy to kill Congressman Leo Ryan, the investigation of Peoples Temple by the Customs Service, and the role and performance of the State Department in the case.[54] According to Rebecca Moore, "The Jonestown tragedy continues because the government will not examine its role in the affair...."[55]

In response to the threats posed by Concerned Relatives, the media, and the American government, draconian measures were instituted within Jonestown to stifle dissent and keep people from defecting. It was feared that defectors would join the outside evil forces attempting to destroy Peoples Temple; therefore, it was all-important to control dissent. At Jonestown, a punishment imposed by Jones was to make the offender chew and swallow hot peppers. Rebellious residents of Jonestown were drugged; some were kept sedated in the "Special Care Unit." Troublemakers, including people who attempted to escape, had to perform hard physical labor or were confined in coffin-sized boxes. Jim Jones manipulated people by pretending to have heart attacks, or by staging gunfire attacks on himself that he attributed to the CIA, mercenaries, or Guyanese soldiers.[56] Jones mediated all information about events in the outside world to Jonestown residents by recounting his version of the news over the public address system. Jones presented reports that made the outside world seem a dangerous place on the brink of nuclear war and/or other conflicts.[57]

Paranoia in Jonestown was increased by the attempts of the Stoens to gain custody of John Victor Stoen. Carolyn Moore Layton wrote about the custody case:

> Pragmatically the issue of John Stoen is not an isolated custody case to us. From the political perspective we know that if we do not get backing on this issue, how could we ever have confidence in the government backing us on far more controversial issues. We also know that if John Stoen were taken from the collective, it would be number one in a series of similar attempts.... It was very much for the good of the collective that we decided as a group to make a stand on the John Stoen issue.... No child here would ever again feel secure if we handed over John Stoen.... [58]

After Grace Stoen was granted custody of John Victor in California, her attorney visited Jonestown at the end of August 1977 to pick up the boy, but John Victor and Jones were nowhere to be found. After the attorney departed, Jones returned to Jonestown and made claims of being besieged by the Guyana Defense Force. For three days and nights, someone fired shots into Jonestown. Talking by shortwave radio to Marceline in the United States, Jones said that they would all commit suicide. Marceline Jones frantically solicited assurances from Guyanese officials that Jonestown would not be assaulted. After another California court decision gave custody of John Victor to Grace and Tim Stoen, they, with Grace's attorney, went to Georgetown, Guyana, to initiate legal proceedings there.[59]

Increasingly, it appeared to Jonestown residents that Jonestown was not the promised land of safe refuge. They explored the possibility of

Kimo Prokes (left) and John Victor Stoen (right) playing in Jonestown. (Photo courtesy of Rebecca Moore)

relocating to Cuba or the U.S.S.R. but received no encouragement from those countries.

Peoples Temple leaders desperately looked for advocates who shared their dualistic and embattled perspective. Their own attorney in the United States, Charles Garry, was discredited in their eyes for reporting that he could find no evidence that the U.S. government was conspiring against Peoples Temple and for advising that Jonestown open itself up to investigators. They found the advocates they wanted in Mark Lane, an attorney noted for his conspiracy theories about the assassinations of John F. Kennedy and Martin Luther King Jr., and in Don Freed, another conspiracy theorist and Hollywood writer. Lane and Freed persuaded Joe Mazor, a private detective who had worked for Concerned Relatives, to visit Jonestown and confess his activities against Peoples Temple. Lane was hired as a Peoples Temple attorney and public relations consultant, and he announced he would file lawsuits against various Concerned Relatives, the U.S. attorney general, the FBI, and the CIA for conspiring to destroy the Peoples Temple.[60]

The confrontation that immediately provoked the murders and mass suicide was the visit of Congressman Leo Ryan to Jonestown on November 17-18, 1978. Ryan's visit brought into Jonestown the enemies most hated by Peoples Temple members: the press, Concerned Relatives, and the American government. Initially, Jones point-blank refused permission for Ryan and his party to visit Jonestown. Peoples Temple members wrote to Ryan asking him not to visit Jonestown, and saying that if he did,

they regarded his visit as intended to destroy Jonestown. Jones grudg-
ingly acquiesed to the visit only when Ryan and his party made arrangements to come anyway. Once in Jonestown, the reporters insisted on
being taken into a building that Peoples Temple members did not want
them to inspect; it was an overcrowded dorm for seniors. At the end of
the visit, while the camera filmed, reporter Don Harris aggressively questioned Jim Jones for 45 minutes about weapons, physical punishment, and
drugs. As the defectors were getting into a truck, a woman remaining in
Jonestown began screaming because her husband was taking their children without telling her of his plans to leave. While Congressman Ryan
informed Jones that his report would be primarily positive, that he saw no
coercion being used to keep people in Jonestown, and that he recommended that Jonestown increase its interaction with the outside world,
Ryan was attacked by a man wielding a knife. Ryan demanded that the
man be arrested, but then the party hastily departed for the airstrip. As
soon as Ryan's party left, a short and unusually violent thunderstorm
eerily blew into Jonestown.[61]

The Failure of the Millennial Goal

Jonestown was already failing to achieve its residents' goal of becoming a
model socialist collective prior to the visit of Ryan, the Concerned Relatives, and the reporters. Mary McCormick Maaga has pointed out that
about one-half of the Jonestown residents were elderly or juveniles.
About 150 people were sixty-five years of age or older, and 340 were nineteen years of age or younger.[62] The able-bodied adults had to work hard
to provide material support, health care, and education to the other residents. By the time of the mass suicide, the adult residents were tired and
despaired of whether their collective was working. This was particularly
true of the women leaders in Jones's inner circle.

The ultimate concern of the Jonestown residents was to preserve their
community. Loyalty to the collective was the primary value. In solidarity,
each person served according to her or his capacity, and each person
received community services according to her or his needs. For the African
American residents, Jonestown was an improvement in quality of life compared to their existence in racist America. For the young, white, college-
educated residents, Jonestown was a sacrifice in standard of living to
achieve their ideal of human unity. Maaga has pointed out that the defectors were primarily whites with the social and financial resources to return
and be integrated back into American mainstream society.

In the dualistic Peoples Temple worldview, people who defected were
demonized as traitors. The traitor was the "most dangerous person of all,"

because he or she appeared to be an insider, but in fact was an outsider.[63] Since the ultimate concern was to maintain the community at all costs, no one wanted to be seen as disloyal.

Every defection was an assault against the ultimate concern, and there were defections beginning when Peoples Temple was located solely in the United States. Eight young people defected in 1973. Al and Jeannie Mills defected in late 1975.[64] Grace Stoen defected in July 1976, before the move to Guyana, and Tim Stoen defected from Guyana in June 1977.[65] Two white women who had been entrusted with Peoples Temple's complex banking arrangements defected from Jonestown: Debbie Layton Blakey in May 1978 and Teri Buford in October 1978. Debbie Layton Blakey reported to the American embassy at Georgetown that Peoples Temple members were rehearsing mass suicide.[66]

When Congressman Ryan departed from Jonestown, his party included sixteen defectors, the majority belonging to the Parks and Bogue families. The Parks and Bogue families were Indiana sect members, so they were some of the earliest members of Peoples Temple. The Parks family helped run the Jonestown medical clinic, and Jim Bogue, an Indiana farmer, was the settlement's agricultural manager and one of Jonestown's founding pioneers. The defection of such long-time and important members was a tremendous blow to the collective, and it was particularly demoralizing to the remaining Indiana sect members.[67] Jim Jones begged Jerry Parks not to leave with the enemies of the Peoples Temple, and he offered to pay for the Parks's travel costs if they would leave a few days after Ryan's party departed. When Jerry Parks refused, Jones was crushed and said, "I have failed." Calling the defectors "traitors," Jones said, "All is lost. I live for my people because they need me. But whenever they leave, they tell lies about the place."[68]

In addition to the looming economic and organizational failure of Jonestown, and the specter of the disintegration of the community caused by defections and the attacks by Concerned Relatives, the news media, and the American government as symbolized by Congressman Ryan, there was also the increasingly obvious failure of Jim Jones to be the messiah. For the majority of the residents of Jonestown: "To love God's justice on earth was to love Jim Jones; to be loyal to socialist values was to be loyal to Jones."[69] The members of the inner circle knew that Jones did not perform miracles, but many of the church members believed that Jones was a messiah who could heal and prophesy. Jones had saved many of them from death in the ghettos of racist America. But Jim Jones was addicted to drugs, and his addiction worsened after he moved to Jonestown. His orders were increasingly erratic, and many knew that wild orders given on the spur of the moment would be reversed later. His speech heard over the public address system was slurred. People saw Jones staggering or urinating in public view.[70] Increasingly, Jones was unable to walk without assistance.

Jim Jones was a messiah in danger of being discredited in the eyes of his followers. In Jonestown, Jim Jones was the patriarch of a dysfunctional family—dysfunctional because no one wanted to acknowledge the mental illness of their beloved and idealized Dad.

The Decision to Commit Violence

Rebecca Moore has argued that the members of Peoples Temple, and especially the residents of Jonestown, were bonded together by their shared participation in the life of the community, which increasingly included participation in rituals of violence. The Peoples Temple's emphasis on violence was not exceptional, but was congruent with the violence committed by mainstream American society and government. In the United States, boxing matches were utilized by Peoples Temple members to punish and humiliate troublemakers. In Jonestown, dissidents were drugged. People who attempted to escape were captured and confined. The level of institutional control and corresponding internally-directed violence and fear of attack escalated as the persecution by Concerned Relatives, federal agencies, and the media intensified. It was all important to preserve the collective from destruction by a hostile external world and internal traitors. Residents of Jonestown began rehearsing to commit "revolutionary suicide" to protect the cohesiveness of their community.[71]

Jim Jones first mentioned suicide as a possible response to the defections of eight young people in 1973. In 1976 the first suicide drill was conducted within Jones's inner circle as a loyalty test. For at least a year prior to fateful November 18, 1978, revolutionary suicide[72] was discussed publicly at Jonestown; residents wrote essays expressing their feelings and thoughts on the subject. A rationale that many found compelling was that it might be necessary to kill the children in order to protect them from being "brainwashed" by capitalists. In 1978 there were drills in which Jonestown residents drank what was purported to be a poisoned beverage. Subsequently, Jones explained that the drill was a loyalty test that prepared them to commit suicide in the future. Jerry Parks, who left with Congressman Ryan, reported that there had been five or six suicide drills during the seven-and-a-half months he had been in Jonestown.[73]

Maaga has pointed out that it is inaccurate to attribute the decision to commit group suicide solely to Jim Jones. She has demonstrated that Jim Jones's power in Peoples Temple, in fact, declined when he moved to Jonestown. Jones knew how to wield power and influence in urban contexts, but he had no skills to run an agricultural settlement in the jungle. The inner circle of leaders close to Jones, mostly young white women, applied their administrative skills to run Jonestown. At Jonestown, the emphasis was on medical health care, and not on Jones's healing power.[74]

There were abuses of authority by Jim Jones at Jonestown, but the community's isolation and will to succeed as a socialist collective prompted people to carry out or overlook coercive measures to control dissidents.

The women within the inner circle at Jonestown were increasingly stressed. The leaders were not privileged in the Jonestown lifestyle; they worked hard and felt the heavy burden of providing for everyone in the collective. They were tired, and they wondered if they were going to fail to achieve their goal of creating a socialist community. They may have thought of leaving Jonestown, but that would have meant repudiating their ultimate concern of preserving the collective. For the leaders, leaving would have meant rejecting the responsibility they had undertaken for the well-being of everyone in Jonestown. This ultimate concern and the demonization of traitors made it unthinkable to give up and leave. As an alternative to passively watching Jonestown disintegrate, the white leaders (the young college-educated NRM members) increasingly thought that perhaps Jonestown could become a symbol of socialist solidarity in protest against corrupt capitalism by committing revolutionary suicide.[75]

The rapid deterioration of Jim Jones's health and behavior increased the stress on the Jonestown leaders. Jones's erratic behavior made it increasingly likely that Jones himself would cause the failure of Jonestown.

The attacks by the Concerned Relatives and the press, and the Concerned Relatives' success in prompting investigations by federal agencies and in getting Congressman Ryan to visit Jonestown increased the pressure on the Jonestown residents. The paranoid, dualistic view within Jonestown was that their beloved community soon would be destroyed by outside evil forces. The possibility that John Victor Stoen might be removed from Jonestown symbolized to them the threat to the community.[76]

Peoples Temple members often stated that they were prepared to die for their ultimate concern. On March 14, 1978, Pamela Moton wrote to the U.S. Congress alleging conspiracies against the Peoples Temple. Moton wrote, "I can say without hesitation that we are devoted to a decision that it is better even to die than to be constantly harassed from one continent to the next. I hope you can...protect the right of over 1,000 people from the U.S. to live in peace."[77] After defecting, Debbie Layton Blakey signed an affidavit stating that there had been a drill in which everyone drank a red liquid and were told that they would all die within forty-five minutes. Then Jones informed them that it had been a loyalty test, but soon they would have to die by their own hands.[78] During the summer of 1978, Mike Prokes wrote to the *San Francisco Examiner*, "We have found something to die for, and it's called social justice. We will at least have had the satisfaction of living that principle, not because it promised success or reward, but simply because we felt it was the right thing to do."[79] Prior to Congressman Leo Ryan's trip to

Guyana, Grace Stoen and Debbie Layton Blakey briefed the U.S. State Department on the possibility of mass suicide in Jonestown.[80]

The defections of Teri Buford and Debbie Layton Blakey demonstrated that members of the inner circle were capable of becoming traitors. The departure of the Parks and the Bogue families was a blow to the Indiana-sect members remaining in Jonestown. The evidence that even founding members of Peoples Temple could abandon the ultimate concern made the Indiana-sect members willing to cooperate in the group suicide in order to preserve the community. At the last community meeting in Jonestown, Jim Jones facilitated the persuasion of the black urban church members to commit suicide, and they agreed that the most important thing in the world was to remain loyal to their community. The black members did not want to be disloyal like the white defectors.[81]

In addition to their decision to direct violence inwardly, a few Jonestown men first directed violence externally to take revenge against those who threatened their community. Prior to his departure, Ryan was attacked by a knife-wielding Jonestown resident. The two Peoples Temple attorneys, Charles Garry and Mark Lane, wrestled the knife away from Don Sly (known in Jonestown as Ujara), and Ryan was not injured. Ryan and his party left immediately. John Victor Stoen (age six) remained in Jonestown. None of the defecting Jonestown residents leaving with Ryan at that time were related to the Concerned Relatives. Larry Layton, the brother of Debbie Layton Blakey and the former husband of Carolyn Moore Layton, pretended to be a defector and left with Ryan's party. Larry Layton probably was a planted assassin, for he fired a gun inside the partially boarded airplane while half a dozen other men from Jonestown opened fire on members of Ryan's party outside the plane. In the attack on Ryan's party, shots were fired at close range to make sure that Congressman Leo Ryan, NBC reporter Don Harris, NBC cameraman Bob Brown, and *San Francisco Examiner* photographer Greg Robinson were killed.[82]

During the final Jonestown gathering, Jim Jones claimed, "I can't control these people. They're out there. They've gone with guns."[83] As the Jonestown physician and nurses prepared the poison and organized its distribution, Jones articulated in a final rambling speech that he, too, believed in the ultimate concern of loyalty to the Jonestown collective. He would stick with his people even when they committed violence, and to preserve their community he would join them in suicide.[84] Jones blamed the ex-members for the necessity of committing suicide, particularly Tim Stoen and Deanna Mertle (Jeannie Mills), for prompting Congressman Ryan to make his unwelcome visit to Jonestown.

The audiotape of Jonestown's final gathering as the poison was prepared, distributed, and given (first to the children) provides a lesson in the

Jim Jones and Peoples Temple members in Jonestown. (Corbis)

danger of succumbing to peer pressure and of uncritically giving authority to a charismatic leader. Christine Miller, a sixty-year-old black woman,
argued with Jones that suicide was not the proper response. Miller suggested that they could relocate to Russia, and Jones claimed to put in a call
to Russia to convince her that Russia would not take them. Miller argued
that the handful of people who defected were not worth the lives of the
whole community. She asserted that she believed that "as long as there's
life there's hope. . . ." Jones did not silence Miller, but he began to remind
her and the members that he was a prophet with all the answers. Miller
stated, "I'm not ready to die," and argued that the babies deserved to live.
She further argued that by committing suicide they were just letting themselves be defeated by their enemies. Jones again said he was "speaking as a
prophet today," and "I cannot separate myself from the pain of my people. You can't either, Christine, if you stop to think about it. You can't
separate yourself. We've walked too long together." Miller then asserted
that "we all have a right to our own destiny as individuals."

   At this direct challenge to the ultimate concern of Peoples Temple —
loyalty to each other as members of a socialist collective — another person
intervened. Jim McElvane, a black man who was the head of Peoples Temple security in California, spoke up. He had arrived in Jonestown only
two days previously. McElvane shifted the focus of the discussion back to
the ultimate concern — communal solidarity — but with the emphasis that

the community identified with Jim Jones and his salvific power: "Christine, you're only standing here because he was here in the first place. So I don't know what you're talking about, having an individual life. Your life has been extended to the day that you're standing there because of him." Another woman acknowledged to Jones, "you've saved so many people." Jones's reply indicated that he still believed himself to be a manifestation of Christ: "I've saved them. I saved them, but I made my example. I made my expression. I made my manifestation and the world was not ready, not ready for me. Paul said, 'I was a man born out of due season.' I've been born out of due season, just like all we are—and the best testimony we can make is to leave this goddamn world. [Applause]" Christine Miller complained that people were becoming hostile toward her, but Jones encouraged her to speak and said that she was not a traitor: "I know you're not a runner." But Miller decided to stop arguing: "That's all I have to say." Christine Miller chose to die with her community.

Other Peoples Temple members continued testifying, and McElvane spoke up again to offer the concept of reincarnation as a comfort to people as they committed suicide together. He claimed that as a therapist who had conducted past-life regressions, he knew that stepping over to the other side "feels good." Numerous other people thanked Dad for his love, for giving them life and also death. Jim Jones reiterated McElvane's statements about reincarnation by saying that dying was "just stepping over to another plane." Toward the end, Jim Jones expressed his conviction that "this world is not our home," and that the Jonestown community by committing suicide was saying, "we don't like the way the world is." Jim Jones's last words on the audiotape were, "We got tired. We didn't commit suicide, we committed an act of revolutionary suicide protesting the conditions of an inhumane world."[85]

Annie Moore, a nurse and the twenty-four-year-old sister of Carolyn Moore Layton, apparently was the last person to die.[86] Annie wrote a final letter that concluded with the following paragraphs:

> Jim Jones showed us all this—that we could live together with our differences, that we are all the same human beings. Luckily, we are more fortunate than the starving babies of Ethiopia, than the starving babies of the United States.
>
> What a beautiful place this was. The children loved the jungle, learned about animals and plants. There were no cars to run over them; no child molesters to molest them; nobody to hurt them. They were the freest, most intelligent children I had ever known.
>
> Seniors had dignity. They had whatever they wanted—a plot of land for a garden. Seniors were treated with respect—something

they never had in the United States. A rare few were sick, and when they were, they were given the best medical care....

Underneath the note, in different colored ink, she added:

We died because you would not let us live in peace. Annie Moore[87]

The Jonestown residents' ultimate concern was preserved.

Notes

1. Mary McCormick Maaga, "Triple Erasure: Women and Power in Peoples Temple," Ph.D. diss., Drew University, 1996, Appendix Two, transcript of audiotape of the final Jonestown gathering, 154.
2. John R. Hall, *Gone from the Promised Land: Jonestown in American Cultural History* (New Brunswick, N.J.: Transaction Books, 1987), 279.
3. Rebecca Moore, "'American as Cherry Pie': Peoples Temple and Violence in America," in *Millennialism, Persecution, and Violence: Historical Cases*, ed. Catherine Wessinger (Syracuse: Syracuse University Press, 2000), 121–37; Maaga, "Triple Erasure," 5.
4. Hall, *Gone from the Promised Land*, 291.
    Mike Prokes and Tim and Mike Carter were not present for the group suicide because the women leaders had sent them off with suitcases filled with the Peoples Temple financial assets to deliver to the Soviet embassy in Georgetown. See Hall, 280-81.
5. Maaga, "Triple Erasure," 5-6; Hall, *Gone from the Promised Land*, 155, 293; Lawrence Wright, "Orphans of Jonestown," *New Yorker*, November 22, 1993, 66-89.
    Jim and Marceline Jones adopted a number of children into their "rainbow family": Agnes was part Native American. Stephanie (who died at age five in a car accident), Lew, and Suzanne were Korean. Their surviving children are Stephan Gandhi Jones, their only natural child who is white, James Warren Jones Jr., who is African American, and Tim Jones, who is white. To a great extent, Stephen, Jimmy, and Tim were saved from the group suicide because they were young men rebelling against their father, and perhaps they perceived their father's insanity more clearly than many other Jonestown residents. See Wright, "Orphans of Jonestown."
6. Hall, *Gone from the Promised Land*, 3-6, 11; Rebecca Moore, *Sympathetic History of Jonestown: The Moore Family Involvement in Peoples Temple* (Lewiston, N.Y.: Edwin Mellen Press, 1985), 148-50.
7. Hall, *Gone from the Promised Land*, 16.
8. Hall, *Gone from the Promised Land*, 17, 144; Moore, *Sympathetic History*, 150.
9. Hall, *Gone from the Promised Land*, 17.
10. Moore, *Sympathetic History*, 151-52.
11. Hall, *Gone from the Promised Land*, 18-22.
12. Hall, *Gone from the Promised Land*, 19-22, 24-26, 146; David Chidester, *Salvation and Suicide: An Interpretation of Jim Jones, the Peoples Temple, and Jonestown* (Bloomington: Indiana University Press, 1991), 38.
13. Hall, *Gone from the Promised Land*, 23-25, 31.
14. Moore, *Sympathetic History*, 155.

15 Hall, *Gone from the Promised Land,* 32, 36, 145, 175-76; Moore, *Sympathetic History,* 157-59.

16. Hall, *Gone from the Promised Land,* 35.

17. Hall, *Gone from the Promised Land,* 37.

18. Maaga, "Triple Erasure," 1-2.

19. Hall, *Gone from the Promised Land,* 45-56, 146.

20. Hall, *Gone from the Promised Land,* 57-9.

21. Chidester, *Salvation and Suicide,* 5, 109-10.

22. Maaga, "Triple Erasure," 2; Hall, *Gone from the Promised Land,* 160, 163; Chidester, *Salvation and Suicide,* 109-10.

23. Maaga, "Triple Erasure," 71-83, 126; Wright, "Orphans of Jonestown," 68.

24. Laurie Efrein Kahalas, *Snake Dance: Unravelling the Mysteries of Jonestown* (New York: Red Robin Press, 1998).

25. Maaga, "Triple Erasure," 70. This situation sounds bizarre but it is a known human organization of power. In Yorubaland in southwest Nigeria, the sovereign of the Oyo kingdom had numerous wives who traveled as his delegates and exercised power in his name; men who performed similar governing functions for the Oyo king were known as his "wives." See J. Lorand Matory, *Sex and the Empire That Is No More: Gender and the Politics of Metaphor in Oyo Yoruba Religion* (Minneapolis: University of Minnesota Press, 1994).

26. Maaga, "Triple Erasure," 76.

27. Maaga, "Triple Erasure," 53.

28. Maaga, "Triple Erasure," 61, note 21. This statement was signed also by Marceline Jones. See Hall, *Gone from the Promised Land,* 127.

29. Moore, *Sympathetic History,* 229.

30. Maaga, "Triple Erasure," 8, 54; Rebecca Moore, *The Jonestown Letters: Correspondence of the Moore Family 1970-1985* (Lewiston, N.Y.: Edwin Mellen Press, 1986), 112. Carolyn Moore Layton and Mike Prokes were married in December 1974 to provide legitimate status to her child. Therefore, Carolyn's son was known as Kimo Prokes. See Moore, *Sympathetic History,* 100.

31. Maaga, "Triple Erasure," 3, 6; Hall, *Gone from the Promised Land,* 133; Moore, *Sympathetic History,* 116.

32. Hall, *Gone from the Promised Land,* 153.

33. Hall, *Gone from the Promised Land,* 153, 163, 166, 168-70.

34. Hall, *Gone from the Promised Land,* 177, 178-89.

35. Maaga, "Triple Erasure," 3; Hall, *Gone from the Promised Land,* 161.

36. Chidester, *Salvation and Suicide,* 51-56, 64-68.

37. Chidester, *Salvation and Suicide,* 56-59, 60-63, 73-78.

38. Chidester, *Salvation and Suicide,* 79-92, 124.

39. Chidester, *Salvation and Suicide,* 109-11.

40. Chidester, *Salvation and Suicide,* 111-13.

41. Chidester, *Salvation and Suicide,* 90.

42. Moore, *Sympathetic History,* 115-16.

43. Hall, *Gone from the Promised Land,* 210-53, 256.

44. Chidester, *Salvation and Suicide,* 142.

45. Maaga, "Triple Erasure," 3, 28.

46. Hall, *Gone from the Promised Land,* 176, 182-83, 207.

47. Moore, *Sympathetic History,* 259, 273-315.

48. After the mass suicide/murder, only ten guns, thirteen small-calibre rifles, seven shotguns, and a flare gun were found in Jonestown. See Hall, *Gone from the Promised Land,* 293.

49. Moore, *Sympathetic History,* 259, 277-82. The content of the report is given in

full on pages 280-81.

50. Moore, *Sympathetic History*, 282.

51. Moore, *Sympathetic History*, 287-88, quote on 288.

52. Moore, *Sympathetic History*, 275, 292-301; Moore, "'American as Cherry Pie.'"

53. Moore, *Sympathetic History*, 399-427; Rebecca Moore, *In Defense of Peoples Temple—And Other Essays* (Lewiston, N.Y.: Edwin Mellen Press, 1988), 152-53.

54. Moore, *Sympathetic History*, 360-61; Moore, *In Defense*, 149-51.

There were numerous federal investigations of Jonestown after the deaths on November 18, 1978. The Bureau of Alcohol, Tobacco, and Firearms (ATF) found that Jonestown had no illegal weapons. In fact, for a community living in the jungle, Jonestown was remarkably underarmed. The Department of Health and Human Services found that Jonestown was not committing welfare fraud. The U.S. Customs Service reported that no customs violations had been committed by Peoples Temple. See Moore, *In Defense*, 146-47.

55. Moore, *In Defense*, 153.

56. Hall, *Gone from the Promised Land*, 233, 240-41; Wright, "Orphans of Jonestown," 72, 77-78, 80; Moore, *Sympathetic History*, 218, 220, 309-11; Moore, "'American as Cherry Pie.'"

In California physical punishments were administered. Offending adults had to box stronger members in literal battles between justice (the collective) and anarchy (individualism); young people were spanked hard with a three-foot paddle. These were punishments that the church members collectively sanctioned against misbehaving members. See Hall, *Gone from the Promised Land*, 123-25, 143.

57. Moore, "'American as Cherry Pie.'"

58. Moore, *In Defense*, 21.

59. Hall, *Gone from the Promised Land*, 217-18, 221; Moore, *Sympathetic History*, 283-87.

60. Hall, *Gone from the Promised Land*, 248-49, 251-53; Moore, "'American as Cherry Pie.'"

61. Hall, *Gone from the Promised Land*, 265-72, 274-77; Moore, *Sympathetic History*, 315, 319-26.

62. In Jonestown, 48 percent of the residents were black women, 22 percent were black men, 14 percent were white women, 10 percent were white men. Fifty women were raising one or two children and eighteen women had three or more children. "Half of the three hundred 'single individuals' at Jonestown were over the age of fifty and nearly all of them were women." See Maaga, "Triple Erasure," 9, 82.

63. Maaga, "Triple Erasure," 28.

64. Hall, *Gone from the Promised Land*, 134; Chidester, *Salvation and Suicide*, 139.

65. Grace Stoen defected with her lover, Walter "Smitty" Jones. Four months prior to her defection, Grace and Tim Stoen had signed a release permitting John Victor to be taken to Guyana. Three months after Grace Stoen defected, Tim Stoen gave the power of attorney for John Victor to Jim Jones, Maria Katsaris, and other Peoples Temple members. In fall 1976, John Victor Stoen, age four, was taken to Guyana. See Hall, *Gone from the Promised Land*, 180-81.

66. Maaga, "Triple Erasure," 117-18, 122.

67. Maaga, "Triple Erasure," 125-26.

Tommy Bogue attempted to escape in 1978, but was captured by the security force. He and friends were shackled in chains and forced to chop wood for 18 hours a day for three weeks. Bogue reported that others who attempted to escape were confined in coffin-sized boxes for several days. See Moore,

"'American as Cherry Pie.'"

68. Hall, *Gone from the Promised Land,* 273-74.
69. Maaga, "Triple Erasure," 65-66, 122.
70. Maaga, "Triple Erasure," 89, 114.
71. Moore, "'American as Cherry Pie.'"
72. The term *revolutionary suicide* came from a 1973 book by that title by Black Panther theorist Huey P. Newton (New York: Harcourt Brace Jovanovich). Jones visited with Newton in Cuba in 1977. See Hall, *Gone from the Promised Land,* 135-36, 205, 218, 295.
73. Maaga, "Triple Erasure," 104-5, 114-15, 120-21; Hall, *Gone from the Promised Land,* 135; Chidester, *Salvation and Suicide,* 130-32.
74. Maaga, "Triple Erasure," 84-87.
75. Maaga, "Triple Erasure," 113-14, 120.
76. Maaga, "Triple Erasure," 105-6.
77. Hall, *Gone from the Promised Land,* 229.
78. Hall, *Gone from the Promised Land,* 246.
79. Hall, *Gone from the Promised Land,* 254.
80. Hall, *Gone from the Promised Land,* 263.
81. Maaga, "Triple Erasure," 123, 126.
    The two Peoples Temple attorneys, Charles Garry and Mark Lane, who remained in Jonestown after Ryan's party left, recounted that they were taken to the guest house so the group suicide could begin. They were told about the plans for revolutionary suicide by two teenagers who passed by. The boys told Garry and Lane how to walk to Port Kaituma, and then returned to the group to commit suicide themselves. See Hall, *Gone from the Promised Land,* 281.
82. Maaga, "Triple Erasure," 124, 142, note 1; Hall, *Gone from the Promised Land,* 276-79; Moore, *A Sympathetic History,* 327.
83. Maaga, "Triple Erasure," Appendix II, 143.
84. Maaga, "Triple Erasure," Appendix II, gives the entire transcript of the final Jonestown gathering, 142-57.
85. Maaga, "Triple Erasure," 142-57.
86. A Jonestown resident hiding in the jungle heard six gun shots. Later it was found that two shots had been fired to kill two dogs, two shots had been fired into the pet chimpanzee, one shot had killed Jim Jones, and one shot to the head killed Annie Moore. The final and sixth shot was heard a good while after the others. Moore, *Sympathetic History,* 335.
87. Moore, *Jonestown Letters,* 286.

CHAPTER FOUR

1993—Branch Davidians

This is where existence is for me in the world.
There is no existence outside this vicinity.
This is where David is, he is revealing the Seals,
and this is what the world should have been waiting for.
—Bernadette Monbelly, March 9, 1993, on videotape made
by the Branch Davidians released to the FBI

Those tanks are not fireproof, you know.
—David Koresh, March 19, 1993, to FBI negotiator[1]

The Violence

The Branch Davidians were a catastrophic millennial group that was assaulted because it was perceived by law enforcement agents to be dangerous. Unlike Jonestown and Aum Shinrikyo, the Branch Davidian community at Mount Carmel Center outside Waco, Texas, was not a fragile millennial group. The Branch Davidian community was not suffering from internal weaknesses that made the believers despair about the accomplishment of their ultimate concern. In 1993, the Branch Davidians were not a threat to the general public or to law enforcement agents.

The Davidians' ultimate concern was to obey God's will, as revealed in the Bible, in order to be included in the millennial kingdom. They were armed for self-protection during armageddon, which they believed was imminent. The Davidians expected to be attacked by evil "Babylon." Former Davidians, who did not believe in David Koresh's messiahship and his interpretation of the Bible, already had left Mount Carmel. The remaining

Davidians formed a cohesive community that was convinced of Koresh's divinely inspired ability to interpret the Bible.

All of the persecutory actions taken against the Davidians by federal agents in 1993 confirmed Koresh's prophecies and enhanced his status as the messiah in the eyes of his followers. Unlike Jim Jones, David Koresh was not in danger of failing to be the messiah. The Davidians had no doubt that the ultimate concern would be accomplished according to God's plan. I think this is why the Davidians were able to withstand so much persecution, which included physical attacks, psychological warfare, and deprivation. Despite all the persecution, the Davidians still attempted to negotiate a peaceful resolution to the siege.

The Davidians did not want to die, and they attempted to negotiate with FBI agents up until the very end. The FBI agents did not understand that the Davidians were not going to do anything unless they believed their actions were in accordance with God's Word as revealed in the Bible. FBI agents tried to force the Davidians to submit to "proper" authority. The Davidians were willing to cooperate with federal agents only to the extent that it conformed to their understanding of God's Word.

Every act of violence in the Branch Davidian case is disputed. The testimonies of Branch Davidians and U.S. federal agents contradict each other. This case involved approximately 123 Davidians[2] and hundreds of law enforcement agents—each with a unique experience and understanding of the cataclysmic events in 1993. In the following summary of events, I report important allegations, but I attempt to steer clear of most of the numerous allegations for which there is no clear evidence. The facts of this case are extremely complex as well as disputed, so I describe the violence involving the Branch Davidians here in considerable detail.

About 9:45 A.M. on Sunday, February 28, 1993, Mount Carmel Center, the residence of a religious community called the Branch Davidians,[3] was raided by seventy-six heavily armed agents of the Bureau of Alcohol, Tobacco, and Firearms (BATF or ATF). In the shootout that followed, four ATF agents were killed, twenty ATF agents were wounded—some severely—five Davidians were killed, and four Davidians were wounded, including their thirty-three-year-old messiah, David Koresh. That afternoon at about 4:55 P.M., three Davidians, who had been away at work, Michael Schroeder, Norman Allison, and Woodrow Kendrick, attempted to return to Mount Carmel Center. Michael Schroeder (29) was shot and killed by ATF agents, Norman Allison was arrested, and elderly Woodrow Kendrick escaped, despite his heart condition.[4]

The next day, FBI agents took control of the site and presided over a siege that lasted fifty-one days. During the siege, fourteen adults and twenty-one children exited Mount Carmel.[5]

The siege of the Branch Davidians concluded on Monday, April 19, 1993, when, beginning at about 6:00 A.M., FBI agents in tanks sprayed and shot rounds of chlorobenzylidene malononitrile (CS) gas into the building and used the tanks to punch holes into the walls and demolish parts of the building. At about noon the residence rapidly caught fire, producing an inferno. Nine Davidians escaped. Seventy-four Davidians died in the fire. Of these, twenty-three were children, including two infants who were born when their mothers expired.[6]

These facts do not even begin to describe the violence in the Branch Davidian tragedy—the preponderance of which was committed by federal law enforcement agents. Federal agents committed physical, mental, symbolic, constitutional, and judicial violence against the Davidians,[7] who were regarded as members of an aberrant cult and were therefore despised and dehumanized.

In addition to the physical violence that resulted in loss of human life, physical violence was committed in the willful destruction of the Davidians' property. ATF agents violated the Davidians' constitutional right to possess legal firearms and to be safe in their home from unwarranted violent entry by law enforcement agents. Mental violence was committed by federal agents against the Davidians in the form of intimidation, threats, and psychological warfare. Symbolic violence was committed by federal agents who told lies about the Davidians to other federal agents, officials, and judges prior to, during, and after the siege. Symbolic violence was committed by the misrepresentation of the Davidians to the American public because of the FBI-controlled information given to the news media. Constitutional violence was committed against the Davidians' First Amendment right to freedom of religion by the FBI agents who dismissed Koresh's communications as being unintelligible "Bible babble." FBI agents assumed that the Branch Davidians were a "cult" and depicted them as such to the media. FBI agents assumed that the Davidians were non-thinking brainwashed cultists under the total control of David Koresh, and they rejected the advice of credentialed scholars of Religious Studies when it was offered. Judicial violence was committed against surviving Davidians by Judge Walter Smith Jr., who in 1994 overturned the lenient verdicts of the jury and convicted a group of Davidians of conspiracy to murder federal agents, giving them extremely lengthy jail sentences. Judicial violence was committed in the failure of the Department of Justice to file charges and try federal agents responsible for the deaths of Davidians.

I include in the total violence committed against the Davidians the willful resolve of ATF commanders to orchestrate the violent raid, despite lack of adequate cause; the trumped-up allegations in the ATF affidavit to obtain the warrants peacefully; the planning of the ATF raid with no provision to serve the warrants peacefully; the acts of intimidation, destruction of property, and psychological warfare waged by FBI agents during the siege; the FBI use of a gas banned by international treaty for use in warfare against a civilian group that included children; the demolition of the building by tanks, and the fire that resulted from that assault.[8]

Symbolic violence was involved in the exaggerated claims made by ex-Davidians prior to and during the siege, and in the prejudiced application of the term *cult* by anticult activists. The "cult" stereotype was perpetuated and the hysteria was amplified by the media—thus encouraging Americans to see the final outcome of the Branch Davidian siege as a just extermination of nonhuman beings; they were brainwashed cultists duped by a false messiah who was really a con man.

Judicial violence occurred when eleven Davidians were tried in 1994 in San Antonio, Texas, for conspiracy to murder federal agents.[9] On February 26, 1994, the jury found all eleven Davidians innocent of conspiracy to murder federal agents. Three Davidians, Clive Doyle, Norman Allison, and Woodrow Kendrick were found innocent of all charges. The jury concluded that Davidians committed violent acts in self-defense. The jury also believed that the Davidians were not totally innocent of contributing to the tragedy, so they found seven Davidians guilty of lesser charges. Members of the jury subsequently told reporters that they believed the Davidians would receive light sentences and credit for time already spent in prison. The jury found seven Davidians guilty of aiding and abetting voluntary manslaughter, five Davidians guilty of carrying a firearm during the commission of a crime of violence, and two Davidians guilty of other arms violations. U.S. District Judge Walter Smith Jr. initially said that the jury's verdicts were inconsistent with innocence of the conspiracy to murder charge, and he set the verdicts aside. However, the violence against the Davidians continued when Judge Smith subsequently said that the Davidians *were* guilty of conspiring to murder federal agents, and gave them harsh sentences. He sentenced five Davidians to forty years each in prison. These were Renos Avraam (31), Brad Branch (36), Jaime Castillo (27), Livingstone Fagan (36), and Kevin Whitecliff (34). Graeme Craddock (34) was sentenced to twenty years, Paul Fatta (37) to fifteen years, and Ruth Riddle (31) to five years. Kathryn Schroeder (35), a witness for the prosecution, was later sentenced to three years.[10] Appeals were filed and lawsuits were filed on behalf of the surviving Davidians and families of the deceased Davidians.[11] But the wheels of justice turned slowly.

Let us shift attention back to the beginning: the initial ATF investigation.

The ATF investigation was triggered by a report from a United Parcel Service (UPS) driver that he had delivered a parcel to Mount Carmel containing hand grenade casings.[12] In June 1992, ATF Special Agent Davy Aguilera was assigned to investigate the acquisition of arms by David Koresh and the Branch Davidians. During his investigation, Aguilera relied heavily on the allegations of disgruntled defectors (apostates)[13] and on information provided by an anticult organization, the Cult Awareness Network, and by Rick Ross, a deprogrammer.[14] Rick Ross had no scholarly credentials in the study of religion.

David Koresh and Paul Fatta were the Davidians who engaged in the gun trade to financially support the community. Although some guns were purchased in preparation for the anticipated armageddon, Koresh and Fatta also bought guns as an investment to sell later when their value increased. They also bought guns to sell at trade shows. On July 30, 1992, Aguilera interviewed gun dealer Henry McMahon about his legitimate business partnership with Koresh. McMahon called Koresh to inform him of the investigation and Koresh said, "If there's a problem, tell them to come out here. If they want to see my guns, they're more than welcome." McMahon offered the telephone to Aguilera so he could speak to Koresh, but Aguilera waved the phone away.[15]

On January 11, 1993, ATF agents, posing as college students, set up an undercover house across the street from Mount Carmel. The Davidians immediately paid a visit to meet their new neighbors, and from the beginning they realized that these men were undercover agents. Agent Robert Rodriguez (42) (known to the Davidians as Robert Gonzalez) made visits to Mount Carmel, participated in Koresh's Bible study sessions, and was invited to move into Mount Carmel. Rodriguez saw no illegal weapons in Mount Carmel.[16]

On January 27, 1993, an ATF undercover agent, posing as a UPS trainee, visited Mount Carmel. It was so obvious that he was an undercover agent that Koresh called the sheriff's office to complain about being under surveillance.[17] Koresh had a good relationship with local law enforcement agents, and it was his policy to address openly any questions they had and to invite them to come by and visit.

At a meeting in Houston on January 27-29, 1993, ATF officials decided to execute a paramilitary raid against the Davidians.[18] This decision was influenced by ex-Davidians, who had adopted the anticult worldview and had stressed that the Branch Davidians were likely to commit group suicide like the Jonestown residents. They asserted that David Koresh would not submit peacefully to arrest or to a search of Mount Carmel. The apostates emphasized that a siege would become a catalyst for group suicide. When the ATF tactical planners met with ATF officials in Washington, D.C., on February 11-12, 1993, they emphasized that "the element of surprise would minimize the threat of mass suicide...." When Treasury Department officials wanted to cancel the raid, ATF director Stephen Higgins explained on February 26 that "the use of scores of heavily armed agents to execute the warrant by force was necessary" to prevent the Davidians from destroying evidence or committing mass suicide.[19] The memory of Jonestown and the "cult" stereotype determined the nature of the ATF raid.[20]

James Moore, a retired ATF agent, has reported the assumptions about David Koresh and the Branch Davidians that shaped the ATF agents' plan for dealing with them:

Along the way, agents were advised by former cult members that Koresh's followers saw him as God, obeying him implicitly to the extent that male followers went celibate, giving him their wives, and that Koresh was sexually abusing children as young as ten. One girl was fourteen when she gave birth to a Koresh son. These reports, *irrelevant to ATF's official mission*, eliminated any possibility that Koresh was a misguided technical violator of federal laws. This suspect was "*a bad guy.*" More relevant was Koresh's teaching that people who attended church on Sunday were worshiping Satan. Any agent dubious about investigating a "religious group" shivered at the prospect of Koresh's sheep invading a church with bombs and machine guns to "deal with the devil." (emphasis added)[21]

This passage illustrates that ATF agents believed that the Davidians were brainwashed followers of David Koresh and were unable to think for themselves. It should be noted that the ATF agents had no evidence whatsoever that Koresh and the Davidians intended to attack a church. The Davidians were armed for self-defense in the anticipated armageddon. The Davidians also participated in the Texas-American culture, in which gun-owning was normal.

ATF officials named the raid "Operation Trojan Horse," but it was known among the agents as "Showtime." By early 1993, the ATF had a very negative reputation for sexism, racism, and for intrusive raids on private homes. The continued existence of the ATF was in question. A Senate Appropriations Subcommittee meeting was scheduled for March 10, 1993, to consider the ATF budget. Some ATF officials may have thought that the agency would benefit from the good publicity generated by disarming a "dangerous cult." At the 1994 trial "several agents stated that a lead ATF agent yelled the very publicity-conscious phrase 'It's showtime!'

as they exited the trailers" to assault the front of the building.[22] Before the raid, an ATF employee informed reporters that a big raid was going to be launched against Mount Carmel Center.[23]

The presence of news reporters on the scene tipped off the Davidians that the raid was imminent. While attempting to get to Mount Carmel, a reporter asked a mail carrier, David Jones (38), for directions. While they were speaking, a vehicle passed by carrying six ATF agents dressed in combat gear. David Jones, who had grown up at Mount Carmel and continued to live there with his father, his three children, and his two sisters and their children, immediately went to alert David Koresh, his brother-in-law.[24]

What law had David Koresh broken that necessitated the ATF raid?

Davy Aguilera wrote the "Probable Cause Affidavit," which secured the warrants from a U.S. magistrate judge. Aguilera's affidavit utilized flimsy circumstantial evidence to allege that the Davidians were converting semiautomatic weapons to fully automatic weapons without filing the required paperwork and paying the fees. Possessing semiautomatic and automatic weapons was not illegal, but paperwork and fees were required by law for conversion. Koresh had purchased semiautomatic weapons legally as an investment for resale at a higher price if, in the future, the government restricted manufacture of the weapons. Most were kept boxed and never fired. During the trial, these weapons in plastic wrap were displayed in the courtroom. The government did not permit x-raying or removal of the wrappers to determine if the weapons were converted. No physical evidence was produced at the trial to prove that the Davidians fired automatic weapons at the ATF agents.[25] Aguilera's affidavit "did not show intent, a requirement of the law."[26]

Aguilera's affidavit did, however, characterize the Mount Carmel community as a dangerous "cult" and David Koresh as a "power-mad, manipulative cult leader"[27] who administered abusive spankings to the children and raped pre-teen girls.

Allegations of child abuse did not come under ATF and federal jurisdiction. David Koresh had been investigated earlier by the Texas Department of Human Services for possible child abuse, and he had cooperated with this investigation by permitting three visits by social workers to Mount Carmel, by allowing the social workers to conduct private interviews with the children, and by visiting Joyce Sparks, the social worker in charge of the case, at her office to answer questions. Aguilera's affidavit to obtain the warrants emphasized the child abuse allegation without reporting that the case had been closed on April 30, 1992, for lack of evidence.[28]

In fact, David Koresh, did have sexual relations with minor females at Mount Carmel—with the permission of their parents. The young women were considered by the community to be David's wives, and they believed that David's children would become rulers in God's kingdom. By producing children for David Koresh, the "Lamb" and messiah, these young women were doing "the Lord's work." David Koresh, then Vernon Howell, legally married Rachel Jones (14) in 1984. Later Koresh began having sex with girls as young as twelve or thirteen. Koresh began having sex with Rachel's sister, Michelle Jones, in 1987, when Michelle was twelve. Also in 1987, Koresh began having sex with Robyn Bunds when she was seventeen. The young women were legally married to other Davidian men in order to protect Koresh from charges of statutory rape, but the young women were considered Koresh's wives by members of the community. In 1989, Koresh presented a "New Light" teaching that all the men, except himself, should be celibate, and that even the women previously married to other men were now his wives. Judy Schneider (41 in 1993), the wife of Steve Schneider (41 in 1993), bore a daughter by Koresh, Mayanah, who was two years old when she died in the fire.[29] Fourteen of David Koresh's children, most from one to four years old, died in the fire.[30]

In February 1993, Texas Child Protective Services investigated the charges by twelve-year-old Kiri Jewell that her mother, Sherri Jewell, left her when she was ten years old in a motel room with David Koresh, who had sex with her. But the state did not prosecute Koresh because Kiri Jewell refused to press charges. Kiri Jewell made the same allegation at the 1995 congressional hearings on Waco.[31]

As to the charge that David Koresh administered abusive physical punishment to young children, there were only a few alleged incidents dating from 1986 to 1990. In examining the evidence, it was not clear if these episodes represented exaggerations by apostates or if David Koresh sometimes went overboard in controlling the community's children. The children who were interviewed by social workers denied being abused. It was the standard Davidian practice to spank misbehaving children with a wooden spoon named "the helper" in a "whipping room." This practice was similar to child-discipline practiced in other conservative Protestant families in the United States. Saving the children was cited as a motivation for both the ATF raid and the FBI tank assault, in which CS gas was inserted into Mount Carmel. Federal agents subjected the Davidian children to a terrifying gun battle, psychological warfare and deprivation during the fifty-one-day siege, and their agonizing deaths in the tank and gas assault and the fire.[32]

Finally, Aguilera's affidavit alleged that there was a methamphetamine laboratory in Mount Carmel. This was a lie told to gain military assistance. The 1996 House of Representatives majority report demonstrated that ATF commanders knowingly lied in the affidavit and to U.S. military personnel when they asserted that there was a methamphetamine lab inside Mount Carmel. By falsely alleging the existence of a methamphetamine lab, the ATF secured four types of military assistance: (1) surveillance overflights made by the National Guard; (2) training of ATF agents by U.S. Army Special Forces; (3) the use of National Guard helicopters in the ATF raid on Mount Carmel; and (4) post-raid support in terms of personnel and equipment to the ATF and FBI.[33]

The ATF undercover agent, Robert Rodriguez, was inside Mount Carmel on the morning of February 28, 1993, when David Jones brought word that a raid was imminent. After speaking privately with David Jones and Perry Jones (64), Koresh returned to Rodriguez, who saw that he was "very nervous and shaking real bad." Rodriguez testified at the trial, "He turned and told me the ATF and the National Guard were coming." Koresh subsequently reported to FBI agents, "I went to the window, and I says, Robert, I says, it's up to you now....And I turned around and he just—his eyes were real big and everything.... And he goes, 'what do you mean?' I says, Robert, you know what I mean....We know they're coming."[34] As Rodriguez left, fearing the Davidians would shoot him in the back, Koresh shook hands with him and said, "Good luck, Robert."

Rodriguez drove his pickup truck down the Mount Carmel driveway and across the street to the undercover house. He immediately telephoned the raid commander, Charles Sarabyn, and said, "Chuck, they know. They know." Sarabyn asked what the Davidians were doing when he left, and Rodriguez said that "they were praying."[35] Sarabyn conferred briefly with other raid commanders, and they decided to hurry up the raid, making remarks such as "Get ready to go, they know we're coming," and "They know the BATF and the National Guard are coming. We're going to hit them now." It took forty minutes for the ATF agents to arrive at Mount Carmel.[36]

John R. Hall has argued that the cultural narrative of mass suicide, derived from Jonestown, may have been an underlying reason the ATF agents felt the need to "hurry up."

> ...even if preventing the imminent event of mass suicide was not a conscious motive for "hurrying up," the narrative of mass suicide was embedded in the de facto fallback position. On the day of the raid, with the media looking on, if the scenario of dynamic entry failed, then a siege—with its latent element of mass suicide— would be the consequence. Presciently, one tactical planner already had understood that with a siege, as the Treasury Department review put it, "BATF probably would have to assault the Compound anyway, once public pressure on BATF to resolve the situation grew and the government's patience wore thin." The only way to avoid a siege was to "hurry up." On the day of

the raid, BATF raid commanders discounted the importance of lost surprise because accepting it would have required canceling the raid, and canceling the raid would precipitate a siege. Because of the specter of mass suicide, a siege was not a fallback option; it was an imminent event to be avoided.[37]

Despite the fact that the search warrant did not authorize a "no-knock" surprise raid, the ATF agents had trained only for a forcible entry.[38]

After Rodriguez left Mount Carmel, David Koresh told the women to go with the children to their bedrooms on the second and third floors and watch. Since it was early in the morning, the mothers were busy getting the children dressed when the gunfire began.

The women subsequently reported that before the shooting began at the front of the building, shots were rained down upon them from overhead by three helicopters. The women and children huddled under beds and in the hallways; the women covered the children with their bodies. The Davidians later claimed that four of the five Davidians killed in the ATF raid died from shots fired from the helicopters, and the controversial autopsy evidence appeared to confirm this allegation. The women who testified to being fired upon by the helicopters were Marjorie Thomas and Kathy Schroeder (both testified for the prosecution in the trial), Victorine Hollingsworth, Catherine Matteson, and Annetta Richards. In the audiotape of the Davidians' 911 call, Wayne Martin and Steve Schneider claimed that helicopters were firing upon Mount Carmel.

The Davidians allegedly killed by shots fired from the helicopters were Peter Gent (24) who was in the water tower, Peter Hipsman (27) who was in a fourth-floor bedroom, and Winston Blake (28) who was sitting on the edge of his bunkbed eating French toast and wearing a knit shirt that said "DAVID KORESH/GOD ROCKS" and a black ammunition vest with the label, "David Koresh Survival Wear." Hipsman was finished off by two bullets in his head fired at close range. Jaydean Wendell (34), mother of four children and a former policewoman, grabbed a rifle and jumped on top of a bunkbed to shoot back at the ATF agents, and was killed by a bullet that struck the top of her head.[39]

With the numerous bullets penetrating the roof, walls, and floors (the ATF agents used armor-piercing bullets and the building was flimsy), it was fortunate that none of the children were killed. Apparently blood did get on a child and Koresh was given information that led him to believe and claim that his two-year-old daughter had been killed.[40] Koresh later dropped this claim, and the surviving Davidians reported that no child was killed in the ATF raid.

During the siege, attorneys for David Koresh and Steve Schneider, the Davidian who spent a great deal of time negotiating with FBI agents, entered Mount Carmel and inspected the bullet holes. Attorneys Dick DeGuerin and Jack Zimmerman testified to the presence of bullet holes in the ceilings with the wood splintered downward, indicating that the shots had been fired from above.[41] These allegations could not be verified after the siege, however, because the entire building was destroyed in the fire.

At the trial in 1994, the three National Guard helicopter pilots, who flew the two small OH-58 helicopters and the large Blackhawk helicopter, testified that the National Guardsmen and ATF agents aboard were armed but had not fired shots. The ATF agents in the helicopters included the raid commander Philip Chojnacki, Ted Royster, an unofficial commander of the raid, and lead investigator Davy Aguilera. The judge prevented defense attorneys from calling to the stand any of the ATF agents in the helicopters.[42]

According to Davidian testimony, the first shots fired in the ATF raid came from the helicopters. But another possibility was that the first shots were fired to kill five dogs (pets) by ATF agents arriving in cattle cars at the front door. ATF agents in this team testified that when they first heard shots, they assumed these were being fired by the agents assigned to take out the dogs.

After the trucks pulling the cattle cars wheeled up to the front door, all the agents jumped off shouting "Police! Search warrant! Lay down!" They saw an unarmed David Koresh in the open door with his unarmed father-in-law, Perry Jones, standing behind him. Koresh had his hands up and shouted, "Go away, there's women and children here, let's talk." Koresh later said that with all the agents shouting simultaneously he could not understand what they were saying: "You've been to a football game and you hear a roar but you don't hear what anybody's saying, right?"[43] When the shooting began, Koresh backed inside and the steel encased double doors were shut. Surviving Davidians have alleged that Perry Jones was wounded in the abdomen by bullets coming through the doors. Armed Davidians standing behind the doors started firing.

The ATF agents have alleged that the Davidians shot first; the Davidians have alleged that the ATF agents shot first. The Davidians, and later attorneys DeGuerin and Zimmerman, alleged that the right-hand side of the front door showed that most of the bullet holes hit the door from the outside and traveled inside the building. During the April 19 fire, a tank driven by an FBI agent pulled the double doors away from the fire (as shown on television), but the right-hand door was never found.[44]

Davidians alleged that Perry Jones was mortally wounded in the stomach. This allegation, as with everything else in the Davidian case, was contested. The autopsy report alleged that Perry Jones had no wound in the abdomen, but died of a single gunshot to the roof of his mouth. Davidians reported that Jones, after being shot in the stomach, was carried into a bedroom and that he was screaming and begging to be put out of his misery. Later, the rest of the Davidians were told that Jones died. Kathy Schroeder subsequently testified that with Koresh's permission, Neil Vaega shot and killed two wounded Davidians, Perry Jones and Peter Hipsman, to end their suffering. It became impossible to verify the autopsy report on Perry Jones's body, because Jones's corpse was one of thirty Davidian corpses stored in the Tarrant County medical examiner's refrigeration unit that somehow was turned off. All the corpses deteriorated, making additional examination impossible.[45]

While the helicopters were overhead and most of the ATF agents on the ground were at the front door, a team of seven agents from New Orleans climbed up on the roof, four to enter a room believed to be Koresh's bedroom, and three to enter a room thought to be an armory. In fact, the gun room was empty because Paul Fatta and his son had left earlier that morning to take the weapons to a gun show. The ATF plan was to break the windows, throw in "flash-bang" grenades (which cause a 175-decibel blast and can cause severe injury), and enter the rooms. Kenneth King, Todd McKeehan, David Millen, and Conway LeBleu were to make the entry into the room thought to be Koresh's bedroom. As they broke the window, shots were fired at them from inside the room wounding Millen and King. A bullet passed through King's right elbow, his chest, and then hit his left elbow. McKeehan (28) and LeBleu (36) were killed. King (48) took four more bullets before he pushed himself off the roof. He nearly died waiting for assistance. King and Millen sustained more wounds. Millen jumped to the other side of the roof where the other three agents, Glen Jordan, Bill Buford, and Keith Constantino, were attempting to enter the other room. They broke the window and threw in a flash-bang grenade and entered the room. Gunfire erupted. Davidian Scott Sonobe (35) was in the hallway shooting at the agents coming in both windows. Millen was able to get off the roof. The three agents in the room returned fire. Bullets hit Buford and Jordan in the legs. Constantino wounded Sonobe in the hand, wrist, and leg. Buford and Jordan exited the room; Buford was hit by a shot that grazed his nose; Constantino got out and dropped off the roof, breaking his hip when he landed on the ground. A New Orleans agent who had remained on the ground to provide cover fire, Robert Williams (27), took cover behind an old safe. When he stood up, he was shot and killed. A KWTX-TV video showed that no shots were being fired from inside the building by Davidians at the time Williams was shot, so he may have been hit by "friendly fire."[46]

If Koresh had surrendered and the agents in front had peacefully entered the building, the team on the rooftop still would have carried out the forcible entry. The men on the roof had no radio communication with the agents at the front of the building. No one on the rooftop team announced to the Mount Carmel residents their reason for forcible entry.[47]

A fourth ATF agent, Steve Willis (32), was killed by the gunfire at the front of the building as he took cover behind a van.[48] A total of twenty ATF agents were wounded, thirteen by bullets and seven by shrapnel.[49]

When the shootout began, Wayne Martin (42), an attorney and father of five children in Mount Carmel, desperately dialed 911 to have the shooting stopped. He spoke with Lieutenant Larry Lynch, the sheriff's deputy assigned to communicate with the ATF agents if the need arose.

> MARTIN: Yeah, there are seventy-five men around our building
> and they're shooting at us in Mt. Carmel!
> LYNCH: Mt. Carmel?
> MARTIN: Yeah. Tell them there are children and women in here
> and to call it off!
> LYNCH: Alright, alright, ah, hello?
> I hear gunfire.
> Oh, Shit!
> Hello? Who is this? Hello?
> MARTIN: Call it off![50]

The sounds of gunfire were clearly heard on the 911 audiotape as Lynch advised Martin that the Davidians should not return fire. Lynch tried to contact the ATF command post on the campus of the Texas State Technical College, but no one responded to the radio. Lynch had to send a campus security officer to the ATF command post to tell ATF agents to call him. Due to the communication problem, a cease-fire was not established for almost an hour.[51]

David Koresh also called and talked to Lt. Lynch, using a cellular telephone.

> KORESH: You see...we told you we wanted to talk. No—How
> come you guys had to be BATF agents? How come you try
> to be so big all the time?
> LYNCH: Okay, David.
> KORESH: There is bunch of us dead, there's a bunch of you guys
> dead. Now, now, that's your fault.
> LYNCH: Okay, let's try to resolve this now. Tell me this,
> now, you have casualties, how many casualties, do you
> want to try to work something out? ATF is pulling back,
> we're trying to uhm—
> KORESH: Why didn't you do that first?
> LYNCH: Okay, all I'm, all I'm doing is handling communica-
> tions. I can't give you that answer, David...

KORESH: Yeah, well, really, let me tell you something.
LYNCH: Okay.
KORESH: In our great country here, the United States, you know
  God has given us a rich history of patriotism. We're not try-
  ing to be bad guys.[52]

Even during the shootout, Koresh launched into an explanation to Lt. Lynch of his interpretation of the prophecies of the New Testament book of Revelation. He explained that God sat on a throne and held in his hand a book sealed with seven seals, and that Koresh had unlocked the symbolism of the seven seals.

KORESH: In the prophecies—
LYNCH: Alright.
KORESH: —it says—
LYNCH: Let me, can I interrupt you for a minute?
KORESH: Sure.
LYNCH: Alright, we can talk theology. But right now—
KORESH: No, this is life. This is life and death!
LYNCH: Okay.
KORESH: Theology—
LYNCH: That's what I'm talking about
KORESH: —is life and death.[53]

David Koresh was seriously wounded by a bullet that struck his side by the hip bone and went out his back. Koresh was also wounded by a bullet that grazed his right wrist and severed the nerve to the thumb. Other Davidians who were wounded were David Jones, whose hard tailbone prevented further entry of the bullet, Scott Sonobe who was wounded in the thigh and hand, and Judy Schneider, wounded when a bullet passed through the length of her right index finger and went through her right shoulder.[54]

Later that afternoon while ATF agents were still in charge of the site and before FBI agents arrived, Michael Schroeder, husband of Kathy Schroeder and father of her fourth child, was shot and killed as he attempted to walk onto the property and return home. The thirteen ATF agents who intercepted Schroeder said that he opened fire on them. Schroeder took three shots to the back and two in the head. Jeffrey Jamar, the FBI special agent who took charge of the site, did not permit Texas Rangers to investigate the scene of Schroeder's death for several days. Schroeder's body was left where it fell.[55]

During the fifty-one-day siege, FBI agents continued to be advised by anticult activists, particularly Marc Breault, a former Davidian and self-styled "cultbuster," the deprogrammer, Rick Ross, and several psychologists and psychiatrists.[56] The anticult activists continued to stress that the siege was likely to conclude with a mass suicide.

The wounded David Koresh, his legal wife, Rachel Jones Howell, and one of their children after the ATF raid. They made statements on a videotape that was given to the FBI. Rachel said, "Thanks a lot for killing my dad." David said about the raid, "It should have been dealt with differently."

During the siege, the efforts of the FBI negotiators to win the David-ians' trust in order to get them to come out peacefully were undermined by the FBI tactical commanders' strategy of intimidation, coercion, and destruction of evidence. Richard Rogers, the FBI agent in charge of the Hostage Rescue Team (HRT), had also been in charge of the HRT at the siege of the Randy Weaver family at Ruby Ridge, Idaho, in 1992 (see chap-ter 6). The FBI's own behavioral scientists, Pete Smerick and Mark Young, concluded that because of their religious beliefs, the Davidians would not react in the same manner as criminals. Smerick and Young advised that tactical pressure would only strengthen the Davidians' religious faith and their cohesion as a group, making them determined to resist the federal government they saw as satanic "Babylon." They advised that aggressive actions taken against the Davidians only confirmed Koresh's prophecies, and thus enhanced his authority in the eyes of his followers. They advised that the FBI agents should pull back the perimeter, keep a low-key armed presence, and rely on time and negotiation to bring the Davidians out.[57] They warned that "tactical presence...if carried to excess, could eventually be counterproductive and could result in loss of life."[58] They recom-mended that the Davidians be encouraged to surrender to Texas Rangers as intermediaries. This advice was not what the tactical commanders wanted to hear, so pressure was put on Smerick and Young to alter their recommendations in order to justify aggressive action. Smerick left Waco in disgust. Only after retiring from the FBI in 1995 did Smerick offer his account to the news media. Smerick testified at the 1995 Waco hearings cosponsored by the House Judiciary and House Oversight and Reform Committees, and said that on several occasions FBI agents destroyed Davidian property after the Davidians had cooperated. More graphically, an interpretive log of the siege, compiled by James Tabor, indicated that whenever Davidian adults began to leave Mount Carmel in significant numbers, FBI agents implemented psychological warfare tactics or destroyed Davidian property. That angered the Davidians and made them more determined not to surrender.[59]

Carol Moore has provided a chronology of the events of the fifty-one-day siege,[60] which forms the framework for my chronology that follows, which has been supplemented with information from additional sources.

On February 28, 1993, after the ATF raid and the subsequent shooting of Michael Schroeder, CNN televised a live interview with David Koresh at 8:00 P.M. At 10:00 P.M., four children were sent out of Mount Carmel.[61]

On March 1, FBI Special Agent in Charge Jeffrey Jamar took command of the site and the FBI Hostage Rescue Team (HRT), headed by Richard Rogers, arrived. During the siege, a total of 668 FBI agents were deployed, as were 6 people from U.S. Customs, 15 from the U.S. Army, 13 from the Texas National Guard, 31 Texas Rangers, 131 from Texas Department of Public Safety, 17 from McLennan County Sheriff's Office, and 18 Waco police. The FBI command post was set up on the campus of Texas State Technical College. All telephone lines from Mount Carmel, except those to the FBI, were disconnected and tanks were brought in.[62] Ten children left Mount Carmel and Koresh promised that if his taped sermon was played on national networks in prime time, they would all leave together.

On March 2, two women, Catherine Matteson (71) and Margaret Lawson (75), and four children came out. Matteson brought out an audiotape made by Koresh. Matteson and Lawson were led away to jail in handcuffs.[63] It was charged that the two old women "did knowingly and willfully use weapons, including machine guns, to commit the violent crimes of murder and attempted murder of federal law enforcement officers."[64] (Every adult Davidian who exited Mount Carmel was made to put on an orange prisoner's jumpsuit and was led away in front of television cameras in handcuffs and leg chains.)[65] Koresh's audiotape was played at 1:30 P.M. by KRLD radio station and the Christian Broadcasting Network. For several hours, Koresh and the Davidians prepared to exit Mount Carmel. A few Davidians considered formulating a suicide plan. After 4:00 P.M., David Koresh relayed to FBI agents that he was instructed by God to wait for further orders from God about when the Davidians should come out.[66] Koresh and the Davidians explained to the negotiators that they had to obey the orders of their commander, God, just as the FBI and ATF agents had to obey the orders of their human commanders. God, through David Koresh, told the Davidians to wait.

On March 3, the charges were dropped against the two harmless old women. One child left Mount Carmel. An ATF agent retrieved a gun from the location of Michael Schroeder's body, but the body was left where it fell. (Texas Rangers and FBI agents finally retrieved Schroeder's body on March 5 or 6.) Koresh spent a total of five hours explaining his theology based on his interpretation of the Bible to FBI negotiators.[67]

On March 4, one child left Mount Carmel. Koresh spent seven hours talking to FBI negotiators attempting to communicate his Bible-based apocalyptic view of the situation.[68]

On March 5, one child exited Mount Carmel. Koresh talked to negotiators most of the day. Koresh stated that he would not come out until he was ordered to do so by God. When asked if he would send out more children, Koresh said, "We're dealing with my children, these are different than the other children."[69] Davidians recovered Peter Gent's body from the water tower and requested permission to bury it.

On March 6, Steve Schneider told an FBI negotiator that he thought the FBI planned to burn the building in order to destroy evidence that the ATF agents had shot at them. David Koresh offered to send out a child, Melissa Morrison (6), if he were permitted to speak with Robert Rodriguez. This deal was refused, and Melissa Morrison was not sent out. That evening Koresh spent two hours explaining his apocalyptic theology to negotiators.[70]

On March 7, Dr. J. Phillip Arnold, a Religious Studies scholar with the Reunion Institute in Houston, attended an FBI press briefing in Waco and extended an offer to FBI spokesman Bob Ricks to interpret Koresh's Bible-based language for the FBI. Ricks brushed off Arnold, saying, "There is nobody who can understand what this man is saying."[71] Koresh spent three hours communicating his religious views to negotiators. Negotiators had conversations with other Davidians. FBI agents offered to send in milk, if more children were sent out. Koresh said, "You're dealing with my biological children now…that's what we've come down to."[72]

After the FBI ignored the Davidians' repeated requests to take Peter Gent's body for burial, on March 8 the Davidians buried Gent's body outside the residence. FBI agents delivered milk to the Davidians. The Davidians sent out a videotape depicting the wounded David Koresh introducing the children.[73]

On March 9, the Davidians sent out a second videotape in which the adults explained why they were choosing to wait on God. FBI agents did not release the videotapes to the press as the Davidians wished. Realizing that they were being dehumanized and demonized by the FBI reports to the media, the Davidians unfurled a sheet from a window on which had been written, "God Help Us We Want the Press." The Texas Department of Protective and Regulatory Services took custody of the twenty-one children who had come out of Mount Carmel away from their parents still inside. This discouraged Davidians from sending more children out, particularly Juliette Martinez (30), who would die in the fire with five of her children, ages three through thirteen. Koresh had no intention of sending his twelve children out. The other children who would die in the fire were the two eldest Martin daughters (13 and 15), Melissa Morrison (6), and Rachel Sylvia (13).[74]

On March 10, FBI agents sent in a videotape of negotiators pleading with the Davidians to come out and end the siege peacefully. Over four hours were spent communicating with Davidians.[75]

On March 11, FBI agents prevented David Koresh's attorney, Dick DeGuerin, and Koresh's mother, Bonnie Haldeman, from entering Mount Carmel. The Davidians were excited by hearing on the radio information about a newly discovered nebula shaped like a guitar.[76] They understood this as a heavenly sign confirming that David Koresh was the messiah.

On March 12, Janet Reno was sworn in as the new attorney general. Davidians Kathy Schroeder and Oliver Gyarfas left Mount Carmel. FBI agents were informed that three more Davidians planned to come out the next day. FBI agents cut off electricity to Mount Carmel, angering Koresh and Steve Schneider. In the days to come, the FBI turned on the electricity briefly so that the Davidians could see on television the FBI press briefings.[77]

All during the siege, family members of the Davidians sent faxes and registered letters to the FBI and Attorney General Janet Reno, offering to negotiate with their relatives. The FBI refused to permit this, and Reno was never shown these letters. Offers received from individuals to serve as third-party intermediaries also were turned down.[78]

On March 13, Schneider informed FBI agents that the three adults who had planned to come out would not do so. The Davidians were angered about the lack of electricity because of the cold nights. Schneider alleged to negotiators that the government wanted to kill them and burn the building down. Dr. Phillip Arnold attended an FBI news conference in Waco and asked questions.

On March 14, the Davidians hung a banner from a window saying, "FBI broke negotiations, we want press." FBI agents began shining bright lights into Mount Carmel to disrupt the Davidians' sleep.[79]

On March 15, Steve Schneider and Wayne Martin met outside with FBI negotiator Byron Sage and Sheriff Jack Harwell. By telephone, Steve Schneider reported to FBI agents the enthusiastic response of Davidians after listening to Dr. Arnold discuss the Bible on a KRLD radio program. Schneider asked that Dr. Arnold be permitted to discuss the biblical prophecies with David Koresh to see if Arnold could offer alternative interpretations. Schneider stated that if Arnold could prove from the Bible that the Davidians should come out, the Davidians would exit Mount Carmel regardless of whether or not David Koresh agreed.[80] Special Agent in Charge Jeffrey Jamar instructed negotiators not to listen to any more of Koresh's "Bible babble."

On the evening of March 16, Davidians used flashlights to flash a message to reporters in Morse code, "SOS, SOS, FBI broke negotiations. Want negotiations from press." The FBI directed bright spotlights at night into Mount Carmel effectively obscuring future SOS messages.[81]

On March 17, the FBI began playing audiotapes of the Davidians who had left Mount Carmel on loudspeakers.

On March 18, negotiator Byron Sage addressed Davidians over the P.A. system. Tanks removed diesel and gasoline storage tanks.[82]

On March 19, the FBI sent in an audiotape of Arnold's radio discussion of the Bible. David Koresh said that the Davidians would come out soon. Brad Branch and Kevin Whitecliff left Mount Carmel and were arrested.

On March 20, David Koresh said two adults would come out on the next day.[83]

On March 21, seven adult Davidians came out: Victorine Hollingsworth, Annetta Richards, Rita Riddle, Gladys Ottman, Sheila Martin, James Lawton, and Ophelia Santoya. The FBI began blasting high decibel sounds at Mount Carmel. Koresh and Schneider angrily said that no one else would exit. During the coming days the sounds blasted at the Davidians included sirens, bagpipes, seagulls, crying babies, dentists' drills, crowing roosters, dying rabbits, Tibetan Buddhist chants, Muslim prayer calls, Christmas carols, a train in a tunnel, songs by Alice Cooper, and Nancy Sinatra singing "These Boots Were Made for Walking." The Davidians panicked when sounds of helicopters were played.[84]

On March 22, FBI agents on site began discussing "stress escalation" and using tear gas. Jamar sent in a letter to Koresh promising a worldwide radio broadcast of his message as well as live news coverage of his exit if he came out, and the ability to preach from jail. Koresh destroyed the letter.

On March 23, Livingstone Fagan came out.

On March 24, conversations between Davidians and negotiators were angry. High decibel sounds were blasted at the Davidians. They refused to talk. At 6:30 P.M., Louis Alaniz sneaked into Mount Carmel to join the Davidians. Bright lights were shone at the building all night. Audiotapes of previous negotiations and of Davidians who had come out were played all night.[85]

From March 25 to 28, FBI agents demanded that the Davidians exit and when they refused, the tanks destroyed vehicles and go-carts belonging to the Davidians. These vehicles could have provided material evidence concerning whether there was shooting from helicopters and the amount

Aerial photo of Mount Carmel Center. (Photo courtesy of the United States Justice Department)

of shots fired by the Davidians and by ATF agents.[86] The Davidians sent out a third videotape of Koresh and the children on March 28. Jesse Amen sneaked into Mount Carmel to join the Davidians.

On March 29, Dr. Arnold heard that the FBI planned a gas assault against the Davidians. Arnold then initiated a plan to communicate with the Davidians, via a radio broadcast, to persuade them to come out based on interpretation of the biblical prophecies.[87] Attorney Dick DeGuerin went inside Mount Carmel and met with his client, David Koresh. Dick DeGuerin went back inside on March 30 and 31.

On March 31, Dr. Arnold called an FBI agent and left a message informing the FBI of the importance of the forthcoming radio discussion of the Bible by himself and Dr. James Tabor. He urged FBI agents not to undertake a violent assault against the Davidians.[88]

On April 1, Dr. Arnold and Dr. Tabor discussed the Bible on the Ron Engelman radio show, to which the Davidians were listening. They offered an interpretation of the book of Revelation to show that God did not will the Davidians to die at the hands of Babylon at that time. The angel holding a "little book" in Revelation 10 was mentioned. Arnold and Tabor argued that Koresh needed to come out to spread the message of God's salvation to the rest of the world.[89] Dick DeGuerin, attorney for David

Koresh, and Jack Zimmerman, attorney for Steve Schneider, spent eight hours inside Mount Carmel. They reported to FBI agents that the Davidians were planning to come out.[90]

On April 2, Steve Schneider told negotiators that the Davidians would come out after Passover. Meanwhile, in Washington, D.C., FBI Director William Sessions approved the plan to gas Mount Carmel.

On April 4, Dick DeGuerin and Jack Zimmerman took an audiotape of the radio discussion of Arnold and Tabor inside Mount Carmel. Jesse Amen came out. Upon exiting Mount Carmel, DeGuerin and Zimmerman alleged to the media that ATF agents shot from helicopters; this story was published the next day in the *New York Times*. The attorneys told FBI agents that the Davidians would come out after Passover.[91]

On April 6, Schneider complained to the FBI about the disturbing lights and music during Passover. FBI stopped the lights and music.[92]

On April 7, Davidians explained to FBI agents that Passover lasted seven days.

On April 8, Schneider said they would come out after Passover. The Davidians hung a banner saying, "Rodney King, We Understand."

On April 9, 10, and 11, Koresh sent out letters concerning prophecies in the Bible and warned of God's retribution in natural disasters. These letters of prophetic warning extensively citing scripture were shown to an anticult psychologist, who concluded that Koresh was psychotic and was not going to come out. This psychologist had no knowledge of the biblical references in the letters. On April 11, the bright lights, music, and noise were directed at Mount Carmel during the night and into the early morning.[93]

On April 12, the plan to gas Mount Carmel was presented to Attorney General Reno. Reno was told that the CS gas was not harmful to children, and she was not informed that CS gas was highly poisonous and flammable.[94]

Passover ended on April 13. At a White House meeting, Assistant Attorney General Webster Hubbell informed White House Counsel Bernard Nussbaum and Deputy Counsel Vincent Foster about the plan to utilize CS gas; Nussbaum informed President Clinton.

On April 14, Koresh sent out a letter saying that at long last God had spoken to him and had instructed him to write down in a "little book" his interpretation of the Seven Seals in Revelation. After he sent the manuscript to his attorney and copies were given to Arnold and Tabor for safekeeping, the Davidians would come out. Schneider requested that a typewriter and typewriter ribbon be sent in. After the Davidians heard David Koresh say that they would come out soon, their cheering was recorded on the negotiation audiotape.[95] Reno was briefed again on the plan to gas the residence, but was not told about Koresh's letter promising to come out.

On April 15, FBI negotiator Byron Sage told Assistant Attorney General Webster Hubbell that negotiations were going nowhere.

On April 16, FBI Director William Sessions urged Reno to approve the plan to gas the Davidians. The Davidians requested a battery-operated wordprocesser to expedite the typing of Koresh's manuscript. Koresh assured a negotiator that all the Davidians would come out as soon as he completed his book on the Seven Seals. He reported that he had already completed his interpretation of the First Seal (see transcript of the negotiation audiotape at the end of this chapter).[96]

On April 17, Louis Alaniz came out of Mount Carmel. Reno approved the plan to gas Mount Carmel. Davidians again asked for a battery-operated wordprocessor and supplies in order to type Koresh's manuscript.[97]

On April 18, Reno informed President Clinton of the plan for the FBI assault against Mount Carmel, and he concurred. Tanks removed and crushed the remaining vehicles that belonged to the Davidians. Koresh called a negotiator and demanded to know what the FBI really wanted, and warned that they were making a tragic mistake in taking aggressive action (see transcript of negotiation audiotape at the end of this chapter). At 5:32 P.M., the battery-operated wordprocessor and related supplies were delivered to the Davidians.[98]

The plan, approved by Attorney General Reno, called for insertion of CS gas into Mount Carmel gradually over 48 hours. If the Davidians did not exit, the tanks would begin dismantling the building. The plan stated that if the Davidians indicated a willingness to negotiate, the assault should halt. The plan called for a team of social workers led by Joyce Sparks to be on site with portable showers that would be used to wash the chemicals off the children as they came out. The children would be dressed in dry clothing and taken to safety. The written plan contained a clause stipulating that if the Davidians fired at the tanks, the process of gassing and demolishing the building would be escalated. The commanders on site had the power to make the decision to accelerate the assault. FBI agents knew that the Davidian adults had gas masks, but that there were no gas masks for the children. Reno and Jamar later testified at the 1995 Waco hearings that they expected the Davidians to fire on the tanks, and, therefore, the assault would most likely be accelerated.[99]

On April 19, Joyce Sparks learned that the FBI assault had begun when she received a call from the governor's office, wanting to know why she and the social workers were not at Mount Carmel. Sparks put in a call to Jeffrey Jamar and was told that the FBI "doesn't know if anyone is coming out." Getting off the telephone Sparks told her husband, "They intend to kill them all."[100]

The FBI assault began at 6:00 A.M., with Janet Reno and other Washington officials watching on CNN. The tanks used grenade launchers to hurl in more than 400 "grenades" or ferret rounds containing CS gas. Some tanks sprayed the gas through holes that the tanks punched in the building walls. FBI agents alleged that after making a call to inform the Davidians the gas assault was beginning, the telephone was thrown out the front door. Surviving Davidians later denied this and said that the tanks severed the telephone line. At 9:10 A.M., the Davidians hung out a banner saying, "We want our phones fixed." Davidian Graeme Craddock went outside and signaled to FBI agents that the telephone line was severed. The FBI agents did not reestablish communications with the Davidians.[101]

At 10:00 A.M. (11:00 A.M. Eastern Standard Time), Reno departed the FBI Operations Center in Washington to travel to Baltimore to deliver an address. Assistant Attorney General Webster Hubbell remained at the Operations Center. Shortly thereafter, the tanks began dismantling the building. FBI agents later claimed that the Davidians had fired on the tanks.[102]

During the assault, the young children and their mothers huddled inside a room on the first floor that was constructed of cement blocks and had contained a walk-in refrigerator and a gun room. They covered themselves with wet blankets to protect the children from the gas. Many of the other adults, including Koresh and Schneider, were on the second floor, while others were scattered around the building in places like the gymnasium and the chapel.[103]

At about 11:19 A.M. the tanks began demolishing the gymnasium, and one tank fully entered the gym. Other tanks smashed the front of the building. A tank pulled the controversial double front doors away from the building. The largest tank entered the front doorway of the building, knocking down the stairway. This tank also may have caused concrete to crash down on women and children in the cement block room, causing some deaths. Elsewhere, tanks destroyed the two other staircases. A tank in the chapel knocked over containers of lantern fuel.[104] At 12:01 P.M. Byron Sage said over the loudspeaker, "David, we are facilitating you leaving the compound by enlarging the front door. David, you have had your fifteen minutes of fame....Vernon is no longer the Messiah. Leave the building now."[105]

A tank smashed into the wall of the east front corner; its boom smashed into a second floor room. A small flame appeared there at 12:07. By 12:08 a large fire was seen in the dining room. At 12:08 another fire was seen in the gymnasium where the roof had collapsed. The separate fires quickly escalated to consume the building. At 12:13 FBI agents called the fire department. Tanks continued demolishing the building as it burned. Fire engines arrived at 12:34, but were held back by FBI agents. From about 12:30 to 12:45, tanks with bulldozer blades pushed the burning walls and debris into a pile of burning rubble. At 12:41 the firefighters were permitted to begin putting out the fire.[106]

The cause of the fire was unclear. An FBI agent said that he saw a Davidian set a fire, and FBI agents alleged that the Davidians had com-

Tanks at the burning Mount Carmel Center. (Photo courtesy of John Mann)

mitted suicide.[107] Surviving Davidians claimed that they had not made a suicide pact. Indeed, John R. Hall, an eminent scholar of Jonestown, concluded: "The mass suicide at Mt. Carmel—if that was what occurred—lacked the ritualistic and collective character of the mass suicide at Jonestown. In the face of the continuing assaults, people at Mt. Carmel died in different parts of the building, some from the fire, others from gunshot wounds, either self-inflicted or 'mercy killings' at the hands of others."[108]

FBI surveillance microphones inside Mount Carmel reportedly picked up a discussion the night of April 18, in which plans were made to fight the tanks with fire. Dr. Phillip Arnold, who has listened to the audiotapes, concludes that the Davidians may have set the fires in self-defense. Based on Nahum 2:13 and Zechariah 2:5 in the Old Testament, the Davidians may have believed that God would permit them to destroy the tanks with fire. If the fire consumed the Davidians, then it would fulfill the prediction in the Fifth Seal of Revelation that Babylon would destroy the community of godly people initiating armageddon leading to God's victory, and the establishment of God's kingdom.[109]

The FBI interpreted certain conversations captured on April 19 on a surveillance device as Davidians discussing the pouring of fuel, but the sound quality of the tape was poor and inconclusive.[110] Surviving Davidians denied this theory, and claimed that the fires were started when the tanks knocked over kerosene lanterns that were used because the electricity had been cut off.

The only fact known for certain was that the fires started in each location where tanks were demolishing the building. There were 30 mph winds and both the CS gas and the solvent with which it was mixed, methylene chloride, were flammable. The building was made of old wood and plasterboard, and in addition to the furniture and clothing in the building, there were bales of hay stacked against the walls to keep out the cold.[111]

Some Davidians escaped the fire. Clive Doyle, Graeme Craddock, David Thibodeau, Jaime Castillo, and Derek Lovelock escaped from the chapel. Ruth Riddle jumped from the second floor. Misty Ferguson escaped from the west front of the building. Renos Avraam escaped from a second floor bedroom onto the roof and from there he jumped to the ground. Marjorie Thomas, who was severely burned, jumped from the second floor. When Ruth Riddle saw FBI agents coming toward her, she was fearful and attempted to run back toward the building. FBI agents caught her. In her pocket was discovered a disk on which was saved David Koresh's interpretation of the First Seal of Revelation, that had been typed the night before.[112]

The fire burned the Branch Davidian flag flying on a flagpole near the building. "By the time that fire trucks had chilled the building's ashes, a new and victorious banner was flying in its place—someone had raised the flag of the ATF."[113]

On May 12, 1993, the FBI leveled the Mount Carmel rubble with bulldozers. Jeffrey Jamar explained, "They're just filling holes so people won't fall in the pits. That's just part of taking care of the scene."[114]

A poll by CNN/Gallup found that 73 percent of Americans believed that the decision to use CS gas on the residents of Mount Carmel was "responsible," and that 93 percent of Americans blamed David Koresh for the deaths of the Branch Davidians.[115] The news reports did not inform the public that the United States had signed an international treaty at the 1993 Chemical Weapons Convention in Paris agreeing not to use CS gas in warfare.[116]

The 1996 House of Representatives majority report on the Branch Davidian tragedy concluded "that CS insertion into the enclosed bunker at a time when women and children were assembled inside that enclosed space could have been a proximate cause of or directly resulted in some or all of the deaths attributed to asphyxiation in the autopsy reports." In using the CS gas, "the FBI failed to demonstrate sufficient concern for the presence of young children, pregnant women, the elderly, and those with respiratory conditions." The majority report concluded that the CS gas "might have impaired the ability of some Davidians to be able to leave the residence had they otherwise wished to do so."[117]

In an addendum to the House of Representatives majority and minority reports, Representative Steven Schiff reported that he believed that the evidence indicated that the demolition of the building by the tanks had cut off most avenues of escape, and that many people were incapacitated by the CS gas.

The Government's use of CS gas in the manner it did, that is, clearly designed to incapacitate men, women and children in a

Judy Schneider and her daughter Mayanah during the seige. In her videotaped statement Judy said, "I think now we need to sit back and see...what is really going on in our government."

confined, unventilated space, after avenues of escape had been deliberately cut off, was unconscionable; as was the cursory manner in which the Government, and especially Attorney General Reno "bought into" the conclusory and simplistic analyses that the use of CS gas posed an "acceptable" level of risk.[118]

Representative Schiff deplored "the militarization of domestic law enforcement and the lack of accountability by Federal law enforcement," and he pointed out that military operations aim to "demolish an 'enemy'" and military tactics run "roughshod over the 'niceties' of caring for the rights of those involved."[119]

David Koresh

The young messiah who died at age thirty-three (the supposed age of Jesus at his death) in the Mount Carmel holocaust, was born on August 17, 1959, and named Vernon Wayne Howell. He was the son of a fifteen-year-old girl, Bonnie Clark. Bonnie did not marry Vernon's father, but she briefly married another man. That marriage ended in divorce because her husband beat two-year-old Vernon. Bonnie left Vernon with her parents in Houston and moved to Dallas. After Bonnie married Roy Haldeman, she brought Vernon, then five, to join them. Roy Haldeman was a carpenter and Bonnie Haldeman operated a construction clean-up service. Vernon's half-brother, Roger, was born shortly thereafter.[120]

Vernon had a learning disability and did poorly in school. In the third grade he was placed in a special education class. When his class joined the other children for recess, the kids shouted "here comes the retarded kids!" Vernon was crushed. During his childhood, other children called Vernon "Mr. Retardo." Vernon learned how to read but had difficulty writing and spelling. An average student, he dropped out of school in the eleventh grade.[121]

Vernon was fascinated with machines, such as radios and cars, and he learned to play the guitar. He was very religious and his grand-mother, Earline Clark, took him to the Seventh-day Adventist Church. Vernon loved listening to the sermons in church and also to the preaching of television and radio evangelists. Vernon memorized large portions of the Bible.[122]

In 1977, when Vernon (18) was working as a carpenter, he fell in love with a sixteen-year-old girl. She became pregnant, but by the time Vernon decided that it was his duty to marry her, she had already had an abortion. They continued their love affair, and when she became pregnant again, her father ran Vernon off. The lovesick Vernon Howell, pining for his lost love, moved into Mount Carmel in 1981 when he was twenty-two.[123]

Mount Carmel had been founded in 1935 by Victor Houteff. It was a religious community that regarded itself as maintaining the true Seventh-day Adventist tradition of expecting the imminent end of the world and God's judgment. The Mount Carmel community was led by a series of prophets beginning with Houteff. When Vernon arrived in 1981 the community's prophet was Lois Roden. Lois Roden (67) liked the young carpenter, apparently took him as her lover, and began to promote him as the prophet who would succeed her. This angered Lois Roden's son, George Roden, who was determined to be the next prophet. But because George Roden's behavior was erratic and obnoxious, the long-time Mount Carmel residents, including Perry Jones and Clive Doyle, began to look to Vernon Howell as their next prophet. In 1984, Vernon married Rachel Jones (14).[124]

Vernon and Rachel (pregnant with their son, Cyrus) visited Israel in January 1985. While in Israel, Vernon received a revelation from God that he was a prophet and a messiah identified with the biblical Cyrus, king of the Persians, and with the Lamb in Revelation. After they returned in February 1985, people noticed a distinctive increase in Vernon's self-confidence. He had achieved maturity as a teacher of the Bible.

In June 1985, George Roden drove Vernon Howell and his followers out of Mount Carmel. They moved to nearby Palestine, Texas, and built a temporary camp. Lois Roden died in November 1986.[125]

In the spring of 1986, Vernon announced that he was married to Karen Doyle (14), daughter of Clive Doyle. Also in 1986 Vernon took Rachel's sister, twelve-year-old Michelle Jones, to be his wife. In 1987 Vernon "married" Robyn Bunds (17), Nicole Gent (16), and Dana Okimoto (20). Vernon's legal wife, Rachel, was initially upset by this development, but God

told her in a dream that this was God's will.[126] Former Davidian Alisa
Shaw explained how these sacred marriages were seen by the Davidians
and particularly by the women:

> A central part of the message [of Revelation] is the marriage of the
> Lamb. That's the way to salvation. There are a few [women] who
> are worthy to be sown with the seed of God and produce chil-
> dren. It's considered an honor to have a baby for Christ. Not
> every woman is worthy of Koresh's loins....A woman who
> becomes "sown with the light" might be worthy, but that doesn't
> mean she will be selected to bear the leader's seed. He's just given
> the inspiration and that's how he knows who's worthy.[127]

Parents of the girls consented to these extralegal marriages to Vernon
Howell, believing that their daughters were "going to have children for
the Lord."[128]

Still angry with Vernon for his competing claim to be prophet of the
Mount Carmel community, in November 1987 George Roden dug up the
casket of Anna Hughes, a resident who had been dead for twenty years.
George Roden challenged Vernon to a contest to see which of the two
prophets could raise the dead.

Vernon went to the McClennan County sheriff's office to lodge a
complaint about the disinterment of Anna Hughes's corpse. Vernon was
told that nothing could be done without evidence of the crime. A friendly
resident of Mount Carmel took photos of the casket, but the sheriff's
deputies said they needed photographs of the corpse. Because George
Roden habitually carried an Uzi semiautomatic weapon, Vernon and some
other men (including Stan Sylvia, Paul Fatta, and David Jones) were armed
when they went to Mount Carmel one night to take the photographs.
When they were confronted by George Roden, a shootout ensued. Vernon and his party were arrested and charged with attempted murder. The
ten-day trial took place in April 1988. The jury acquitted Vernon's com-
panions but could not reach a verdict about Vernon. All were released.[129]

George Roden continued to get in trouble with the law. While Roden
was in jail, Vernon and his followers paid $62,000 in taxes owed on Mount
Carmel and took possession of the property. George Roden was committed to a mental hospital after he murdered a man in 1989.[130]

In August 1990, Vernon Howell legally changed his name to David
Koresh, identifying himself with the "Cyrus message" that he had
received from God while in Israel in 1985. Cyrus (Koresh in Hebrew)
was the king of Persia who in 539 B.C.E. conquered Babylon and then
permitted the captive Jews to return to their promised land. In the
Hebrew Bible (the Old Testament for Christians), the term *messiah*

("christ" in Greek) referred to someone who was anointed and thus designated to carry out a special mission for Yahweh. Psalms 105:15 referred to the patriarchs Abraham, Isaac, and Jacob as messiahs; the Hebrew kings and priests were also messiahs. In Isaiah 45:1, Cyrus the king of Persia was termed a messiah.[131]

David Koresh related the references to Cyrus in Isaiah 40-54 to the conqueror of evil Babylon in Revelation (the rider on the white horse and the Lamb), and he identified himself as the christ or messiah who would die in armageddon, be resurrected, and then conquer evil to establish God's kingdom. Koresh identified himself, and not Jesus, with the suffering servant described in Isaiah 53. Isaiah 53:10 stated, "He shall see his seed, he shall prolong his days." Since Jesus did not have children, Koresh argued that this figure could not be Jesus Christ. Psalms 45 spoke of a messiah who married virgins and whose children ruled the earth. Koresh saw his marriage to young women and the birth of his children as fulfilling this prophecy.[132]

Koresh taught that Yeshua (Jesus) was Christ, a messiah, but that Koresh was also a messiah, or God's anointed, who would participate in the catastrophic events of the endtime that would result in the establishment of God's kingdom. Jesus Christ was in heaven, and the Davidic Christ was currently on Earth.[133]

Koresh revealed to his followers a "New Light" teaching in the summer of 1989, that all the women in the community were his wives, even those women already legally married to other men. Koresh thus claimed all Davidian women as his "wives" and rightful sexual partners. Correspondingly, Koresh taught that all the men, except himself, should be celibate. Utilizing various biblical texts (1 Corinthians 7:29; Luke 20:35; Galatians 3:28; 2 Corinthians 5:17; Matthew 19:12; Revelation 14:4; Isaiah 2:19-22), Koresh taught that in the kingdom of God there would be no sexual relations, and that the elect who followed the Lamb to establish God's kingdom were celibate. In God's kingdom the separation of masculinity and femininity would be healed in androgynous wholeness. The Lamb had to propagate children, however, because these special souls would become rulers in God's kingdom in Palestine (the 24 elders in Revelation 4:4 and Revelation 5:10).[134]

According to Koresh, all the Davidians, male and female, were married to him, the Lamb. The Christ Spirit in Koresh was the feminine Shekinah, the presence of God. The Davidian men, therefore, were united with their alienated femininity by their spiritual love for Koresh. A male Davidian's love for David Koresh was expressed in the following statement by Oliver Gyarfas, father of Aisha Gyarfas, one of Koresh's young wives: "David Koresh has a beautiful message, like a silver thread running through the scripture....I believe he is an inspired modern-day prophet.... He has a message for us, his brethren, but also for the whole world....I love David Koresh above all."[135] The return to androgynous wholeness was accomplished by Davidian women through sexual union with the Lamb.[136]

Koresh taught that the Branch Davidians at Mount Carmel were the "firstfruits" (Revelation 14:4) or the "wave sheaf" (Leviticus 23:10-11), who, through their faith, had come to the truth before others who would be included God's kingdom. The Branch Davidians separated themselves from corrupt Babylon to live lives dedicated to God at Mount Carmel. They considered themselves to be part of one Koresh family.[137]

The King James Version of the Bible was the ultimate source of authority for the Davidians. The Davidians believed that David Koresh's special status was proved by his unique ability to interpret the Bible. The Davidians believed that Koresh, through divine inspiration, had unlocked the secrets of the Bible; specifically, he revealed the meaning of the symbolism of a scroll sealed with seven seals in Revelation, and therefore he predicted the events of the endtime. Koresh was the Lamb described in Revelation as the only person who could reveal the secrets of the Seven Seals. Livingstone Fagan wrote about David Koresh, "The *only* one who can open The Seals to you is The Lamb, Who like The Spirit, is an aspect of God who comes to join with each of those betrothed to 'Him,'" and "According to Yeshua's Revelation, as shown to His beloved friend John; only one being in earth or heaven is worthy to open the seals—The Lamb."[138]

By his divine inspiration to interpret the Bible (the King James Version), David Koresh drew on Daniel 11, Matthew 24, Revelation 7-16, Ezekiel 38, Zechariah 14, Psalm 89, and Isaiah 53 to predict that in the future the Davidians would move to Palestine/Israel and help the Israelis fight in armageddon against a United Nations force led by the United States. Koresh, the Lamb, would be slain. After his death the Lamb would be resurrected and would return in power to judge and establish God's Kingdom.[139]

Until the time for armageddon, Koresh concentrated on giving his teachings to gather the faithful into God's kingdom. The ATF raid appeared to the Davidians to initiate armageddon, and Koresh's apparently mortal gunshot wounds appeared to fulfill the prediction of the slaying of the Lamb. That David Koresh honestly believed his teachings about himself was indicated by the homespun message he left on his mother's answering machine on February 28, 1993: "Hello, Mamma. It's your boy. They shot me and I'm dying, alright? But I'll be back real soon, okay? I'm sorry you didn't learn the Seals, but I'll be merciful, okay? I'll see ya'll in the skies."[140]

The Branch Davidians at Mount Carmel

Most of the Branch Davidians were former Seventh-day Adventists. Seventh-day Adventism grew out of the Millerite movement, which during the nineteenth century in the United States generated intense excitement over the imminent Second Coming of Jesus Christ. This movement was initiated by William Miller's interpretations of the King James Version of the Bible. Out of the confusion and necessary reinterpretation after the Great Disappointment on October 22, 1844, Seventh-day Adventism developed with Ellen G. White as its living prophet.

The Branch Davidians shared the distinctive characteristics of Seventh-day Adventism: (1) apocalyptic beliefs about the imminent end of the world; (2) the view that the prophecies and statements in the King James Version of the Bible were applicable to the events of our day and could be deciphered to predict the imminent events of the endtime; (3) reliance on living prophets to interpret God's Word in the Bible, and to reveal more of God's Word; and (4) observance of the Saturday Sabbath.

The schismatic group of Seventh-day Adventists, which became known as the Branch Davidians, originated in 1929 when Victor Houteff, a Bulgarian immigrant living in Los Angeles, decided that, regrettably, the Seventh-day Adventist Church had tempered its expectation of the imminent Second Coming of Jesus Christ. The Seventh-day Adventist Church was becoming too much like a denomination and was accommodating to the sinful world that Revelation termed Babylon. Houteff saw himself as a prophet whose role was to call out of the Seventh-day Adventist Church the 144,000 "servants of God" (Revelation 7), and prepare for the imminent coming of Christ. Houteff spread his teachings by publishing a journal called *The Shepherd's Rod*.[141]

In May 1935, Houteff and twelve followers bought 189 acres near Waco, Texas, which they named Mount Carmel, and moved there. They saw Mount Carmel as a temporary residence, for soon they would move to Palestine where they would participate in the final events leading to the reestablishment of the Davidic messianic kingdom. Houteff's group was named the Davidian Seventh-day Adventists. To symbolize that the end-time was near, Houteff had a clock set in the floor of the main building with its hands close to 11:00. In 1937 at age fifty-two, Houteff married Florence Hermanson (17), the daughter of two devoted followers.[142]

The Davidians lived at Mount Carmel longer than they expected. Houteff wrote numerous tracts that were mailed to more than 100,000 Seventh-day Adventists. Missionaries were sent to the West Indies, England, Australia, and India.[143] Houteff was a noted teacher of the Bible, and his hermeneutical method would be adopted later by David Koresh.

This constant blending of literal and symbolic readings left room for an infinite amount of "play" and adjustment of interpretation as events unfolded. This method allowed every line, every word, every symbol in the entire Bible to serve, on some level, as a coded indicator for the contemporary situation, often directly addressing Houteff and his group. Even in cases where a text had an obvious historical fulfillment or point of reference, it could always have a "double" hidden meaning, revealed only through the "Spirit of prophecy."[144]

When Victor Houteff died in February 1955 at age sixty-nine, Florence Houteff briefly became the group's prophet. In December 1957, the Davidians sold their property and relocated to 941 acres that they purchased nine miles east of Waco. They named this place the New Mount Carmel. This property later became the Mount Carmel of David Koresh's Branch Davidians. In 1955, Florence Houteff announced that on April 22, 1959, armageddon would break out in the Holy Land followed by the establishment of God's kingdom in Jerusalem. Between 500 to 1,000 people sold their possessions and gathered at Mount Carmel for this great event. William L. Pitts described what followed as the "second great disappointment." From 1955 to 1959, Florence Houteff reaped the benefits of her followers' heightened expectations, commitment, and enthusiasm, but after April 22, 1959, most of the disappointed left, leaving only about fifty followers. Three years later Florence Houteff announced that her prophecies were in error. She got out of the prophet business, sold all but a few hundred acres of the Mount Carmel property, and moved away.[145]

Ben and Lois Roden had moved to Mount Carmel in 1955, and Ben Roden became the next Mount Carmel prophet. Ben claimed to be the Davidic messiah, the anointed "Branch" predicted in Zechariah 3:8 and 6:12, whose task was to "organize the theocratic kingdom in preparation for Christ's return."[146] Ben Roden's followers were also called "Branches" based on John 15:1-3, where Jesus tells his followers, "I am the vine, and you are the branches."[147] In the 1960s, Ben Roden's group gained legal control of Mount Carmel, which by that time consisted of seventy-seven acres. Roden named his group the General Association of Davidian Seventh-Day Adventists (GADSA).[148]

Israel as the site of God's kingdom continued to play an important role in the Davidians' mental landscape. Ben Roden claimed to be the successor to King David, and because his role was to reestablish the Davidic kingdom, he and his wife Lois founded a community in Israel in 1958. In addition to observing the Sabbath on Saturday, Roden's Davidians began to observe Jewish sacred holidays. Ben Roden died in 1978, and four years later Lois Roden had his body buried on the Mount of Olives overlooking Jerusalem.[149]

After Ben Roden's death, there was a power struggle for the prophet's mantle between Lois Roden and their son, George. Lois Roden successfully established herself as the next prophet by utilizing female images of God to legitimize her authority. In 1977, Lois Roden received a revelation that the Holy Spirit was feminine, the Shekinah, the immanent feminine presence of God, and she began publishing a journal called *SHEkinah*. Lois Roden gained the loyalty of Davidians, who subsequently would accept Vernon Howell/David Koresh as their prophet: Perry Jones, Catherine Matteson, Woodrow and Janet Kendrick, and Clive Doyle. Lois Roden called her group the Living Waters Branch. It was this Davidian community that Vernon Howell joined in 1981,[150] and Lois Roden's teachings about the femininity and masculinity of God influenced David Koresh's teachings about the holistic, androgynous unity from which humans were fallen and which would be restored in God's kingdom.

David Koresh saw himself as the culminating figure in a lineage of prophets going back to William Miller, who in the 1830s and 1840s taught the imminent Second Coming of Christ and who sparked the Adventist movement that gave birth to the Seventh-day Adventist Church. Koresh taught that the lineage of prophets, in which he stood, was predicted in Revelation in the symbolism of seven angels announcing the endtime. William Miller fulfilled the role of the first two angels "by proclaiming that the 'end times' had arrived and that 'Babylon' was ready to fall."[151] Ellen G. White was the third angel, who proclaimed the message that the Sabbath should be observed on the seventh day of the week, Saturday. David Koresh was a student of Ellen G. White's teachings and cited her often. Koresh asserted that Victor Houteff was the fourth angel, who brought the message that "there would be a literal, earthly Davidic Kingdom of God in Palestine."[152] The fifth angel was Ben Roden, whose message was the restoration of biblical sacred holidays such as Passover, Pentecost, and the feast of Tabernacles. The sixth angel was Lois Roden, who revealed that the Holy Spirit was feminine, thus "recovering a vital 'lost' aspect of the understanding of God."[153] David Koresh was the seventh angel, the designated messiah (christ), who was the rejected and despised suffering servant (Isaiah 53) who would inaugurate armageddon by battling Babylon.[154] Koresh would be killed, but would then return in power and glory to defeat God's enemies, judge, and then establish God's kingdom in Palestine where his children would be rulers.

The Davidians were convinced that David Koresh was the messiah, the Lamb, who would usher in God's kingdom by his inspired ability to unlock the secrets of the Bible. David Koresh interpreted the meaning of the Seven Seals in Revelation and, thus, unveiled the events of the endtime. Paul Fatta testified, "I believe David is the Messiah….He has shown me over and over that he knows the book [the Bible], and he presented Scriptures showing how the last day's events would happen."[155]

The ultimate source of authority for the Davidians was the Bible (King James Version). As long as David Koresh appeared to be divinely inspired to interpret the prophecies of the Bible, the Davidians put their faith in him. The Davidians believed that obeying God's commandments in the Bible was critical for being included in God's kingdom. On April 9, 1993, Steve Schneider explained to negotiator Byron Sage that he tested the validity of Koresh's teachings every day by the Bible. When Sage asked whether Schneider was waiting on God or David to tell them to leave Mount Carmel, Schneider answered,

I'm waiting on God. But, see, if you read through the *Bible*, you know, the prophets were the ones that came to Israel who thought they knew God and had to walk with God, but the prophets came saying you're, you're this, you're that, God's going to destroy you. And God—if you look at Second Peter, Chapter 1, verses 19 through 21, those three verses, Byron, you'll find out that God has chosen men and women, contrary to what you and I think, throughout the ages, given them inspiration, and it has always been in line with those that have preceded before them, the prophets, the apostles of old. So, if David's out of sink [sic] with the apostles and prophets, there are tests in the *Bible*, Isaiah 20, Jeremiah 28, verse 9, Matthew 7, verses 15 through 20, that test this kind of phenomena by those that came before, those that have preceded. So, I've tested and retested this man over and over again and I can't find—I mean, and I've tried. Like I've told many other negotiators, this is a day-by-day thing with me. I don't make up my mind adamantly, you know, like say a month ago or yesterday. It's a new day today. I'll look at the facts, the information I have, and, and make a decision based on what's before me (emphasis in the transcript).[156]

The Branch Davidians living at Mount Carmel chose to separate from Babylon and to study God's message in the Bible with David Koresh. They did not identify themselves by a particular name, such as Branch Davidians, but they identified themselves as being "students of the Bible" or as simply being "in the message."[157] Koresh taught that this message was "the most important subject matter since the foundation of the world,"[158] because it told how to gain salvation in God's kingdom, how God's kingdom would be established after a series of cataclysmic events, and how the young David Koresh as the messiah was God's agent to create God's Kingdom.

In order to recruit more individuals to this elect group, David Koresh and talented apostles such as Steve Schneider and Marc Breault traveled throughout the United States, especially to California and Hawaii. They also traveled to England, Canada, Australia, and Israel. Koresh's manner of converting people was to take them through concentrated and lengthy Bible study sessions in order to show them that he could reveal the prophetic secrets of the Bible.[159] Koresh had the greatest success in converting people who were Seventh-day Adventists.

The Mount Carmel community on February 28, 1993, consisted of about 130 people: 42 men, 46 women, and 43 children. The Davidians' multi-ethnic composition reflected the demographics of the Seventh-day Adventist Church. One-third of the Davidians were from Great Britain. There were also Davidians from Canada, Australia, New Zealand, Jamaica, the Philippines, Mexico, and Israel. Over half were persons of color, with about 45 blacks and about 25 Asians or Hispanics.[160]

Initially David Koresh's Mount Carmel community was financially supported by donations from Davidians. In this manner, a house was purchased in Pomona, California, and the back taxes were paid on Mount Carmel. The Davidians operated a car repair and renovation business called the Mag Bag. Paul Fatta financed and managed the trade in guns and survival supplies[161] that attracted the attention of the ATF.

It should be noted that there are other Davidian and Branch Davidian groups, who do not believe in David Koresh. These Davidians, who

Bernadette Monbelly was a British citizen. In her videotaped statement Bernadette said, "We are a big family here. We are very happy."

are part of the tradition started by Victor Houteff, see David Koresh as a false prophet.

After April 19, 1993, the surviving Koresh Davidians had diverse views about David Koresh. Some concluded that Koresh was a false prophet or a manipulative religious leader who "brainwashed us all."[162] Others were confirmed in their faith that David Koresh was the messianic Lamb who would be resurrected and return in glory. Some believed that David Koresh would return in power on December 13, 1996.[163] Koresh Davidians derived this date by utilizing Daniel 12:7-12, which stated that the power of the holy people would be scattered for 1,355 days after the "daily" was taken away. They understood "daily" to be David Koresh's daily morning and evening Bible studies. Counting 1,335 days after Koresh's death on April 19, 1993, yielded the date of December 13, 1996.[164]

As the early followers of Jesus had to adjust their expectation that Christ would return before that generation died out (Matthew 24:34), Branch Davidians also will have to cope with the delay in David Koresh's return.

Catastrophic Millennialism

By 1987, David Koresh had developed detailed teachings about the final events and his own role based on his interpretations of Daniel 11, Matthew 24, and Revelation 7-16. Koresh taught that the Branch Davidians would move to Palestine and fight on the side of Israel against a United Nations army led by the United States. He taught that this final battle was described in Ezekiel 38 and Zechariah 14. Koresh drew on Psalm 89, Isaiah 53, and Revelation 5 to predict that he would be slain in armageddon, and he expected these events to take place in 1995.[165]

However, the Persian Gulf War in 1991, and cultural opposition experienced by the Davidians in 1992, convinced Koresh that it was possible that armageddon would begin at Mount Carmel in Texas and that the Davidians would be killed there. This was confirmed for Koresh and the Davidians on February 28, 1993, by the ATF attack on their home. They understood their situation to be predicted in the Fifth Seal of Revelation.[166] Koresh announced this to the public in his message broadcast on KRLD radio on February 28, "We are now in the Fifth Seal."[167] The Fifth Seal in Revelation 6:9-11 in the King James Version of the Bible reads:

> And when he had opened the fifth seal, I saw under the altar the souls of *them that were slain* for the word of God, and for the testimony which they held; and they cried out with a loud voice, saying, How long, O Lord, holy and true, dost thou not judge

and avenge our blood on them that dwell on the earth? And white robes were given unto every one of them; and it was said unto them, that *they should rest yet for a little season, until their fellow-servants also and their brethren, that should be killed* as they were, should be fulfilled.[168]

The murder of God's people predicted in the Fifth Seal would lead to the catastrophic events predicted in the Sixth Seal (Revelation 6:12-17), involving an earthquake and heavenly signs of God's wrath and judgment.

Religious Studies scholars Dr. Arnold and Dr. Tabor realized that David Koresh's predictions were not rigidly fixed and that Koresh was constantly adjusting his biblical interpretations in response to events. Koresh was waiting during the siege, because the Fifth Seal mentioned a waiting period before the entire godly community was slaughtered, and because he was waiting for God's instruction about what he should do and whether they were actually in the Fifth Seal.[169] David Koresh was not going to do anything unless it followed his understanding of the biblical script, and Koresh's understanding of the biblical script was not set in stone.

Despite being rebuffed by FBI agents, Arnold and Tabor continued to study Koresh's theology by listening to Koresh's audiotaped sermon that was played on KRLD, and also by speaking by telephone with Livingstone Fagan in jail. "Fagan had stressed to them that from the Davidian viewpoint the outcome of the crisis was completely open-ended and undetermined. According to Fagan, what would transpire depended on how the government authorities responded to Koresh's efforts to communicate his biblical faith. Fagan saw the Mount Carmel siege as a kind of spiritual trial, or test, for our culture, to determine whether or not we would listen to God's final messenger."[170]

David Koresh's many hours of preaching his interpretation of the Bible to various FBI negotiators was an effort to save their souls, so they too could be included in God's kingdom. Koresh wanted to offer his message to a wider audience,[171] but FBI agents systematically blocked Koresh's access to the public, and they did not understand Koresh's Bible-derived language and worldview. FBI agents complained that Koresh "refused to discuss matters of substance" when in fact Koresh constantly discussed what was to him the most important matter of all—salvation in God's kingdom. On March 15, FBI negotiators were ordered not to listen any longer to Koresh's "Bible babble."[172] This was the same day that Steve Schneider asked that Dr. Arnold be permitted to discuss the Bible with Koresh and the Davidians. Schneider said that if Dr. Arnold could demonstrate from the Bible, that God wanted the Davidians to come out of

Mount Carmel, they would do so no matter what David Koresh thought.[173] This request was denied by the FBI.

On April 1, Arnold and Tabor discussed the biblical prophecies on a KGBS radio program. They offered an alternative interpretation of scripture to suggest that it was not foreordained that the Davidians die at that time at the hands of Babylon. They argued that the "waiting period" of the Fifth Seal would be years, and not merely a few months.[174] Arnold and Tabor suggested that David Koresh should come out of Mount Carmel to spread his message of God's imminent judgment and salvation in God's kingdom.

On April 14 after Passover, Koresh sent out the following letter to his attorney, Dick DeGuerin, promising that after he wrote down his interpretation of the Seven Seals in a "little book" (Revelation 10 refers to an angel with a little scroll or book), he and the Davidians would come out.

I am presently *being permitted* to document, in structured form, the decoded messages of the Seven Seals. Upon completion of this task, I will be *free of my "waiting period."* I hope to finish this as soon as possible and to stand before man to answer any and all questions regarding my actions.

This written Revelation of the Seven Seals *will not be sold*, but is to be available to all who wish to know the Truth. The Four Angels of Revelation are here, now ready to punish foolish mankind; but, the writing of these Seals will cause the winds of God's wrath to be held back a little longer.

I have been *praying so long* for this opportunity; to put the Seals in written form. Speaking the Truth seems to have very little effect on man.

I was shown that as soon as I am given over into the hands of man, I will be made a spectacle of, and people will not be concerned about the truth of God, but just the bizarrity of me in the flesh.

I want the people of this generation to be saved. *I am working night and day to complete my final work* of the writing out of these Seals.

I thank my Father, He has finally *granted me the chance* to do this. It will bring New Light and hope for many and they will not have to deal with me the person.

I will demand the first manuscript of the Seals be given to you [Dick DeGuerin]. Many scholars and religious leaders will wish to have copies for examination. I will keep a copy with me. As soon as I can see that people like Jim Tabor and Phil Arnold have a copy *I will come out* and then you can do your thing with this beast.[175]

Attorney General Janet Reno was never informed of Koresh's April 14 promise to come out after writing his little book,[176] nor was she informed that on April 16, Koresh reported to FBI agents that he had completed writing his interpretation of the First Seal of Revelation.[177] Working at that rate, Koresh would have completed his little book on the Seven Seals in twelve days.

The effort of Arnold and Tabor to communicate with Koresh in his own Bible-derived language, in a respectful manner, that took Koresh's ultimate concern seriously, was a success. This was confirmed by the disk carried out of the fire by Ruth Riddle containing Koresh's interpretation of the First Seal.

The Branch Davidians believed that they would be martyred in the violent events of the endtime, but the Davidians did not want to die. The Davidians' constant effort to communicate with FBI agents and to reach an audience beyond the barriers set up by the FBI indicate that the Davidians did not want to die. Until their very final moments, the Davidians strove to achieve a peaceful resolution of the siege. The Bible was the ultimate source of authority for the Davidians, and they were not going to do anything contrary to what they believed God willed them to do as revealed in the Bible. The Davidians requested that Bible scholars be permitted to show them alternative interpretations of biblical prophecies; David Koresh was persuaded by the alternative biblical interpretation offered by Arnold and Tabor. But the tank and CS gas assault launched by FBI agents on April 19 probably convinced Koresh that his original understanding of the situation had been correct—the Davidians were going to be martyred at Mount Carmel.

Perhaps Koresh ordered that fires be lit to battle the tanks, but there is no conclusive evidence that this was the case. If the tanks had not assaulted and entered the building, the fires never would have erupted. I do not believe there was a suicide pact, as evidenced by the nine Davidians who escaped the burning building. It was very likely that the women and children in the concrete block room were trapped (and some were crushed) by the falling debris, and that most of the people on the second and third floors could not escape because the tanks had destroyed the staircases and the fire engulfed the building so rapidly.

The ATF and FBI played the role of satanic Babylon perfectly and confirmed Koresh's catastrophic millennial prophecies.

The Persecution

The Branch Davidians viewed themselves as the target of a number of attacks, which prompted them to prepare for self-defense, but the Davidians' sense of being persecuted—prior to the ATF attack—never seemed to have been very strong. This was probably because they did not perceive themselves as failing to achieve their ultimate concern, and their messiah was not in serious danger of losing his authority based on charisma (divine revelation). If anything, actions taken by federal agents confirmed David Koresh's prophetic powers and his status as the Lamb. Nevertheless, the sense of being threatened by enemies—Babylon—increased during 1992, and the Davidians, therefore, prepared to defend themselves against the predicted attack against their community.

Prior to February 28, 1993, the Branch Davidians were besieged by a coalition of "active opponents"[178] who shared the prejudiced "cult" stereotype promoted by the anticult movement. Indeed, apostates, who embraced the anticult perspective and tactics of targeting a group and aggressively utilizing government agencies, law enforcement, and the media to pressure the group, sparked the persecution of the Branch Davidians. This is not to say that the Branch Davidians did not have problematic features—David Koresh's sexual intercourse with underage girls being the most significant. However, the typical tactic taken by apostates of exaggerating the facts and disseminating "atrocity tales"[179] "to magnify the dangers of the group"[180] had the effect of motivating law enforcement agents to use excessive force, which inevitably killed the children and young women who were supposedly in need of being saved from David Koresh.

It must be noted that Marc Breault, the apostate who was most active against the Davidians as a "cultbuster,"[181] acted out of concern for the children and adults whom he saw as Koresh's victims. Breault was critical of the use of excessive force by the ATF and FBI agents.

When the [B]ATF approached me (I did not approach them) they told me that they believed Vernon had amassed a huge arsenal of weapons and that some of those were illegal. I am not a weapons expert and I can't say whether they did have illegal weapons or not. I wouldn't be surprised....It was for this reason I strongly advised the [B]ATF that if they were going to arrest Vernon, they do so with no force, that they somehow lure Vernon away from Carmel....I must say that it hurts both my wife and I when Branch Davidians accuse us of murder. We repeatedly advised the [B]ATF to use this tactic....I am outraged that government mishandling, along with Vernon's own delusions of grandeur, contributed to the deaths of all those children I knew and loved, not to mention the adults....The FBI mishandled a lot of things during the siege. They did not take sufficient note of Vernon's religion and its teachings. They assumed they were the experts....The FBI and [B]ATF lied to the public numerous times.[182]

However, John R. Hall pointed out that "cultural opponents have never seriously weighed their own roles in negative outcomes of pitched conflicts with alternative religious movements,"[183] and have neglected to consider how their own actions exacerbated a group's potential for volatility.

> This static view of predispositions is based on a tendency that governmental authorities share with the anticult movement, a tendency to see the dynamics of "cults" as internal to such groups, rather than examine external social interaction in conflict between a sectarian group and opponents and authorities themselves.[184]

Thus in this book, we see that cultural opposition played significant roles in the tragic outcomes of Jonestown and the Branch Davidians, and in a more complicated manner, in the violent acts committed by Aum Shinrikyo devotees (see chapter 5). Hall pointed out that cases in which there was *no* adversarial involvement of anticult activists were resolved peacefully. But he pointed out that in the cases he has studied, in which anticultists were very active in highlighting the threat of the "cult" and enlisted government agents and the media to oppose the "cult," "there have been truly devastating and disastrous results...."[185]

Marc Breault became a Branch Davidian in 1986, but he and his wife left Mount Carmel in September 1989, because of Koresh's teaching that even married women were Koresh's wives, and over concerns about Koresh having sex with underage girls. Breault and his wife moved to Australia, and there Breault used Bible study sessions to convince Australian Davidians that Koresh was a false prophet.[186] Breault devoted himself to saving the Branch Davidians and reportedly claimed that he was a prophet in order to win believers from David Koresh.[187] Eugene V. Gallagher has shown that David Koresh felt severely threatened by Breault's rejection of him as the messiah who was divinely inspired to interpret the Bible's prophecies, and by Breault's use of Bible study sessions to convince other Davidians to give up their faith in him.[188]

Breault worked with former Davidians in Australia and California to bring the attention of authorities to the threat posed by David Koresh. Robyn Bunds in California, who had a child by David Koresh, Shaun (also called Wisdom), was an important ally in this effort. In 1990, Marc Breault and Robyn Bunds alleged to Davidians in Australia and California, to U.S. immigration officials, to California police, and to law enforcement agents in Texas that David Koresh was planning to commit child sacrifice. This was alleged in a brief custody battle in which Robyn Bunds successfully regained custody of Wisdom. In September 1990, a detective hired by Breault, carrying affidavits signed by Australian defectors, flew to the United States and met with local authorities in LaVerne, California, and Waco, Texas, and also spoke with Internal Revenue Service officials and officials of the U.S. Immigration and Naturalization Service.[189]

Marc Breault worked with Martin King of the Australian television program, *A Current Affair*, to expose Koresh. King and his television crew visited Mount Carmel in January 1992, posing as objective reporters, when in fact their agenda was to make a documentary showing Koresh to be "a cruel, maniacal, child-molesting, pistol-packing religious zealot who brainwashed his devotees."[190]

Furthermore, Marc Breault was involved in the custody battle over Kiri Jewell, the daughter of Davidian Sherri Jewell and David Jewell, who lived in Michigan and had never been a Davidian. On October 31, 1991, Marc Breault in Australia called David Jewell to warn him that Kiri was destined to become one of Koresh's wives. The custody hearing was held in Michigan in February 1992. Koresh sent Steve Schneider to assist Sherri Jewell, and Marc Breault testified on behalf of David Jewell. Joint custody was given to David Jewell and Sherri Jewell. Sherri Jewell left Kiri with her father and returned to Mount Carmel.[191]

In February 1992, Marc Breault, David Jewell, and others alerted the Texas Department of Human Services to alleged child abuse, which was investigated by Joyce Sparks of Texas Child Protective Services. The case was closed for lack of evidence.[192]

In March 1992, Marc Breault, David Jewell, and others began to allege that the Davidians were planning to commit mass suicide on or about April 18, 1992. They alleged that if no action were taken, Mount Carmel would become "another Jonestown." They wrote to Michigan Congressman Fred Upton, who passed the letter to Texas Congressman Chet Edwards, who passed it to the FBI. The FBI closed the case for lack of evidence. The mass suicide allegation made by Breault, Jewell, and Australian Bruce Gent prompted the *Waco Tribune-Herald* to begin an investigation of the Davidians. These anticult activists never explained why the mass suicide, allegedly planned for April 1992, never materialized.[193]

According to John R. Hall, all these activities of anticultists, particularly in early 1992, led David Koresh to conclude that an attempt would be made to remove his children from his custody, and so he prepared to resist by force. According to Hall, "the efforts of Koresh's opponents precipitated a distinctively heightened siege posture at Mt. Carmel."[194]

The ATF investigation of Koresh's activities involving arms began in May 1992. On July 23, 1992, agent Davy Aguilera sent a report to ATF headquarters. On November 2, 1992, ATF headquarters responded that there was not enough evidence to justify a search warrant. Aguilera then began to interview defectors to bolster the allegations of probable cause in his affidavit to obtain search and arrest warrants. Aguilera interviewed Isabel and Guillermo Andrade, who had two daughters at Mount Carmel; Jeannine Bunds and David Bunds, the mother and brother of Robyn Bunds; and Marc Breault, all of whom he met in California. Breault put Aguilera in touch with the deprogrammer Rick Ross, who was a "cult expert" adviser during the siege. Ross put Aguilera in touch with former Davidian David Block, whom Ross had deprogrammed. The apostates stressed to ATF investigators that David Koresh would not surrender peacefully, and that a siege would culminate in mass suicide.[195] These allegations by anticultists did not conform to Koresh's actual behavior when he was arrested and prosecuted for attempted murder in 1987. The former district attorney in that case, Vic Feazell, said, "[I]f they'd [the BATF] called and talked to them, the Davidians would have given them what they wanted.[196]

The first installment of the *Waco Tribune-Herald* series on David Koresh, entitled "The Sinful Messiah," appeared on February 27, 1993, the day before the ATF raid.[197] The series presented a one-sided view, reflecting only the perspective of the anticultists who were interviewed, including Rick Ross, Priscilla Coates, and Marc Breault. Sociologist Stuart A. Wright has stated that relying on the anticult movement for information on new religious movements (NRMs) is analogous "to suggesting that Ku Klux Klan materials are dispassionate assessments of racial minorities.[198] Scholars who specialize in the study of NRMs were not consulted for the newspaper series, nor were David Koresh and the Davidians. The views of non-hostile former Davidians were not reported.[199] The *Waco Tribune-Herald* series became the first source of information used by reporters who came to Waco to cover the Branch Davidian story.

This demonization of Koresh and the Davidians was increased when the FBI prevented the Davidians from communicating with the public. The Davidians and their children were not seen on television; their views were not reported in the media. The media presented the FBI's perspective on the Branch Davidians, and made no effort to investigate beyond what they were told by FBI spokespersons.[200] The reporters swallowed whole and regurgitated the stereotype of the Branch Davidians as a "cult."

> The media, feeling that an appropriate story line was in place, chose to settle for this arrangement. They basically adopted the government's narrative of why its actions were justified. As the siege went on, and as the media reported a government-fed account of events at Waco, the media were increasingly faced with a loss of credibility if anomalies and hard questions about government strategy that they failed to report and examine earlier were raised.[201]

Tabor and Gallagher pointed out that in such media stories, "Labeling takes the place of analysis. The term 'cult' brings with it a ready-made interpretive framework...."[202]

A significant persecution of the Branch Davidians, perpetuated by the media, was the fact that people "living at Mt. Carmel, including even the children, were never fully humanized in the eyes of the general public. We know little about them as individuals, including details of their lives — their hopes and desires, their hobbies, their goals. We did not see many depictions of them as real human beings."[203] The FBI did not release to the media the videotapes made by the Davidians during the siege to avoid creating public sentiment favorable to the Davidians.[204] According to James T. Richardson, the "dehumanization of those inside Mt. Carmel, coupled with the thoroughgoing demonization of Koresh, made it easier for those in authority to develop tactics that seemed organized for disaster...."[205] Richardson pointed out the problematic results of the "dichotomization" of subjects in which the media presents stories in simplified, conflictual, black-and-white terms. Presenting news stories in this manner leads to depicting victims as either "worthy" or "unworthy." Richardson quoted Edward S. Herman and Noam Chomsky, *Manufacturing Consent: The Political Economy of the Mass Media* (1988: 35):

> Our hypothesis is that worthy victims will be featured prominently and dramatically, that they will be humanized, and that their victimization will receive the detail and context in story construction that will generate reader interest and sympathetic emotion. In contrast, unworthy victims will merit only slight detail, minimal humanization, and little context that will excite or outrage.[206]

Richardson continued, "As Herman and Chomsky point out, the politically correct side can literally get away with murder, for its cause is deemed just, whereas those designated the aggressors can do only evil, receiving no credit for any good deeds they might do."[207]

The persecutory acts committed by federal agents against the Branch Davidians were amply documented in the first section of this chapter. These acts involved physical, mental, social, constitutional, and judicial violence against the Davidians. Here I recount only one more report. Louis Alaniz, who was not a Davidian, but who surreptitiously entered Mount Carmel, where he remained until two days before the FBI tank and gas assault, said that during the siege the tank drivers mooned the Davidians and made obscene hand signals at them. The tank drivers shouted over their loudspeakers, "Why don't ya'll just get the hell out of here? Why are ya'll making us stay here?" "Once," Alaniz asserted, "they didn't know that they hadn't turned off their speakers. I heard one of them say, 'Why don't we just kill them all?' "[208]

The Success of the Millennial Goal

From February 28 to April 19, 1993, the Branch Davidians did not perceive that they were failing to achieve their ultimate concern. I believe that this accounts for how the Davidians were able to persist through a siege during which they were subjected to escalating intimidation and psychological warfare without resorting to violent action. This is how the Branch Davidians differ from the Jonestown residents. Within Jonestown, cultural opposition was interpreted as threatening the ultimate concern, because the actions of Jim Jones and weaknesses internal to Jonestown had already endangered the ultimate concern. Violent acts were committed by residents of Jonestown to preserve their ultimate concern, because there were simultaneous internal and external threats to its success.

This was not the case with the Branch Davidians. Earlier, David Koresh felt threatened by the activities of Marc Breault in persuading Davidians to give up their faith, but Breault had moved to Australia and left Koresh in Mount Carmel with a group of very committed Davidians. It is questionable whether the Davidians committed suicide at the end of the siege. *If* some Davidians lit the fires, it was more likely a defense measure against the tanks than a mass suicide. This interpretation is reinforced by the fact that the Davidians attempted to communicate with FBI agents until the bitter end, and highly-committed Davidians managed to escape the fire. The Branch Davidians did not want to die, but they saw whatever happened as the unfolding of God's plan to establish his millennial kingdom.

The Davidians' ultimate concern and David Koresh's charismatic authority were not endangered by the actions of federal agents. In fact, all the violent actions committed by ATF and FBI agents served to validate Koresh's power of prophecy and thus his role as the messiah. After the fire, Ruth Riddle stated that the sense of community among the Davidians was strengthened by the FBI's tactics during the siege, and that the events validated Koresh's authority. According to Riddle, that time in her life was: "The very best. Some of my best times. Companionship was closer,...our commitment was stronger, our desire to study was more, and the more we studied the more we could see how plainly what David had taught."[209]

There was only one time during the siege when *some* Davidians contemplated group suicide, and this was when the wounded David Koresh was preparing to surrender to the FBI, and the leaderless Davidians would have had to turn themselves over to Babylon. *Some* Davidians may have entertained thoughts of suicide and made suicide pacts at that time, because they were failing to achieve their ultimate concern; the scenario as it was unfolding did not fit their understanding of the biblical script for the accomplishment of God's millennial kingdom. But survivors reported that there was no general agreement to commit suicide, and many stated that if they had known about a suicide pact, they would have refused to participate. Koresh salvaged the situation on March 2 by refusing to surrender, saying that they would wait for God's word about their proper course of action.[210] The doubt entertained by some—perhaps by Koresh himself—that they would fail to achieve the ultimate concern was safely put to rest. Also, Koresh's need to wait was likely due to his need to recover from his wounds. Koresh needed time, and as it turned out, some help, in determining which biblical script they were going to follow.

All the events during the siege and even the final assault affirmed that God was carrying out the salvation plan to achieve the ultimate concern, and that David Koresh was the messiah who would create the millennial kingdom. Surviving Davidians, who remain faithful to David Koresh's teachings, and new converts will determine how Branch Davidian theology will interpret the deaths of Davidians on February 28 and April 19, 1993.

I believe that the Davidians were able to endure severe persecution throughout the siege, because at no point was their ultimate concern endangered by the actions of their leader or by their opponents. David Koresh utilized the "waiting period" between February 28 to April 19, 1993, to attempt to get his message of God's impending judgment and salvation out to the public, and when that was effectively barred, he tried to convert the FBI agents with whom he spoke.[211]

The Branch Davidians at Mount Carmel differed from Jonestown and Aum Shinrikyo, because they never—except perhaps in their very final moments—gave up on their missionary outreach to the rest of humanity. They did not give up their attempts to offer the message of salvation to humanity, and this, prior to their enforced isolation by federal agents, effectively prevented the Davidians from being a community isolated from the rest of society. The dogged optimism that at least *some* individuals in Babylon would accept God's message given by Koresh prevented the Davidians from resorting to violent actions to destroy themselves or their attackers. This is how the Davidians differ from Jonestown and Aum Shinrikyo, both of which were fragile millennial groups. In Jonestown, persecution from the outside coupled with internal weaknesses, including those generated by the charismatic leader, caused believers to give up on the corrupt outside world as hopeless, and to commit violent acts to preserve their ultimate concern. It will be seen in the next chapter that internal weaknesses caused by the leader of Aum Shinrikyo threatened the ultimate concern. Due to the internal weaknesses, Aum Shinrikyo leaders were hyper-sensitive to any cultural opposition. The violent acts committed by Aum Shinrikyo devotees also were aimed at preserving their ultimate concern.

During the FBI assault did the Davidians despair of their ultimate concern? I do not think so. Events were unfolding according to God's plan, and that, regrettably, called for their collective martyrdom. They were assured of their eternal salvation. The persistent efforts of Koresh and the Davidians to negotiate and communicate their religious message tells us that *they did not want to die.* Unfortunately, ATF and FBI agents played the part of Babylon perfectly.

The Decision to Commit Violence

In light of the cultural opposition experienced by the Davidians prior to the ATF raid, Koresh and the Davidians prepared for the possibility that armageddon would begin in Texas instead of Israel. They stockpiled dried food and military MREs (meals ready to eat), weapons and ammunition, and filled a large tank with propane gas in the event of electricity loss.[212] Opposition prompted Koresh to move the anticipated battle "closer in time and space" and began "the implementation of survivalism." According to Bromley and Silver, there "is little doubt that Koresh felt increasingly vulnerable and embattled...."[213] During the summer of 1993, the men at Mount Carmel cut six-inch openings in the sheetrock walls on the front of the building, two feet from the floor, and filled the space between the sheetrock and the outside wall with cement, thus making slots through which Davidians could shoot at attackers from behind a reinforced wall.[214]

Koresh taught that although Jesus did not resist his own torture and execution, shortly before his death Jesus instructed his followers to buy weapons. In Luke 22:36 Jesus is reported to have said, "But now, he that has a purse let him take it, and likewise his money, and he that has no sword, let him sell his garment and buy one."[215] Koresh, drawing on the very violent passages about armageddon in Revelation, Zechariah 14, and Ezekiel 38, taught that the Davidians should be armed and prepared to fight in self-defense against evil.[216] Eugene V. Gallagher's study of the audiotapes of Koresh's Bible study sessions and of the negotiation transcripts reveals that Koresh did not encourage Davidians to initiate apocalyptic violence. The Davidians would fight on the side of God in armageddon, but only God would determine the time for armageddon and initiate that violence.[217] Unlike Aum Shinrikyo, to be discussed in the next chapter, the Branch Davidians armed themselves for self-defense, not to initiate armageddon. Koresh and the Davidians relied on God's action above all to establish the millennial kingdom, and to utilize Koresh and the Davidians in doing so.

Although God was first in the allegiance of the Davidians, they were not averse to cooperating with civil authorities. As Koresh said to Lt. Lynch in the February 28, 1993, 911 call: "We will serve God first. Now, we will serve the God of truth. Now, we were willing, and we've been willing all the time to sit down with anybody. You've sent law enforcement out here before."[218] Nevertheless, the Davidians were ready and willing to resist an attack with violence.

The decisions by ATF and FBI agents and Washington officials to assault the Davidians were discussed in the lengthy first section of this chapter. The intent of FBI tactical commanders to resolve the siege peacefully remains in doubt. Carol Moore's thesis in her book, *The Davidian Massacre*, is that FBI tactical commanders aimed to destroy evidence that on February 28, 1993, ATF teams at the front door of Mount Carmel, on its roof, and overhead in helicopters shot into the residence without first attempting to serve the warrants peacefully. All of the evidence that would have supported the allegations made by the Davidians and their two attorneys is now gone: the building and its roof, the right side of the steel-encased front door, the Davidians' parked vehicles, and even corpses of the Davidians. In 1997, a movie was released, entitled "Waco: The Rules of Engagement," which showed overflight infrared film (FLIR) taken during the tank and gas assault. An expert interpreted flashes, originating from behind the tanks, as evidence that federal agents fired on the Davidians during the gas assault, and that federal gunfire ignited the flammable tear gas, but this opinion was disputed by other experts.[219]

It is unclear whether some Davidians, acting on Koresh's orders, lit fires to combat the tanks that were demolishing their home. It is possible that they did, but the evidence does not unequivocally indicate that the Davidians intended to commit mass suicide. The Davidians exercised remarkable restraint in the face of excessive force used by ATF and FBI agents.

In contrast to Jonestown and Aum Shinrikyo, the Branch Davidians were not in danger of failing to achieve their ultimate concern, and the events of 1993 involving federal agents' use of excessive force only enhanced the authority of their messiah. The Davidians were prepared to defend themselves against attack by Babylon, but it remains unclear whether the Davidians committed group suicide, were massacred, or died as a result of a tragic chain of misjudgments made by federal law enforcement agents. It *is* clear, however, that because the Davidians were believed to be dangerous "cultists," the Davidians were subjected to violence ranging from the abrogation of their constitutional rights to mental, physical, symbolic, and judicial violence.

Transcript: Waco Negotiations, April 10, 1993

The following conversation between Steve Schneider and FBI negotiator Byron Sage is taken from audiotape 204 of the Waco negotiations.

Byron Sage asks Steve Schneider if the Davidians will go back on their intention to come out by committing mass suicide. In answering, Schneider articulates the Davidians' ultimate concern and gives their reason for not committing group suicide. Schneider also expresses frustration at the difficulty of communicating with FBI agents. (Emphasis added to the transcript.)

BYRON: This isn't some doomsday letter that's sent out and then, all of a sudden, you'll elect to go back on everything, every precept that we've discussed, is it?

STEVE: Explain — I'm not sure I know what you're saying.

BYRON: I'm, I'm talking straightforward *about doing injury to one another, to yourself, to others in there.*

STEVE: Oh, oh. Well, no, you know that's — How many times — I don't — Do you need to have me reiterate those things every day to you?

BYRON: Well —

STEVE: *We're not a suicide bunch. We love life.*

BYRON: Steve.

STEVE: *We hold life so highly. That's why I want it eternally. And no one cannot go break the commandments by taking their own life* —

BYRON: Okay, that's, that's —

STEVE: — because that's blasphemy against the Holy Ghost.

BYRON: I understand.

STEVE: One cannot —

BYRON: I, I agree with that and I'm glad to hear you say that.

STEVE: Well, I've said it almost — I have to say frequently —

BYRON: Okay, but let me ask you this.

STEVE: *— because people on that end of the line are not understanding plain English.*

Transcript: David Koresh and FBI Negotiators, April 16 and 18, 1993

The following is transcribed from an audiotape entitled "The Last Recorded Words of David Koresh, April 16-18, 1993," with introduction and commentary narrated by James Tabor.

On April 16, 1993, David Koresh enthusiastically reported to an FBI negotiator that he had completed writing his interpretation of the First Seal of the book of Revelation. Koresh reiterated that he and the Davidians would come out once he had committed his interpretation of the Seven Seals to writing and after the manuscript was safely in the hands of James Tabor and Phillip Arnold. From April 16 to April 18, the Davidians persistently requested a battery-operated wordprocessor, so that Koresh's manuscript could be typed. This represented obvious progress in the negotiations.

> FRIDAY, APRIL 16, 1993 (Italics reflect the emphasis of the speaker.)
>
> DICK: Are you telling me, David—I want to get this clear in my own mind. Are you telling me, here and now, that as soon as you reduce the Seven Seals to a written form, that you're coming out of there? I don't mean two days later...
>
> DAVID: I have no reason not—I have no reason not to...
>
> DICK: I know what you're saying, but answer my question if you would please. Definitely. I mean, I want to get an answer to this. Are you coming out as soon as you're done, or are you saying you're coming out afterwards at some point in time?
>
> DAVID: After I get the thing—See, Dick, you don't seem to *understand. We are going to fulfill our commitment to God.* Now, if you would allow me to show you [in the Bible] what has been prewritten by the prophets you would know what I'm doing.
>
> DICK: Well, I'm asking you a simple question.
>
> DAVID: And I'm giving you the simple answer. *Yes, yes, yes. I never intended to die in here.*

The following transcript for April 18, 1993, gives the last recorded words of David Koresh. Koresh called an FBI negotiator to complain about the tanks destroying the remaining vehicles outside Mount Carmel. Their conversation is very heated, and at times Koresh is solemn and depressed. Koresh realizes that an attack that will result in their deaths is imminent, which he wishes to avoid.

The reader should note that the negotiator on April 18 made the assumption promoted by the "cult" stereotype, that the leader of the group has total control over the followers. This overlooks the independent agency and ability of the members of the group to make decisions.

APRIL 18, 1993, ABOUT 2:00 P.M.—LAST RECORDED WORDS OF DAVID KORESH

DAVID: Henry, this is Dave.

HENRY: Hi Dave.

DAVID: Look. The generals out here, right? You have a hard time controlling them, right?

HENRY: I don't control them, no.

DAVID: O.k. Well, look. We have done everything we can to be able to communicate in a nice, passionate way. We've told you what our work with God is, and we've been kind. We've not been your everyday kind of cult. We've not been your everyday kind of terrorists, which I'm sure you're familiar with having to deal with.

HENRY: Uh huh.

DAVID: And a lot of the things the FBI, or these generals, are doing is just kind of way beyond the scope of reason. They are not only destroying private property, they are also removing evidences. And this doesn't seem like these are moves that should be made by a government who says to a people that we're going to be able to take this up in a court of law. They're not going to be able to replace a lot of things here. Like that '68 SS El Camino that belonged to Paul Fatta; they'll never be able to replace that. They don't have any more of those. And the '68 Camero and other things out here in the front; they can't replace that. They just can't replace it. And they keep doing these kind of things. It's just proving to us that they're not showing good faith on their part, and I just suggest they shouldn't do it.

HENRY: I understand what you're saying, and I will impart that…

DAVID: In all courtesies, please impart that, because it's come to the point to where, uh, you know, God in heaven has somewhat to do also. And it's really just come to the point of *what do you men really want?*

HENRY: I think what—I'm just imparting to you what my perception is. And my perception is that what they want is that they want you and everybody to come out. You know...

DAVID: I don't think so. I think what they're showing is they don't want that.

HENRY: I think that's exactly what they want.

DAVID: They're not going to get that—They're not going to get that by what they're doing right now. They're going to get exactly the opposite. Exactly the opposite. They're going to get wrath on certain people, they're going to get anger from certain guys. Now I can't control everybody here.

HENRY: I think you can.

DAVID: No, I can't. You got to understand, John.

HENRY: Henry.

DAVID: Henry, I'm sorry. In 1985 I presented a truth, and everybody's that's here I had to debate, and I had to talk to, and I had to show from the scriptures. I had to prove my point for many hours and days and months, and sometimes years with certain people here. They weren't the scholars, they weren't the theologians. I have a very unique group here.

HENRY: Yes you do.

DAVID: Not ignorant people, not stupid people. Now there's some people that in the beginning that went out, like Kevin and Brad, individuals that were, you know, people that were out there—bar rollers and stuff like that. Rough and tough guys. They're not the theologians of the world, but they're guys that need a lot of patience, you know, with a little bit of refinement and a little bit of proof to them, they can be good people.

But I would really in all honesty and in good faith tell these generals to back up. They don't need to tear up any more of this property. You tell us out of one side of the mouth that we're going to be able to come back here, and all this, and we're going to take this up in court, and on the other hand, you're showing us that there is not going to be nothing to come back to.

HENRY: I think the problem on this, on this thing, David, is that this thing has lasted way too long.

DAVID: Oh, it *has*. It should have never gotten started this way, and that was *not our fault*.

HENRY: O.k., but...

DAVID: You don't wish to speak of the issues of the beginning of this...

HENRY: No, I don't, and what the issues were at that time is something else. The problem is not what the issues were at that time. The problem is this has lasted way too long.

DAVID: I'm going to finish my book, or I'm not going to finish my book.

HENRY: I hope that you do.

DAVID: Well, let me tell this. These men, who everyday we've tried to show them good faith, they've walked out in front of us, they've driven their tanks up to us, they've busted the side of the building a little bit one time. You said that was a mistake. It was not under your control. It wasn't the commanders' wishes. All of this has been showing us that these guys want to fight. Now I don't want to fight.

HENRY: Good.

DAVID: I'm a life, too, and there's a lot of people in here that are lives, and there's children in here.

HENRY: That's right.

DAVID: And we're also Americans, and I think that America has a patronage [heritage], a very clear patronage of individual citizens who have a breaking point. The government has gotten this strong to where it can come on to something that we have worked for *hard*. We worked hard when we got on this property. A lot of *hard* hours. This place was a dump. We fixed it up. We built this little house here. It's not extravagant. There's a lot of people here with a high commission [commitment] and a lot of love and concern, and not just for our own lives, but for everybody's lives. And if this is the way our government is showing the world that its tactics are to get someone to do as they wish when realistically our rights have been infringed upon right and left.

HENRY: But there's a way to resolve that, David. The way to resolve that is for you to come out, and lead the people out.

DAVID: You're going to keep destroying our property.

HENRY: This probably would not have had to happen.

DAVID: It never did have to happen.

HENRY: That's right, and then, you know, if you had come out on the day that you indicated, that you promised that you were going to come out, none of this would have taken place.

DAVID: Look, you denounce the fact that I have a God that communicates with me. That's the first mistake...

HENRY: Nobody is saying anything about your religious beliefs, your thoughts, your ideas, or anything like that.

DAVID: But you *are*.

HENRY: The same things you can do there, you can do out here.

DAVID: That's what you say. I think that you are lying. As a matter of fact, I know that in the first month or so that I'm out, I'm going to be bombarded all the time with nothing but people wanting to know questions, asking this, asking that—

HENRY: And if you were working on the Seven Seals, I mean, nobody would bother you. Why would that have to happen?

DAVID: I have my responsibility, also. *Come on.* Look at the realities of things.

HENRY: And the reality of things is that there are priorities, and your priority and everybody's priority should be in the safety of the children, in the safety of the women...

DAVID: All right. You are fixing to ruin that. These commanders are fixing to ruin the safety of me and my children. My life, the lives of my wives, the lives of my friends, *my family*. You are fixing to step across the ribbon.

HENRY: I think that, that was something that you brought on. It has nothing to do with the commanders, David.

DAVID: All right—*I* brought on. If this is the corner of the box that you place me in to...

HENRY: I think that you are placing yourself in that, David.

DAVID: No, you're the one moving forward. You're the one who has violated—your generals are violated our constitutional rights. You have made us guilty before proven so.

HENRY: I don't think so.

DAVID: You actually brought a band of people who didn't announce themselves. They came. I was at the front door. I was willing to talk to them. They shot at me first.

HENRY: Now, you're talking about...

DAVID: About something that you don't want to prove as a matter of the fact. You're telling me that *I'm* under arrest. *I* have to come out.

HENRY: When somebody's under arrest, that doesn't mean that— that you've already been proven guilty. It just means that you've been charged.

DAVID: No, I'm being punished. We've already been *punished*. We've been placed in jail. We're being *punished* as guilty.

HENRY: Well, that is something that you chose for everybody inside.

DAVID: That is not correct. That is something *you* chose as a confinement.

HENRY: Because if you had walked out on that day as you promised, by now, who knows where we would have been? You know, you'd probably be out on bail, for goodness sakes.

DAVID: John, [sighs] all I can say is that if you want to place this in the history books as one of the saddest days in the world...

HENRY: Well, I think that the rules for your safety still apply. There's no reason to think that they shouldn't apply.

DAVID: O.k., I understand your rules. I'm just simply asking you in all good faith, and in all good manner, that you tell the generals it's *enough* to tear up our property.

HENRY: I will tell them exactly what you said, but you need to understand that, uh, I'm talking *up*. It's not, you know, talking down. So you know, what I suggest, and what I will suggest is exactly what you said. I've suggested that, and I've suggested other things. I have no problem in, uh, you know [unintelligible]...

DAVID: You tell we love 'em, we love 'em, and you know...

HENRY: And you're willing to send out 30 people.

DAVID: Look...

HENRY: Fifty?

DAVID: Whoever wants to go out can go out.

HENRY: No, no, no, no. Don't tell me *that.* Tell me that you're sending somebody out.

DAVID: I'm not going—You see, you don't understand about these people yet.

HENRY: And you don't understand about the people here yet, *either.*

DAVID: O.k., well, if this is the way we want to play it, then we come to a point where, to where...

HENRY: I'm not wanting to play *anything*...

DAVID: Look, you *are* playing...

HENRY: No I'm not...

DAVID: Everyone in the tanks up there is playing...

HENRY: No, nobody is. People just want to see some progress.

DAVID: Look, some progress is being *made*—You don't realize what kind of progress is being made. There are people all over this world who are going to benefit from this book of the Seven Seals. You don't seem to understand...

HENRY: And what you don't seem to understand is, is that the people here want to see *that* kind of progress, but *other* kind of progress. There is no reason why you couldn't be doing the same very thing you are doing now within the place out here...

DAVID: That's not true. What you are saying is not based on the truth.

HENRY: Why not? Why not? What do you mean it's not?

DAVID: Because it's just not.

HENRY: Your attorney is going to be your attorney whether you're in there or out here. Anything that you want, all you'd have to do is, is furnish it to him.

DAVID: An attorney...

HENRY: Why would he not comply with your wishes?

DAVID: That's—The legal system is *not* the majority of the attorney. The legal system is a completely sophisticated, lots of Indian chief, uh... system. It's not just where you got one guy who is hired to speak in your behalf in a court case in front of a jury.

HENRY: Yes, but, but what I'm saying...

DAVID: There's more to it—I was in jail in 1988.

HENRY: And how did it come out?

DAVID: It came out wonderful, because it...

HENRY: Well, there you go! There you go!

DAVID: Well, the thing of it is—You don't understand the amount of cost it takes to get, to get that legal representation, too. And this was something, this was something that the sheriff's department got us in.

HENRY: Well, that was then. You have an attorney now. You know the same work that you're doing there, you could be doing out *here*.

DAVID: This is a different, more high profile type situation. I just, I just suggest that it would be a very bad thing for you to keep destroying all this evidence out here.

HENRY: Well, you know, I really...

DAVID: I mean: What are they doing? Are you covering up the ATF? That's exactly what it appears you're doing.

HENRY: David, what we're trying to do...

DAVID: It's *wrong!* You're doing *wrong* before *God!* Before *man! You are doing wrong! You're adding to your wrong!*

HENRY: David, you're the one that's doing wrong...

DAVID: No, no, no, no...

HENRY: You seem to have...

DAVID: no, no, no...

HENRY: ...no concern about anybody in the place except yourself!

DAVID: You know that we've [unintelligible]...

HENRY: Well, then o.k., send 50 people out! Send 50 people out right now!

DAVID: [To Davidians.] Do 50 of you want to go out?

HENRY: You don't have to ask. All you have to do is say, "Look, I want 50 volunteers," and they'll come out. If you send 50 people out...

DAVID: [To Davidians.] Huh?

[Voices in background. Unintelligible.]

DAVID: They're saying that because of these things, they want to stay the more.

HENRY: And I guess *you* have *no control* over anybody.

DAVID: You've got to understand...

HENRY: This is your responsibility!

DAVID: ...what I have control...

HENRY: This is your responsibility, because you're the *leader. Their* safety is in *your* hands. These people look...

[The tape breaks off.]

Notes

1. Dick J. Reavis, *The Ashes of Waco: An Investigation* (New York: Simon & Schuster, 1995), 228, 274.

2. The community of 123 persons included 43 children. See James D. Tabor and Eugene V. Gallagher, *Why Waco? Cults and the Battle for Religious Freedom in America* (Berkeley: University of California Press, 1995), 3.

3. The followers of David Koresh did not at that time call themselves Branch Davidians. They regarded themselves as students of the Bible or "students of the Seven Seals" described in the biblical book of Revelation (Apocalypse). The term Branch Davidian was derived from earlier prophets and their followers at Mount Carmel near Waco, Texas. Reporters applied the name Branch Davidians to the group because they found on the property deed that the name of the ownership group was Branch Davidian Seventh-day Adventist Association. The name was applied to the David Koresh group by outsiders, but it was not inconsistent with the self-understanding of the group. See Tabor and Gallagher, *Why Waco?* 213, note 1; and Reavis, *Ashes of Waco,* 85.

4. Tabor and Gallagher, *Why Waco?* 1, 3; Carol Moore, *The Davidian Massacre: Disturbing Questions about Waco Which Must Be Answered* (Franklin, Tenn.: Legacy Communications, and Springfield, Va.: Gun Owners Foundation, 1995), 110-11.

5. Tabor and Gallagher, *Why Waco?* unnumbered final pages entitled "List of Mount Carmel Davidians."

6. Tabor and Gallagher, *Why Waco?* 3; Moore, *Davidian Massacre,* xiii-xiv; Reavis, *Ashes of Waco,* 277. The two pregnant women were Aisha Gyarfas, who died of a gunshot wound; and Nicole Gent, who was killed by falling cement as she huddled with other women and the children in a room made of concrete blocks.

7. I thank Eugene V. Gallagher for encouraging me to specify the range of violence that occurred; email message dated September 24, 1996.
8. The precise cause of the fire is unknown and fiercely disputed. The available evidence and conflicting claims are reviewed later in this chapter. It is clear that the fire would not have started if the FBI agents had not launched the tank and CS gas assault.
9. Tabor and Gallagher, *Why Waco?* 2.
10. Moore, *Davidian Massacre,* xiv, 449-53; Reavis, *Ashes of Waco,* 295-300.
    The details of the 1994 trial are too complex to recount in this chapter. See Reavis, *Ashes of Waco,* 278-300; Moore, *Davidian Massacre,* 437-61; Tabor and Gallagher, *Why Waco?* 112-16; and Albert Bates, "Waco: Trial By Fire," *Natural Rights: News of the Natural Rights Center* 9, no. 3 (Fall 1994): 1-7. I thank Timothy Miller for forwarding to me the issues of *Natural Rights* that discuss the Branch Davidian case.
11. Bates, "Waco: Trial By Fire," 6-7.
12. Reavis, *Ashes of Waco,* 33.
13. Former members who aggressively oppose a religious group are called *apostates.*
14. Moore, *Davidian Massacre,* 38-40.
15. Reavis, *Ashes of Waco,* 38.
16. Moore, *Davidian Massacre,* 40; Reavis, *Ashes of Waco,* 73.
17. Moore, *Davidian Massacre,* 40.
18. Moore, *Davidian Massacre,* 40.
19. John R. Hall, "Public Narratives and the Apocalyptic Sect: From Jonestown to Mt. Carmel," in *Armageddon in Waco: Critical Perspectives on the Branch Davidian Conflict,* ed. Stuart A. Wright (Chicago: University of Chicago Press, 1995), 225.
20. The ATF agents explored several options for luring Koresh away from Mount Carmel, but these did not work out. See Hall, "Public Narratives," 225. If the undercover operation had been effective, the ATF agents would have observed that Koresh frequently left Mount Carmel on business and entertainment trips into town.
21. James Moore, *Very Special Agents: The Inside Story of America's Most Controversial Law Enforcement Agency—The Bureau of Alcohol, Tobacco, and Firearms* (New York: Pocket Books, 1997), 286.
22. Reavis, *Ashes of Waco,* 33; Moore, *Davidian Massacre,* 89-90.
23. Videotape entitled "Waco: The Rules of Engagement," produced by Dan Gifford, William Gazecki, and Michael McNulty (Los Angeles: Fifth Estate Productions, 1997).
24. Reavis, *Ashes of Waco,* 44-47.
25. Tabor and Gallagher, *Why Waco?* 100-101, Reavis, *Ashes of Waco,* 34-35; Moore, *Davidian Massacre,* 47-48, 443-44, 446, 468, 473.
    During the congressional research relating to the 1995 Waco hearings, the Justice Department did not permit examination of the Davidians' legal semi-automatic weapons to see if they had been illegally converted to automatic weapons, nor did the Justice Department conduct its own official examination of the weapons. See House of Representatives, *Investigation into the Activities of Federal Law Enforcement Agencies toward the Branch Davidians: Thirteenth Report by the Committee on Government Reform and Oversight Prepared in Conjunction with the Committee on the Judiciary together with Additional and Dissenting Views* (Washington, D.C.: U.S. Government Printing Office, 1996), 9.

26. Reavis, *Ashes of Waco,* 35.
27. Tabor and Gallagher, *Why Waco?* 102.
28. Tabor and Gallagher, *Why Waco?* 101-2; Moore, *Davidian Massacre,* 22.
29. Tabor and Gallagher, *Why Waco?* 66-68; Christopher G. Ellison and John P. Bartkowski, "'Babies Were Being Beaten': Exploring Child Abuse Allegations at Ranch Apocalypse," in Wright, *Armageddon in Waco,* 126.
30. In the number fourteen I am including the two infants born when their mothers, Nicole Gent (24) and Aisha Gyarfas (17), died. The other children were Chanal Andrade (1), Dayland Gent (3), Paige Gent (1), Cyrus Howell (Koresh) (8), Star Howell (Koresh) (6), Chica Jones (2), Latwan Jones (2), Serenity Sea Jones (4), Bobbie Lane Koresh (2), Mayanah Schneider (2), Startle Summers (1), Hollywood Sylvia (2).
31. Moore, *Davidian Massacre,* 96-97, 297, 470; Hall, "Public Narratives," 225.
32. Ellison and Bartkowski, "'Babies Were Being Beaten,'" 111-49; Larry Lilliston, "Who Committed Child Abuse at Waco?" in *From the Ashes: Making Sense of Waco,* ed. James R. Lewis (Lanham, Md.: Rowman & Littlefield, 1994).
33. Reavis, *Ashes of Waco,* 122-28; Moore, *Davidian Massacre,* 101; House of Representatives, *Investigation,* 30-55.
34. Reavis, *Ashes of Waco,* 7.
35. Reavis, *Ashes of Waco,* 72.
36. Hall, "Public Narratives," 227.
37. Hall, "Public Narratives," 228.
38. Reavis, *Ashes of Waco,* 139.
39. Reavis, *Ashes of Waco,* 130-36, 162-66; Albert Bates, "What Happened at Waco?" *Natural Rights: News of the Natural Rights Center* 9, no. 1 (Spring 1994): 1-2; Moore, *Davidian Massacre,* 144-48, 157-60.
40. Moore, *Davidian Massacre,* 142.
41. Moore, *Davidian Massacre,* 149-50.
42. Moore, *Davidian Massacre,* 147, 149-55.
43. Reavis, *Ashes of Waco,* 139-41.
44. Reavis, *Ashes of Waco,* 139-42.
45. Reavis, *Ashes of Waco,* 145-49; Moore, *Davidian Massacre,* 129-31.
46. Reavis, *Ashes of Waco,* 152-54, 176; Moore, *Davidian Massacre,* 165, 175.
47. Reavis, *Ashes of Waco,* 154.
48. Reavis, *Ashes of Waco,* 158-59, 286-87.
49. Moore, *Davidian Massacre,* 176. For another version of the ATF raid and resulting deaths and injuries to ATF agents, see James Moore, *Very Special Agents,* 294-301.
50. Reavis, *Ashes of Waco,* 170.
51. Reavis, *Ashes of Waco,* 169-73.
52. Reavis, *Ashes of Waco,* 174.
53. Reavis, *Ashes of Waco,* 175.
54. Reavis, *Ashes of Waco,* 154-55, 244-45; and Judy Schneider's statement on a videotape made by the Branch Davidians kindly provided to me by J. Phillip Arnold.
55. Reavis, *Ashes of Waco,* 191-97; Moore, *Davidian Massacre,* 177-82.
56. Marc Breault and Martin King, *Inside the Cult: A Member's Chilling, Exclusive Account of Madness and Depravity in David Koresh's Compound* (New York: Signet Books, 1993); Moore, *Davidian Massacre,* 258-62.
57. Nancy T. Ammerman, "Waco, Federal Law Enforcement, and Scholars of Religion," in Wright, *Armageddon in Waco,* 290-92.
58. Moore, *Davidian Massacre,* 252.
59. Moore, *Davidian Massacre,* 252-54, 475-76; Ammerman, "Waco," 296, note 7;

James Tabor, "The Events at Waco: An Interpretive Log," located at <http://home. maine.rr.com/waco/ww.html>.

60. Moore, *Davidian Massacre,* 209-15.
61. Tabor, "Events at Waco. "
62. Moore, *Davidian Massacre,* 223. There were two Abrams (M1A1) tanks and five M728 Combat Engineering Vehicles (CEVs). The CEVs were converted M-60A1 tanks equipped with bulldozer blades and battering rams. To conform to the *posse comitatus* prohibition against using U.S. military against civilians, the tanks were not equipped with ammunition. However, whenever a Davidian was seen looking out of Mount Carmel, the tank driver pointed the barrel directly at the Davidian, convincing the Davidians that the tanks were loaded with ammunition.
63. Reavis, *Ashes of Waco,* 214; Bates, "What Happened at Waco?" 2.
64. Reavis, *Ashes of Waco,* 219.
65. "Waco: The Rules of Engagement" videotape.
66. Reavis, *Ashes of Waco,* 216-20; Tabor, "Events at Waco. "
67. Tabor, "Events at Waco. "
68. Tabor, "Events at Waco. "
69. Tabor, "Events at Waco. "
70. Tabor, "Events at Waco. "
71. Reavis, *Ashes of Waco,* 253.
72. Tabor, "Events at Waco. "
73. Reavis, *Ashes of Waco,* 259; Tabor, "Events at Waco. " Subsequently, the Davidians were very distressed by the tanks repeatedly running over and tearing up the grave of Peter Gent. See "Waco: The Rules of Engagement" videotape.
74. Reavis, *Ashes of Waco,* 230-35; Tabor and Gallagher, *Why Waco?* final unnumbered page listing the Davidians dead.
75. Tabor, "Events at Waco. "
76. Moore, *Davidian Massacre,* 255; Tabor, "Events at Waco. "
77. Reavis, *Ashes of Waco,* 222.
78. Moore, *Davidian Massacre,* 254-56.
79. Tabor, "Events at Waco. "
80. Negotiation tape no. 129, March 15, 1993. I thank Dr. J. Phillip Arnold for kindly forwarding this audiotape to me.
81. Moore, *Davidian Massacre,* 256.
82. Tabor, "Events at Waco. "
83. Tabor, "Events at Waco. "
84. Reavis, *Ashes of Waco,* 259-60.
85. Tabor, "Events at Waco. "
86. Moore, *Davidian Massacre,* 256-57.
87. Tabor, "Events at Waco. "
88. Tabor, "Events at Waco. "
89. Audiotape of discussion of James Tabor and J. Phillip Arnold on the Ron Engleman radio talk show, station KGBS, on April 1, 1993. I thank Phillip Arnold for kindly forwarding this tape to me.
90. Tabor, "Events at Waco. "
91. Tabor, "Events at Waco. "
92. Tabor, "Events at Waco. "
93. Tabor, "Events at Waco"; Tabor and Gallagher, *Why Waco?* 17-18, 111, 217, note 40.
94. Reavis, *Ashes of Waco,* 264-65.
95. House of Representatives, *Investigation,* 165.
96. Moore, *Davidian Massacre,* 275; audiotape entitled, "The Last Recorded Words

of David Koresh April 16-18, 1993," narrated by James Tabor. I thank J. Phillip Arnold for kindly forwarding this tape to me.

97. Tabor, "Events at Waco."
98. Tabor, "Events at Waco"; "Last Recorded Words of David Koresh."
99. Moore, *Davidian Massacre*, 325, 340, 346; House of Representatives, *Investigation*, 81.
100. Moore, *Davidian Massacre*, 325-26.
101. Moore, *Davidian Massacre*, 318-19, 338-39, 340-43, 364; Reavis, *Ashes of Waco*, 268-70.
102. Moore, *Davidian Massacre*, 335-36, 337-38, 344-45.
103. Moore, *Davidian Massacre*, 340, 350, 355.
104. Moore, *Davidian Massacre*, 320, 346-53, 368; Reavis, *Ashes of Waco*, 275.
105. Moore, *Davidian Massacre*, 320.
106. Moore, *Davidian Massacre*, 318-22, 366-67, 369-70, 415-16; Reavis, *Ashes of Waco*, 277.
107. Moore, *Davidian Massacre*, 333, 375-76, 406-13.
108. Hall, "Public Narratives," 230.
109. Nike Carstarphen, "Third Party Efforts at Waco: J. Phillip Arnold and James Tabor," unpublished paper, Institute for Conflict Analysis and Resolution, George Mason University (1995), 7-8; Moore, *Davidian Massacre*, 378.
110. Moore, *Davidian Massacre*, 379-84.
111. Moore, *Davidian Massacre*, 362-63, 365-66, 390-92; Reavis, *Ashes of Waco*, 268-69.
112. Moore, *Davidian Massacre*, 334-36, 355, 367, 368, 377, 387-88, 390-91; Reavis, *Ashes of Waco*, 275-76.
113. Reavis, *Ashes of Waco*, 277.

The Branch Davidian flag depicted a Star of David and a serpent with blazing wings. For the Davidians, the serpent represented higher wisdom and salvation. The fiery serpent on a pole was also a reference to Numbers 21: 8-9 and Isaiah 15:29. "The more transparent scripture reads, 'And the Lord said unto Moses, Make thee a fiery serpent, and set upon a pole: and it shall come to pass, that every one that is bitten, when he looketh upon it, shall live. And Moses made a serpent of brass, and put it upon a pole, and it came to pass, that if a serpent had bitten any man, when he beheld the serpent of brass, he lived.'" (pp. 149-50.)

114. Moore, *Davidian Massacre*, 418.
115. Stuart A. Wright, "Introduction: Another View of the Mt. Carmel Standoff," in Wright, *Armageddon in Waco*, xv.
116. Moore, *Davidian Massacre*, 293.
117. House of Representatives, *Investigation*, 71, 75, 83.
118. House of Representatives, *Investigation*, 94.
119. House of Representatives, *Investigation*, 93.
120. Reavis, *Ashes of Waco*, 23-25; Tabor and Gallagher, *Why Waco?* 58.
121. Reavis, *Ashes of Waco*, 25-26.
122. Reavis, *Ashes of Waco*, 26.
123. Reavis, *Ashes of Waco*, 27-30.
124. Reavis, *Ashes of Waco*, 75-76; Tabor and Gallagher, *Why Waco?* 41.
125. Tabor and Gallagher, *Why Waco?* 42; Reavis, *Ashes of Waco*, 76.
126. Tabor and Gallagher, *Why Waco?* 42.
127. Quoted in David G. Bromley and Edward D. Silver, "The Davidian Tradition: From Patronal Clan to Prophetic Movement," in Wright, *Armageddon in Waco*, 59.
128. Bruce Gent, quoted in Bromley and Silver, "Davidian Tradition," 60.
129. Reavis, *Ashes of Waco*, 77-81; Tabor and Gallagher, *Why Waco?* 43.

130. Reavis, *Ashes of Waco,* 81-82. George Roden (60) died of a heart attack on the grounds of the Big Spring State Hospital on December 7, 1998. It was erroneously reported in the media that Roden had escaped the mental health facility. I thank James Tabor for kindly forwarding to me the December 7, 1998, article by Mark England that appeared in the *Waco Tribune-Herald.*

131. Tabor and Gallagher, *Why Waco?* 59-60.

132. Tabor and Gallagher, *Why Waco?* 59-63.

133. Tabor and Gallagher, *Why Waco?* 63.

134. Tabor and Gallagher, *Why Waco?* 68-72.

135. Quoted in Bromley and Silver, "Davidian Tradition," 57.

136. Tabor and Gallagher, *Why Waco?* 72.

137. Tabor and Gallagher, *Why Waco?* 60-61, 74.

138. Livingstone Fagan, "The Sevenfold Manifestation of God to Man," quoted in Bates, "What Happened at Waco?" 5.

139. Tabor and Gallagher, *Why Waco?* 76-77, 79.

140. Reavis, *Ashes of Waco,* 24.

141. Bromley and Silver, "Davidian Tradition," 44; Tabor and Gallagher, *Why Waco?* 33-35.

142. Tabor and Gallagher, *Why Waco?* 33-37; William L. Pitts Jr., "Davidians and Branch Davidians, 1929-1987," in Wright, *Armageddon in Waco,* 25.

143. Tabor and Gallagher, *Why Waco?* 37.

144. Tabor and Gallagher, *Why Waco?* 36.

145. Bromley and Silver, "Davidian Tradition," 49-50; Tabor and Gallagher, *Why Waco?* 38-39; Pitts, "Davidians and Branch Davidians, 1929–1987," 30-31.

146. Tabor and Gallagher, *Why Waco?* 39.

147. Tabor and Gallagher, *Why Waco?* 39.

148. Bromley and Silver, "Davidian Tradition," 51.

149. Tabor and Gallagher, *Why Waco?* 39-40; Bromley and Silver, "Davidian Tradition," 51.

150. Tabor and Gallagher, *Why Waco?* 40; Reavis, *Ashes of Waco,* 85.

151. Tabor and Gallagher, *Why Waco?* 49.

152. Tabor and Gallagher, *Why Waco?* 50.

153. Tabor and Gallagher, *Why Waco?* 50.

154. Tabor and Gallagher, *Why Waco?* 50-51.

155. Quoted in Bromley and Silver, "Davidian Tradition," 61.

156. Transcript of negotiation tape no. 201, April 9, 1993. I thank Eugene V. Gallagher for kindly forwarding to me the Waco negotiation transcripts.

157. Tabor and Gallagher, *Why Waco?* 30.

158. Quoted in Tabor and Gallagher, *Why Waco?* 31.

159. Tabor and Gallagher, *Why Waco?* 24-28.

160. Tabor and Gallagher,*Why Waco?* 23-24.

161. Bromley and Silver, "Davidian Tradition," 55.

162. Comment by Victorine Hollingsworth, quoted in Bates, "Waco: Trial By Fire," 4.

163. Personal letter from Rev. Robert L. Uzzel, dated August 1, 1996.

164. Tabor and Gallagher, *Why Waco?* 79.

165. Tabor and Gallagher, *Why Waco?* 76; Marc A. Breault, "Vernon Howell and the 1995 Deadline" (Marc Breault, 1992), obtained at <http://www.ime.net/~mswett>.

166. Tabor and Gallagher, *Why Waco?* 10, 77.

167. Tabor and Gallagher, *Why Waco?* 5.

168. Quoted in Tabor and Gallagher, *Why Waco?* 9-10, their emphasis added.

169. Tabor and Gallagher, *Why Waco?* 8-9, 11-12.

170. Tabor and Gallagher, *Why Waco?* 13.

171. Tabor and Gallagher, *Why Waco?* 13.

172. Tabor and Gallagher, *Why Waco?* 6.
173. Negotiation tape no. 129, March 15, 1993.
174. Tabor and Gallagher, *Why Waco?* 14-16.
175. Quoted in Tabor and Gallagher, *Why Waco?* 15-16, their emphasis added.
176. Tabor and Gallagher, *Why Waco?* 18.
177. Transcript of audiotape entitled "The Last Recorded Words of David Koresh April 16-18, 1993," with introduction and commentary by James Tabor. I thank J. Phillip Arnold for forwarding this audiotape to me. See transcript appended to this chapter.
178. Hall, "Public Narratives," 206.
179. Stuart A. Wright, "Construction and Escalation of a Cult Threat: Dissecting Moral Panic and Official Reaction to the Branch Davidians," in Wright, *Armageddon in Waco,* 83.
180. Hall, "Public Narratives," 218.
181. Breault and King, *Inside the Cult.*
182. Interview of Marc Breault by James Tabor, in Tabor and Gallagher, *Why Waco?* 87.
183. Hall, "Public Narratives," 230.
184. Hall, "Public Narratives," 230.
185. Hall, "Public Narratives," 231.
186. Hall, "Public Narratives," 213.
187. Wright, "Construction and Escalation," 84; Breault and King, *Inside the Cult.*
188. Eugene V. Gallagher, "'Theology Is Life and Death': David Koresh on Violence, Persecution, and the Millennium," in Wessinger, *Millennialism, Persecution, and Violence,* 82–100.
189. Hall, "Public Narratives," 213-14.
190. Breault and King, 256-57, quoted in Hall, "Public Narratives," 215; Wright, "Construction and Escalation," 86.
191. Hall, "Public Narratives," 215-17; Wright, "Construction and Escalation," 84.
192. Hall, "Public Narratives," 217.
193. Hall, "Public Narratives," 218-19.
194. Hall, "Public Narratives," 220.
195. Hall, "Public Narratives," 223-25; Wright, "Construction and Escalation," 85-86.
196. Quoted in Wright, "Construction and Escalation," 86.
    Vic Feazell also said on March 2, 1993, "The Feds are preparing to kill them [noting the mobilization of military equipment into nearby staging areas]. That way they can bury their mistakes and they won't have attorneys looking over what they did later....I'd represent these boys for free if they'd surrender without bloodshed, but I'm afraid I'm going to wake up and see the headlines that say they all died." See p.91, note 1.
197. Wright, "Construction and Escalation," 89.
198. Wright, "Construction and Escalation," 90.
199. Tabor and Gallagher, *Why Waco?* 135-38.
200. Anson Shupe and Jeffrey K. Hadden, "Cops, News Copy, and Public Opinion: Legitimacy and the Social Construction of Evil in Waco," in Wright, *Armageddon in Waco,* 196-99.
201. Shupe and Hadden, "Cops, News Copy, and Public Opinion," 199.
202. Tabor and Gallagher, *Why Waco?* 139.
203. James T. Richardson, "Manufacturing Consent about Koresh: A Structural Analysis of the Role of Media in the Waco Tragedy," in Wright, *Armageddon in Waco,* 163.

204. "Waco: The Rules of Engagement" videotape.
205. Richardson, "Manufacturing Consent about Koresh," 163-64.
206. Quoted in Richardson, "Manufacturing Consent about Koresh," 163.
207. Richardson, "Manufacturing Consent about Koresh," 169.
208. Reavis, *Ashes of Waco,* 249-50. In describing the events that led to the massacre of a band of Lakota Sioux at Wounded Knee in 1890 by United States soldiers, Michelene E. Pesantubbee reports that the soldiers first engaged in ritualized taunting and demeaning of the Lakota men. See Michelene E. Pesantubbee, "From Vision to Violence: The Wounded Knee Massacre," in Wessinger, *Millennialism, Persecution, and Violence,* 62–81.
209. Interview of Ruth Riddle by Stone Phillips on *Dateline NBC,* quoted in Bates, "Waco: Trial by Fire," 5.
210. Reavis, *Ashes of Waco,* 215-20.
211. Tabor and Gallagher, *Why Waco?* 109-10.
212. Bromley and Silver, "Davidian Tradition," 61.
213. Bromley and Silver, "Davidian Tradition," 65-66.
214. Reavis, *Ashes of Waco,* 188.
215. Quoted in Tabor and Gallagher, *Why Waco?* 65.
216. Tabor and Gallagher, *Why Waco?* 65-66.
217. Gallagher, "'Theology is Life and Death.'"
218. Tabor and Gallagher, *Why Waco?* 99.
219. Charles Richards, Associated Press, "FBI trapped cult, started inferno, Waco film claims," *New Orleans Times-Picayune,* April 23, 1997, A-6; Stephen Holden, "'Waco: The Rules of Engagement': A Documentary Indictment of the FBI," *New York Times* (AOL), June 13, 1997.

CHAPTER FIVE
1995—Aum Shinrikyo

*If asked why we are oppressed, it is because we are the true
religion that liberates people from the current mistaken world.*
—Yoshinobu Aoyama, head of Aum Shinrikyo Justice Ministry[1]

Aum is a mighty obstacle to the evil that rules this world.
—Shoko Asahara[2]

The Violence

The Japanese new religion known as Aum Shinrikyo stands in contrast to
Jonestown and the Branch Davidians, because Aum devotees detained,
coerced, tortured, and killed people, and pursued the development of
weapons of mass destruction in a national context in which the activities of
religious organizations were not scrutinized by law enforcement agents.
Aum's guru, Shoko Asahara, and his devotees saw themselves as belonging
to a persecuted religious organization, but the activities of their cultural
opponents were miniscule compared to the violence perpetrated by Aum
devotees. Aum leaders were anxious to block investigation of Aum Shinrikyo because of crimes that members had committed before serious cultural opposition had developed. In terms of financial resources and
violence against members and outsiders, Aum Shinrikyo makes Jim Jones's
Jonestown and David Koresh's Mount Carmel Center appear small-scale.

Aum Shinrikyo leaders and members were preparing to commit revolutionary violence, but the violent acts committed by Aum members
were motivated by the fragility of their millennial group. The combination
of a lack of monitoring by law enforcement agents, internal weaknesses

within Aum, and Aum members' sense of being in conflict with external opponents prompted a group of Aum devotees to coerce and/or murder people to protect their ultimate concern, the creation of the Buddhist millennial kingdom, Shambhala. As at Jonestown, high-level Aum devotees became bonded by their shared participation in rituals of violence, which prepared some of them to commit ever-escalating acts of violence. The dualistic millennial theology taught by Asahara provided a justification for committing murder.

The name of this Japanese new religion includes the Hindu and Buddhist sacred syllable "Om" (pronounced "aum"). Shinrikyo can be translated as "teaching of the supreme truth." Asahara taught that "Aum" in Sanskrit referred to the creation, preservation, and destruction of the universe. Therefore, Aum Shinrikyo was an organization that taught the truth about creation and destruction.[3] This was no ordinary truth; it was the *supreme* truth for which devotees were asked to kill or die.

On Monday, March 20, 1995, at 7:45 A.M., five members of Aum Shinrikyo boarded five subway trains at different stations in Tokyo. Each of the trains was scheduled to converge at 8:15 A.M. at the Kasumigaseki station located near the headquarters of the National Police Agency and other government buildings. At 8:00 A.M., these devotees deposited plastic bags containing sarin[4] on the floor, punctured the bags with sharpened umbrella tips, and immediately disembarked. People began coughing, choking, and vomiting, and those closest to the sarin collapsed. The fumes of the deadly nerve gas injured over 5,000 Tokyo commuters, and twelve people died.[5] The Aum members who released sarin gas on the Tokyo subway were a cardiovascular surgeon, Dr. Ikuo Hayashi (48), a former graduate student in particle physics, Toru Toyoda (27), a specialist in applied physics, Masato Yokoyama (31), another applied physicist, Kenichi Hirose (30), and an electronics engineer, Yasuo Hayashi (37). They were all members of Aum's Science and Technology Ministry.[6]

This was not the first instance of murder committed by Aum Shinrikyo members, nor was it the last. The March 20, 1995, gas attack on the Tokyo subway was merely the most dramatic and large-scale act of violence committed by Aum devotees. It had been preceded by an attempt to release botulinus bacteria at Kasumigaseki station five days prior to the sarin gas attack. That effort failed because equipment placed in a briefcase did not work.[7]

Subsequently, Aum Shinrikyo devotees confessed to a variety of violent crimes, and evidence of murders was discovered.

Purposeful and accidental gas releases had occurred prior to the Tokyo subway attack. In July 1993 residents near an Aum Shinrikyo center in Kameido in Tokyo complained about a foul-smelling gas. Aum officials refused entry to police seeking to investigate. On June 27, 1994,

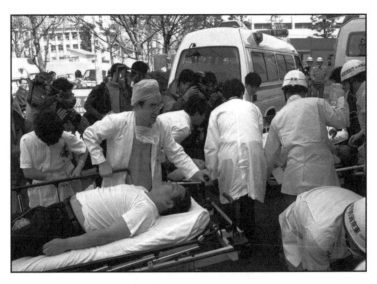

Victims of the gas attack on the Tokyo subway are taken to St. Luke Hospital in Tokyo. (AP Photo/File/Chiaki Tsukumo)

after 10:00 P.M., a cloud of sarin gas wafted through Matsumoto, a town in Nagano Prefecture. About 600 people were injured and seven died. The alarm was first raised by Yoshiyuki Kono, a machinery salesman. Kono and his children were made ill by the gas, and his wife succumbed to a coma. Feeling pressured to quickly identify a guilty party, the police alleged that Kono released the poisonous gas by mixing chemicals for fertilizer. Kono possessed chemicals for photography, not gardening, and he did not possess the chemicals necessary to make sarin, but the police and the news media made Kono the scapegoat. Kono's reputation was damaged, but he was never charged. In fact, the sarin gas was released by Aum devotees from a truck. Two weeks after the Matsumoto gas attack, a cloud of chlorine (used in the manufacture of sarin) was emitted from Aum headquaters in Kamikuishiki village at the foot of Mount Fuji. Neighbors were made ill, and they observed Aum members wearing gas masks rushing around the commune. Aum devotees refused to permit firemen and police to enter the grounds to investigate. A week later, a poisonous gas was emitted from the Aum headquarters and members again were observed wearing gas masks. Tree leaves and plants in the surrounding area died. Much later, a police investigation revealed that the gas had been sarin.[8]

Aum Shinrikyo's path of escalating violence began with Asahara's insistence that devotees practice asceticism; the ascetic acts themselves were so extreme that they constituted violence. In addition to standard Buddhist practices such as meditation, chanting, and prostrations, devotees had to submit to immersion in very cold water for extended periods to cool down their minds, and also to submersion in very hot water to raise internal heat to produce psychic experiences. Physical beatings were sometimes applied to exorcise impure thoughts. (In Japanese religious culture, beatings sometimes are utilized to exorcise bad spirits.) If Aum devotees were reluctant to engage in these extreme forms of asceticism, they were coerced or beaten to make them do so. Salvation in the Shambhala millennial kingdom was dependent on their ascetic practice and devotion to the guru.[9]

In 1988, Terayuki Majima died while being subjected to cold water immersion. Since Aum Shinrikyo had applied to become a legally registered religious organization, Majima's death was kept secret. Another member, Shuji Taguchi (25), was frightened by Majima's death, wanted to defect, and thus raised the possibility that he might report Majima's death to the police. Taguchi was murdered at Aum headquarters in February 1989. Taguchi was strangled, his neck broken, and his body was burned in a metal drum. The Taguchi murder may have been the first premeditated murder committed by Aum devotees.[10]

In early November 1989, an attorney who represented the Aum Shinrikyo Victims' Society (Aum Shinrikyo higaisha no kai), Tsutsumi Sakamoto (33), his wife Satoko (29), and their son Tatsuhiko (14 months) were murdered in their Yokohama apartment by Aum devotees. The murders were carried out by Aum's chief scientist, Hideo Murai (30), a martial arts expert, Satoru Hashimoto (28), a physician, Dr. Tomomasa Nakagawa (29), and Kazuaki Okazuki. The sleeping Sakamotos were held down, beaten, smothered, and Dr. Nakagawa injected them with potassium chloride. The bodies were carried out of the apartment wrapped in their futons and blankets, and were buried in separate locations in the countryside. The confession of Okazuki in 1995 after the Tokyo subway gas attack enabled police to locate the remains of the Sakamoto family.[11]

In late June 1993, Aum scientists tested the first weapon they had developed for mass murder. They used a large fan on the rooftop of an Aum building in Tokyo to spray a biological agent they believed was anthrax across the city. Birds, pets, and plants died, people got sick, there was a nauseating odor, and cars and pedestrians' clothes were stained. Aum devotees refused to permit inspectors to investigate the building.[12]

On January 30, 1994, two former members, a pharmacist, Kotaro Ochida (29), and Hideaki Yasuda (26), sneaked into the Aum headquarters in Kamikuishiki to rescue Yasuda's ill mother. They were captured and brought into the presence of Shoko Asahara and his wife. Asahara gave Yasuda the choice of either killing Ochida or being killed himself. A plastic bag was placed over Ochida's head, and Yasuda was forced to spray Mace into it. A rope was wound around Ochida's neck and Yasuda was made to strangle him. Yasuda was permitted to leave with instructions to tell his father that his mother was well and that Ochida had decided to rejoin Aum.[13]

On September 20, 1994, phosgene, a lethal gas used in World War I, was released in the apartment of a journalist, Shoko Egawa, who had written two anti-Aum books as well as critical articles. Egawa required hospitalization, but she was not killed.[14]

On December 2, 1994, a Tokyo parking lot attendant, Noboru Mizuno (83), was injected with VX nerve agent when he went outside his home. Mizuno was hospitalized for over six weeks, but he recovered. Mizuno's crime against Aum was that he had provided shelter to five defectors. The person who attempted to execute Mizuno was Tomomitsu Niimi (30), the Aum security chief, who had also released the phosgene into Egawa's apartment.[15]

On December 12, 1994, Takahito Hanaguchi (28) was killed on a street in Osaka when Niimi injected him with VX. Hanaguchi, who had visited Aum headquarters numerous times, was believed by Aum leaders to be a police undercover agent.[16]

On January 4, 1995, the head of the Aum Shinrikyo Victims' Society, Hiroyuki Nakaoka (57), was struck by a stream of VX as he walked across a parking lot. Again, Niimi was the assassin. Nakaoka was in a coma for several weeks, but he recovered.[17]

Kiyoshi Kariya (68), a businessman who was hiding his sister Aiko Nishina (62) after she had defected from Aum Shinrikyo, was abducted from a Tokyo street on February 28, 1995. The sister had donated money earlier to Aum amounting to about $600,000. Kariya was injected with sodium thiopental by Drs. Nakagawa and Hayashi, and he died during the interrogation. An industrial-size microwave oven was used to incinerate Kariya's body; probably other corpses were disposed of in the same manner.[18]

An Aum hospital located in Tokyo was utilized as a place where dissenting and disruptive members were incarcerated and drugged. The Aum Supreme Truth Hospital in Tokyo was supervised by Dr. Ikuo Hayashi, the son of a Ministry of Health official and a graduate of a prestigious Japanese medical school. Unorthodox treatments consisted of Aum ascetic practices and gaining good karma by making large donations to Aum. Patients there had a high death rate for a small nine-bed clinic—nine deaths within an eighteen-month period beginning in 1993—and patients were systematically isolated from contact with their families. The physicians and nurses working there were Aum devotees. They carried out coercive medical practices and administered drugs in religious initiations.[19]

Japanese police later concluded that Aum devotees killed 31 people between October 1988 and March 1995. Some were being coerced into making financial donations. At least eight died from Aum's extreme ascetic practices. People were coerced and killed for doubting Asahara's "supreme truth" and for wanting to defect. Two people committed suicide.[20]

On March 22, 1995, two days after the Tokyo subway gas attack and the day about 3,500 Japanese police and soldiers launched a massive raid against the twenty-five Aum Shinrikyo centers in Japan,[21] a videotaped message from Shoko Asahara was broadcast to Japan by Aum devotees in Russia. In this message, Asahara said, "It is time for you to carry out the plan of salvation. Let us prepare to meet our death without any regrets."[22] This message apparently motivated additional violent actions by Aum members.

On March 30, 1995, Police Chief Kunimatsu, the head of the National Police Agency, was shot outside his residence as he left for work. He was seriously injured but not killed. An anonymous call to a television network two hours after the shooting warned that more police officers would be assassinated if the investigation of Aum was not halted. A police officer who was an Aum devotee, Toshiyuki Kosugi (30), later confessed, but the embarassed National Police Agency refused to regard his confession as genuine. In June 1997, the Tokyo District Public Prosecutor's office decided not to press charges against Kosugi due to lack of material evidence.[23]

Shoko Asahara predicted that a catastrophe worse than the January 1995 Kobe earthquake (which killed about 5,500) would occur in Tokyo on April 15, 1995. On that date two shopping complexes in the Shinjuku area of Tokyo were closed, and the usually bustling Shinjuku station was silent. Nothing happened, probably because about 20,000 police were deployed in Tokyo.[24]

On April 23, 1995, as television cameras filmed outside Aum's Tokyo headquarters, a man with gangster (*yakusa*) connections stabbed to death Hideo Murai, the head of Aum's Science and Technology Ministry. It has been speculated that mobsters had purchased illegal drugs manufactured by Aum's scientists, and that they wanted to silence Murai.[25]

On May 5, 1995, an attempt to release hydrogen cyanide (Zyklon B, used in Nazi death camps) at Tokyo's busiest station at Shinjuku failed when the device burst into flames.[26]

The intensive police hunt led to the arrest of about 200 Aum members, but Shoko Asahara remained at large until May 16, 1995. A search of a building at the Aum headquarters in Kamikuishiki village discovered Asahara with yen amounting to over $100,000 hiding in a secret cubicle located between the second and third floors. Asahara was charged with murder in relation to the Tokyo subway gas attack and the Matsumoto gas release, and with the murders of the Sakamoto family and Kariya. He was charged also with production of illegal drugs.[27]

On the evening of May 16, a letter bomb was sent by Aum devotees to the Tokyo Governor's office and exploded in the hands of a secretary. The Governor had previously announced his intention to revoke Aum's status as a registered religion.[28]

Shoko Asahara

The man who became known as Shoko Asahara was born on March 2, 1955, as Chizuo Matsumoto. He was the fourth son of seven children of a very poor couple living on the island of Kyushu. His father was a maker of *tatami* mats. Chizuo, as an infant, suffered from glaucoma and his eyesight was permanently impaired; he was totally blind in one eye and had about 30 percent of his vision in the other eye. At age six Chizuo and two of his brothers were sent to board at a school for the blind. Chizuo became a leader among the blind children because he had the advantage of being partially sighted and served as a guide for the other children.

After graduating from the Kumamoto Prefectural School for the Blind, Matsumoto moved to Tokyo in 1977 with great ambitions. He earned his living by working as a licensed masseur and acupuncturist. Matsumoto wanted to attend medical school, but was not admitted because of his impaired eyesight. Matsumoto then aimed to enter law school at Tokyo University, but he failed the entrance exam. In 1978, he married Tomoko Ishii and they started a family that would grow to include six children. Matsumoto began a business selling Chinese herbal medicines in July 1978, and he studied Chinese forms of divination and asceticism to acquire supernatural powers. Matsumoto read works on Buddhism and books by Shinji Takahashi, founder of God Light Association (GLA), whose teachings drew on Spiritualism and the New Age movement. In 1981 Matsumoto joined the Japanese new religion Agonshu, and learned about meditation and yoga. In June 1982, Matsumoto's herbalist license was revoked for selling bogus herbal medicines and he had to close his shop.[29] As a student of mysticism and popular religion, Asahara probably read interpretations of the prophecies of the sixteenth-century French astrologer and seer, Nostradamus, whose prophecies had been popularized in Japan since 1973. The founder of Agonshu published a book on Nostradamus's prophecies in 1981, the year that Asahara joined Agonshu. In Japan, interest in Nostradamus's prophecies focused on quatrain CX-72, which stated that in July 1999, "From the sky will come a great King of Terror."[30]

In 1984, Matsumoto left Agonshu with fifteen followers and founded his own meditation and yoga group. In 1985, Matsumoto gained public attention for claiming in an occult journal that he could levitate. A photograph was published of Matsumoto seated in lotus position, propelling himself about a foot into the air.

Matsumoto's spirituality was a syncretic blend of Hindu yoga and ideas (with special emphasis on the Yoga Sutra) and his understanding of Buddhism with Japanese concerns with asceticism and belief in gods. Matsumoto took as his tutelary deities the Hindu gods Shiva and Vishnu, particularly Shiva, a deity of asceticism and yoga. In 1985, Asahara claimed that when he was engaged in ascetic practice on Miura beach in Kanagawa Prefecture, a deity descended from the sky and said, "I appoint you as *abiraketsu no mikoto*. Asahara came to understand *abiraketsu no mikoto* as meaning "the god of light who leads the armies of gods." He thus understood that he was divinely appointed to wage warfare to create the Buddhist millennial kingdom called Shambhala, that, according to Asahara, would be inhabited by spiritual adepts with advanced psychic powers.[31]

It is noteworthy that Matsumoto, who achieved leadership among blind schoolchildren because he was partially sighted, increasingly achieved exalted religious leadership because he claimed to have fully developed psychic senses. Matsumoto began to publish books on asceticism and the acquisition of superhuman powers. His first book, whose title in English translation was *A Secret Method to the Development of Psychic Power* (1986), claimed that Matsumoto could levitate, prophesy, heal, and control the weather, and that he had powers of clairvoyance and telekinesis. This book contained a brief reference to Nostradamus's prediction of disaster in 1999.

In 1986, Matsumoto visited India, and upon returning, he claimed to be the only person in Japan who had achieved *gedatsu* or "final liberation," and said that he had achieved this full enlightenment by two months of solitary meditation in the Himalayan mountains. In April 1986, Matsumoto founded Aum Shinsen no Kai (Aum wizards [or Daoist sage] society), and established a commune near Tokyo. At the end of 1986, Matsumoto published *Transcending Life and Death*, in which he identified yoga with early Buddhist teachings. In February 1987, Matsumoto visited Dharamsala, India, the settlement of Tibetan refugees led by the Dalai Lama, who practice Vajrayana or Tantric Buddhism. Matsumoto had his photo taken with the Dalai Lama, and he later published this photo in his books to convey legitimacy to his religious leadership. In 1987, Matsumoto changed his undistinguished name to Shoko Asahara—Asahara being a classy family name and Shoko being a homonym for the word meaning "an offering of incense." The organization's name was changed to Aum Shinrikyo, and it was registered in 1989 under the Religious Corporations Law.[32]

From 1987 on, Shoko Asahara styled himself as a Buddha who possessed psychic powers. Asahara claimed to have the power to levitate and to soul-travel out of the body, and to have an infallible power of prophecy. Although he did not use the Sanskrit term *siddha*, the doctrine that he taught was very similar to the concept of the *siddha* (a perfected human possessing *siddhis*, superhuman powers) found in Hinduism and in Mahayana or Vajrayana Buddhism. The *siddha*, the perfectly enlightened guru, is believed to convey enlightenment to his devotees by instructing them in meditation and yoga, but most importantly, by conveying the energy of enlightenment by *shaktipat* when the guru awakens higher consciousness by touch. *Shaktipat* is believed to awaken the *kundalini*, a spiritual energy dormant at the base of the spine. Through spiritual discipline and the grace of the guru, the devotee aims to experience the rising of the *kundalini*, activating the *chakras*, centers of energy along the spinal column, to achieve enlightenment. In the Hindu *siddha* tradition, the guru is God and the devotee receives enlightenment by surrendering totally to the guru.[33]

Asahara conveyed his understanding of the *siddha* tradition in the popularized language of twentieth-century science and computer technology. According to Asahara, each devotee should strive to become a clone of the guru. Devotees should purify and empty their minds of thoughts—associated with the deluded lower-self—and fill themselves with the "guru's data." Claiming that this was Vajrayana Buddhism, Asahara wrote, "In the teachings of Vajrayana, disciples regard the guru as the absolute, and devote themselves to him. They make every effort to empty themselves, and fill their empty vessel with the experience and energy of the guru. That is, it is the cloning of the guru...." Terming *shaktipat* "empowerment," Asahara explained it in the following terms: "From time to time the savior should utilize a dangerous method called shaktipat.... This is a technique to squeeze out someone's bad thought and karma and infuse good karma into them."[34]

In his book, *Initiation* (1987), Asahara claimed that *shaktipat* given by himself to the devotee was necessary to awaken the *kundalini*.[35] In 1994, Aum scientists began producing drugs, LSD, sodium thiopental, mescaline, methamphetamine, and PCP, for use in religious initiations. Even those chemically-induced mystical experiences were attributed by Aum believers to the *shakti* (spiritual power, energy) of the guru.[36]

At a seminar in May 1987, Asahara predicted that armageddon (Japanese, *harumagedon*) was imminent. Asahara said, "Between 1999 and 2003, a nuclear war is sure to break out. I, Asahara, have mentioned the outbreak of nuclear war for the first time. We have only fifteen years before it." Asahara asserted that armageddon could be averted if every country contained an Aum center led by a Buddha, an "awakened one." "Spread the training of Aum on a global scale and scatter Buddhas over the world. Then we can avoid World War III for sure. I guarantee it."[37]

Shoko Asahara expressed his alienation from Japanese culture by wearing Indian clothing and by keeping his hair and beard long in the style of an Indian ascetic. Congruent with the Indian *siddha* tradition, Aum devotees believed that their own enlightenment would come from their submission to Asahara as the guru. Devotees were encouraged to repeat 16 to 20 hours each day: "I pledge faithfulness to Aum, the Guru and the god Shiva. Please lead me, [name], quickly to *gedatsu* [enlightenment]."[38]

Shoko Asahara identified himself as the Buddha of the current age and claimed to be teaching Mahayana Buddhism, and later, Vajrayana Buddhism. In 1992, Asahara published a book entitled *Declaring Myself the Christ* in English translation. He claimed to be the Lamb of God, who absorbed the bad karma of his disciples, even though it made him ill. *Karma* is the Hindu and Buddhist term for "action" and the doctrine that all actions produce results leading to rebirth in good or bad circumstances. Asahara taught that people who rejected him as the guru were destined for rebirth in the lower realms of the animals, hungry ghosts, and the hells due to their bad karma. Acceptance of Asahara as the incarnation of Shiva, as the guru was necessary to attain good karma and salvation.[39]

In Hinduism, the guru or a deity is considered to be so pure that disciples may eat food from his plate, drink his dirty bath water, or touch his feet—normally polluting acts—and be purified. Carrying on in this tradition, Asahara's bath water was sold to disciples to be drunk. Vials of Asahara's blood were sold so that devotees could "absorb the Master's DNA by drinking his blood." A devotee explained the Aum blood initiation:

> The Initiation of Blood comes from a secret Tantric rite wherein the blood of the guru is taken into one's own body. The introduction of the guru's internal tissue implies the introduction of the guru's holy karma, and hastens progress in purifying one's own karma, thus elevating one's practice....[40]

It was claimed that Asahara's blood had been analyzed at Kyoto University and found to contain a unique DNA. Drinking Asahara's blood conveyed his enlightened consciousness to the disciple.

Special caps equipped with electrical wires and electrodes known as PSI (Perfect Salvation Initiation) were rented by devotees and worn to bring their

Shoko Asahara. (Photo courtesy of
Uchitel)

thoughts into harmony with the thoughts of the guru.[41] Members who lived
and worked at the Aum communes wore the PSI caps as they went about
their duties, including the scientists, physicians, and medical personnel.

Asahara taught a cosmology in which the highest spiritual existence is
the realm of Mahanirvana, ruled by Shiva. Asahara was the earthly incarnation (*avatar*) of Shiva. Below the Mahanirvana realm were the causal
and astral worlds, which contained influences that manifested as events in
the phenomenal (material) world. "True Selves" belong to the Mahanirvana existence, but, due to delusion, had become caught up in rebirth in
the lower realms. Devotees could recover their "True Selves" by identifying themselves with Asahara as Shiva, the one ultimate "True Self."[42]

Asahara claimed to have the ability to travel psychically through the
astral and causal worlds and to discern there the influences that would
manifest as events in the material world. Being fully enlightened, a perfected Buddha, Asahara was said to be incapable of mistakenly interpreting information gained in the causal and astral worlds. Any disconfirmed
prophecy would have discredited Asahara's claimed status as a Buddha.

Aum Shinrikyo

When Aum Shinrikyo became a legally registered religion in 1989, it had
about 4,000 members. By 1995 it had about 10,000 members, twenty-five

centers in Japan, and about 30,000 members in Russia. The devotees in Japan included 1,247 *shukkesha* (renunciants). In Japan, about 75 percent of the devotees were in their 20s and 30s. Nearly 40 percent of the *shukkesha* were women.[43]

Aum Shinrikyo was attractive to educated, urban young people dissatisfied with being cogs in the Japanese economic system and interested in cultivating mystical experiences. Aum offered an alternative to lifetime employment in unfulfilling work for modest wages. In the 1990s, many young adults lived with their parents because of the slowing Japanese economy, low starting salaries, and the high cost of living. Aum Shinrikyo offered an alternative of communal living in an exotic environment. Aum devotees were given Indian names. They built up the organization's assets with their free labor. In Aum, young people could pursue mystical experiences by meditating, practicing yoga, and also by listening to music, dancing, and by taking drugs such as LSD. It was believed that by these methods, and the grace of the guru, it was possible to become a superhuman (*shinkajin*).[44]

Aum was not unusual in Japan for drawing on Mahayana/Vajrayana Buddhism for the practice of meditation, ascetic disciplines, and initiations. Aum Shinrikyo's members *were* unusual—indicating their alienation from Japanese society—for adopting Indian names, dress, practices, and deities.

Japan has been hospitable to religious disciplines taught within the Buddhist tradition, but Japan also has its indigenous tradition of asceticism. In Japan, ascetic practices are termed *gyo*, and these are arduous practices designed to purify the soul in order to stimulate possession by *kami* (the indigenous gods), to cultivate healing power and clairvoyance, to be able to

An Aum Shinrikyo devotee in Tokyo on March 16, 1999. (AP Photo/Itsuo Inouye)

see and communicate with spirits, and to cure oneself of illness. A typically Japanese ascetic practice is to stand praying under an ice cold waterfall, or in lieu of a waterfall, to repeatedly pour buckets of cold water over one's head and shoulders under the coldest possible conditions, such as in the middle of the night in the dead of winter. Not many Japanese are hardy enough to practice *gyo*, but those who do become noted as shamans, healers, and sometimes as prophets who found new religions.[45] Aum Shinrikyo appealed to an authentically Japanese concern to practice asceticism in order to develop superhuman powers. This concern is conspicuous in Japanese animated videos, in which characters possess a variety of superhuman powers.

The religious imaginations of the young members of Aum Shinrikyo were influenced by Japanese comics (*manga*) and animated videos (*anime*) of the 1970s and 1980s. "The Space Battleship Yamato" was particularly influential. On one occasion an Aum devotee sang the theme song of "The Space Battleship Yamato" while driving Asahara's car. Asahara then said, "Yamato was a ship carrying the last hope for the earth. It's like us, isn't it?" In the Yamato story, a device named the Cosmos Cleaner was brought from another planet to clean the earth of radioactivity. Aum Shinrikyo's buildings were equipped with devices termed Cosmos Cleaners to purify the air of chemicals, and members were told that chemicals were being deployed against them by enemies.[46]

Aum's resonance with Japanese popular culture was also seen in its use of animated videos for promotional purposes, depicting Asahara levitating and flying through the astral and causal worlds.[47] In one Aum-produced animated video, Asahara was depicted as the captain of Spaceship Mahayana.[48]

The Japanese animated videos often possess a plot set in an apocalyptic or post-apocalyptic period. The typical plot emphasizes the conflict between good and evil that characterizes a radical dualistic worldview: Humanity is threatened by overwhelming evil, and young warriors (male and female) possessing superhuman powers must eradicate that evil to survive. Very often a messiah with superhuman powers arrives to bring salvation by destroying the enemies. Helen Hardacre describes the typical *anime* plot: "This evil force is bent on destruction, and only a complete commitment to destroy it can save the earth before the righteous themselves are destroyed. One side or the other must perish; coexistence is impossible. Aum's portrayal of immense forces bent on its destruction, whether the Jews, the Freemasons, or other imagined enemies, clearly parallels this motif."[49]

Aum Shinrikyo attracted highly-educated young men with training in the sciences and technology. These men became the Aum leaders who researched and developed a variety of weapons for mass destruction.

Hideo Murai had graduated from Osaka University with a major in physics, and attended graduate school specializing in cosmophysics. He was working in the research and development department of Kobe Steel Ltd. when he began reading Asahara's books. Murai became head of Aum's Science and Technology Ministry. Kiyohide Hayakawa, head of Aum's Construction Ministry, had earned a masters degree in architecture from Osaka Prefectural University. Fumihiro Joyu, head of Public Relations, had a masters degree in artificial intelligence from Waseda University. He worked briefly as an engineer at National Space Development Agency. Masami Tsuchiya, head of the chemical team, possessed a master's degree in organic chemistry from Tsukuba University. He was said to have joined Aum because it had better research facilities than his university. After the Tokyo subway gas attack, Tsuchiya confessed that he had led the team that produced sarin.[50]

Most of the male leaders in Aum Shinrikyo were young. At midnight on June 27, 1994, the date of the Matsumoto sarin gas attack, which was aimed at killing three judges scheduled to decide a lawsuit involving Aum, Asahara and about one hundred Aum leaders met in an Aum-owned Tokyo restaurant to form the government of a sovereign nation. Immediately after the ceremony, in which the leaders swore oaths of determination to Asahara, some left to prepare to release sarin in Matsumoto, Aum's first act of war against Japanese society. In the new Aum government, Shoko Asahara (39) was titled *shinsei hoo* ("sacred emperor" or "sacred master of the law"). Hideo Murai (35) was in charge of the largest ministry, Science and Technology. Kiyohide Hayakawa (44) was the head of the Construction Ministry. Seiichi Endo (34) was head of the Health and Welfare Ministry. Dr. Tomomasa Nakagawa (34) headed the Household Agency of the Supreme Master of the Law. Dr. Ikuo Hayashi (47) headed the Medical Healing Ministry. Tomomitsu Niimi (30) headed Home Affairs (security and intelligence), Yoshihiro Inoue (24) headed the Intelligence Ministry, attorney Yoshinobu Aoyama (34) headed the Justice Ministry, and Fumihiro Joyu (31) headed Public Relations. The average age of the Aum ministers was thirty-two.[51]

Additionally, there was "a significant cadre of young female leaders, [who] were involved in fields as diverse as accounting, medicine and nursing, overseeing factory work, and the daily administration of communes housing hundreds of 'ordained' members."[52] Recent scholarly publications in English have focused on the male Aum leaders, but women found that their association with Asahara empowered them to positions of leadership unusual in Japanese society. For instance, Asahara brought Russian musicians to Japan to play in an Aum orchestra conducted by a teenage girl who was close to Asahara. Another one of Asahara's lovers, Hisako

Ishii, was the Aum treasurer.[53] Asahara had sex with a number of Aum women until they became pregnant. His explanation was that the guru knew how to catch the good souls floating in the air and bring them into physical incarnation.[54] More scholarly work needs to be done on women's roles in Aum Shinrikyo.

There also needs to be scholarly investigation of the treatment of children within Aum; currently the information available in English is sketchy. Children were separated from their parents and raised communally. They had to wear the PSI electrode caps, and they were taught to chant mantras and practice yogic disciplines. Reportedly, the children were given little education and were generally neglected. Authorities found that one little girl did not know the purpose of a pair of socks. Children removed from the communes were malnourished, and some suffered from pneumonia.[55]

Aum recruited members from Japan's military, the Self-Defense Force (SDF). In 1994, Aum's members included forty active-duty SDF members and sixty SDF veterans. Additionally, about six police officers were Aum members, including two officers with the Tokyo Metropolitan Police Department. A special squad was formed within Aum, consisting of former SDF personnel. These individuals with military training in conventional arms and chemical weapons participated in Aum's preparations for armageddon.[56]

Every member of Aum Shinrikyo was encouraged to meditate and practice a variety of yogic disciplines, and the most committed disciples became *shukkesha* (renunciants). Becoming a renunciant involved cutting off all contact with one's family, turning over all property and assets to Aum, pledging devotion to Asahara, living communally, and practicing rigorous asceticism. By these means, *shukkesha* believed they would develop superhuman powers of clairvoyance, levitation, and the ability to travel through the spiritual realms.[57] The *shukkesha* aimed to become superhuman beings, the only ones who would not be destroyed in armageddon.

From 1986 to 1990, 537 people became Aum *shukkesha*. Only 43 people became *shukkesha* during 1991 through 1992. From January 1993 to summer 1994, Aum gained 524 *shukkesha*. These relatively low numbers were significant because Asahara had predicted that armageddon would occur in 1999 unless 30,000 people became *shukkesha*.[58] It is likely that Asahara brought the date for armageddon closer to enhance recruiting efforts and to strengthen the commitment of existing Aum members.

The practice of extreme asceticism to obtain salvation was considered so important that people were forced to undergo it.[59] Some of the severe ascetic practices included fasting or living on a meager diet, being lowered into scalding or near-freezing water, and being hung upside down. Drugs such as LSD were used to stimulate altered consciousness. Majima's death, due to asceticism, occurred at the end of 1988. This led to a *shukkesha*, Shuji Taguchi (25), wanting to leave and raised the threat that he would inform the police of Majima's death. Taguchi became the first person known to be murdered by Aum members for turning against the guru, the supreme truth organization, and its methods to obtain salvation.

Aum Shinrikyo received financial income from a variety of sources. Aum reportedly acquired more than a billion dollars worth of real estate, stocks, and other assets by selling Asahara's blood (300,000 yen or over US$3,000 for a vial), renting PSI headgear (one million yen for one month), charging fees for initiations, meditation classes (300,000 yen), membership, *shaktipat* (more than 30,000 yen in 1989), and receiving donations from members, and all the worldly goods of *shukkesha*. Aum Shinrikyo's numerous small businesses included computer shops, noodle restaurants, a health club, a dating club, and a babysitting service.[60]

From 1993 onward, members of Aum Shinrikyo were pressured to donate more financial resources. Armageddon was fast approaching, and preparations had to be made for survival. Aum Shinrikyo increased its acquisition of land to build communes, whose residents would inherit the new world after armageddon destroyed the old world. These communities were known as Lotus Villages and they would constitute Shambhala, the Buddhist millennial kingdom.[61]

Society outside the Aum communes was believed to exert an "evil mind control" over people. The claim was that Aum counteracted society's brainwashing with "good mind control" that taught the supreme truth. By replacing their own thoughts with the enlightened consciousness of Asahara, devotees could overcome society's brainwashing. To this end, Aum members listened to many hours of audiotaped affirmations. For instance, an Aum pamphlet suggested that devotees listen to the following statement on audiotape:

> Even if I should begin to doubt, that is only an illusion caused by earthly desire. My doubts are illusions caused by earthly desire. My doubts are illusions caused by earthly desire. I will thus shut off those doubts. I will thus shut off those doubts. What should I do when I can't shut them off? Then I should just leave them alone. If there comes a time when I'm captured by such doubts then I should chant the mantra repeatedly and perform memory training. I'm going to train my memory for the truth! I'm going to train my memory for the truth![62]

Catastrophic Millennialism

Asahara claimed that he was the savior who would establish the perfect Shambhala kingdom on earth. The aim was to make Japan into Shambhala, and then to make the whole world into Shambhala. According to Asahara, this was an "incomparably grand" plan "to extend the divine space of Aum all over Japan, and to make Japan the base of world salvation."[63] This millennial kingdom would be established by Asahara's creation of Lotus Villages inhabited by persons of high spiritual attainment. The initial theme of Aum Shinrikyo thus appears to have been one of progressive millennialism: personal spiritual attainment within spiritual communities would accomplish the collective earthly salvation. In Asahara's 1987 book, *Initiation*, he predicted that a nuclear war would occur between 1999 and 2003, but this could be averted if Aum established centers overseas and gained 30,000 renunciants. Even if armageddon occurred, Aum devotees would be saved because they would have the ability to consciously abandon their physical bodies for existence in the astral world. Until about 1988 the creating of Lotus Villages was a noncatastrophic means of progressively establishing the millennial kingdom. But Asahara's thought began to take a more pessimistic turn as he studied the New Testament book of Revelation, on which he produced two commentaries, *Doomsday* (1989) and *From Destruction to Emptiness: A Sequel to Doomsday* (1989). By 1990 the Lotus Villages were seen as places of refuge from armageddon, which needed to be equipped with shelters for protection from nuclear, bacterial, and chemical weapons.[64]

Asahara read the book of Revelation in 1988 while he was ill in bed and believed that his sickness was caused by giving more than 8,000 initiations and *shaktipat*. Asahara had set himself the goal of single-handedly saving humanity, and his illness caused him to despair over whether he would achieve that impossible goal. Asahara identified with Revelation's depiction of the Lamb of God, the suffering savior,[65] who defeated evil in the final great battle.

The 1989–1990 shift to catastrophic millennialism, involving a pessimistic evaluation of society and unredeemable humanity, corresponded with Aum's increasing conflicts with the world outside its communes. Some of the conflicts arose from Aum's attempts to purchase land in rural areas in order to build Lotus Villages. When purchasing land, the identity of Aum Shinrikyo was often concealed. Aum leaders refused to compromise in disputes, and did not attempt to become good neighbors and citizens. There was controversy about Aum's application for legal status as a religious organization in the Tokyo Prefecture. Aum leaders believed the application was initially refused because of the protests of the parents of Aum members and Sakamoto, the attorney who represented them. After vigorous protests, Aum Shinrikyo gained the legal status. In October 1989, a series of highly negative news articles on Aum were published in the *Sunday Mainichi*.[66]

Ian Reader explains that, because of the hiding of criminal secrets beginning with the deaths of Majima in 1988 and Taguchi in 1989, Aum leaders were exceptionally sensitive to cultural opposition and anxious to prevent any investigation of Aum's activities.[67] All of the conflicts were interpreted by Aum leaders and members as persecutions. Increasingly, Aum members were taught that enemies identified as the United States military, Freemasons, the Japanese government, and Jews, were conspiring to destroy them.[68] Goodman and Miyazawa have shown that belief in a Jewish conspiracy to take over Japan and the world is a mainstream belief in Japanese society promoted by popular anti-Semitic literature sold in bookstores and advertised in major newspapers. These views are espoused by political leaders in Japan. Many Japanese believe that Jews control international banking, multinational corporations, and the U.S. government, and that Jews plot to enslave the Japanese by demolishing their economy and by introducing foreign workers to threaten Japanese racial purity. Often the Japanese version of the One World Government conspiracy theory (see chapter 6) equates Jews with Freemasons, and equates the post–World War II American occupation of Japan with Jewish occupation. Anti-Semitism in Japan dates back to the early twentieth century and especially harkens back to World War II and Japanese admiration of Hitler and his program. These are not marginalized and stigmatized ideas in Japan as they are in the United States, because there are few Jews in Japan to protest this bigoted stereotype. As in the United States, a number of Japanese believers in a Jewish One World Government conspiracy believe that Jews are the children of Satan. This belief ultimately derives from the Christian gospel of John 8:44, in which Jesus reportedly said to Jews rejecting his message, "Your father is the devil...."[69] By 1990 Asahara was preaching that society outside Aum communes was ruled by the devil, and that Aum was being attacked by agents of evil.[70]

In 1992, Asahara gave public lectures at universities, where he predicted that 90 percent of the world's population would be killed by ABC weapons (atomic, biological, and chemical) in the imminent armageddon. He pointed to the 1991 Persian Gulf War as initiating armageddon whereby the United States would destroy Japan.[71] Asahara utilized the predictions of Nostradamus, the New Testament book of Revelation, Hitler's statements about a thousand-year Reich, and his own purportedly infallible psychic powers to predict armageddon. His 1992 book, *The Ideal Society, Shambala*, opened with the caption, "The messiah who will come at the end of the century will be blind: the Master Asahara Shoko, as prophesied by Nostradamus."[72]

In 1992, Asahara predicted that armageddon would occur in 1999. Asahara's role as the messiah was to enable persons to attain a superhuman condition. Aum Shinrikyo was an organization of superhumans, who would survive armageddon and then establish Shambhala on Earth, which would be a "1000 year kingdom."[73] Asahara's 1993 book, a collection of his public talks, entitled *The Frightening Prophecies of Asahara Shoko*, stated that armageddon would occur in 1997 without fail. The United States would destroy Japan with weapons more destructive than the atomic bomb. On April 9, 1993, Asahara made his first public mention of sarin when he asserted that Japan needed to develop chemical weapons for self-defense. In his 1995 book, published eighteen days before the Tokyo subway gas attack, *Disaster Approaches the Land of the Rising Sun*, Asahara predicted that armageddon would take place in 1995 as a result of the bad karma of the world's population. Since Asahara's prophecies were unerring, there was no doubt that 1995 would mark the total destruction of the old materialistic world to make way for the building of a new civilization of spiritual adepts, who would have extremely long and healthy life spans, led by Christ (Asahara).[74]

Asahara's initial predictions put armageddon in 1999 or later, and said that armageddon could be averted if 30,000 people became renunciants. But as Aum Shinrikyo failed to achieve this impossible goal set by the guru, Asahara taught that armageddon was inevitable and brought the date closer to help recruitment and increase members' commitment. Asahara's claim to be an infallible Buddha meant that Asahara's prophecies had to be fulfilled, and his scientists set about to find the means to accomplish that.

The Persecution

Asahara taught that evil forces, including the Jews, Freemasons, and the United States were conspiring to destroy Aum Shinrikyo. Some allegations of conspiracies—for instance, that the U.S. military was attacking Aum communes with sarin—appear to have been covers for Aum's activities in developing weapons of mass destruction and for the accidental poison gas releases. Many of the activities of outsiders, which were perceived within Aum as persecutions, were actions taken by individuals and families who were injured by Aum. Some of the extreme activities of news reporters were genuinely persecutory. Aum's dualistic worldview, in which Aum Shinrikyo was identified with truth and seen as being attacked by diabolic forces, enhanced what one member called a "persecution complex" within Aum Shinrikyo.[75] Aum had a severe persecution complex because Aum leaders had to cover up Aum's criminal secrets. Much of Aum's persecution was imaginary,[76] but there was indeed cultural opposition to Aum Shinrikyo.

Aum Shinrikyo's application in 1989 for registration under the Religious Corporations Law was initially rejected because of the numerous complaints from families whose offspring had become *shukkesha*. Aum responded with aggressive protests, demonstrations, and legal action, and was granted legal status as a religious organization.[77]

The complaints from relatives led to newspaper investigations. Beginning in October 1989, the *Sunday Mainichi* published a seven-part series on Aum entitled, "Give Back My Child!" describing how Aum alienated young people from their families, coercively acquired financial assets from its members, and raised large sums of money by questionable means, for instance, by selling Asahara's blood. Aum again responded with a vigorous attack. Aum devotees distributed leaflets criticizing the *Sunday Mainichi* and its editor, bombarded the editor's home with telephone calls, and congested traffic in his neighborhood. Nevertheless, the *Sunday Mainichi* put aggrieved family members in touch with each other, and the Aum Shinrikyo Victims' Society (Aum Shinrikyo higaisha no kai) was formed. An attorney, Tsutsumi Sakamoto, was hired to represent this organization.[78]

Sakamoto's investigation revealed that Aum's claim that Asahara's blood had been tested by Kyoto University and was found to have a unique DNA was untrue. Sakamoto was preparing to publicize this fact when he, his wife, and his young son disappeared on November 4, 1989. An Aum badge was found at the Sakamoto home, but Aum leaders claimed that it was planted to persecute the organization. While to an outsider the murder of the Sakamoto family may appear to be an extreme response to pressures from Sakamoto,[79] the Victims' Society, and the *Sunday Mainichi*, it should be recalled that Asahara was regarded by Aum devotees as the living Buddha, the Christ, whose assertions and prophecies were infallible. Salvation could only be obtained through the guru's grace. If Asahara was shown to have made untrue claims, the basis for Aum Shinrikyo as a religion would have crumbled. Perhaps Asahara recalled how he was put out of business in 1982 for making false claims about the healing properties of herbal concoctions.

In 1990, Aum Shinrikyo members formed a political party, Shinrito (Supreme Truth Party), and put up twenty-five candidates, including Asahara, in the Upper House elections. The goal was to publicize Asahara's predictions of armageddon and offer salvation within Aum to the public. The campaign tactics made Aum the laughing stock of Japan. Aum devotees appeared in public wearing Ganesha (Hindu elephant-headed deity) and Asahara masks. They sang a song *ad nauseam* chanting Asahara's name.[80] All of the Shinrito candidates lost badly, with Asahara getting only 1,783 votes—a smaller number of votes than those gained by the good-looking Fumihiro Joyu.[81] After the election defeat, Aum-bashing "became almost a national pastime and a media-obsession." One observer reacted, "They lost: but why did their noses have to be rubbed in the dirt?"[82]

After the election debacle, Asahara called a meeting of about 1,000 devotees on the remote Okinawan island of Ishigaki. There Asahara announced that Aum Shinrikyo would no longer teach Mahayana Buddhism, which, according to him, strove for the enlightenment of all beings.

Thenceforth, Aum would teach Vajrayana Buddhism, which, according to Asahara, recognized that not all people would be saved. From that point on, Aum Shinrikyo focused on the salvation of its own members as an elect who would inherit the Earth after armageddon. Asahara announced that in preparation to survive armageddon, Aum would focus on building communes equipped with protective shelters. Numerous Aum members at Ishigaki decided to become *shukkesha*. Intensifying the persecution complex within Aum, hundreds of news reporters followed the group to Ishigaki and disrupted the meeting, and, in obnoxious interviews, asked if Aum devotees planned to commit mass suicide.[83]

From 1990, Aum experienced increased conflicts with neighbors over buying land and building communes. On August 12, 1990, there was a riot when residents of Namino in Kumamoto Prefecture tried to block five buses bringing in Aum devotees. The Namino Municipal Government refused to grant residential registry to Aum members. Leaders Yoshinobu Aoyama and Kiyohide Hayakawa and six other members were arrested. Four years later, Kumamoto Prefecture agreed to pay Aum 920 million yen in damages on the condition that Aum close its Namino commune. The sensationalized treatment of Aum in the news media continued.[84]

Shoko Asahara, in *Declaring Myself the Christ*, asserted that this persecution was occurring because he was the New Testament Lamb (I Peter 1: 18-20), who would suffer and be slain for the salvation of a remnant of humanity. Conflating his identity with his religious organization, Asahara wrote:

> Let us look at the situation of Aum Shinrikyo now. When did the slaying happen to Aum? It began when Aum got involved in the election and declared freedom, equality, and benevolence for every being, especially for the Japanese, spreading the hospice movement and campaigning against the consumption tax at the same time. Since then, just like a Lamb who was slain, Aum has sacrificed its honor and position in the society for the sake of its teaching.[85]

With armageddon increasingly imminent, and the outside world believed to be totally evil and seeking to destroy Aum, it became imperative to inhibit internal dissent and prevent defections. Salvation was found only within Aum Shinrikyo. Numerous defectors were kidnapped, drugged, and imprisoned in Aum facilities. Defectors were captured and brought back and kept under sedation in Aum's Tokyo hospital. Others were drugged and incarcerated to prevent them from leaving. A woman (29) tried to escape twice because she objected to being separated from her two-year-old son. She was captured both times; she was handcuffed and confined in a freight container. A woman (23) who wanted to leave was beaten and drugged. Some comatose persons, found by police in the March 22 raid, had been given pentobarbital.[86] According to Ian Reader, "the closer and more inevitable Armageddon was, the more dangerous it would be to leave the movement, and the greater the external threat to it, the more important it would be to remain inside it."[87]

From the time of the murder of the Sakamoto family in 1989, allegations of conspiracies against Aum became prominent themes in Aum publications and in Asahara's talks. In the 1990s, conspiracy allegations appear to have been used to deceive rank-and-file Aum members about Aum's development of chemical weapons and the resulting chemical accidents. In October 1993, it was alleged that sarin was being used to attack members living at Aum communes. On March 11, 1994, Asahara publicly stated that sarin was used in attacks against him. On March 21, 1994, Asahara publicly claimed again that sarin was being used by the American and Japanese governments against him and Aum members, and that these attacks began in 1989. Aum publications claimed that since 1992, the residents at the Kamikuishiki headquarters were ill from sarin attacks. In April 1994, it was claimed that the American air force was dropping poison gas on Aum centers.[88]

Aum's conspiracy theories also alleged that Jews, Freemasons, the Japanese new religion Soka Gakkai, and others were conspiring against Aum Shinrikyo. In 1994, an Aum magazine published a "blacklist" of twelve Japanese and two foreigners living in Japan who were "wanted" for having "sold their souls to the devil" in the conspiracy against Aum. These included the Emperor, who was alleged to be an agent for Jews, and the popular Crown Princess Masako.[89]

Aum found itself involved in a conflict in Matsumoto, in central Japan, where it had attempted to purchase property. The property owner wanted to cancel the sale when he discovered the identity of the purchaser. On June 27, 1994, sarin gas was sprayed in the area where the three judges who would decide the case resided. Two of the judges were among the seven people who died, and the third judge was among the hundreds who were injured. The case was postponed.[90]

Over the New Year holiday in 1995, negative news stories were published about Aum Shinrikyo. On January 1, the lead article for the *Yomiuri Shimbun* linked the Matsumoto sarin gas poisonings with the July 1994 gas incident in Kamikuishiki that had damaged vegetation. On January 3, the *Asahi Shimbun* published a story noting that Aum had its headquarters in Kamikuishiki, and that there had been conflict between Aum and its neighbors.[91]

At the beginning of 1995, the talk among journalists was that police would soon raid the Aum headquarters. About March 17, 1995, police leaked to the media that a raid, deploying 2,000 police, would take place on March 20. Aum leaders may have been tipped off that a raid was imminent by Aum members who were in the Self-Defense Force and whose units were put on alert. Numerous people knew about the impending raid, and Aum leaders easily could have learned of it. By March 19, journalists were at Kamikuishiki waiting for the raid. On March 19, police raided the Aum center in Osaka and arrested four members for abducting a university student and holding him against his will.[92]

The sarin gas attack on the Tokyo subway was carried out March 20, 1995, to avert the imminent police raid and to prevent investigations of Aum Shinrikyo's activities. The hardest hit subway station was Kasumigaseki near the National Police Agency's headquarters. Two days later the police made the raids on Aum headquarters and other communes in Japan.[93]

The Failure of the Millennial Goal

Ian Reader has pointed out that Aum Shinrikyo suffered the stress of failing to achieve its ultimate concern to create Shambhala, the Buddhist millennial kingdom, consisting of enlightened adepts possessing psychic powers. In 1987, Asahara announced that if 30,000 people became *shukkesha* (renunciants), their positive energies would counteract the bad karma bringing armageddon in 1999. Only about 1,200 people became *shukkesha*. Furthermore, Aum membership in Japan was only about 10,000, which was very small compared to other Japanese new religions with membership in the hundreds of thousands. Aum Shinrikyo was particularly in competition with two other new religions to convert educated young people in the urban areas. Agonshu was the new religion to which Asahara previously belonged. Kofuku no Kagaku was a new religion with a leader who made claims similar to those of Asahara. Both Agonshu and Kofuku no Kagaku were more successful in gaining members than Aum Shinrikyo. The Kofuku no Kagaku leader, Ryuho Okawa, and Asahara insulted one another, each claiming to know the previous lives of the other. Okawa said that Asahara was an infamous criminal, who was executed by being boiled in a cauldron. Asahara said that Okawa was a badger in a previous life. In the rivalry, Aum Shinrikyo was failing to achieve the one million members claimed by Kofuku no Kagaku.[94]

Asahara increased the internal stress to Aum by moving the date for armageddon closer. Moving the date of armageddon from 1999 to 1997, and then to 1995, had the effect of increasing the commitment and fervor of Aum devotees, but it also meant that armageddon *had* to occur.

According to his own teachings, the Buddha Asahara could not err in his prophecies. If Asahara's predictions proved false, then the whole Aum Shinrikyo edifice would crumble. The necessity for armageddon to arrive as predicted led to the decision within Asahara's inner circle to develop weapons to create armageddon.

The Decision to Commit Violence

Aum's extreme ascetic practices were acts of violence, and they prepared the members to commit increasingly violent acts. Asceticism was practiced either voluntarily or involuntarily, as members were coerced into enduring arduous experiences. Thus, ascetic practices became rituals of violence that bonded the most committed Aum members to each other. They shared the suffering of the ascetic experiences and some of them shared the experience of coercing others to endure the practices. These shared rituals of violence prepared a number of Aum members to commit escalating and more frequent acts of violence.

Asahara developed a theology that justified the assassination of unbelievers as being "altruistic murder."[95] Asahara taught that a person must submit to him as the guru, the savior, who was the incarnation of Shiva, in order to gain good karma and achieve salvation. People who did not accept him as their savior had bad karma and would inevitably be reborn in the lower realms. According to Asahara, *poa* murders committed on orders of the guru released unbelievers from their bad karma and enabled them to go to a higher world. Asahara thus took on their bad karma and *poa* was "salvational murder." According to Watanabe,

> It is paradoxical that Aum Shinrikyo believed that the evil people, that is, the enemies of Aum Shinrikyo, are worthy of salvation in the sense of poa. In other words, just because those enemies will certainly accumulate bad karma furthermore and go to hell, Aum should exterminate those people for their salvation. In Aum's internal logic this should be a positive act of salvation. Based on this kind of logic, many people who were regarded as Aum's enemies were killed or injured in various ways.[96]

The first murders committed by Aum devotees were desperate measures to prevent defections, and then to prevent the revelation of Aum's criminal secrets. Aum was viewed as the supreme truth organization following a perfect Buddha, and nothing could contradict him. Majima, the young man who died in 1988 from forceable immersion in ice-cold water, had wanted to leave. After this, Shuji Taguchi had been openly critical of

Aum beliefs and practices, and he wanted to defect. Asahara prescribed purification in cold water, but Taguchi declined. When Taguchi continued to insist that he wanted to leave, Asahara instructed devotees to commit their first *poa* killing; Taguchi was strangled and his neck was broken.[97]

Asahara inaccurately utilized the Vajrayana term *poa* (*phowa*) for his doctrine justifying murder. According to Asahara, *poa* meant being "sent to Shiva." Asahara asserted that *poa* was a kindness to the murdered persons by releasing them from incurring more bad karma in that life.[98] Asahara claimed that he, as a perfectly enlightened person, had the ability to see a person's karma and determine when it was necessary to save a person from creating more bad karma by murdering him or her. "Looked at objectively, that is from the viewpoint of human objectivity, this is murder. According to Vajrayana, however, this would be a splendid *poa*. A person with true wisdom, that is [an enlightened person] with the supernatural powers that I talked about earlier, would see this as being of benefit to both the person killed and his murderer."[99]

Also in 1989, the activities of Tsutsumi Sakamoto, in representing the Aum Victims' Society, threatened to destroy Asahara's credibility as a perfect Buddha. An interview with Sakamoto had been videotaped by the Tokyo Broadcasting System. Aum devotees were permitted by TBS to view the unbroadcast interview, after which the Sakamoto family was murdered.[100] Sakamoto planned to reveal evidence that Asahara's blood had not been tested by Kyoto University and, therefore, Aum's claim of scientific proof that Asahara's blood contained a unique DNA was false. This directly threatened Asahara's claimed status as a Buddha as well as Aum's methods based on the belief that salvation could only be achieved through the grace of the guru.

By 1990, Asahara had ordered his scientists to develop weapons of mass destruction to ensure that his prophecies of armageddon would come true. The scientists enthusiastically, and with great ingenuity, complied. Dr. Ikuo Hayashi later testified to their motivation: "We thought we could serve the world through our work for Asahara."[101]

By 1990, Aum's scientists and technicians were pursuing the development of a variety of weapons. Endo, a molecular biologist, worked on biological weapons. Tsuchiya worked to develop chemical weapons. Murai oversaw the weapons research of the scientists, and he himself worked on acquiring nuclear, laser, microwave, and electromagnetic weapons. Hayakawa acquired information and technology during his numerous trips to Russia.

In 1990, under the supervision of Endo, Botulinus Toxin A was manufactured in a lab at the Kamikuishiki headquarters. But when the powder was tested on animals, none died.[102]

In 1992, Shoko Asahara carried out his Russian Salvation Tour, the first of his visits to Russia. With the 1991 collapse of the Soviet Union, numerous Russian scientists and weapons experts were either out of work or ill paid. Asahara visited Moscow, bearing cash and computer equipment to leave as donations. Asahara visited the Moscow State University, the Russia-Japan University, and the Moscow Institute of Engineering and Physics. Asahara gained Russian converts who worked at the I.V. Kurchatov Institute of Atomic Energy and the Mendeleyev Chemical Institute. These and other Russian contacts may have been sources of equipment, materials, and expertise in Aum's quest to gain weapons of mass destruction. Seichi Endo, the Aum microbiologist, and Masami Tsuchiya, the Aum chief chemist, visited Russia to do research in their respective fields. The information on how to produce sarin nerve gas was probably obtained in Russia. In 1997, Yoshihiro Inoue testified that he witnessed Asahara pay 10 million yen to Oleg Lobov, Russia's former Security Council secretary, and in return for that sum Hideo Murai brought a blueprint for a sarin production plant and information on how to manufacture sarin from Russia.[103]

In October 1992, Asahara and a team of scientists, physicians, and nurses traveled to Zaire on a purported medical mission of mercy and visited hospitals there in an attempt to acquire the Ebola virus. They were unsuccessful.[104]

In spring 1993, Clear Stream Temple was instituted at the Kamikuishiki commune, which was actually the facility for the Supreme Truth Research Institute of Science and Technology. Machinery was set up there to manufacture AK-47 Russian automatic rifles. About $10 million was spent on equipment and parts to build automatic rifles.[105]

In 1993, Murai and Hayakawa visited a Russian weapons-research facility to learn about bazookas and missiles. Hayakawa researched and attempted to acquire numerous Russian weapons and military equipment. In 1993, a meeting was requested of the Russian minister of nuclear energy, perhaps with the intent of purchasing a nuclear warhead, but the minister's office declined to set up the meeting.[106]

In June 1993, Aum set up another biolab in a building in Tokyo, from which devotees made the failed attempt to spray Tokyo with anthrax. Endo continued his work to develop biological weapons. From a poisonous mushroom, he made cultures of Q fever.[107]

By October 1993, a new and improved facility for the Supreme Truth Research Institute of Science and Technology was ready at the Kamikuishiki headquarters. The building was named Satian 7 (from the Sanskrit word, *satyam*, "truth"). Tsuchiya manufactured sarin in Satian 7 as well as mustard gas, cyanide gas, and VX.[108]

Around 1993, the Aum office in Manhattan, New York, was used to purchase American high-tech equipment, including a $400,000 laser and a $500,000 lens grinder, as well as equipment and materials from all over the world. Dr. Hayashi went to the United States to research chemical weapons and immunizing agents in American libraries.[109]

In April 1993, Aum Shinrikyo purchased a 500,000-acre sheep ranch in western Australia, and Asahara and twenty-four devotees went there in September 1993. They brought through Australian customs ditchdiggers, gas masks, protective clothing, generators, chemicals, and laboratory equipment. They may have tested sarin on sheep at the Australian ranch; in May 1995 twenty-four buried sheep carcasses were discovered. They also began mining for uranium at the ranch. But after the group left the country, Australian authorities learned that Aum Shinrikyo was under investigation for kidnapping and detaining people. Asahara and other Aum members were refused visas to return to Australia.[110]

In the spring of 1994, forty-five Aum devotees including Yoshihiro Inoue, Tomomitsu Niimi, and former SDF soldiers received training by former KGB agents in firearms, intelligence gathering, kidnapping, and assassination.[111]

In 1994, about twenty-five people succeeded in defecting. In response, Tomomitsu Niimi, the Minister for Home Affairs, created a team called the New Followers Agency, to make sure there were no defections and no internal dissent. Suspected traitors were murdered in a variety of ways—gassing, poisoning, strangling. One man who wanted to leave to get married was purified in scalding hot water. When he tried to get out of the water, Niimi held him under until he passed out and his body was burned. Niimi told a shocked nurse, "He had a lot of bad karma." The man was taken to the Aum hospital, where he died. His corpse was incinerated in the industrial microwave at the Kamikuishiki headquarters. By the end of 1994, about twenty Aum members had disappeared permanently.[112]

Niimi and his team became experts at kidnapping defectors. Once returned to Aum facilities, defectors were imprisoned, drugged, and indoctrinated in Aum teachings. A young mother, who became a renunciant with her husband in 1994, decided she wanted to leave when she realized that her young son, staying with the other Aum children, was being neglected. She was subjected to a "Bardo Initiation" in which she was confined to a small room with a television depicting scene after scene of gory violence and death, followed by an animated depiction of hell, followed by constant drumbeating by an Aum priest. She subsequently escaped, but was captured and imprisoned with five other handcuffed victims in a freight container in which the heat reached over 100 degrees. The container was unsanitary, they were ill-fed, deprived of sleep, and forced to sit in the lotus position chanting, "I am going back to Asahara." She was also given sodium thiopental in an attempt to reprogram her thoughts. After being judged a compliant devotee and released from the container, she managed to escape again, and with the assistance of an attorney regained custody of her son.[113]

Defectors were considered "betrayers of the guru's love." Dr. Hayashi administered electric shocks to uncompliant members to cause memory loss. One defector, a former soldier, was abducted, and injected over 120 times with amylobarbitone, a drug that suppresses REM sleep. For four months he was subjected to this drug, lack of sleep, little food, immersed in scalding water, and given electric shocks. When rescued, he had lost his memory, lost 66 pounds, and his right side was paralyzed, and he could barely speak. Police discovered about fifty others in debilitated condition.[114]

A young woman was imprisoned in the Kamikuishiki commune in December 1994, when she went there to visit friends. She was drugged and placed in a tiny cargo container with no room to stand. On a rare trip outside to shower, she found and concealed a screwdriver with which she attempted to pry her way out of the container. She remained in the container until she was rescued by police in March 1995.[115]

A notebook belonging to Hayakawa indicated plans for a *coup* against the Japanese government to take place in November 1995. Ikuo Hayashi, the head of Aum's Treatment Ministry, later testified that Aum planned to wage "urban guerilla war" in November 1995 against government offices and the prime minister's residence.[116]

Throughout 1994, Hayakawa continued to shop in Russia for a nuclear warhead. The weapons factory at Clear Stream Temple was producing parts for the AK-47 automatic rifle. In September 1994, Hayakawa and fourteen other Aum members were trained in the use of weapons at a military base near Moscow. Hayakawa succeeded in purchasing in Azerbaijan an Mi-17 cargo-carrying helicopter that could be equipped with weapons. Apparently, the plan was to spray sarin from the helicopter. The helicopter was brought into Japan in June 1994 and taken to the Kamikuishiki headquarters.[117]

On December 15, 1994, Aum members at the Kamikuishiki commune attempted to use drugs, electric stimulation, and recorded mantras to brainwash 120 Russian orchestra musicians and make them Aum devotees. The frightened Russians revolted and thus lost their employment in Asahara's orchestra, but they were returned home.[118]

On the evening of December 28, 1994, Yoshihiro Inoue, the head of the Ministry of Intelligence, and three SDF paratroopers made their first intelligence-gathering visit into Mitsubishi Heavy Industries (MHI) in Hiroshima with the help of Hideo Nakamoto (38), a senior MHI researcher. MHI is Japan's leading defense contractor, and there Inoue's team gathered information on laser weapons and how to use lasers to enrich uranium.

Inoue and his team of SDF paratroopers also broke into a driver's license center to steal data to forge driving licenses. They broke into a facility of NEC, Japan's top computer manufacturer, to steal data on laser technology. They also took an inside tour of a U.S. naval base near Tokyo.[119]

At the end of 1994, Asahara predicted in a radio broadcast, "From the end of 1995, Japan will be repeatedly hit by great changes. They will lead to armageddon and World War III."[120]

By early 1995, an Aum team named Time Tunnel had constructed a two-meter-long rail gun, that fired 20-mm caliber shells. A rail gun is a type of cannon that operates using electromagnetic force.[121]

When a news story appeared on New Year's Day 1995, linking the gas leaks at the Kamikuishiki headquarters with the Matsumoto sarin attack, Asahara ordered the destruction of Aum's stockpile of sarin. But Dr. Nakagawa buried three pounds of sarin precursor, and this was used later to make the sarin released in the Tokyo subway trains.[122] Satian 7 was renovated hastily to make it appear to be a temple, and a large styrofoam statue of the Buddha was installed. At a press conference Aum leaders and devotees declared that the United States was spraying Aum members with sarin and mustard gases. Aum even released a video, entitled "Slaughtered Lambs," to the news media making this claim. It was claimed that just as the FBI had used poison gas to eradicate the Branch Davidians at Waco, gases were being used to attack Aum communes.

That month's issue of the Aum journal, *Vajrayana Sacca*, provided a list of the "Black Aristocracy," Aum's enemies, who had "sold their souls to the Devil." The list of fourteen included Emperor Akihito, Masako, the Crown Prince's wife, and her father, the ambassador to the United Nations, and a rival religious leader, Daisaku Ikeda of Soka Gakkai, and Ichiro Ozawa, a politician perceived to have ties to the United States. This issue contained a lengthy article, entitled "Manual of Fear," in which Aum declared war on "the world shadow government" controlled by Jews. The article claimed that the members of the Black Aristocracy were Freemasons who were the tools of Jews. It quoted extensively from an anti-Semitic work popular also among American anti-Semites, *Protocols of the Elders of Zion*. The article claimed that Jews were behind the genocides in Cambodia, Bosnia, and Rwanda, and warned the Japanese to awaken to the plot that threatened to destroy them. It claimed that Jews planned to brainwash those Japanese who weren't killed.[123]

After the Great Hanshin Earthquake struck Kobe in central Japan on January 17, 1995, Asahara quickly published a book, *Disaster Approaches the Land of the Rising Sun*, proclaiming, "The war has already begun." Hideo Murai claimed to the press that the earthquake, which killed over 5,500 people, was caused by the United States military using an electromagnetic device. Murai and other Aum scientists explored the possibility of making such a weapon by visiting the Nikola Tesla museum in Belgrade, Serbia, to study his theories on electromagnetism and seismology.[124]

Disaster Approaches the Land of the Rising Sun included a dialogue between Asahara and Hayakawa, in which Hayakawa said:

> There are no shelters in Japan. If you want to survive, you have to provide your own defense. People of noble virtue, and people who...have overcome hardships and privations, and who possess [good] karma, will survive. We will see the creation of a world populated by a new race that surpasses the human race in its present form.[125]

The decision to create weapons of mass destruction to orchestrate armageddon to fulfill Asahara's prophecies and achieve the millennial goal of establishing Shambhala was made within Asahara's inner circle. In their respective trials, the Aum leaders claimed that they were ordered to take these actions by Asahara, while Asahara claimed that he was a blind man kept in the dark by his lieutenants. Ordinary members who asked about these activities were told to get back to their work and not to ask questions. The sense of being besieged by outside conspirators and persecutors, and the urgency generated by the imminent armageddon, probably created an atmosphere in which rank-and-file members did not question the "secret work" to which Asahara referred in his talks.[126] Open disagreement was impossible due to the silencing measures taken against dissidents. According to Reader, "Aum's closed, communal and hierarchic structure, and its increasing focus on an explosive, conspiracy-bound rhetoric infused with predictions of violence (either of the end of the world or of violence against Aum) produced the momentum toward violence, while providing internal rationalisations of this process."[127]

The radical dualism of the Aum worldview caused members to view the cultural opposition they experienced as persecution. Aum's dualism dehumanized nonbelievers and made them dispensable. In *Declaring Myself the Christ*, Asahara wrote that an Aum member was a "warrior of truth" waging a war to destroy the totally corrupt and impure society outside Aum:

> Now let us look at today's situation: we have reached the peak of materialism;...socialism has collapsed and only...materialism seems to thrive. I have made the following prediction of polarization. It is the polarization between the genuine materialists and the genuine spiritualists. Now that socialism has collapsed, the polarization is really to take place. The genuine spiritualists will grow full and shine like the sun, while the genuine materialists will be collected to be burned.[128]

The failure of Aum Shinrikyo to achieve its ultimate concern and to establish the millennial kingdom by recruiting large numbers of people to become *shukkesha* led Asahara to resort to the tactic of recruiting new members and increasing the fervid commitment of devotees by preaching the imminent end of the world. Predicting armageddon and moving its date closer led to the necessity of preparing to create armageddon, because, according to Asahara, a Buddha could not err in his prophecies. Asahara and the other leaders became bold in their quest to destroy existing Japanese society, since there were no repercussions from the death of Majima in 1988 or the murders of Taguchi and the Sakamoto family in 1989. The violent coercion of members and even nonmembers to donate large sums of money to Aum was spurred by the sense that armageddon was imminent; extreme measures were necessary to build the Shambhala kingdom. Their dualistic perspective, us versus them, the good warriors of spirituality versus the evil world contaminated by materialism, dehumanized people whom Aum members deemed unworthy or who were blocking the accomplishment of the salvation kingdom. Asahara's *poa* doctrine rationalized that killing unbelievers, traitors, or enemies of Aum benefited the victims, since the guru took on their bad karma and, thus, enabled them to achieve rebirth in the higher realms.

Shoko Asahara drew on two distinct religious traditions highly conducive to authoritarianism—the Judeo-Christian apocalyptic tradition that radicalizes one's relationship with the ordinary world and has given tremendous authority to messiahs in many times and places, and the Hindu and Buddhist *siddha* tradition, in which the guru cannot be questioned because the guru is God (in Hinduism) and one's salvation depends on total surrender and obedience to the guru. The remarkable degree of death and destruction accomplished by Aum Shinrikyo devotees resulted from the combination of these two religious traditions within the cultural context of respect for authority in Japan.[129]

In contrast to the American context, Aum Shinrikyo had free rein in Japanese society to kill numerous people and develop weapons of mass destruction due to lack of scrutiny by law enforcement agents. In reaction to government abuses prior to and during World War II, Japanese law enforcement agents did not typically investigate religious organizations or conduct covert intelligence gathering by undercover work or wiretapping.[130] The report of the National Police Agency in 1996 concluded that police officers lacked expertise in religious groups and in the types of weapons Aum's scientists were developing. It also noted that Japanese police were not centralized and did not have authority to conduct investigations in other prefectures. The Tokyo Metropolitan Police were unable to search Aum's Kamikuishiki headquarters in Yamanashi Prefecture.

There was no national investigative unit in Japan, such as the FBI in the United States.[131]

While Japanese law enforcement agents were oblivious to the criminal activities of Aum devotees, Aum Shinrikyo acquired the means and the will to carry out armageddon. The sarin gas attacks in Matsumoto on June 27, 1994, and on the Tokyo subway on March 20, 1995, had the short-term aims of neutralizing Aum's enemies and protecting Aum's mission of creating the Shambhala kingdom. Therefore, the violence committed by Aum devotees was motivated by the organization's fragility and the endangerment of the ultimate concern. Fortunately, Aum devotees did not have the opportunity to carry out their revolutionary plan to fight armageddon in November 1995.

Notes

1. Aoyama also said, "There is worry that the authorities would murder en masse the Aum members, making it look like a mass suicide—we have been oppressed that severely." Sheryl WuDunn, "Sect Says Government Staged Attack," *New York Times*, March 22, 1995, A-6.
    In this chapter, I follow the English-language journalistic convention of reversing the order of Japanese names to put the given name first and the family name last.
2. Quoted in David E. Kaplan and Andrew Marshall, *The Cult at the End of the World: The Terrifying Story of the Aum Doomsday Cult, from the Subways of Tokyo to the Nuclear Arsenals of Russia* (New York: Crown Publishers, 1996), 217.
3. Mark R. Mullins, "Aum Shinrikyo as an Apocalyptic Movement," in *Millennium, Messiahs, and Mayhem: Contemporary Apocalyptic Movements*, ed. Thomas Robbins and Susan J. Palmer (New York: Routledge, 1997), 315.
4. Sarin is a nerve gas developed from an insecticide in Germany prior to World War II. Murray Sayle, "Nerve Gas and the Four Noble Truths," *New Yorker* 72, no. 6 (April 1, 1996): 66.
5. Ian Reader, *A Poisonous Cocktail? Aum Shinrikyo's Path to Violence* (Copenhagen: NIAS Books, 1996), 86-87; Sayle, "Nerve Gas and the Four Noble Truths," 69-70; Mullins, "Aum Shinrikyo as an Apocalyptic Movement," 313-14.
6. Kaplan and Marshall, *Cult at the End of the World*, 1-2, 240-41, 242-52.
    In December 1995, Dr. Ikuo Hayashi, Toru Toyoda, and Kenichi Hirose pleaded guilty to releasing sarin on the subway cars. In October 1996, Kenichi Hirose testified to the following motivation, "In the end, we were going to build a kingdom of Aum." "Japan Cult Member Pleads Guilty to Attack," Reuters (AOL), December 26, 1995; Associated Press, "Gas Attack Called Part of War," Reuters (AOL), October 4, 1996.
7. "Ushering in Armageddon," *Japan Times* special report, "Terror in the heart of Japan," July 1995, 21; Kaplan and Marshall, *Cult at the End of the World*, 235-36; Associated Press, "Asahara predicted 'panic' in March 1995: AUM's Inoue," Reuters (AOL), January 17, 1997. I thank the editor of *AMPO* for kindly forwarding to me the *Japan Times* special report in English.
8. Reader, *Poisonous Cocktail?* 77, 82-83; Kaplan and Marshall, *Cult at the End of*

the World, 142-48.

9. Ian Reader, "Imagined Persecution: Aum Shinrikyo, Millennialism, and the Legitimation of Violence," *Millennialism, Persecution, and Violence: Historical Cases,* ed. Catherine Wessinger (Syracuse: Syracuse University Press, 2000), 158–82.

10. Kaplan and Marshall, *Cult at the End of the World,* 36-37.

11. Kaplan and Marshall, *Cult at the End of the World,* 37-43; email message from Robert Kisala dated August 26, 1997. Nakagawa subsequently pleaded guilty to the murders of the Sakamoto family. See Sayle, "Nerve Gas and the Four Noble Truths," 61. Kyodo News Service, "Ex-AUM member testifies, Asahara interrupts," Reuters (AOL), June 20, 1997.

12. Kaplan and Marshall, *Cult at the End of the World,* 94-96.

13. Kaplan and Marshall, *Cult at the End of the World,* 113-17.

In 1996 Hideaki Yasuda was convicted of strangling Kotaro Ochida to death, but was given a light sentence, because Yasuda was ordered to kill Ochida or be killed himself. Yasuda was sentenced to three years in prison, but the sentence was suspended. "Ex-cult member forced to kill, judge says," *New Orleans Times-Picayune,* June 27, 1996, A-2.

In May 1998, Asahara's wife, Tomoko Matsumoto, was sentenced to seven years in prison for conspiring with her husband to murder Ochida. Kyodo News Service, "Asahara's wife given 7-year prison term for '94 murder," America Online News, May 17, 1998.

14. Kaplan and Marshall, *Cult at the End of the World,* 185-86.

15. Kaplan and Marshall, *Cult at the End of the World,* 211.

16. Kaplan and Marshall, *Cult at the End of the World,* 211-12.

17. Kaplan and Marshall, *Cult at the End of the World,* 218.

18. Kaplan and Marshall, *Cult at the End of the World,* 227-28.

19. Kaplan and Marshall, *Cult at the End of the World,* 77-83.

20. Mullins, "Aum Shinrikyo as an Apocalyptic Movement," 320.

21. Helen Hardacre, "Aum Shinrikyo and the Japanese Media: The Pied Piper Meets the Lamb of God," Columbia University, East Asian Institute, 1995, 4.

Hundreds of tons of chemicals and a laboratory were discovered at Aum headquarters, as well as equipment and parts to make 1,000 automatic rifles. See Brian Williams, "Japanese cult leader linked to new crimes," Reuters (AOL), July 16, 1995.

22. Mullins, "Aum Shinrikyo as an Apocalyptic Movement," 318.

23. Kaplan and Marshall, *Cult at the End of the World,* 261-63; Kyodo News Service, "Ex-police officer in police chief shooting to be freed," Reuters (AOL), June 9, 1997.

24. Reader, *Poisonous Cocktail?* 88; "Nightmare Come True," *Japan Times* special report, "Terror in the heart of Japan," July 1995, 16; Teruaki Ueno, "Fear grips Tokyo as sect guru predicts disaster," Reuters (AOL), April 15, 1995.

25. Reader, *Poisonous Cocktail?* 7, 81, 108-9; Sayle, "Nerve Gas and the Four Noble Truths," 70. On the power of the *yakusa* in the Japanese economy, see Michael Hirsh and Hideko Takayama, "Big Bang or Bust? Mobsters slow Tokyo's plan to join world markets," *Newsweek,* September 1, 1997, 44-45.

26. Kaplan and Marshall, *Cult at the End of the World,* 279-80.

In June 1997, Yasuo Hayashi pleaded guilty to releasing sarin on the Tokyo subway in March 1995, to planting the device to release cyanide at the Shinjuku station in May 1995, to helping to equip the vehicle to release sarin in the Matsumoto gas attack in June 1994. Kyodo News Service, "AUM's Hayashi pleads guilty to gas attack murder charge," Reuters (AOL), June 6, 1997.

27. Mullins, "Aum Shinrikyo as an Apocalyptic Movement," 319; "A New Form

of Terrorism Is Unleashed," *Japan Times* special report, "Terror in the heart of Japan," July 1995, 5; Kaplan and Marshall, *Cult at the End of the World*, 280-81.

28. Kaplan and Marshall, *Cult at the End of the World*, 282.
29. Sayle, "Nerve Gas and the Four Noble Truths," 58; Reader, *Poisonous Cocktail?* 19-23; Susumu Shimazono, "In the Wake of Aum: The Formation and Transformation of a Universe of Belief," *Japanese Journal of Religious Studies* 22, no. 3-4 (1995): 384-86; Hardacre, "Aum Shinrikyo and the Japanese Media," 10; Robert Kisala, "The AUM Spiritual Truth Church in Japan," in *Wolves Within the Fold: Religious Leadership and Abuses of Power*, ed. Anson Shupe (New Brunswick, N.J.: Rutgers University Press, 1998), 33-48.
30. Robert Kisala, "1999 and Beyond: Use of the Nostradamus Prophecies by Japanese Religions," paper presented November 8, 1997, at the Society for the Scientific Study of Religion, San Diego, kindly forwarded by the author via email.
31. Manabu Watanabe, "A License to Kill: Aum Shinrikyo's Idea of Buddhist Salvation," paper presented November 8, 1997, at the Society for the Scientific Study of Religion, San Diego, kindly forwarded by the author by email.
   The identity of the deity that appeared to Asahara on Miura beach is vague in the early Aum literature. Watanabe's opinion in the paper cited above is that the deity was an indigenous Japanese deity. Ian Reader's opinion is that the deity was the Hindu god Shiva. See Ian Reader, "Imagined Persecution."
32. Sayle, "Nerve Gas and the Four Noble Truths," 58; Reader, *Poisonous Cocktail?* 19-23; Shimazono, "In the Wake of Aum," 391; Kisala, "AUM Spiritual Truth Church in Japan"; Kaplan and Marshall, *Cult at the End of the World*, 13-14; Watanabe, "License to Kill."
33. For a description of Siddha Yoga, a Hindu *siddha* tradition brought to the United States and other countries outside India, see Gene R. Thursby, "Hindu Movements Since Mid-Century: Yogis in the States," in *America's Alternative Religions*, ed. Timothy Miller (Albany: State University of New York Press, 1995), 191-213; Gene R. Thursby, "Siddha Yoga: Swami Muktananda and the Seat of Power," in *When Prophets Die: The Postcharismatic Fate of New Religious Movements*, ed. Timothy Miller (Albany: State University of New York Press, 1991), 165-81, 232-38; Catherine Wessinger, "Woman Guru, Woman Roshi: The Legitimation of Female Religious Leadership in Hindu and Buddhist Groups in America," in *Women's Leadership in Marginal Religions: Explorations Outside the Mainstream*, ed. Catherine Wessinger (Urbana: University of Illinois Press, 1993), 125-46.
34. Quoted in Watanabe, "License to Kill."
35. Kisala, "AUM Spiritual Truth Church in Japan," 37. Asahara ceased performing *shaktipat* in 1988, saying that it depleted his energy, but delegated his leading disciples to perform the initiation for which a large donation was required. See Shimazono, "In the Wake of Aum," 394-95.
36. Kaplan and Marshall, *Cult at the End of the World*, 162-65.
37. Kaplan and Marshall, *Cult at the End of the World*, 16.
38. Shimazono, "In the Wake of Aum," 404.
39. Sayle, "Nerve Gas and the Four Noble Truths," 65; Reader, *Poisonous Cocktail?* 56; Watanabe, "License to Kill."
40. Quoted in Shimazono, "In the Wake of Aum," 405.
41. Reader, *Poisonous Cocktail?* 31-34, 38.
42. Watanabe, "License to Kill."
43. Sayle, "Nerve Gas and the Four Noble Truths," 61; Mullins, "Aum Shinrikyo as an Apocalyptic Movement," 317.

Aum Shinrikyo became active in Russia in 1992, and had five chapters in Moscow. It broadcasted a weekly TV program and a daily hour-long radio program. The government seized Aum's assets in 1994 when a group of parents, the Committee to Rescue Youth, brought a criminal suit alleging that their offspring were brainwashed. Aum was disbanded by the Russian government. See Hardacre, "Aum Shinrikyo and the Japanese Media," 33, note 18.

44. Sayle, "Nerve Gas and the Four Noble Truths," 59; Reader, *Poisonous Cocktail?* 62.
45. Carmen Blacker, *The Catalpa Bow: A Study of Shamanistic Practices in Japan* (London: George Allen & Unwin Ltd., 1975).
46. Richard Gardner, "Aum Shinrikyo's Use of Animated Scriptures and a Panic about Popular Culture," paper presented at the American Academy of Religion, San Francisco, November 1997. I thank Dr. Gardner for kindly forwarding this paper to me.
47. Video clips shown by Richard Gardner, Sophia University, Tokyo, in a session on Aum Shinrikyo, November 18, 1995, at the American Academy of Religion meeting in Philadelphia.
48. Gardner, "Aum Shinrikyo's Use of Animated Scriptures."
49. Helen Hardacre, "Aum Shinrikyo and the Japanese Media," 28. The *anime* discussed by Hardacre include "The Voyage of the Battleship Yamato," "Conan, Youth of the Future," and "Great Battle with Genma."
50. "The Talents of Aum," *Japan Times* special report, "Terror in the heart of Japan," July 1995, 13.
51. Hardacre, "Aum Shinrikyo and the Japanese Media," 17; Reader, *Poisonous Cocktail?* 81-82; "Aum's quasi-governmental structure," in *Japan Times* special report, "Terror in the heart of Japan," July 1995, 14-15.
52. Hardacre, "Aum Shinrikyo and the Japanese Media," 3.
53. Kaplan and Marshall, *Cult at the End of the World,* 161, 201.
54. Conversation with Shannon Higgins, reporter for *Asahi Shimbun,* April 4, 1997.
55. Kaplan and Marshall, *Cult at the End of the World,* 62-63.
56. "Ushering in Armageddon," 21-22; Kaplan and Marshall, *Cult at the End of the World,* 188.
57. Reader, *Poisonous Cocktail?* 25.
58. Reader, *Poisonous Cocktail?* 29.
59. Reader, *Poisonous Cocktail?* 28.
60. Sayle, "Nerve Gas and the Four Noble Truths," 61; Reader, *Poisonous Cocktail?* 32-33; Richard Young, "Lethal Achievements: Fragments of a Response to the Aum Shinrikyo Affair," *Japanese Religions* 20, no. 2 (1995): 238; "New Form of Terrorism Is Unleashed," 7-8; "The Cost of Devotion," *Japan Times* special report, "Terror in the heart of Japan," July 1995, 13; "Breaking Up a Cult," *Japan Times* special report, "Terror in the heart of Japan," July 1995, 34.
61. Reader, *Poisonous Cocktail?* 32-33; Mullins, "Aum Shinrikyo as an Apocalyptic Movement," 316-17.
62. Aum pamphlet, "Precious words in answer to the prayers of new members," quoted in Shimazono, "In the Wake of Aum," 410.
63. Quoted in Watanable, "License to Kill."
64. Mullins, "Aum Shinrykio as an Apocalyptic Movement," 316-17; Reader, *Poisonous Cocktail?* 46; Shimazono, "In the Wake of Aum," 395-400; Kisala, "AUM Spiritual Truth Church in Japan."
65. Reader, "Imagined Persecution"; Kisala, "AUM Spiritual Truth Church in Japan," 39.
66. Reader, *Poisonous Cocktail?* 46-49; Shimazono, "In the Wake of Aum," 398.
67. Reader, "Imagined Persecution."

68. Reader, *Poisonous Cocktail?* 62-63.
69. David G. Goodman and Masanori Miyazawa, *Jews in the Japanese Mind: The History and Uses of a Cultural Stereotype* (New York: The Free Press, 1995). The most influential source of the One World Government Jewish conspiracy theory is the spurious book purporting to be *The Protocols of the Elders of Zion* (ca.1897–98). *The Protocols* was brought to Japan about 1918–22 by Japanese soldiers returning from service in Siberia. *The Protocols* was republished in Japan in 1972 as *The Jews and World Revolution.*
Beginning in 1991, the League of National Socialists, a group of small business owners, plastered Tokyo with flyers bearing swastikas warning about the Jewish plot to destroy Japanese culture and economy. A 1993 flyer read: "Remember Kristallnacht! Get the illegal aliens in Japan who threaten Japan's security! Fight the Zionist occupation government! Smash international Jewish power and free the world from diabolical Judaism!"
In 1992, the Global Restoration Party (Chikyu ishin to), an anti-Semitic political party, put up candidates for election to the Upper House Diet. The party aimed to "smite the traitors who are selling out Holy Japan to the diabolical Jewish cult." Goodman and Miyazawa, *Jews in the Japanese Mind*, 76-86, 182, quotes on 255-56. For similar anti-Semitic ideas in the United States, see the following chapter on the Montana Freemen.
70. Shimazono, "In the Wake of Aum," 399.
71. Reader, *Poisonous Cocktail?* 55-56; Shimazono, "In the Wake of Aum," 402.
72. Reader, *Poisonous Cocktail?* 56-58.
73. Reader, *Poisonous Cocktail?* 57-58.
74. Reader, *Poisonous Cocktail?* 60-65.
75. Reader, *Poisonous Cocktail?* 9. This member was Naruhito Noda, who became spokesman for Aum after the arrest of Fumihiro Joyu in October 1995, who had served as primary spokesman after the arrests of Asahara and other leaders.
76. Reader, "Imagined Persecution."
77. Reader, *Poisonous Cocktail?* 35-37.
78. Reader, *Poisonous Cocktail?* 37-38; Sayle, "Nerve Gas and the Four Noble Truths," 62; Hardacre, "Aum Shinrikyo and the Japanese Media," 11-12.
79. Reader, *Poisonous Cocktail?* 37-41; Sayle, "Nerve Gas and the Four Noble Truths," 61.
80. This may have been a magic ritual to ensure success in the election, since Ganesha is the "remover of obstacles" to any successful undertaking.
81. Reader, *Poisonous Cocktail?* 44-45; Sayle, "Nerve Gas and the Four Noble Truths," 62; Young, "Lethal Achievements," 232.
82. Young, "Lethal Achievements," 233.
83. Reader, *Poisonous Cocktail?* 45-46; Sayle, "Nerve Gas and the Four Noble Truths," 62; Hardacre, "Aum Shinrikyo and the Japanese Media," 14.
84. "New Form of Terrorism Is Unleashed," 9; Reader, *Poisonous Cocktail?* 47-48.
85. Hardacre, "Aum Shinrikyo and the Japanese Media," 14.
86. Kaplan and Marshall, *Cult at the End of the World*, 212, 226-27; Reader, *Poisonous Cocktail?* 49-51; "Aum Hierarchy," *Japan Times* special report, "Terror in the heart of Japan," July 1995, 14-15.
87. Reader, *Poisonous Cocktail?* 51.
88. Reader, *Poisonous Cocktail?* 66-67.
89. Reader, *Poisonous Cocktail?* 67.
90. Reader, *Poisonous Cocktail?* 78-80; Hardacre, "Aum Shinrikyo and the Japanese Media," 15.
91. Reader, *Poisonous Cocktail?* 83.

92. WuDunn, "Sect Says Government Staged Attack"; David Van Biema, "Prophet of Poison," *Time,* April 3, 1995, 32; Kaplan and Marshall, *Cult at the End of the World,* 239.

93. Reader, *Poisonous Cocktail?* 85-87.

94. Reader, *Poisonous Cocktail?* 24, 29, 42.

95. Watanabe, "License to Kill."

96. Watanabe, "License to Kill." For an accurate account of the Tibetan Buddhist doctrine of *phowa,* see Sogyal Rinpoche, *The Tibetan Book of Living and Dying,* ed. Patrick Gaffney and Andrew Harvey (San Francisco: HarperSanFrancisco, 1993).

97. Kaplan and Marshall, *Cult at the End of the World,* 35-37.

98. Sayle, "Nerve Gas and the Four Noble Truths," 65.

99. Translated and quoted in Kisala, "AUM Spiritual Truth Church in Japan," 40-41.

100. Kyodo News Service, "TBS ex-president to become affiliate's chief," Reuters (AOL), June 6, 1997; *Yomiuri Shimbun,* "PRESS DIGEST—Top Japan business news—March 26," Reuters (AOL), March 25, 1996.

101. Eric Talmadge, Associated Press, "Cult Doctor Testifies on Guru," Reuters (AOL), September 19, 1996.

102. Kaplan and Marshall, *Cult at the End of the World,* 51-54.

103. Kaplan and Marshall, *Cult at the End of the World,* 69-76, 106-8; Kyodo News Service, "Former AUM member says sarin data came from Russia," Reuters (AOL), April 23, 1997.

104. Kaplan and Marshall, *Cult at the End of the World,* 97; Sayle, "Nerve Gas and the Four Noble Truths," 67.

105. Kaplan and Marshall, *Cult at the End of the World,* 84-88; Brian Williams, "Japanese cult leader linked to new crimes." A usable rifle was never produced. Email message from Robert Kisala, August 26, 1997.

106. Kaplan and Marshall, *Cult at the End of the World,* 109-12.

107. Kaplan and Marshall, *Cult at the End of the World,* 94-97.

108. Kaplan and Marshall, *Cult at the End of the World,* 119-25, 132, 150.

109. Kaplan and Marshall, *Cult at the End of the World,* 99-103.

110. Sayle, "Nerve Gas and the Four Noble Truths," 66; Hardacre, "Aum Shinrikyo and the Japanese Media," 18; Kaplan and Marshall, *Cult at the End of the World,* 126-34.

On the evening of May 28, 1993, an explosion caused the sky in the area of the Aum sheep ranch to blaze and the ground to shake. This mysterious event prompted the Senate Government Affairs Committee, led by Senator Sam Nunn, to hold hearings in Washington, D.C., to explore whether Aum had detonated a nuclear bomb. The explosion had the force of a small nuclear blast or 2,000 tons of high explosives. The Incorporated Research Institution for Seismology (IRIS) reported that the explosion had the characteristics of an earthquake or meteor impact (no crater was found), and that Aum members were not present at the ranch when the explosion occurred. William J. Broad, "Seismic Mystery in Australia: Quake, Meteor, or Nuclear Blast?" *New York Times* (AOL), January 21, 1997.

111. Kaplan and Marshall, *Cult at the End of the World,* 110.

112. Kaplan and Marshall, *Cult at the End of the World,* 172-73.

113. Kaplan and Marshall, *Cult at the End of the World,* 175-81.

114. Kaplan and Marshall, *Cult at the End of the World,* 184-85, 226-27.

115. Kaplan and Marshall, *Cult at the End of the World,* 226.

116. Wahei Sakurai, "Doomsday cult plotted urban war on Japan—report," Reuters (AOL), May 26, 1995; Kisala, "AUM Spiritual Truth Church," 44.
117. Kaplan and Marshall, *Cult at the End of the World*, 190-94.
118. Kaplan and Marshall, *Cult at the End of the World*, 201-5.
119. Kaplan and Marshall, *Cult at the End of the World*, 206-8, 210.
120. Kaplan and Marshall, *Cult at the End of the World*, 214.
121. Kaplan and Marshall, *Cult at the End of the World*, 220-21.
122. The sarin released on the Tokyo subway trains was manufactured in the private labs of Tsuchiya and Endo. Email message from Robert Kisala, August 26, 1997.
123. Kaplan and Marshall, *Cult at the End of the World*, 215-20.
124. Kaplan and Marshall, *Cult at the End of the World*, 222-25.
125. Kaplan and Marshall, *Cult at the End of the World*, 223.
126. Reader, *Poisonous Cocktail?* 76-77.
127. Reader, *Poisonous Cocktail?* 101.
128. Hardacre, "Aum Shinrikyo and the Japanese Media," 27.
129. Ian Buruma, "Lost Without a Faith: In the spiritual vacuum of the postwar years, some Japanese seek new gods," *Time*, April 3, 1995, 34.
130. Kaplan and Marshall, *Cult at the End of the World*, 149.
131. Yvonne Chang, "Japan police admit poor handling of subway gassing," Reuters (AOL), August 20, 1996; Mari Yamaguchi, Associated Press, "Police Say Cult Probe Bungled," Reuters (AOL), August 20, 1996.

CHAPTER SIX

1996—The Montana Freemen

I am only here because of my mom.
This is not something I am willing to die for.
I haven't even started to live.
—Ashley Taylor (16) as reported by Bo Gritz[1]

The Potential for Violence

The standoff on a wheat farm in Garfield County, Montana, from March 25 to June 13, 1996, between FBI agents and a group of Christian Patriots known as Freemen corralled a group of people who had been waging war for approximately four years against law enforcement agents and the government. The Freemen were part of a revolutionary movement that aimed to overthrow the federal government, which they regarded as oppressive and satanic. As revolutionaries, the Freemen had sympathizers, but they had not gained a sufficient number of people willing to fight the revolution. Aware of being small in comparison to the armed law enforcement establishment, the Freemen utilized "paper warfare" to achieve their goal. The Freemen possessed guns and threatened violence against their enemies, but their primary weapons were "Common Law" documents; the Freemen placed liens against the property of government officials, judges, sheriffs, attorneys, and then issued Comptroller Warrants (drafts) against the liens.[2]

The Freemen's worldview was derived from the Christian Patriot interpretation of the Bible, the Magna Carta, the Declaration of Independence, the pre–Civil War American Constitution, and other legal documents that they regarded as authoritative. The Freemen utilized their liens and drafts—which they regarded as valid—as weapons to battle the federal government and the Federal Reserve System, which they regarded as satanic "Babylon." As Christian Patriots and believers in a theology called

Christian Identity, the Freemen believed they were living in the period of the tribulation, the time of violence leading to armageddon, the final battle against Satan's agents. This would be followed by the Second Coming of Christ and the establishment of God's kingdom.[3]

The ultimate concern of the Freemen was to establish an association of sovereign state republics free from federal authority, in which Yahweh's laws, given in the Old Testament, would be enforced. The Freemen emphasized the illegitimacy of centralized federal government and, conversely, the legitimacy of local governing structures, such as independent townships, Common Law courts, and the authority vested in sheriffs by these local institutions.

As revolutionary millennialists, the Freemen were part of a contemporary Euro-American nativist millennial movement, or what scholars often call a "revitalization"[4] movement. A *nativist millennial movement* consists of individuals who feel oppressed by a foreign colonizing government, believing that the government is removing the natives from their land and eradicating their traditional way of life. Nativists hope for an elimination of their oppressors and a restoration of their idealized past way of life. The idealized past way of life may be highly embellished, as is the case with Identity Christians, who identify themselves with the biblical Israelites and seek to create a government that enforces God's laws given in the Old Testament.

Nativist millennialists are not necessarily violent; they display a range of behaviors, and they may fall into the categories of millennial groups discussed in this book—fragile groups, assaulted groups, and revolutionary groups. Nativist millennial groups may become fragile and therefore initiate violence.[5] Nativist groups may await divine intervention but find themselves assaulted by law enforcement agents who perceive them as being dangerous.[6] Nativists may be revolutionaries,[7] such as the Montana Freemen and their kindred in the diffuse contemporary Euro-American nativist movement.

Euro-Americans certainly were not the original "natives" of North America. But the white Americans who participate in this Euro-American nativist millennial movement regard America as their native land from which they are being dispossessed.

The Freemen were part of a Euro-American nativist millennial movement that is ongoing; they considered themselves to be an indigenous group that was being colonized and oppressed by a foreign government bent on exterminating their families, race, religion, and culture. The Freemen were fighting for survival and independence, and to establish a millennial kingdom they viewed as a return to their earlier culture. They aimed to restore the "united States of America," an association of sovereign state republics governed by Common Law derived from the Bible and the American Constitution. To accomplish this it was necessary to demonstrate the illegitimacy of the "United States," which they believed had come under the control of the World Bank.[8] They believed that international banking institutions and the United States federal government were under the control of conspiratorial Jews. The Freemen were waging a war to regain control of their sacred promised land, America. If necessary, the Freemen were willing to kill or die for their ultimate concern.

The Freemen were part of a grassroots nativist movement of white Americans, many of whom call themselves Christian Patriots, and who may affiliate with Constitution and Common Law study groups, militias, and a variety of white supremacist organizations and religions including the white supremacist religion known as Christian Identity.[9] The most committed of the Montana Freemen were Identity Christians, who advocated white supremacy and believed that Jews, identified as the offspring of Satan, controlled international banking institutions and the United States government. The Freemen utilized their Common Law documents to wage paper warfare in order to destroy the federal government and its economic institutions.

The Freemen's Common Law documents and financial instruments may be analyzed in terms of magic, which often is used in nativist millennial movements. Magic consists of rituals (often involving speaking or writing words of power) that are believed to have the power to effect changes in the physical world. Magic, like other religious methods, is aimed at securing well-being. Participants in nativist millennial movements often "imitate the behavior or organizational patterns" of the group that has conquered them in order to gain power over that government and its agents.[10] The nativist aims to gain and utilize the invisible power that the dominating group appears to possess. The nativist aims to acquire that power in order to defeat the controlling government and to establish the natives' idealized past golden age.

Michael Adas has pointed out that nativist millennial movements[11] originate among people who feel oppressed by a foreign colonizing regime. They feel oppressed by taxation and other "extraction" methods utilized by the dominating government. These extraction methods result in the natives' loss of land, wealth, and their traditional way of life, and cause their downward mobility. The natives are in the position of losing the status and economic well-being that was available in their earlier way of life. They see their traditional way of life, often in villages and agrarian communities, disappearing. A nativist millennial movement may arise when the bureaucratic structures of a dominating government are viewed as oppressive and unresponsive to the needs and petitions of the natives. The natives do not believe they will receive a fair hearing or an adequate response from the courts and agencies of the oppressing government. Adas points out that nativist movements are often characterized by hostility toward ethnic groups who are perceived as benefiting from the dominant government and its economy. If possible, the nativists will attempt to purge their land and culture of the hated ethnic people. Adas also points out that networks of communication are crucial for the development of a nativist millennial movement.[12]

While scholars have been accustomed to identifying and studying nativist millennial movements in undeveloped parts of the world where natives have responded to colonialism, the Freemen and the Euro-American nativist millennial movement of which they are a part are a nativist movement of white people utilizing the means of communication available in the post-industrial world: radio, television, telephone, fax, Internet, email, and the World Wide Web. Although distinctive among nativist millennial movements because of their use of advanced technology, like other nativists, Euro-Americans are responding to deprivation of economic and social advancement in the "highly mobile society"[13] presided over by the hated dominating government.

Journalist Joel Dyer locates an important source of this contemporary Euro-American nativist movement in the hardships experienced by farmers and rural small business operators and workers during the 1980s. During the 1970s, farmers were encouraged by bankers and Farm Home Administration agents to take out large loans to increase the size of their farming operations. But, in 1979, Federal Reserve Chairman Paul Volcker decided to curb inflation by raising interest rates. Property values dropped while the interest rates on loans increased. Farmers were unable to make profits on their produce, and they were subjected to high taxes. Multinational corporations took advantage of the farmers' plight by buying up their repossessed farms at low prices and consolidating much of American farmland into the holdings of a few corporations. These same multinational corporations determined the prices farmers could obtain for their produce. The farm crisis also caused the failure of numerous businesses related to the farming industry. Dyer highlights the fact that federal decision makers typically live in cities and are unconcerned and unresponsive to the plight of rural people. He also criticizes the news media for failing to report the ongoing crisis in rural America.[14]

Due to the continuous anxiety and unending work, resulting only in the loss of one's farm, way of life, and identity, the rate of suicide among farmers has gone up dramatically. Dyer argues that while suicide is an expression of anger turned inward, numerous rural people have begun to turn their anger outward and direct it against the federal government, its policies, and agents. American farmers' despair was expressed in the following letter written by Darrell and Sally Frech in 1989. Darrell Frech subsequently became a Common Law activist and teacher.

Dear Sir:

No one can ever begin to imagine the stress, strain, frustrations, and total helplessness that the American farmer has had and felt the last few years in trying to stay afloat and fight the farm credit system. You get so desperate you do not know what to do or even where your next meal for your kids will come from.

We personally have been fighting Federal Land Bank of Enid and Wichita for the last seven years. FLB lied, cheated, and frauded us. One farmer by themselves can not fight them through the courts. So where do you turn to for help?

We wanted to give up so many times and walk away. You take your frustrations out on each other and on your family. You are always under tension. You can't afford insurance, doctors, or anything. This stress and strain causes arguments, divorces, and extra problems with children. This desperation often causes murder and suicides. They can not face failure and losing the family farm.

Our Plea is this, make the Farm Credit System, especially the FLB accountable to someone! No entity should be allowed to do these things to anyone and not be punished. If a borrower was free to sue the Farm Credit system and for punitive damages, they would straighten up their act. A federal grand jury investigation needs to be called to investigate their dealings, contracts, and why their illegal charges, debits, and credits appear and disappear at the touch of a button. Please make the Farm Credit System accountable to someone!

Darrell and Sally Frech, 1989[15]

Increasingly, instead of turning their anger inwards, farmers, small-business owners, and other Americans threatened with downward mobility have become receptive to the message of the radical right that their hardship is the result of an international conspiracy of Jewish bankers, who have gained control of the federal government and who aim to profit from the suffering of hardworking Americans. In the 1990s, a California farmer named Tim explained this view. According to Tim, "This kind of injustice [death and foreclosure] is going on all over the country...."

It's what happened to the folks in Montana [referring to the antigovernment group called the Freemen, who were involved in an eighty-three-day [sic] standoff with the FBI in 1996, and it's what happened to me. That's why LeRoy [LeRoy Schweitzer, the leader of the Freemen] was arrested. He was teaching people how to keep their farms and ranches. He was showing them that the government isn't constitutional. They foreclose on us so they can control the food supply. What they want to do is control the Christians. They'd like to kill us all.[16]

The Freemen's resistance to the federal government began in 1992 when Rodney Skurdal, a former Marine, bought a farm in Musselshell County, near Roundup, Montana, and initiated paper warfare by filing Common Law documents. His documents included a "Citizens Declaration of War" against "foreign agents" in the "country of Montana." The Musselshell County attorney became so frustrated in dealing with Skurdal's cases that she resigned. In July 1994, the Montana Supreme Court limited Skurdal's access to the courts and fined him $1,000 for filing "meritless, frivolous, vexatious" documents.[17] Because Skurdal did not pay federal taxes, his property was legally siezed in 1993 and put up for sale, but no one attempted to remove Skurdal from his farm.

In late 1994, LeRoy M. Schweitzer moved in with Skurdal, and in early 1995 Daniel and Cherlyn Petersen did as well. They collaborated in waging war against Babylon by filing legal documents that expressed their understanding of Common Law. A sign on Skurdal's property warned, "Do Not Enter Private Land of the Sovereign.... The right of Personal Liberty is one of the fundamental rights guaranteed to every citizen, and any unlawful interference with it may be resisted." They taught other people their understanding of the Common Law and how to fight the federal government with Common Law documents. In late 1995, fifteen drafts issued by Schweitzer ranging in value from $2,600 to $91,000 were successfully passed. The Schweitzer drafts were used by individuals to make child support payments and to buy trucks and cars. The Freemen issued threats against law enforcement officers who attempted to limit what the Freemen considered to be legal activities. The local sheriff did not attempt to move against Skurdal and his colleagues, saying, "These people want to be martyrs."[18]

The Freemen in Roundup became acquainted with the Clark family, who lived on a 960-acre wheat farm near Jordan in Garfield County, Montana. In 1981, after accepting almost $700,000 in federal aid, the Clarks stopped making payments on federal loans, and by 1995 owed $1.8 million. The bank foreclosed and sold the farm at a sheriff's auction in April 1994, but the Clarks refused to vacate their family farm.[19]

In January 1994, the Freemen, including Skurdal and Petersen, seized control of the Garfield County courthouse and held a meeting to set up a local government. Richard Clark presided as judge and charged the judge who had ruled against the Clark family with contempt. According to Richard Clark, "We've opened our own common law court and we have the law back in the county now." Shortly thereafter, the Freemen posted flyers in Garfield County advertising a bounty of $1 million for the arrest of the sheriff, the county attorney, and the judge. The sheriff asked a Freeman if he could turn himself in and collect the reward. The Freeman replied that he could do that, but the sheriff would be tried, convicted, and hung. The sheriff in Jordan arrested Freemen every now and then but made no attempt to take all of them into custody. Garfield County attorney Nick Murnion filed charges against the Freemen for impersonating public officials and committing "criminal syndicalism," defined as "advocating violence or terrorism for political purposes." The Freemen continued their revolution against the government.[20]

In February 1995, Murnion successfully prosecuted William Stanton (64) for criminal syndicalism. Stanton had lost his ranch in foreclosure and blamed his misfortune on the government. After Stanton's conviction, the FBI alerted Murnion, the Musselshell County attorney, and the judge who had convicted Stanton, that the Freemen were planning to kidnap a judge, try, convict, and hang him. On March 3, 1995, a Musselshell County deputy stopped Freemen Dale Jacobi and Frank Ellena for driving without a license plate and driver's license. The deputy discovered in the vehicle thirty sets of handcuffs, rolls of duct tape, $60,000 in gold and silver, and $26,000 in cash. After Jacobi and Ellena were arrested, three Freemen came to the Roundup jail and demanded the items that had been seized. Other armed Freemen were outside in two cars. After all were arrested, the sheriff's office received hundreds of threatening calls. Most of the charges were dropped because of the search procedures.[21]

FBI agents kept the Freemen under surveillance, but they attempted to avoid violence subsequent to their botched handling of the Branch Davidian (see chapter 4) and Weaver family cases.

The cabin of Randy and Vicki Weaver at Ruby Ridge, Idaho, was under surveillance in August 1992, when two federal marshals got into a gunfight that killed Deputy U.S. Marshal William F. Degan (42) and the Weavers' son, Sammy (14). The gunfight began when the Weavers' yellow Labrador, Striker, discovered the armed marshals dressed in camouflage combat suits. Striker was killed, and shots were exchanged between the marshals, Sammy Weaver, and a Weaver family friend, Kevin Harris. Sammy was shot in the back as he tried to run away. Randy Weaver was an Identity Christian and an army veteran who had trained his children in the use of firearms. The Weaver family had taken refuge in the Idaho mountains and were armed for self-defense during the expected tribulation. Randy Weaver was wanted for failing to appear in court on a charge that he had illegally sawed off two shotguns and attempted to sell them. The FBI Hostage Rescue Team (HRT), commanded by Richard Rogers, surrounded the Weavers' cabin and did not notify the Weavers of their presence or ask them to surrender. Nor were the Weavers apprised that the FBI had changed its normal rules of engagement; the FBI snipers were instructed to shoot to kill any armed male adult they saw. An FBI agent fired shots at Randy Weaver and Kevin Harris when they came outside, and this resulted in the killing of Randy Weaver's wife, Vicki (42), as she stood behind the cabin's front door, holding their baby. After a ten-day siege, Randy Weaver, his friend Kevin Harris, and Weavers' three young daughters surrendered. Subsequently, Randy Weaver and Kevin Harris were acquitted of murder and conspiracy charges in a federal court. In 1995, the federal government, without admitting wrongdoing, paid the Weavers' three daughters $1 million each and gave Randy Weaver $100,000 in settlement.[22]

The killings of Randy Weaver's wife and son at Ruby Ridge in 1992 and the deaths of the Branch Davidians in 1993 provoked a strong reaction among right-wing white Americans, some of whom organized into militias and prepared to do battle with federal agents utilizing excessive force against civilians. The majority Christian Patriot view is that militia members are law-abiding citizens "who only want to protect themselves and their neighbors should federal agents begin breaking down doors in their neighborhoods. The militia are the law enforcement when the government becomes lawless."[23] But revolutionary individuals commit acts of domestic terrorism. In October 1995, sabotage caused the derailment of an Amtrak passenger train, and a note nearby, signed "Sons of Gestapo," condemned federal handling of Ruby Ridge and Waco.[24] On April 19, 1995, the second anniversary of the Branch Davidian fire, a federal office building in Oklahoma City was ripped apart by a bomb that killed 169 and injured about 600. The Oklahoma City victims were depicted in the news media as worthy victims, and the world was shocked by a photograph of a rescuer carrying out the bloodied corpse of an infant. In 1997, Timothy McVeigh (29), an Army veteran of the Persian Gulf War, was found guilty of committing the Oklahoma City bombing and given the death penalty. At his trial, McVeigh's defense attorney presented evidence concerning the Branch Davidian tragedy, implying that McVeigh was motivated to take revenge against federal agents for the deaths of the Davidians.[25]

FBI agents did not move quickly against the Montana Freemen, despite pleas for assistance from the local sheriffs and county attorneys.[26] The Freemen continued their Common Law and financial activities and continued making threats against law enforcement agents. In April 1995, Skurdal wrote in a document, "This is a holy war." He saw it as a conflict involving "God's laws vs. man-made laws."[27]

In September 1995, Skurdal, Schweitzer, and other Roundup Freemen formed a convoy of six vehicles and drove 150 miles to the Clark farm near Jordan. The Clark farm was designated "Justus Township," with its own Common Law court and officials. Justus Township became a center, where seminars were given on the Freemen tactics of issuing liens and drafts. There the Freemen taught an estimated 700 to 800 people their understanding of the Common Law. The primary teachers were LeRoy Schweitzer, Rodney Skurdal, Daniel Petersen, and Dale Jacobi.[28] The Freemen attracted like-minded locals and outsiders to settle in Justus Township.

Finally, neighbors became fed up with the Freemen. They planned a meeting to discuss taking action against the Freemen, such as cutting their telephone lines and closing the county road to the Clark farm. The Freemen resolved to fight back to defend themselves and their government. Reportedly, at a meeting, Schweitzer outlined the plan: "We'll travel in units of about 10 outfits, four men to an outfit, most of them with automatic weapons, whatever else we got—shotguns, you name it…. We're going to have a standing order: Anyone obstructing justice, the order is shoot to kill."[29] An undercover agent, Special Agent Timothy J. Healy, saw "Wanted, dead or alive" posters for public officials inside Justus Township.[30]

On Monday, March 25, 1996, LeRoy Schweitzer and Daniel Petersen were arrested by Healy and four other agents while they were away from the farm's main buildings inspecting a newly installed ham radio antenna. On the following Saturday, Richard Clark, who had been away from Justus Township when the standoff began, turned himself in.[31]

FBI agents took a totally different approach with the Freemen standoff than the one taken with the Branch Davidians. Attorney General Janet Reno announced that there would be "no armed confrontation, no siege and no armed perimeter."[32] FBI checkpoints were established out of sight of the Clark farm houses. Relatives were permitted to visit regularly. The Freemen and news reporters were able to meet at the perimeter and exchange information. FBI agents brought in about forty-five third-party intermediaries.[33] Two sympathizers, Stewart Waterhouse and Jon Barry Nelson, drove to Justus Township and joined the Freemen.[34] At his hearing, Daniel Petersen predicted that the Freemen standoff would be "worse than Waco."[35] The Freemen were revolutionaries prepared to fight against evil Babylon and the "Agents of Satan."[36] After the eighty-one-day standoff concluded, Colorado state Senator Charles Duke, who had served as a third-party intermediary, released to the media an audiotape he had recorded in Justus Township. On it Freeman Russell Landers said, "We're not here in this logistically defendable position as fools. We're guerilla warfare and I'm sorry, Charlie, but I feel very strongly about this, and they can take their (expletive) warrants and shove 'em right up their (expletive) where that 30-0-6 [sic] (rifle) of mine is gonna drill 'em." Duke reported that each of the Freemen was armed. Duke also recorded Freeman Edwin Clark expressing his fears of falling into federal custody. Clark asserted that when LeRoy Schweitzer was temporarily taken to a prison medical facility, Schweitzer had an encounter with a physician: "A doctor from New York City come in and told Leroy: he says, you'll never see the light of day. And he says, I'll guarantee you before you leave here I'm gonna inject you with a, with a deadly ah...dose of cancer." Edwin Clark made the following assertion about another jailed comrade: "They gave him a lethal dose of 'no brains' when he come back."[37]

The Freemen counted on help from revolutionary allies in the diffuse Euro-American nativist millennial movement. A Michigan militia leader, Norm Olson, told the media that the "second American Revolution" would begin at Justus Township, and he called on militiamen across the nation to prepare to do battle, but militia support for the Freemen did not materialize in significant strength.[38]

The eighty-one-day Freemen standoff was handled in a low-key manner by FBI agents and, thus, it ended peacefully, but throughout the standoff there was the possibility of violence. The FBI resolved the standoff peacefully when they offered terms to the Freemen that permitted them to remain true to their ultimate concern—the most important thing in the world to them—while being taken into custody.

The Cast of Characters

The Freemen were a group of individuals, some more assertive than others, who held the opinions of jailed LeRoy Schweitzer in particular esteem, and acknowledged his expertise in Freemen Common Law.

Russell Landers stands before the Justus Township seal as he explains principles of Freeman Common Law in a videotape given to reporters. (AP Photo)

LeRoy M. Schweitzer (57) was one of the leaders arrested on March 25, 1996, and he had a reputation among Christian Patriots as a foremost expert of Common Law. The charges against Schweitzer included threatening to kill a federal judge, threatening public officials, and issuing false financial documents. Schweitzer was formerly a crop duster. One year in the 1970s, he claimed what he thought was a legitimate deduction on his federal income tax form. He was subsequently audited by the Internal Revenue Service. In 1977, Schweitzer refused to pay a $700 tax bill. In turn, the Internal Revenue Service froze $6,000 in his business banking account. This marked Schweitzer's loss of faith in banks and the government. He told a friend, "The IRS can steal my money, but nobody else can." Schweitzer was audited again by the Internal Revenue Service in 1978. In 1992, the Internal Revenue Service seized his airplane and his home in Bozeman, Montana, to pay taxes dating back to the 1970s. He had frequented meetings of the anti–federal government movement known as Posse Comitatus.[39] Schweitzer perfected the Freemen technique of waging paper warfare in the following steps: (1) a "true bill" enumerating crimes in confession format was sent to the targeted enemy; (2) if the targeted person did not respond to the true bill, he or she was judged guilty; (3) a lien was filed against the target's personal property; (4) Comptroller Warrants (drafts) were issued based on the lien.[40] Schweitzer explained how he utilized liens against public officials:

> We sent this little UCC 4 out to them, this confession sheet we call it, the true bill, as an agreement. And when they don't answer, it becomes a binding contract. Now we get 'em for failure of consideration, breach of covenant. That has value to it. Every time they breach a covenant with me, it's a hundred million. And if I'm feeling a little bit bad that day, I charge them a billion that day.
>
> My liberty is worth a lot more than their hanging. So we're not hanging them yet. We don't have enough people to make the arrest, yet.... So what we're doing is going after the property first. We're attaching the property. We'll get to the cleanup later.[41]

The Freemen believed their liens and drafts were legal, since the same documents were utilized by Federal Reserve banks and the Internal Revenue Service. They felt that the news media misrepresented their activities by reporting that the Freemen were issuing "bogus checks." According to Freemen logic, the Freemen were utilizing the documents and legal strategies of the satanic federal system to destroy that system; if the Freemen documents were illegal, so were those of the federal government.[42] As noted earlier, these methods can be viewed as magic, by which nativists appropriate the enemy's power by imitating their actions and their use of words possessing power. The Freemen had total confidence in the magical power of their Common Law documents to acquire the condition of well-being for them.[43]

Daniel E. Petersen (53)[44] was arrested with Schweitzer on March 25, which left his wife, Cherlyn (51) in Justus Township during the standoff. Cherlyn appeared to be following her husband on the Freemen path. After she was taken into custody, Cherlyn told a judge, "My husband will speak for me."[45] Cherlyn probably played no role in the standoff negotiations.

Rodney O. Skurdal (43) was one of the primary ideologues in Justus Township during the standoff. He was a former Marine and had served in a military honor guard for Presidents Nixon and Ford. Since 1983 Skurdal had refused to have a driver's license or license tags on his car, or to use his Social Security number.[46]

Dale Jacobi (54), a Canadian and a former police officer, was also an important Justus ideologue during the standoff.[47]

Russell Landers (44) and Dana Dudley Landers (46) of North Carolina came to Justus Township with their sixteen-year-old daughter, Ashley Taylor. The Landers couple were students of Roy Schwasinger, leader of an anti-federal government group called "We the People," from whom they learned about radical right interpretations of Common Law and the analysis of the American economic system. Both were wanted in Colorado for conspiracy and securities fraud.[48] They taught seminars on the economic system based on their interpretation of the Bible and their belief that God willed Americans to follow the laws given in the Old Testament. Like the other Freemen, they saw their legal and financial battle against the federal government as a holy war.[49] After the Freemen were taken into custody, Dana Dudley Landers asserted in court that she was "a Christian woman," and since the Bible forbade her to speak, her husband would speak for her. But Dana Dudley Landers was an outspoken woman—even when she claimed that she would not speak. Dana Dudley Landers was probably a person to be reckoned with during the standoff negotiations. Their sixteen-year-old daughter, who was variously known as Ashley Taylor, Ashley Landers, or Amanda Michele Kendricks, came out of Justus Township immediately prior to the Freemen's exit.[50]

Other residents of Justus Township when the standoff began were Agnes Stanton (51), her son Ebert Stanton (23), Ebert's wife Val Stanton, and their five-year-old daughter, Mariah. Agnes and her husband William Stanton became interested in Freemen ideas when they began having financial problems. During the standoff, William Stanton was serving a ten-year-term for criminal syndicalism and passing a bad check. Val and

Mariah Stanton left early in the standoff, and Agnes and Ebert surrendered shortly thereafter.[51]

Steven Hance (46), and his two sons, James Hance (24) and John Hance (19), were wanted in North Carolina for assaulting a police officer and for resisting arrest in a chase that began because the Hances were driving a vehicle without a license plate. They faced federal charges for failing to appear in court. After the standoff concluded, Steven Hance emerged as one of the most belligerent Freemen in court, who vehemently rejected the jurisdiction of the federal courts.[52]

Other committed Freemen arrested at the conclusion of the standoff were Jon Barry Nelson (40)[53] and Cornelius John Veldhuizen (49).[54]

Justus Township was the temporary residence of Elwin Ward (55)[55] and his Common Law wife, Gloria Ward (35), also known as Tamara Mangum. With them were two of Gloria's daughters, Jaylynn Joy Mangum (8) and Courtnie Joy Christensen (10). The Wards belonged to a schismatic Mormon sect led by a prophet, John Chaney (39), who taught that girls should be married at puberty. Chaney did not have ties with the Freemen, but his group and the Freemen shared a literalist manner of interpreting the Bible. Gloria Ward was involved in a custody battle with her ex-husband, Steve Mangum, and she faced charges in Utah for felony custodial interference for taking the children out of state. Earlier, Gloria had married her eldest daughter, Ariel, formerly known as Leslie Joy Christensen, to John Chaney. Toward the conclusion of the standoff, Ariel (15), who was in foster care in Michigan, gave birth to John Chaney's child. During the standoff, Chaney was in a Utah prison for marrying his own thirteen-year-old daughter to a forty-eight-year-old follower.[56]

Elwin Ward's Pentecostal background, and Gloria Ward's Mormon background, and their joint involvement in a schismatic Mormon group, indicated that the Wards had beliefs similar to those of the Freemen concerning the Bible and identification with the biblical Israelites, but the Wards were new to the Freemen's revolutionary activities and Christian Identity beliefs. The Wards felt they were led by God to take refuge in Justus Township, and that meant that a message from God might prompt them to come out with Gloria's daughters.[57]

Justus Township was the Clark family farm. The Clark family members were deeply attached to the land and brought to the Freemen group a concern for the sacred land typical of nativist millennial movements. The Clark family members present on the farm during the standoff were the two brothers, Ralph Clark (65) and Emmett Clark (67),[58] Ralph's wife, Kay Clark (65), and Emmett's wife, Rosie Clark (70). At the conclusion of the standoff, the two wives were not charged with any crime and were permitted to drive away. Also present during the standoff was Edwin Clark (45),[59] the son of Ralph and Kay Clark. Edwin's wife, Janet Clark, was not a Freeman and did not stay in Justus Township during the standoff. Janet Clark was permitted to visit Justus Township regularly during the standoff to administer shots to their son, Casey Clark (21), who had a pituitary gland disorder.[60] Janet Clark probably played an important role as intermediary during the negotiations. Richard Clark, the son of Emmett and Rosie Clark, turned himself in shortly after the standoff began.[61]

The members of the Clark family involved in the standoff were Christians with a reverence for the Bible, who were attracted to the Freemen ideology as a means to save their family farm. The Clarks' ultimate concern during the standoff was to preserve their ownership of their land.

The Clarks' attachment to their land resonated with the Christian Identity belief that America was the "promised land." The Clark family farm was located near Jordan, Montana. The name Jordan recalled the purported homeland of white Israelites near the Jordan River in Palestine. Drawing on Christian Identity teachings, the Freemen believed that white Europeans or Scan*din*avians were descendants of Adam and the Israelite tribe of *Dan*, who were promised land in the Jor*dan* region. Justus Township for the Freemen was a sacred space protected by Yahweh, in which the Freemen obeyed Yahweh's laws. Justus Township was the home base the Freemen used to do battle against the sinful outer world that followed Satan.[62] The standoff was brought to a peaceful conclusion in part because the Clark family members decided that their commitment to each other's well-being was greater than their commitment to their land.

Justus Township was the Clark family farm. (Photo courtesy of the United States Justice Department)

The Clark family saga was complicated by the fact that the farm and adjacent lands had been purchased by Dean Clark (29), the son of Richard Clark and the grandson of Emmett and Rosie Clark. Dean Clark thought that by buying the land, he was keeping it within the Clark family, but Emmett Clark and Richard Clark saw Dean as a traitor. During the stand-off, Dean Clark had 14,000 bushels of wheat in storage on the land that he desperately needed to sell, but his father and grandfather had driven him off with a warning not to return. Further, the standoff prevented Dean Clark from doing his spring planting in a timely manner. Dean Clark's ability to pay his mortgage and his own continued ownership of the land was endangered by the Freemen standoff.[63]

The most strongly committed Freemen in Justus Township during the standoff were Skurdal, Jacobi, the Landers couple, and Steven Hance. These people were fully committed to the Freemen understanding of Common Law as deriving from Yahweh and Yahweh's laws in the Old Testament. Their ultimate concern was to reestablish the association of sovereign state republics governed by the pre–Civil War American Constitution. For the Freemen and other Identity Christians, the Fourteenth and other Amendments, giving full rights of citizenship to people of color and women, constituted a "fall" from the divinely revealed Constitution and Bill of Rights, which guarantee the sovereignty of free white men. The Freemen expressed a willingness to die or kill to achieve their ultimate concern.[64] If the Freemen had been pressured during the standoff, the highly committed individuals might have killed the other residents of Justus Township to effect a collective "suicide" and make a statement about their ultimate concern. The Freemen expressed their readiness to do battle with federal agents. The Freemen were willing to be martyrs to spark the "second American Revolution" and to overthrow Babylon, the illegitimate and oppressive federal government and its agencies.

The Montana Freemen—Part of a Euro-American Nativist Movement

In 1996 the Freemen of Justus Township were the most visible portion of a white supremacist, nativist movement in the United States. A *nativist movement* is a millennial movement responding to colonization, either by an outside culture or by a ruling bureaucratic class internal to a culture. The colonized people are economically oppressed, pressured by the government's law enforcement agents and tax collectors, and systematically removed from their land. The oppressed group feels enslaved by the ruling class, and they believe that their ethnic group and way of life are threatened with extinction. Millennial expectations of catastrophe instill hope among the oppressed that the dominant class will be eliminated violently and that the oppressed will be restored to their previous idyllic way of life.[65] Nativist millennialists may attempt to withdraw from the dominant society in order to build their millennial kingdom. If they experience success at building their millennial kingdom, their millennialism may begin to emphasize themes of progress. If they feel persecuted, nativist catastrophic millennialists may wage war to defeat the dominating class.[66] As with other nativist millennial movements, the broad movement that includes the Freemen manifests both options.

Due to the accessibility of the Christian Bible in many areas around the world, members of a number of nativist millennial movements have identified themselves with the Israelites and their salvation history in the Old Testament. Other such Israelites, besides the white American Israelites of Christian Identity, include the self-identified Israelites among the Maoris of New Zealand, Kikuyus and Bantus of Africa, and Native Americans of North[67] and South America.

A nativist millennial movement is a "culture clash" movement.[68] There have been numerous nativist movements among third-world peoples who have reacted to colonization by Europeans with advanced technology and developed economies. The nativist movement that heightened Jewish expectations of a messiah was a response to colonization by the Roman Empire. The contemporary Euro-American nativist movement in the United States, which includes the Freemen, Identity Christians, Neo-Nazis, Odinists (racist neopagans), the Ku Klux Klan, and other white supremacists, is a movement of white Americans who possess education and advanced technology, and who believe that the Aryan (white) race is being subjected to genocide and is being dispossessed of its sacred land by an illegitimate government controlled by foreign and satanic beings identified as Jews. Hence, these American nativists often refer to the federal government as ZOG (Zionist Occupation Government). Jews are seen by many in this nativist millennial movement as conspirators who control the media, Hollywood, the nation's schools and universities, the economy, the Federal Reserve system, and the international banking industry, all with the aim of enslaving and ultimately eliminating the white race. This Euro-American nativist movement demonstrates that education and advanced technology are compatible with nativist millennial thinking.

While this contemporary Euro-American nativist movement has strong roots in the economic crisis that affects rural America as described earlier, it is not restricted solely to farmers and blue-collar workers, and these are not uneducated people. James Aho's survey of Christian Patriots in Idaho found that Patriots were slightly better educated than the average Idahoan and American. The Christian Patriots surveyed by Aho included fewer high school drop-outs than the U.S. population as a whole. The Christian Patriot leaders in Aho's survey had college educations.[69] This indicates, I believe, that a broad range of American citizens feel oppressed by the federal government, its unresponsive bureaucracies, and its burdensome tax system. College-educated people also are experiencing downward mobility or, at least, a lack of upward mobility.

This contemporary Euro-American nativist millennial movement includes the broad right-wing Christian Patriot movement as well as the Christian Constitutionalist and Common Law movements, the militia movements, various Christian Identity churches and communities, tax protesters, anti-abortion extremists, and individuals who identify themselves with the Phineas Priesthood. This white nativist movement also includes non-Christian millennialists who may affiliate with Odinists, Neo-Nazis, or other white supremacist neopagan groups. The non-Christian members of this white nativist movement have been very influential in stirring individuals to take violent actions.[70] Similar to their Christian counterparts in this Euro-American nativist movement, Odinists expect imminent Ragnarök, the final battle that will cleanse the world of evil.[71] My focus in this chapter is on Christian Identity and the Christian Patriot movement.

The Christian Patriot movement involves a range of opinions and orientations to action. Mormon Christian Patriots and Constitutionalists are less likely to be anti-Semitic, while fundamentalist Protestant Christian Patriots are more likely to be anti-Semitic and are more likely to become Identity Christians or to join other white supremacist religions.[72]

Christian Patriots who are Mormons or members of other mainline Christian churches are more likely to participate in electoral politics to return America to being a Christian nation.

Constitution study classes convinced numerous Christian Patriots that the post–Civil War amendments to the Constitution were unconstitutional. Barristers' Inn in Idaho and others taught seminars on Common Law, and taught people how to represent themselves in court (*pro se* litigation). Independent townships, applying a Christian Patriot interpretation of the Common Law, were established in as many as thirty states by the 1990s. Independent posses, and later militias, were formed to enforce the judgments of the Constitutionalist Common Law courts and to be ready to fight the "second American Revolution" against the illicit federal government.

Some persons willing to commit terrorist actions based on Christian Identity doctrines consider themselves to be part of the Phineas Priesthood.[73] Individuals identifying with the Phineas Priesthood aim to kill mixed-race couples, abortionists, homosexuals, all considered polluting to the pure Aryan race. The Bruders Schweigen or The Order, founded by Robert Mathews in Idaho in 1983, was the most well-organized group of men who affiliated with Christian Identity or Odinism, which were committed to violent action. The Order's members waged war against ZOG. Order members were responsible for armored car robberies in Seattle (netting $500,000) and Ukiah, California ($3 million); the murder of Alan Berg, a Denver radio talk show host; the murder of a man they suspected of being an undercover agent; bombing a synagogue in Boise, Idaho; and counterfeiting money. In 1984, Robert Mathews, who was in a house on Whidbey Island in Puget Sound, Washington, was surrounded by FBI agents. A gun battle ensued; Mathews died in the fire that resulted when FBI agents fired flares into the house.[74]

The Christian Constitutionalist movement teaches that the Fourteenth Amendment, extending citizenship to all persons born in the United States or those naturalized, is illegitimate because it was ratified by the Union states in 1866, while the Confederate states were under military occupation. Participants in the Constitutionalist movement, consisting of numerous Constitution study groups, regard all amendments to the Constitution beginning with the Thirteenth Amendment abolishing slavery as invalid. Christian Constitutionalists recognize the validity of what they term the "organic Constitution," consisting of the Constitution and the Bill of Rights. They regard the organic Constitution to be a divinely inspired document to be interpreted in light of the Bible and its laws.[75] The Freemen and other Constitutionalists believe that only Fourteenth Amendment citizens are subject to the laws and regulations of the federal government. White Freemen do not owe their citizenship to the illicit Fourteenth Amendment. By rescinding all contracts with the illegitimate "United States" government, the Montana Freemen claimed to be Common Law Citizens with rights protected by the Constitution of the Republic of Montana and the Constitution of the "united States of America."[76]

The Common Law township movement grew out of Posse Comitatus ("force of the county"), an anti–federal government movement founded in 1969 by Henry L. "Mike" Beach, who was a Silver Shirt (pro-Nazi) in the 1930s, and by William P. Gale, a retired Army colonel. According to Posse Comitatus doctrine, the county is the only valid unit of government. It asserts that the Internal Revenue Service draws its authority from the Eighteenth Amendment, which was not properly ratified. Therefore, the federal income tax is unconstitutional, and payment is optional for individuals. The Federal Reserve System is seen as a private monopoly that is unconstitutional and is controlled by a cabal of Jewish international bankers. The local sheriff can organize posses of armed male citizens to enforce the Common Law derived from the organic Constitution. Mike Beach's "Blue Book," distributed by Posse Comitatus, is a manual for establishing small sovereign townships with their own Common Law courts. Posse Comitatus established a township at Tigerton Dells, Wisconsin. In the 1970s, there were perhaps 12,000 to 50,000 members of Posse Comitatus. Foreclosures on farms made Posse Comitatus attractive to small farmers. Its ideology blames the economic system, the federal government, and the courts—all believed to be controlled by Jews—for the farmers' problems. The townships established Common Law courts, which typically issued threats against conventional law enforcement agents. Posse members wore small gold hangmen's nooses on their lapels indicating the manner in which they aimed to enforce the Common Law. Posse members and the Common Law townships flooded the legal system with documents expressing their interpretation of the Constitution and Common Law, and placed liens on the property of public officials.[77] These tactics were adopted by the Montana Freemen. A related movement is the tax protest group, "We the People," of Roy Schwasinger. Schwasinger taught seminars throughout the country on "how the Federal Reserve was illegitimate, the money system worthless, and debts irrelevant."[78]

While one segment of this contemporary Euro-American nativist millennial movement is exemplified by the Freemen's paper warfare against the federal courts and the national economy, another segment is the militia movement. Christian Patriot Common Law experts, such as the Freemen, are armed and declare themselves willing to resort to physical violence to enforce their legal decisions. The militiamen explicitly advocate the right of American citizens to bear arms to protect themselves against excessive and illegal actions by law enforcement agents. The Branch Davidian and Weaver tragedies are regarded as wake-up calls by many in the militias. Many militia members see themselves as called to fight in a second American Revolution against the tyrannical and illegitimate federal government. The widely distributed *Field Manual of the Free Militia* cites passages in the New Testament to show that Jesus advocated the use of arms to fight an unjust government and teaches that such battles will occur in the endtime tribulation.[79] A variety of terrorist acts committed between 1994 and 1996, were thought to have been committed by radical militia members,[80] or by individuals who regarded themselves as members of the Phineas Priesthood. Citing Jeremiah 51:1 (Yahweh raised up a "destroying wind" against Babylon)[81] and Numbers 25:1-9 (the priest Phineas carried out Yahweh's will by killing an Israelite man and his woman for the sin of race-mixing instigating a massacre of 24,000),[82] persons who identify with the Phineas Priesthood make violent strikes against abortionists, mixed-race couples, Jews, homosexuals, and law enforcement agents in their warfare to establish Yahweh's laws as the law of the land. The novels by William Pierce, *The Turner Diaries* and *Hunter,* also enjoin terrorists to destroy the federal government. *The Turner Diaries* may have inspired Timothy McVeigh to commit the Oklahoma City bombing in 1995.[83]

Philip Lamy has demonstrated that there is a strong secular segment to this Euro-American nativist movement, that is expressed in the pages of the

Soldier of Fortune magazine read by military veterans and a wide range of survivalists, militiamen, and Christian Patriots. *Soldier of Fortune* utilizes apocalyptic images such as the Four Horsemen of the Apocalypse in the book of Revelation (6:1-8) to express the expectation of imminent violence and destruction of the present social order. *Soldier of Fortune* readers are suspicious of the intentions of federal agents toward American citizens and believe they must be armed and prepared to defend themselves and their families. Lamy observed at the 1995 *Soldier of Fortune* convention a bumper sticker that read, "I Love my Country, but I Hate my Government." The most frequently seen bumper sticker declared, "Remember Waco." Many *Soldier of Fortune* readers believe that there is an international conspiracy of power elites (some believe these are Jews) to enslave white Americans to the "New World Order." Secular readers of *Soldier of Fortune* share with their Christian Patriot brothers and sisters the conviction that a violent period is at hand, and military preparedness is vital in order to survive.[84]

An important segment of this contemporary Euro-American nativist movement is Christian Identity. Christian Identity is an intepretation of the Bible and Christianity that provides religious sanction to white supremacy. Identity Christians believe that white people are descendants of Adam and are the true Israelites who migrated to Europe. Not all Identity Christians are racist and anti-Semitic, but those who are believe that Jews are the descendants of Cain (Canaanites), who was begotten by Satan on Eve; people of color are seen as subhuman beings, animals, or the "beasts of the field" in Genesis. Christian Identity doctrines assert that Jesus was a Christian, meaning he was white, and that white supremacy is ordained by God.[85] Jews are regarded as satanic beings who are implementing a worldwide conspiracy to exterminate all Christian (Anglo-Saxon, or Aryan) people. Jews are believed to do this by working in various arenas, including the Zionist Occupation Government (ZOG), the Federal Reserve and international banking, and among the Freemasons, the Illuminati, and communists.[86] During the standoff, the Freemen released a document stating:

> Certain power mad individuals, commonly known today as the Directors of the Board of The Federal Reserve, or the twelve (12) major international banking families, have used the so-called 14th Amendment to commit "legal genocide" upon the class of Common Law Citizens known as the Citizens of the Several States. This has been accomplished by the application of Social Security through fraud, deception and non-disclosure of material facts for the simple purpose of reducing the Union of States to a people once again enslaved to puppet masters, and simply for the gathering of revenue for the profit of the bankers.[87]

The Freemen asserted that "the Common-Law white State Citizens are an endangered species, on the verge of extinction...."[88]

Catastrophic Millennialism

A great deal of the Freemen worldview is derived from the white supremacist religion known as Christian Identity, which identifies Anglo-Saxons with the biblical Israelites. A common Christian Identity claim is that Euro-Americans are the "true" Israelites, Jews are imposters and the children of Satan, and people of color are subhuman. Christian Identity claims the myth of the promised "land of milk and honey"—America—for Euro-Americans. Based on statements found in the Old Testament, Skurdal wrote in his 1994 Edict: "It is the colored people, and the jews, who are the descendants of Cain...when We move into a new land, We are to kill the inhabitants of all the other races...nor are We to allow other races to rule over us."[89]

The Freemen in Justus Township saw themselves as creating a community set apart from sinful Babylon, in which Yahweh's laws given in the Old Testament were obeyed. The New Testament book of Revelation's prediction of the destruction of Babylon and its sinful economic system in the endtime was important to the Freemen. The Freemen hoped that they would defeat the babylonian economic and legal system through their paper warfare, and that their biblically-based society in Justus Township would become the model of life and law for the rest of the nation.[90] Thus the Freemen's hope for Justus Township paralleled the hope embodied in Jonestown; the ideal community could become the model others would follow in creating the millennial kingdom.

The Freemen saw things in dualistic terms: they were fighting a holy war against evil Babylon, and they were armed and threatened violence. If FBI agents had applied intense pressure during the standoff, it would have confirmed the Freemen's belief that the federal government was Babylon. The Freemen threatened to resort to violence and they easily could have found biblical warrant to do so. As Identity Christians, the Freemen believed they were living in the tribulation period, in which Christians must be prepared to defend themselves and/or actively wage war against the satanic government.

Dr. Jean Rosenfeld, one of a team of Religious Studies advisers to the FBI during the standoff, analyzed the Freemen as a nativist movement in a revolution against a perceived foreign colonizing culture. She found the Freemen to have features in common with a Maori millennial movement, Pai Marire ("good and peaceful"), in nineteenth-century New Zealand. Pai Marire was a diverse grassroots movement with several prophets. It alternated between peaceful and violent phases. When civil authorities permitted Pai Marire believers to concentrate on building their millennial kingdom, they were peaceful. When violently oppressed by civil authorities, Pai Marire believers and prophets responded with violence to protect themselves, to establish their millennial kingdom, and to exact vengeance. According to Rosenfeld, "civil police may unwittingly play out the role of God's enemies and elicit a violent response from a community that views itself as allied to God against Satan."[91]

On May 1, 1996, the Freemen told a third-party intermediary that they had made an "affirmation" to Yahweh, that they would not surrender, and that they had been told by Yahweh that an invisible barrier surrounded Justus Township and protected the Freemen from enemies.[92] This belief in divine protection from the oppressor's weapons is typical of nativist millennial movements that feel threatened by the government's armed forces. This belief in divine protection from the superior military power of the oppressing government is essential in encouraging nativists to develop the courage to fight a war against a government with overwhelmingly superior fire power.[93]

Jean Rosenfeld, in her advice to the FBI during the standoff, stressed that a nativist group might defend itself violently against aggression when inhabiting a sacred space set apart from the polluted world by a divinely-sanctioned boundary. Belief that their God had rendered them immune to harm was a typical feature of nativist movements, and when faced with a militant enemy, they would respond according to their own internally consistent worldview, not in a commonplace or "rational" fashion. Over time, when the perceived threat to their existence diminished, even some very violent groups might become benign.[94]

The Freemen were a nativist millennial group that was revolutionary; they saw themselves locked in a battle with Babylon, the American government and economy. Their enemy was identified clearly. If FBI agents had used excessive force in dealing with the Freemen, in all likelihood there would have been loss of life. Had they experienced aggressive opposition, the Freemen could have called upon resources in the Bible to justify their taking violent action.

Events of the Standoff—Avoiding Persecution

There is no doubt that the Freemen, prior to the standoff, felt persecuted by the federal government, the American economy, and related institutions. A key to peacefully concluding the standoff was for the FBI agents to avoid exacerbating the Freemen's sense of persecution.

Since the horrifying Branch Davidian tragedy, scholars had warned the FBI about the danger of provoking religiously committed groups.

Actions were taken by members of the scholarly community to make its expertise more readily available to news reporters, law enforcement agents, and the general public. The executive secretary of the Society for the Scientific Study of Religion (SSSR) wrote to Attorney General Janet Reno on April 29, 1993, advising her of the availability of sociologists with expertise on new religious movements.[95] The American Academy of Religion (AAR) took steps to make reporters affiliated with the Religion Newswriters Association aware of its existence, and to encourage reporters to call the AAR when in need of experts on religion. Dr. J. Phillip Arnold organized the Religion-Crisis Task Force, a group of sociologists, historians of religions, political scientists, and theologians willing to advise law enforcement agents. In November 1995, the executive director of the American Academy of Religion met with FBI negotiators and behavioral scientists, and an FBI negotiator attended a session at the 1995 meeting of the AAR in Philadelphia. In late 1995, Dr. Michael Barkun, a political scientist and expert on millennialism, was asked to be a member of the Select Advisory Commission for the FBI's Critical Incident Response Group. The commission met at the FBI Academy in early 1996 and formulated recommendations. There were quite a few scholars who were anxious to help prevent future Wacos.

On October 20, 1995, I wrote to Attorney General Janet Reno to respond to news reports that changes had been made within the FBI in response to criticism of the handling of the Weaver case. In my letter, I asked why changes had not been made in response to the tragic Branch Davidian case.[96] In response, I received a letter, dated November 20, 1995, from Robin L. Montgomery, Special Agent in Charge of the Critical Incident Response Group (CIRG), FBI Academy, Quantico, Virginia. Montgomery assured me that the FBI was seriously engaged in efforts to deal constructively with future incidents involving religion.[97]

On January 26, 1996, I received a telephone call from Reno's assistant, John Hogan. Reno had asked Hogan to call me because she did not think Montgomery's letter had addressed my concerns completely. Hogan told me that an important change had been made by putting behavioral scientists on an equal footing with the tactical experts on the FBI crisis response team. Reno also had instructed the FBI to bring in outside experts for training sessions on millennial groups.[98] In response, I wrote a letter, dated February 5, 1996, to John Hogan making general remarks on the current status of millennialism studies. On March 7, 1996, I received a telephone call from an FBI agent, asking if I would speak on millennialism at a seminar for the critical incident negotiation team at some point in the future. I agreed, and subsequently I received a letter of confirmation from Robin Montgomery, dated March 21, 1996.[99] The fax number enclosed therein came in handy during the Freemen standoff that began March 25, 1996.

On April 2, 1996, during the Freemen standoff, I sent a fax to Robin Montgomery advising that the FBI should consult Michael Barkun, a political scientist at Syracuse University, because of his expertise on Christian Identity and militia groups, and to utilize his advice in dealing with the Freemen.[100] I received a call back from the FBI Academy saying that the FBI had already received a memo from Dr. Barkun with his recommendations, and that they would call him. Dr. Barkun was in frequent contact with FBI agents, especially between May 8-17, and they sent him information about the Freemen to analyze. After leaving for London about May 18, Barkun continued to be in touch with FBI agents by telephone.[101] The nature of Barkun's recommendations to the FBI were indicated in an interview Barkun gave to Laurie Goodstein of the *Washington Post*, which appeared on April 9, 1996.

> "They've done precisely what they should be doing with a group of this kind, namely being very careful not to act in a way that confirms the group's beliefs," Barkun said. "That suggests that some very important lessons have been learned."[102]

Unlike the Branch Davidians, the Freemen refused to negotiate with the FBI agents, because the Freemen believed that the FBI, as a federal agency, had no legitimacy. By April 4, 1996, a number of initiatives were undertaken to attempt to persuade the Freemen to come out. A granddaughter of Emmett Clark visited the Freemen and delivered a community petition asking them to surrender peacefully. After this, visits by relatives to Justus Township became a normal occurrence. Also on April 4, four Montana state representatives, Joe Quilici (Democrat), John Johnson (Democrat), Karl Ohs (Republican), and Dick Knox (Republican) met with four Freemen. They sat outside on folding chairs and talked. On Saturday, April 6, Val Stanton, who was not charged with any crime, left Justus Township with her five-year-old daughter. Val's husband, Ebert Stanton, and his mother, Agnes Stanton, departed Justus Township on April 11.[103]

This marked the beginning of Representative Karl Ohs's involvement as a third-party intermediary. Val Stanton's father had worked on Ohs's ranch, and Ohs considered Val Stanton to be a second daughter. Karl Ohs (49) continued working as a third-party intermediary to resolve the standoff peacefully. He related to the Freemen as human beings—even as friends. Ohs said, "You can't spend that much time with those people and not become...friends." In an interview given near the end of the standoff, Ohs explained: "I want people to understand and I've made it very clear to the Freemen—I am part of the other system. I believe in the other system, but that doesn't mean to say you haven't got some things here that maybe we should hear and that we can't work out a solution." Ohs reported that in his many visits to Justus Township, he never felt threatened by the Freemen: "Fanatics? I think the people in there are very committed to their cause and thus have become fanatics about it." "They think about nothing else. Every second of every minute of their lives I think this issue...occupies their minds."[104]

Toward the end of April, Randy Weaver, retired Green Beret Colonel James "Bo" Gritz, and retired police officer Jack McLamb travelled to Montana and offered to serve as intermediaries. Randy Weaver was turned down by the FBI. Bo Gritz, who had successfully negotiated Randy Weaver's surrender at Ruby Ridge, and Jack McLamb entered Justus Township on Saturday, April 27. Gritz and McLamb were part of the Christian Patriot movement. Gritz had run for president in 1992 as a Populist Party candidate, and he had founded a separatist community called "Almost Heaven" near Kamiah, Idaho. Also on Saturday, Stewart Waterhouse (37) left Justus Township and was charged with being an accessory after the fact and with felony intimidation.[105]

On Sunday, April 28, Gritz and McLamb brought out of Justus Township a videotape and a document explaining the Freemen's views. FBI agents confiscated the videotape and it was not released to the media. The document asserted that Justus Township was a sovereign entity and not bound by federal laws. Gritz told reporters, "They are willing to walk out—everyone of them—right now if the U.S. government can prove the documents are not the law."[106]

On April 30, in addition to Gritz, the Freemen met with Representative Karl Ohs and state Assistant Attorney General John Conner Jr. to discuss dropping state charges. A proposal was made to the Hance family that federal charges for failing to appear in court would be dropped. A proposal was made to Gloria Ward that the charges relating to child custody would be dropped. The Freemen responded by requesting the presence of a full-time third-party intermediary, and named former Supreme Court nominee Robert Bork or Chief Justice Rehnquist as their choices.

On Wednesday, May 1, Gritz and McLamb angrily gave up on the Freemen and left. Gritz said that the twenty-one people in Justus Township made an affirmation to Yahweh that they would not leave and were told by Yahweh that they were protected by an invisible barrier. The Freemen told Gritz that they would submit themselves only to the judgment of a Common Law grand jury consisting of twenty-three "Freeholders" (defined as "non-14th Amendment citizens," i.e. white males) at least 21 years of age, who were not in debt to anyone and were not employed by the government. Again, the Freemen declared that the FBI had no legal authority. A frustrated state Assistant Attorney General Conner said, "I'm dealing with people who have issues I don't understand. They're convinced of their rightness."[107]

On Thursday, May 2, the Freemen abandoned negotiations with the FBI and communicated directly with the media. Twice the Freemen brought items to the edge of the property for reporters, first a videotape, and second a letter from Robin Montgomery to Edwin Clark requesting a meeting. Montgomery's letter stated that if negotiations did not resume the "FBI will reserve the right to take whatever action it deems necessary to resolve this matter." The Freemen stamped the letter "REFUSAL FOR CAUSE WITHOUT DISHONOR" and wrote on it, "The FBI does not exist as a government agency." Excerpts of the videotape were broadcast on television, depicting Russell Landers wearing a Western shirt and cowboy hat standing in front of the Justus Township seal explaining the Freemen's understanding of Common Law. The Freemen refused to acknowledge the authority of the Montana Bar Association, the Internal Revenue Service, Garfield County, the Justice Department, the State of Montana, and the United States, because they were illegally constituted corporations with no jurisdiction in the Republic of Montana. The FBI was not constitutionally part of the government and was illegally in Montana. Landers alleged that FBI agents had kidnapped LeRoy Schweitzer and Daniel Petersen.[108]

On May 3, Phillip Arnold and I spoke by telephone about the need for the Religion-Crisis Task Force to become involved in the Freemen standoff. Arnold had already spoken with James Tabor, who agreed that the Task Force should attempt to advise the FBI. (See chapter 4 on the role played by Dr. Phillip Arnold and Dr. James Tabor in the Branch Davidian case.) On May 6, Dr. Arnold called an agent at the FBI Academy, offering to assist.

On May 7, I received a call from an agent asking what the FBI should do: Should they tighten the perimeter? I said the FBI should absolutely not do anything that the Freemen would construe as persecution. I stressed that it was important not to initiate a siege with a group that believed God's authority overruled the authority of law enforcement. I said that the FBI should consult with Dr. Arnold of Reunion Institute for his expertise in Bible and apocalyptic groups, Dr. Jean Rosenfeld for her expertise on nativist movements, and Linda Collette, a graduate student writing her dissertation on Christian Identity.[109]

On May 8, I confirmed my advice in a fax to the FBI Academy. Referring to Jonestown, Aum Shinrikyo, and the Solar Temple, I stressed that a group with "this dualistic mindset [good vs. evil, us vs. them] will resort to violence when they believe that they are being persecuted." The violence might be directed toward enemies outside the group, or might be directed inwardly as in group suicide/murder. The violence might take both forms. I noted that the Freemen's belief in a protective invisible shield was typical of the beliefs of violent nativist millennial groups. I mailed a copy of this fax to John Hogan and Janet Reno in the Justice Department.[110] Also on May 8, Phillip Arnold, coordinator of the Religion-Crisis Task Force, sent a fax to Robin Montgomery at the FBI Academy, offering to analyze the data to determine the Freemen's beliefs and help devise a plan for peaceful surrender.[111]

On May 9, 1996, Phillip Arnold, Jean Rosenfeld, and I were put in touch with FBI negotiators in Montana. I spoke with negotiation coordinator Dwayne Fuselier, and he gave me a short description of each of the Freemen, characterizing most of them as not being very religious. After comparing notes with Jean Rosenfeld about her conversation with Fuselier, we agreed that he seemed to want us to conclude that the Freemen were not religious.

When I attempted to call Fuselier on May 10, he was not available. I left a message with another negotiator, but I was not confident that he understood my recommendation. Therefore, I put my recommendation in writing and faxed it to the negotiators with copies by mail to John Hogan and Janet Reno. In this fax I attempted to introduce the discipline of Religious Studies to the negotiators.

> Before I state my recommendation, let me make some explanatory statements about my academic discipline which is Religious Studies. Those of us who are trained in Religious Studies are trained to study other people's worldviews and to understand the content of those worldviews as if from within. In other words, we seek to empathetically understand how reality appears to people possessing a particular worldview. A worldview will be constructed from a variety of elements—ideas, doctrines, content of scriptures, etc. We aim to understand how all those pieces fit together to make what the believer regards as a coherent worldview. Even though we seek to be empathetic about imagining how someone else's worldview appears from within, we are also trained to maintain a critical distance so that we can analyze worldviews. This is the case even when the scholar is studying his or her own worldview. For a good scholar, this critical distance will be maintained even when studying one's own worldview. For instance, there are plenty of Christian scholars who study Christianity, and do an excellent job at it.
>
> Sending in someone like Bo Gritz to mediate, on the surface, appears to have been a good idea, because this is a person who speaks the Freemen's language and understands their worldview. But the problem with Bo Gritz's mediation was that Bo Gritz had no critical distance from the worldview that he shares to a great extent with the Freemen. I suggest that the same problem will

probably arise if other mediators are used who participate in the militia, patriot, or writ writing movements.

On the other hand, sending in mediators who not only do not understand the Freemen's worldview, but who are not trained to study and analyze other people's worldviews, seems unlikely to produce the desired results. I am NOT saying you should no longer permit various mediators to visit the Freemen. I think this process of letting people visit the Freemen is good, because it illustrates that the perimeter is permeable, and it makes the standoff appear not to be a siege. I'm suggesting, however, that it appears unlikely that such people will be able to significantly resolve the standoff.[112]

I concluded the fax by urging the FBI to bring in a scholar to serve as third-party intermediary.

On May 10, 1996, the *Billings Gazette* reported that members of the Eastern Oregon militia were preparing for "Operation Clean Sweep" to defend the Freemen. Walt Hassey asserted that they planned to hit targets outside Montana, but would not harm civilians: "We are not a threat to the people. We are a threat to the government."[113]

On May 11, Jean Rosenfeld sent a fax to the negotiators explaining the Freemen as a nativist movement similar to the Native American Ghost Dance in the nineteenth century. As in other nativist movements, the Freemen were concerned to preserve their sacred land, and to preserve barriers between their pure godly community and the impure outer world. They saw themselves locked in a struggle between good and evil, and believed they had divine favor and protection. Rosenfeld explained that the phenomenon of claiming to be Israelites had occurred cross-culturally in a variety of nativist movements. She cautioned that rogue acts of violence could be committed by members of a group with no authoritative leader. Rosenfeld explained that the Freemen were "ultimately concerned," which meant "they hold certain truths or values so dear they will die for them. This is what makes them different from criminals although they may mistakenly be assessed as mere criminals." Rosenfeld advised the FBI negotiators to assume that all residents of Justus Township were equally religious. She also urged that more data be provided to Religious Studies scholars for analysis.[114] Rosenfeld, by this time, was engaged in locating significant data on the Freemen from a variety of sources available on the World Wide Web. The information provided by the FBI was quite limited.

On Saturday, May 11, the Freemen added a second sentry post in preparation for a possible assault.[115]

Montana state Representative Karl Ohs visited Justus Township on Tuesday, May 14, and on Wednesday Colorado state Senator Charles Duke, a Christian Patriot leader, began his efforts as third-party intermediary. Duke was running in Colorado for the Republican nomination for the U.S. Senate. Representative Ohs remained involved in the negotiations.[116]

On Thursday, May 16, 1996, four Freemen, Edwin Clark, Rodney Skurdal, Russell Landers, and Dale Jacobi met face-to-face with FBI negotiators for the first time; two FBI negotiators, along with Charles Duke, met with the Freemen near the farm's gate. At this time, the media quoted Bo Gritz, advocating a "coordinated nonviolent strike against all four areas [houses] deep on a moonless night" and saying that it "might well result in capture of all 21 occupants without bodily injury to either side."[117]

Also on May 16, Jean Rosenfeld recommended to the FBI that a small team of experts be brought on site to work with negotiators. Rosenfeld specifically recommended that Phillip Arnold be brought to Montana. She explained that to be effective, negotiations had to address the Freemen's "ultimate concerns."[118]

The May 18, 1996, *Billings Gazette* reported Duke excitedly announcing a possible deal between the Freemen and the federal government, but the FBI responded that no deal had been made.[119] The nature of the Freemen's creative proposal was never made public.

FBI agents set up a table and folding chairs on May 18, 1996, for negotiations with the Freemen with Duke as intermediary. Again, Edwin Clark, Skurdal, Landers, and Jacobi were the Freemen who came to negotiate.[120]

Also on May 18, 1996, the *New York Times* carried an article, in which Bo Gritz shared his impressions of the Freemen. He reported that the Freemen were convinced that the federal government was the pawn of Jews—the Zionist Occupation Government (ZOG). The Freemen leaders believed that an FBI attack on them would provoke an American revolution to overthrow the ZOG-dominated government. According to Gritz, "Skurdal announced in a loud voice that their forceful capture would ignite a multimillion-man militia revolution that would sweep ZOG out of America."[121]

On Sunday, May 19, Gloria Ward and her two daughters were seen at the negotiation table with the FBI agents and Duke. But on Monday, the fifth day of talks, the discussion between Duke, three FBI agents, and three Freemen was heated.[122]

On May 20, with the Duke-mediated negotiations obviously breaking down, Jean Rosenfeld sent a fax to Dwayne Fuselier advising that to be successful, the negotiators needed to address the Freemen's ultimate concern, and that offers to drop some charges or to let them tell their story to the media would not be enough to get the Freemen and the children safely out of Justus Township. She contradicted Gritz's calling some of the Justus residents "hostages": "Neither hostage nor criminal models are a sufficient 'fit' in this particular case." Rosenfeld concluded by asking for more information to analyze.[123]

On Tuesday, May 21, it was announced that negotiations had ceased. Duke asserted, "The time for negotiation is over at this point. They need to feel some pain in order to get back to the table." Duke told the media, "In my opinion, the FBI have tried everything possible to come to a peaceful resolution."[124]

On May 21, 1996, I sent a fax to Dwayne Fuselier in Montana advising that taking aggressive action would be counterproductive. "These people have an ultimate concern, something for which they are ready to die if need be. They do not want to die, but they will not give up their ultimate concern, because it is the most important thing in the world to them."[125] I advised Fuselier that he had not provided Religious Studies scholars with enough information to analyze, and I urged him to utilize more fully the expertise of Religious Studies scholars by bringing them on site, providing them with more data, and letting them interpret the Freemen's worldview and ultimate concern for negotiators.[126]

On May 21, 1996, Jean Rosenfeld faxed a memo to the Montana negotiators reiterating a number of points: The Freemen sounded rambling and incoherent, but they had a coherent worldview that made sense to them; confronting a nativist movement would likely provoke violence; the Freemen standoff was not a hostage or a criminal situation; the Freemen had an attitude of ultimacy and they were "ready to live or die for their 'faith'"; negotiations to be successful had to address the Freemen's ultimate concerns. Rosenfeld again recommended that a team of scholars be brought on site to analyze and translate the Freemen's worldview for negotiators; the FBI would never convince the Freemen that their worldview was not true.[127]

On May 22, the Freemen raised an upside-down American flag as a signal of distress and a call for help.[128] Also on May 22, Phillip Arnold sent a fax to Dwayne Fuselier in Montana, urging that the Freemen's views not be assumed to consist of "Bible babble" (see chapter 4), or "mere rhetoric," or attributed to psychological "defects." "If their beliefs about God are not given the primary role their importance demands, all other negotiation techniques and appeals will fail to resolve the crisis." Arnold added, "Current tactics seem to suggest that the Freemen are being told to 'surrender' *despite* their religious beliefs." Arnold offered three final cautions:

A. It is necessary to refrain from reductionistic thinking, which reduces the Freemen beliefs (political and religious) to mere rhetoric and jail-avoidance tactics. For some of them, their beliefs are a life and death matter.

B. It is necessary to realize that "religious" and "ethical" are not synonymous. Freemen may be very "immoral" or "unsavory," but very religious. Religion appears to be the primary button which controls decision making for a number of these "unsavory" people.

C. Any escalation of the use of force will definitely convince the religious Freemen that the enemies of God's true people are coming against them. This will increase religious fervor among them and result in their drawing closer together and hunkering down to withstand the perceived threat, like martyrs for their faith.

Arnold concluded by offering to "analyze firsthand the Freemen's religious motivations in order to facilitate a 'surrender plan.'"[129]

On May 23, 1996, I sent a fax, entitled "ultimate concerns, something to die or kill for" to Dwayne Fuselier in Montana, with copies faxed to John Hogan in the Justice Department, and to the FBI Academy. I defined ultimate concern as "the most important thing in the world, either for an individual or a group," and stressed that even people who appeared to be secular, such as communists or Nazis, had ultimate concerns. The Freemen's ultimate concern, "the restoration of the 'true' constitutional government," was derived from their understanding of the Bible and God's will. The Freemen did not want to die, but they were willing to do so if necessary. "They believe what they are doing is necessary to achieve well-being, if not for themselves, then for their loved ones." It was possible that different individuals in Justus Township had different ultimate goals. For instance, the Clarks appeared to have the ultimate goal of maintaining ownership of their land. I stressed, "Any negotiation with the Freemen has to make offers to them that will enable them to be true to their ultimate goal(s)." Otherwise, the Freemen would not come out. I stressed that if actions taken by the FBI convinced the Freemen of the impossibility of achieving their ultimate goal, the Freemen might choose to resort to violence, rather than give up their ultimate concern. They might commit a group suicide/murder and/or attempt to kill FBI agents. I emphasized that, although the Freemen had committed crimes, it did not mean they were not religious: "They are so committed to achieving their ultimate goal(s) that they view criminal acts as legitimate methods to achieve their ultimate concern(s)." Negotiations to be successful *must* "address the Freemen's ultimate concern(s) and enable the Freemen to remain true to what they deem to be the most important thing in the world."[130]

On May 23, Jean Rosenfeld sent a fax to John Hogan in the Justice Department stating that intermediaries such as Gritz and Duke had no "critical distance" on the right-wing Christian Patriot worldview and that professionals trained to analyze worldviews were needed on site. More information needed to be provided to Religious Studies scholars. Rosenfeld also recommended that the scholars be involved in debriefing after the standoff was resolved "to optimize policy for future events...."[131]

On May 23, the FBI brought in generators in preparation for cutting off electricity to Justus Township. The portable generators were to keep electricity flowing to nearby farms.[132]

On May 24, I spoke with John Hogan by telephone and advised him that the Religious Studies scholars had not been given sufficient data to analyze and that the FBI negotiators had not made optimum use of our expertise. In this conversation, I utilized Anthony F. C. Wallace's term *revitalization movement* to explain that the Freemen were a nativist millennial movement seeking to overthrow an oppressive government in order to return to their idealized golden age. To indicate the manner in which government agents typically react to revitalization movements, I mentioned the execution of Jesus by the Romans because they believed that Jesus was a "Zealot" who advocated the violent overthrow of Roman rule.

On May 24, Representative Karl Ohs rode on horseback into Justus Township and spoke with the Freemen.[133] Arnold, Rosenfeld, and I did not realize it at the time, but Ohs was emerging as the third-party intermediary who could simultaneously empathize with the Freemen's worldview and maintain the necessary cognitive distance to analyze it. That Ohs was able to do this is a tribute to his intelligence, humaneness, and honor. Ohs concluded that Gritz and Duke had failed as intermediaries because they were more concerned with their own political agendas. Ohs, who was running unopposed for his second term in the state House of Representatives, said he had no motive other than to prevent loss of life.[134]

On May 25 in a *New York Times* article, Duke and Gritz warned militiamen and Christian Patriots not to come to the aid of the Freemen. Gritz again called for a "nonviolent" strike against Justus Township and was quoted as saying, "It's time the FBI began to act like the FBI."[135]

Michael Barkun was invited by the FBI to come on-site in Montana, but he was unable to do so because of prior commitments in London.[136] Phillip Arnold was invited to come to Montana. Coincidentally, while Arnold was on-site in Montana from May 28–31, the Freemen refused to communicate with the FBI. FBI agents offered Arnold the chance to speak by telephone with the Freemen in preparation to going inside Justus Township, but the Freemen refused all calls. Arnold served as a liaison with Jean Rosenfeld and other members of the Religion-Crisis Task Force during that time. The FBI did not provide additional information to Jean Rosenfeld directly, but relied on Arnold to communicate with her. Rosenfeld continued to fax her analyses to the FBI.[137]

While in Montana, Arnold was given more information about the Freemen and their views. He was put in touch with Lynn Nielsen, Gloria Ward's sister, and he was able to speak with Janet Clark, who was still making regular visits to Justus Township. Arnold spent a great deal of time discussing the importance of religion and religious worldviews with FBI negotiators. Arnold protested the agents' tendency to discount religion as *only* a cover for illegal activities or as *only* the product of psychological needs. Arnold stressed again that religion was ultimate concern and that the Freemen's beliefs had to be taken seriously for negotiations to be successful. Arnold advised that terms offered to the Freemen had to take into account the Freemen's religious beliefs and ultimate concern.[138]

Prior to cutting the electricity to Justus Township on May 31, 1996, the FBI brought in armored cars and helicopters, stating that they would stand ready in case a rescue became necessary. The June 1 Associated Press report stated: "The FBI stressed that it has continued to consult a variety of non-federal experts in a bid to persuade the Freemen to negotiate a peaceful solution."[139]

The FBI cut the power to Justus Township on Monday, June 3, 1996. Justus Township had its own generator, but it could provide electricity for only a few hours a day. Meanwhile a local rancher was circulating a petition urging the FBI to use "reasonable force" to end the standoff.[140]

A major breakthrough occurred on Thursday, June 6, when Elwin and Gloria Ward left Justus Township with Gloria's two daughters, Jaylynn and Courtnie. What had it taken to get Gloria Ward to exit Justus Township? When Phillip Arnold was in Montana, he had spoken at length with Gloria Ward's sister, Lynn Nielsen. Initially, Nielsen denied that her sister was religious, but after speaking with Arnold, Nielsen went to Utah to ask the jailed John Chaney, the Wards' spiritual leader, to encourage the Wards to come out. Chaney asked for time alone so that he could pray. Afterward he wrote a letter to the Wards saying that God had revealed to him that the Ward family should come out of harm's way. The FBI permitted the letter to be delivered to the Wards inside Justus Township. This revelation from God mediated through the FBI was the primary factor prompting the Wards to come out.

Gloria Ward found that her fortune changed quickly once she was outside Justus Township. To induce Gloria Ward to come out, the Utah state charges were dropped against her, and Lynn Nielsen was given temporary custody of the girls, but on June 7, a Utah judge gave the girls into the custody of Robert Gunn, the father of Courtnie. Gloria Ward angrily predicted that her predicament would adversely affect the outcome of the standoff, but it did not seem to have an influence.[141]

The negotiations with the remaining Freemen, particularly with Edwin Clark, continued. Both the elderly Clark brothers had medical problems, and there was the on-going health problem of Edwin's son,

Gloria Ward (on right) is escorted out of Justus Township with her two daughters, Courtnie Joy Christensen (10) and Jaylynn Joy Mangum (8). Americans who said the FBI should have used force against the Freemen overlooked the fact that children were inside Justus Township. (AP Photo)

Casey. The Clark family finally decided that their ultimate commitment was to each other's well-being instead of to their land. Subsequently in court, Edwin Clark and Casey Clark continued to demonstrate commitment to Freemen ideology, but the Clark family's primary commitment was to each other. Edwin Clark from this point emerged as the Freeman who persuaded the others to leave Justus Township.

How were the other Freemen—the "do or die" ideologically committed Freemen—persuaded to come out? Phillip Arnold had recommended that the FBI bring in as intermediaries attorneys familiar with Freemen Common Law interpretations. On June 10, three attorneys affiliated with the rightwing CAUSE Foundation, Kirk Lyons, Dave Holloway, and Lourie Salley, were brought to Justus Township. In 1993, Kirk Lyons had offered to assist the FBI in the Branch Davidian siege but had been rebuffed. Ever since the beginning of the Freemen standoff, the CAUSE attorneys had been offering to assist the FBI. They were able to serve successfully as third-party intermediaries because they understood and spoke both the language of the Freemen's Common Law and the legal language of the federal establishment. By their account, the three CAUSE attorneys quickly discerned that the Freemen would exit Justus Township only if they had the approval of LeRoy Schweitzer. On June 11, the three attorneys accompanied Edwin Clark as he was flown to Billings, where he met in jail with LeRoy Schweitzer. An unnamed government source told the Associated Press that "Edwin had to become at peace with LeRoy about it. He didn't want to go forward without checking with LeRoy first." Schweitzer approved the five terms for the Freemen's exit, and sent an audiotaped message to his colleagues in Justus Township saying that it was time to take their fight into the courts.[142]

On Wednesday, June 12, a self-assured sixteen-year-old Ashley Taylor, also known as Amanda Michele Kendricks, came out of Justus Township. She looked relaxed with the FBI agents and very happy to be out. But the plan to resolve peacefully the standoff was endangered on June 12, when Dean Clark and a friend drove tractors onto the property and began plowing. They left when FBI agents asked them to stop.[143]

On June 13, 1996, the sixteen remaining Freemen peacefully exited Justus Township. Prior to coming out, they spent the entire day cataloguing and packing up all their papers, evidence for their defense. The boxes were put on a Ryder rental truck driven onto the property by Representative Karl Ohs. Ohs was the person they trusted with their evidence. About 11:00 A.M., Kirk Lyons and Lourie Salley lowered the upside-down American flag and raised a Confederate battle flag taken from the wall of the Freemen's schoolroom. Thus, the CAUSE attorneys signaled to their friends that they had successfully answered the Freemen's distress call; the Freemen were coming out. At about 6:00 P.M., Edwin Clark escorted the Freemen, two at a time, to FBI vehicles. The Freemen did not consider themselves to be surrendering, because they did not acknowledge the authority of the FBI or the federal government. As the Freemen were arrested by the FBI agents, the Freemen delivered arrest warrants to the FBI agents for operating outside the FBI's jurisdiction. Unlike the FBI's treatment of the Branch Davidians in front of the news cameras, the Freemen left with dignity and were not handcuffed, put in leg irons, or dressed in prison clothing. An FBI agent in a Suburban at the end of the caravan discreetly waved a small American flag for the news cameras. After the convoy left for Billings, FBI agents lowered the Confederate flag.[144]

The FBI received immediate public criticism for being "too nice" to the Freemen and for not taking aggressive action, but FBI agents achieved a breakthrough in dealing with a revolutionary nativist millennial group. The FBI avoided exacerbating the Freemen's dualism (us versus them perspective) and sense of persecution, and they found a way for the Freemen to be taken into custody while simultaneously permitting the Freemen to preserve their allegiance to their ultimate concern.

The Millennial Goal Preserved

The Freemen were never made to feel that it was utterly impossible to achieve their ultimate concern. After the angry departures of Bo Gritz and

Charles Duke, the Freemen realized that the Christian Patriot militias were not going to come to their aid, and therefore they would not be able to ignite the second American Revolution. FBI agents maintained a low-key presence and applied pressure cautiously. The primary reason the Freemen agreed to come out of Justus Township was that they were enabled to do so in a manner in which they could remain true to their ultimate concern. They did not surrender to the authority of the United States's federal government. The Freemen did not abandon their battle to establish the true "united States" consisting of sovereign state republics and townships; they merely changed the venue of their fight from Justus Township to the federal courts.

After the resolution of the standoff, CAUSE attorney Kirk Lyons revealed to the press the five terms that had been negotiated:

1. Representative Karl Ohs would take custody of the Freemen's evidence and publish a signed statement to that effect in the three Montana newspapers.

2. Each of the Freemen who wished an attorney's assistance would retain 51 percent control of his or her own case with co-counsel. Co-counsel would have to agree to be sworn in according to the Freemen's Common Law system, and swear to fight for "unfettered and unobstructed subpoena power."

3. The federal government would not oppose bond for Emmett and Ralph Clark if their health warranted release from prison.

4. Supporters and co-counsel would work to ensure that the incarcerated Freemen could meet together.

5. Arraignment would be with co-counsel after being sworn in.

Lyons reported that CAUSE Foundation attorneys would not represent the Freemen, but that they had agreed to look for attorneys with whom the Freemen could work.[145] As one official summarized the deal, "They wanted to choose their own public defenders outside the government system and control their own evidence—which of course were things they were already entitled [to] under the law."[146] Once assured they would retain control over their court defenses, and that their evidence, or what I would term their "scripture,"[147] was in safekeeping, the Freemen came out of Justus Township to argue in court that the federal legal system was illegitimate—just as other Freemen were already doing. The Freemen's battle against Babylon would be fought within the belly of the beast—the federal court system.

During the Freemen standoff, a student of LeRoy Schweitzer, Elizabeth Broderick, who had been teaching seminars on Common Law and the federal financial system in southern California, was charged and brought to trial. On April 25, Elizabeth Broderick and four others were arrested and indicted. When she appeared in court, Broderick threw the indictment on the floor and denied that the court had jurisdiction over her.[148] This type of defiant and dramatic refusal to cooperate with the legal process would be displayed also by the Montana Freemen.

In their first courtroom appearance on June 14, 1996, in Billings, the fourteen Freemen pointed out that the yellow-fringed American flag in the courtroom was "a military flag with an [sic] maritime/admiralty jurisdiction under which no common law rights to the people exist."[149] Steven Hance declared, "This is not my flag, and this is not my court." Judge Robert M. Holter retorted, "My brother died for that flag." Steven Hance also asserted, "My venue is the common law and my only lawgiver is Yahweh." All the Freemen except Ralph Clark refused to accept court-appointed attorneys. Rodney Skurdal vehemently renounced U.S. federal authority over him and claimed Common Law rights. Dale Jacobi attempted to argue, but the judge cut him off by saying, "I run a tight ship. I do the talking around here." Russell Landers wore a red-white-and-blue stars-and-stripes shirt to court, and Dana Dudley Landers asserted, "I am a Christian. My flag is red, white and blue, it's an American flag. The holy Scriptures are my law. I'm not familiar with your tribunals." Cherlyn Petersen was close to tears.[150]

On June 20, 1996, U.S. Magistrate Richard Anderson arraigned Dale Jacobi, Casey Clark, Ralph Clark, Rodney Skurdal, Cherlyn Petersen, and Emmett Clark. Casey Clark told the judge that he wanted to stay in jail: "I don't trust Nick Murnion [Garfield County attorney]. I ain't going nowhere." The judge ordered that Casey Clark be held in Yellowstone County jail until trial. Ralph Clark refused to enter a plea, but permitted his court-appointed attorney to speak for him. Rodney Skurdal objected to the judge reading the indictment, saying, "I did not give you power of attorney." The judge said, "That is true," and read the indictment, after which Skurdal replied, "I charge you with one count of perjury and one count of treason." Dale Jacobi voiced his objection vehemently, "I didn't want to go to Australia and have a kangaroo court." He said to the judge, "I hope your mother is really proud of you...." Jacobi was removed from court and taken to a holding cell.[151]

The June 25, 1996, hearing before U.S. Magistrate Richard Anderson was raucous. Steven Hance threatened the judge, "You're going down, son." As Hance was led from the courtroom, he shouted, "Contempt? That's not a strong enough word!" Edwin Clark peacefully stated, "I stand on my objection that you have no jurisdiction. So I will make no plea." Jon Barry Nelson was ejected from the courtroom and taken to a holding cell.[152]

Also on June 25, Gloria Ward represented herself in a Utah courtroom in an attempt to regain custody of her two daughters. Ward argued that she was a law-abiding woman, "I haven't even had a ticket in my life, let alone any criminal activity." Ward noted the yellow fringe on the court's flag saying that it indicated an admiralty court subject to the Emergency War Powers Act of 1933, and that act gave custody to mothers who were neither immoral or unfit. The judge retorted, "Fringe or no fringe, this court is not a military tribunal or an admiralty court. It is a court of law of the state of Utah."[153]

In a Billings courtroom on July 10, 1996, Steven Hance again was removed and taken to a holding cell. Hance objected to being represented by a court-appointed attorney.[154]

On July 17, 1996, a courtroom drama unfolded that demonstrated the power of the Freemen worldview to interpret reality differently from conventional views. This incident prompted jubilation nationwide among Christian Patriots because it was seen as a significant Common Law victory.

U.S. District Judge James M. Burns decided to get acquainted with the Freemen in groups of six. He appeared in the courtroom without his judge's robes, and he told the Freemen about his personal background. Burns stressed the importance of civil behavior, and the Freemen spoke respectfully. At these sessions, a number of the Freemen appointed LeRoy Schweitzer as their counsel. The news reporter noted that during the July 17 meeting, Schweitzer, "stood, declared himself chief justice of their supreme court and started to talk about extradition proceedings." Judge Burns interrupted him and moved the conversation to other matters. The reporter noted that "Schweitzer and the judge seemed to establish a rapport."[155]

Subsequently, Schweitzer as "chief Justice" of the "united States of America" issued a "Protective Order of Release" to "hearing officer James M. Burns" to release the Freemen and transport them back "to our Church (asylum) state."[156] The word was put out on a World Wide Web site maintained by a Freeman in Alaska, that because Judge Burns had appeared with no robes he had acknowledged the authority of Schweitzer as chief justice of Justus Township's Common Law court: "We have Won a major step in the road of thousands of steps to restoration of the Common Law!!!!!!! Say a prayer tonight for the Republic!"[157] On July 24, 1996, the *Billings Gazette* reported that it had received excited calls from people in California, Florida, Oklahoma, and North Carolina, who had heard on radio shows or had received faxes that the Freemen had won their cases and were being released. These reports were denied by the Montana attorney general and the Yellowstone County sheriff, the latter having been appointed by Schweitzer as special bailiff and ordered to appear before the Freemen's supreme court to release the Freemen.[158]

A Christian Patriot writer, J. Patrick Shannan, subsequently reported how the incident was viewed by the Freemen.

On Wednesday, July 17, 1996, six justices were seated in a Billings, Montana, courtroom and became the first common law grand jury to be heard in 135 years in America. Their purpose was to pass judgment over a lower jurisdiction. With apparent deference, Federal District Judge James Burns appeared on the bench without his black robe in the United States Courthouse to direct the proceedings. After an introductory statement he yielded to the superior court in the charge of Chief Justice Leroy Schweitzer.

The other five justices were Stuart Waterhouse, Russ Landers, Elwin Ward, Rod Skurdal, and Emmitt [sic] Clark. They flashed a smile of pride each time Judge Burns referred to their old friend, Leroy, as "Chief Justice Schweitzer." In a complete turnaround, Burns recognized the authenticity of the common law court while insinuating that even he was disappointed in the American public for falling into a slumber and allowing the nation to reach the point it has. Chief Justice Schweitzer then took over the proceedings and presented facts to the board of the other five justices. He admonished the prosecution attorneys not to object, because "I will only overrule you."

All of the names above are those of six of the Freemen arrested last month and incarcerated without bail by the federal judiciary. The common law venue is what they had been asking for since long before any confrontation with law enforcement. Amazingly, it was granted.

Chief Justice Schweitzer cited the national Constitution and that of Montana, and dozens of sections from USC Titles 26 and 28, and supplemental United States Codes to prove the judicial authority of this court to act. The justices conferred for a short time before issuing the order of this superior court *to abort the forthcoming trial of the Freemen by the federal judiciary and to release them from custody. This meant that the 22 American nationals had now been acquitted of all charges,* and unless someone from the federal side of this legal fracas could quickly find something unlawful about this proceeding, this common law grand jury decision would prevail.

The following Monday, July 22nd, the written order of this court was served upon the Yellowstone County Sheriff, the clerk of the county court, and the aforementioned District Judge James

M. Burns. The sanguine Freemen expected to be released in a matter of days. (Emphasis in the original)[159]

Other Christian Patriots across the nation were in various ways battling Babylon, and federal agents were busy attempting to contain the revolution. At the end of June 1996, the Texas attorney general filed suit against twenty-six leaders of the Republic of Texas, who were flooding Texas courts with thousands of liens and documents.[160] In early July 1996, twelve members of the Viper Militia were arrested in Phoenix, Arizona, for allegedly plotting to blow up federal buildings. On July 18, 1996, the *New York Times* reported that about 600 New York City employees had made false declarations on their W-4 forms so that no federal or state taxes were withheld from their paychecks. Of these people, fifteen were city housing police officers who had declared up to 99 dependents on their W-4 forms. Others included city police officers and correction officers. Some claimed they owed no taxes because they lived in the Republic of New York. In court, some of the officers stated that they did not recognize the court's authority; they were not citizens as defined by the federal tax code. Other officers refused to be fingerprinted or have their photos taken, and they refused to give their home addresses and telephone numbers. A detective, Jose Lugo, who had recently served federal warrants and had the job of arresting and booking criminals, said, "I have no standing in this court. I am not here voluntarily. I have committed no crime. This court has no jurisdiction, and I demand to be released immediately."[161] At the end of July 1996 in Seattle, eight people including four militia members were charged with constructing pipe bombs and converting rifles into automatic weapons in preparation for war. During the hearing, William Stanton (not the convicted Montana Freeman) objected to the yellow-fringed American flag in the courtroom.[162]

Once they were in federal custody, the Freemen's utilization of their Common Law was excluded. On August 13, 1996, U.S. District Judge James M. Burns stated that documents filed for the Freemen by sympathizers were "bunkum," ordered that they be removed and that future attempts to file Freemen Common Law documents be refused. Warren Stone, who had been filing documents for the Freemen, despaired, "We've lost our law."[163] Repeatedly, whenever a Freeman spoke up to defend himself with the Freemen Common Law, he was removed from the courtroom to a holding cell where he watched on a closed-circuit television a court-appointed attorney represent him.

The Freemen's papers stored in the Ryder rental truck were seized, and Judge Burns hired an expert to computerize the documents' contents so they could be available to defense attorneys.[164] After the documents were organized and saved on CD-ROMs, audiotapes, and videotapes, they were offered to the Freemen for use in preparing their cases.

In September 1996, LeRoy M. Schweitzer was convicted by a federal jury of failing to file income tax forms in the 1980s. Schweitzer defended himself by arguing that as an "American National who [had] expatiated himself from the United States, he was not subject to the jurisdiction of the federal government or its court system." Schweitzer attempted to enter as evidence various Common Law documents including the Bible and an $8 million lien against the judge. The judge refused to admit these as evidence, prompting Schweitzer to declare, "This court is a sham proceeding." In turn, the judge declared Schweitzer's arguments as having "no more bearing in law than an ounce of sand."[165]

In 1997, it was clear that federal agents were continuing to work to contain the second American Revolution. In January it was reported that federal authorities had arrested or were investigating 151 people with Freemen ties in twenty-three states. Many of these persons had taken classes with LeRoy M. Schweitzer, in which he taught that the banking system was illegal. These individuals had issued financial instruments totaling $2.17 billion. In February, two men were convicted in California for utilizing Freemen financial documents.[166] In Seattle, evidence was presented in the U.S. District Court in the trial of members of the Washington State Militia that they had planned to "go to war" with the federal government if it took aggressive action against the Freemen during the standoff. In March, three Christian Patriots from Sandpoint, Idaho, linked to Christian Identity and calling themselves "ambassadors of the kingdom of Yahweh," were put on trial in Spokane, Washington, for twice robbing a U.S. Bank branch and pipe-bombing a newspaper office and a Planned Parenthood clinic, all in Spokane. They were found guilty.[167] In June 1997, the FBI released to the press copies of two letters signed by the "Army of God" declaring "*total war*" on federal agents, "the ungodly communist regime in New York and your legaslative-bureaucratic [sic] lackey's [sic] in Washington." One letter concluded with, "Death to the New World Order." The Army of God was a name used by anti-abortion militants since the 1980s. FBI agents speculated that the Army of God letters were probably linked to the perpetrator(s) of three bombing incidents in the Atlanta area: the Centennial Olympic Park bombing in summer 1996; the bombing of a family planning and abortion clinic on January 16, 1997; and the bombing of a lesbian bar on February 21, 1997.[168] In July, five men and two women with militia connections were arrested and charged with plotting and arming themselves to attack U.S. military bases beginning with Fort Hood at Killeen, Texas, where they believed United Nations troops were stationed preparing to take control of America.[169]

On January 23, 1997, U.S. District Judge James M. Burns asked the Freemen if they were ready for trial, and most of them replied that they still did not acknowledge the federal court's jurisdiction over them. Seventeen of the twenty-four defendants were representing themselves, but only Dana Dudley Landers was working on her defense by utilizing the Freemen documents that had been put on 40 CD-ROMs, 5,000 audiotapes, and 172 videotapes.[170]

Russell Landers was tried in a North Carolina U.S. District Court beginning on January 14, 1997. On the first day of trial, Landers came to court waving a postage stamp with the American flag on it, saying, "I'm here under my American flag of peace. Since I don't see any flag in the room, I brought my own with me."[171] LeRoy Schweitzer, identifying himself as "chief justice LeRoy Michael of Justus Township," testified in Landers's North Carolina trial. Schweitzer explained that the Freemen regarded their "comptroller warrants" as valid documents. "'I explicitly told the people the warrants were good and why they were good,' he said. 'We had the proof. How could they not believe?'" Schweitzer denied that the Freemen had plans to kill anyone. But Schweitzer explained that the Freemen could make "lawful arrests" and after due process a person could be executed for treason. "'Lawful arrests are part of the supreme court duties,' he said. 'But only under lawful process. We do everything lawful.'"[172] Russell Landers also faced a trial in Montana.

In January 1997, there were news reports about the Republic of Texas (RoT), which claimed to be a sovereign nation, led by Richard L. McLaren (43) in west Texas. McLaren filed liens against Texas Governor George W. Bush, state officials, businesses, and individuals, and issued drafts drawn on the Republic of Texas Trust. When a reporter told McLaren that state officials considered his activities "paper terrorism," McLaren retorted, "This is not paper terrorism. It's a paper war. It's our only real ability to fight." McLaren warned the reporter, "If they [the feds] try to cut this embassy off, there will be a military reprisal, I promise you. Within six hours, probably 2,000 men will hit this site to defend the Republic."[173] The Republic of Texas had a chief of security, and militia members lived nearby. McLaren's computer screen displayed two messages:

Rule #1: Texas is an independent nation.
Rule #2: We will never surrender.[174]

Information on how to become a citizen of the Republic of Texas provided at a web site expressed the following ultimate concern:

Becoming a Citizen of the Republic vests you with all the rights and freedoms of Citizenship, as well as placing you under the jurisdiction of the Common Law. You will then experience lib-

200 HOW THE MILLENNIUM COMES VIOLENTLY

erty and freedom, rather than a life filled with oppression, regulation, and government red tape.[175]

On April 27, 1997, a standoff ensued between McLaren's Republic of Texas and Texas Rangers. When RoT members were arrested, other RoT members retaliated by forcibly breaking into the home of two neighbors (whom they identified as FBI informants and as enemies), and took them into custody. After a peaceful exchange of prisoners between the RoT and the Texas Rangers occurred, the standoff continued. The standoff concluded on May 3, 1997, when McLaren and the head Texas Ranger signed a cease-fire agreement that promised that McLaren would be given the opportunity to argue his case for Texas sovereignty in a federal court. The cease-fire agreement resolved the RoT standoff quickly, because it permitted McLaren to maintain his commitment to his ultimate concern, even while being taken into custody by the Texas Rangers. McLaren and other members of the Republic of Texas continued their efforts to have Texas recognized as a sovereign state.[176] Two RoT men fled into the countryside before McLaren was taken into custody. Mike Matson (43) was killed in a confrontation with Texas law enforcement agents on May 5, 1997. Richard Frank Keyes III (22) was taken into custody by FBI agents on September 19, 1997.[177]

During 1997, attorneys and judges in Yellowstone County, Montana, noted an increase in the number of incarcerated defendants dismissing their court-appointed attorneys and conducting their own defenses according to the principles of Freemen Common Law. The Freemen in Yellowstone County jail were teaching their understanding of Common Law to other inmates, who were charged with a variety of crimes. According to Yellowstone County Public Defender Sandy Selvey, "They read the statutes very literally but don't know how to interpret." U.S. Attorney Sherry Matteucci said, "These ideas are very, very, almost seductive to incarcerated individuals," because they purported to give autonomy to those who felt helpless at being imprisoned and charged with crimes. Matteucci said that prison inmates were entitled to discuss ideas, but predicted, "I think the attraction to these ideas will diminish as people continue to be unsuccessful in their application." Defendants in other parts of the United States likewise attempted to utilize Freemen Common Law to escape their difficulties. Some of these defendants were Native Americans and African Americans.[178] Freemen Common Law methods, a type of imitative magic, could be extrapolated from the racist Christian Identity ideology and utilized to attempt to secure well-being by a variety of oppressed persons.

Early in May 1998, Freemen supporters attempted to utilize Common Law magic again to obtain the release of the Freemen scheduled for trial in U.S. District Court beginning on May 26, 1998. Four men claimed to be special marshals and gave the Yellowstone sheriff "appointment papers" and a list of the Freemen to be "self deported back to the great state of Montana, Garfield County." The sheriff refused to comply in releasing the Freemen from jail.[179]

The Decision Not to Commit Violence and Subsequent Developments within the FBI

During the 1996 Freemen standoff, the FBI negotiators tended to continue to interpret the Freemen according to their familiar FBI worldview, which discounted religious talk as being a "cover" for criminal activities or as *only* an expression of psychological needs and pathology. FBI agents continued to want to use punitive measures that work when applied to criminals. The Freemen were fortunate that the standoff occurred during a presidential election year and that Attorney General Janet Reno was determined to keep the standoff nonviolent. It was likely that FBI agents consulted outside experts on religion upon orders from the Justice Department.

The persistent advice given by Barkun, Arnold, Rosenfeld, and myself, that aggressive action not be taken against the Freemen and that the Freemen's religious worldview be taken seriously, paid off. The Freemen were *not* severely pressured to the point of despair in achieving their ultimate concern. Ways finally were found for the Freemen to surrender without compromising their commitment to their religious goal. This was a tremendous breakthrough for law enforcement—to refrain from wiping out a revolutionary nativist millennial group with its clear challenge to civil authority. The Freemen were offered terms that permitted them to remain true to their ultimate concern and exit Justus Township and be taken into custody. The Freemen believed that they had received assurance that they would be able to continue their battle against the federal government in the federal courts.

The successful terms offered to the Freemen permitted them to remain true to their ultimate concern and be taken into custody.[180] The Freemen standoff was resolved peacefully because the Freemen believed that they had the nonviolent means to achieve their ultimate concern after leaving Justus Township. FBI agents, in accordance with our advice, had refrained from taking aggressive actions against a millennial group possessing a dualistic, apocalyptic worldview.

For some time after the Montana episode, the signs were ambiguous about whether FBI agents realized the significance of religion in resolving the Freemen standoff peacefully. The roles played by Barkun, Arnold, Rosenfeld, and myself were not mentioned by FBI agents to the media. In an interview given to the Associated Press, Dwayne Fuselier did not mention the importance of understanding religion in peacefully concluding the standoff.[181] But the Religious Studies scholars each received letters from Robin Montgomery thanking us for our input, and Mr. Montgomery verbally declared to Dr. Arnold that our method (taking religion seriously) "works."[182] FBI consultants attended the national meetings of the Society for the Scientific Study of Religion (SSSR) and the American Academy of Religion (AAR) in November 1996, and I was asked to compile a list of religion scholars for the FBI. The relatively speedy resolution of the Republic of Texas standoff suggested that lessons might have been learned, by the FBI agents, about how to deal with ultimately concerned persons. (Texas Rangers were in charge of the RoT standoff, but they were advised by FBI agents.[183]) Subsequently, however, FBI negotiators told Jayne Seminare Docherty, a conflict resolution expert, that they found the Religious Studies advice to be irrelevant to resolving the Freemen standoff, and that they found that the Religious Studies scholars required "high maintenance" because we kept asking for more data to analyze.[184]

To explore the issue further, I organized a Special Topics Forum for the 1998 meeting of the American Academy of Religion in Orlando, Florida, entitled "Believers, Law Enforcement Agents, and Religion Scholars: Communicating across Worldviews of Religious and Professional Disciplines."[185] I invited the FBI to send a negotiator to participate on this panel, but the invitation was declined.

On June 5, 1998, Barbara DeConcini, executive director of the American Academy of Religion, Eugene Gallagher, and I met in Washington, D.C., with Roger Nisley, the current director of the Critical Incident Response Group, and other agents. In this productive meeting, the agents said they were receptive to using Religious Studies scholars as advisers and as "worldview translators"[186] in cases involving religious groups. I was surprised and pleased when I saw the agents smiling and their heads nodding when I discussed "ultimate concern."

FBI agents attended the 1998 meeting of the American Academy of Religion where they attended sessions and engaged in conversations with Religious Studies scholars. Also in 1998, four Religious Studies scholars visited the FBI Academy in three separate visits. Ian Reader is an expert on Aum Shinrikyo, Massimo Introvigne is an expert on European and American new religions, Jean-François Mayer is an expert on the Solar Temple, and James T. Richardson is a sociologist of new religious movements. There were additional meetings between scholars and FBI agents in 1999.

These face-to-face meetings between FBI agents and Religious Studies scholars have begun to promote communication across our divergent professional worldviews. Given the nature of the institution that is the FBI, the agents will determine the extent to which they make use of the Religious Studies expertise that is relevant to their work. The peaceful resolution of the Freemen standoff is a breakthrough and major accomplishment for law enforcement agents dealing with millennial groups. If FBI and other law enforcement agents actively develop professional contacts with scholars of the religions, Religious Studies advice will be useful to them as they attempt to avoid future Wacos.

Notes

1. James Brooke, "Some Freemen Are Called Hostages of the Leaders," *New York Times* (AOL), May 18, 1996.
2. J. Patrick Shannan, *The Montana Freemen: The Untold Story of Government Suppression and the News Media Cover-Up* (Jackson, Miss.: Center for Historical Analysis, n.d.), 32.

    According to *Webster's New World Dictionary* a *lien* is "a legal claim on another's property as security for the payment of a just debt."
3. Jeffrey Kaplan, *Radical Religion in America: Millenarian Movements from the Far Right to the Children of Noah* (Syracuse, N.Y.: Syracuse University Press, 1997), 49-53.

    Christian Identity theology developed out of nineteenth-century British Israel theology, which claimed that the British constituted one of the lost tribes of Israel. Both theologies were developed by a number of theorists ranging from philo-Semitic British Israel thinkers to anti-Semitic American Christian Identity thinkers. North American Christian Identity achieved its full expression after World War II. See Michael Barkun, *Religion and the Racist Right: The Origins of the Christian Identity Movement*, rev. ed. (Chapel Hill: University of North Carolina Press, 1997).
4. Anthony F. C. Wallace, "Revitalization Movements," *American Anthropologist* 58, no. 2 (April 1956): 264-81; Vittorio Lanternari, *The Religions of the Oppressed: A Study of Modern Messianic Cults*, trans. Lisa Sergio (New York: Alfred A. Knopf, 1963); Michael Adas, *Prophets of Rebellion: Millenarian Protest Movements against the European Colonial Order* (Chapel Hill: University of North Carolina Press, 1979).

    I find Wallace's definition of *revitalization movement* to be too broad to be of great use. Wallace uses that phrase to refer to any new worldview articulated by any individual (guru, prophet, messiah, buddha) that revitalized a culture. Wallace considers Buddhism as articulated by that tradition's founder, Gautama Buddha, to be a revitalization movement. Buddhism in its origins was not a millennial movement, although Buddhist forms of millennialism developed later in the tradition. Early Buddhism was a fresh approach to the problem of suffering (which all religions address) that was simultaneously innovative and continuous with the Hindu tradition out of which Buddhism developed.

    Revitalization movement is most often used by scholars (for example, Adas) to refer to what I term in this book a *nativist millennial movement* or simply *nativist movement*.
5. For example, see Christine Steyn's discussion of the Xhosa Cattle-Killing movement in South Africa in "Millenarian Tragedies in South Africa: The Xhosa Cattle-Killing Movement and the Bulhoek Massacre," and my discussion of the Xhosa culture as fragile in "The Interacting Dynamics of Millennial Beliefs,

Persecution, and Violence," in *Millennialism, Persecution, and Violence: Historical Cases*, ed. Catherine Wessinger (Syracuse, N.Y.: Syracuse University Press, 2000).

6. See Christine Steyn's discussion of the massacre of the Israelites at Bulhoek, South Africa, in "Millenarian Tragedies in South Africa," 185–202; and Michelene E. Pesantubbee's discussion of the massacre of a Lakota Sioux band at Wounded Knee in "From Vision to Violence: The Wounded Knee Massacre," in Wessinger, *Millennialism, Persecution, and Violence*, 62–81.

7. In *Millennialism, Persecution, and Violence*, the Freemen are discussed in Jean E. Rosenfeld's chapter, "The Justus Freemen Standoff: The Importance of the Analysis of Religion in Avoiding Violent Outcomes," 323–44. Other revolutionary nativist movements discussed in *Millennialism, Persecution, and Violence* are the Russian Old Believers by Thomas Robbins, the Taiping Revolution by Scott Lowe, the German Nazis by Robert Ellwood, and American Neo-Nazis by Jeffrey Kaplan. American Neo-Nazis and the Montana Freemen are cousins in the contemporary Euro-American nativist millennial movement discussed here.

8. Freemen, "Argument in Support of Notice to Abate/Etc. Attached Here by Reference and Made an Official Part of This Record, Nunc Pro Tunc," in Shannan, *Montana Freemen*, 101-4.

9. Allen D. Sapp, "Ideological Justification for Right Wing Extremism: An Analysis of the Nehemiah Township Charter Document," Center for Criminal Justice Research, Central Missouri State University, 1996; Patrick Minges, "Apocalypse Now! The Realized Eschatology of the 'Christian Identity' Movement," *Union Seminary Quarterly Review* 49, nos. 1-2 (1995): 83-107. I thank Jean Rosenfeld for forwarding these articles to me.

10. Adas, *Prophets of Rebellion*, 156.

11. Adas calls these millennial movements "revitalization" movements.

12. Adas, *Prophets of Rebellion*, 42, 63, 75-91, 115, 136.
     Based on the nativist movements that he studied (the Java War of 1825-30, led by Prince Dipanagara; the 1930-32 movement in Burma, led by Saya San; the Maji Maji rebellion initiated in 1905 in German East Africa, and led by Kinjikitile Ngwale; the Munda uprising in India led by Birsa; the Pai Maire movement among the Maori of New Zealand, initially led by Te Ua Haumene), Adas believes the prophet is "*the* critical determinant" in the development of a nativist movement. I disagree on this point, because no single prophet or messiah has yet arisen in the amorphous Euro-American nativist movement discussed in this chapter.

13. Adas, *Prophets of Rebellion*, 77.

14. Joel Dyer, *Harvest of Rage: Why Oklahoma City Is Only the Beginning* (Boulder, Colo.: Westview, 1997). I thank Jean Rosenfeld for kindly providing me with this book.

15. Dyer, *Harvest of Rage*, 170.

16. Dyer, *Harvest of Rage*, 38.

17. Mark Pitcavage, "Every Man a King: The Rise and Fall of the Montana Freemen," modified May 6, 1996, <http://www.greyware.com/authors/pitman/freemen> [7-8]. This document was kindly forwarded to me via email by Phillip Lucas. Page numbers are my own because this document was downloaded from the Internet. Therefore I indicate page numbers in brackets.

18. Pitcavage, "Every Man a King," [9], [11-12].

19. Pitcavage, "Every Man a King," [12-13].

20. Pitcavage, "Every Man a King," [13-14].

21. Pitcavage, "Every Man a King," [15-17].

22. "Weaver moving to state," *Billings Gazette Online*, June 1, 1996; David Johnson

(*New York Times*), "Study: FBI violated rules in standoff," *New Orleans Times-Picayune,* December 14, 1994, A-4; Associated Press, "Informant denies he tricked Weaver," *Atlanta Journal-Constitution,* September 9, 1995, A-7; Pete Yost (Associated Press), "Militant's claim disputed by ATF," *New Orleans Times-Picayune,* September 8, 1995, A-19; David Johnston, "Report Shows FBI Officials Blocked Access to Documents," *New York Times* (AOL), July 16, 1995; Pierre Thomas and Ann Devroy, "Probe of FBI's Idaho Siege Reopened, Official Accused," *Washington Post* (CompuServe), July 13, 1995; Tom Morganthau, Michael Isikoff, and Bob Cohn, "The Echoes of Ruby Ridge," *Newsweek,* August 28, 1995, 25-28; Jess Walter, "'Every Knee Shall Bow': Exclusive Book Excerpt," *Newsweek,* August 28, 1995, 28-35; Jess Walter, *Every Knee Shall Bow: The Truth and Tragedy of Ruby Ridge and the Randy Weaver Family* (New York: HarperPaperbacks, 1995), 193, 201-12, 218-24, 230-32, 238-46, 267, 348-55, 440, 442, 453; Gerry Spence, *From Freedom to Slavery: The Rebirth of Tyranny in America* (New York: St. Martin's Press, 1993), xix-xx, 11-14, 30, 30-37.
    After Ruby Ridge, FBI officials in Washington covered up just who had approved the altered rules of engagement. No one stepped forward to admit they had read and approved the revised rules of engagement. E. Michael Kahoe, who during Ruby Ridge was the head of the violent-crimes division, pleaded guilty to destroying copies of the internal FBI report on Ruby Ridge. Deputy Director Larry Potts was demoted, suspended, and put on administrative leave with pay. Potts at the time of the Ruby Ridge siege was head of the FBI's criminal division. Also suspended with pay were Daniel O. Coulson, deputy assistant director of the criminal division, George M. Baird, supervisory special agent, and Gale R. Evans, unit chief of the violent-crimes division. The Justice Department announced in August 1997 that no more criminal charges (other than the obstruction of justice charge against Kahoe) would be brought against FBI agents in the Ruby Ridge case. This news was followed immediately by an announcement that an Idaho county prosecutor was filing first-degree murder charges against Kevin Harris for killing U.S. Marshal Degan, and involuntary manslaughter charges against Lon Horiuchi, the FBI sniper who shot Vicki Weaver. In October 1997, an Idaho judge ruled that Kevin Harris could not be tried a second time on first-degree murder charges. In May 1998, a federal judge dismissed state involuntary manslaughter charges against Lon Horiuchi, ruling that Horiuchi was acting in the line of duty when he fired the shot that killed Vicki Weaver. See Jerry Seper, "4 FBI officials escape charges in Weaver death," *Washington Times,* August 16, 1997, A-3; Tim Weiner, "U.S. Won't Bring More Charges Against F.B.I. Officials in Ruby Ridge Siege," *New York Times* (AOL), August 22, 1997; Timothy Egan, "Idaho Prosecutor Charges 2 in Killings at Ruby Ridge," *New York Times* (AOL), August 22, 1997; "Ruby Ridge state murder charge axed," *New Orleans Times-Picayune,* October 3, 1997, A-2; Associated Press, "Charge in Ruby Ridge Dismissed," *New York Times,* email text kindly forwarded by Carol Moore.
23. Shannan, *Montana Freemen,* iv.
24. "Weaver moving to state," *Billings Gazette Online,* June 1, 1996; David Stout, "F.B.I. Memorandum on Crime was Mistakenly Sent to Press," *New York Times* (AOL), September 4, 1997.
25. "Letter Describes Aliases, Money in Okla. Blast," Reuters (AOL), October 15, 1995; Mike Irish, ed., *Heroes of the Heartland* (Boca Raton, Fla.: Globe International, Inc., n.d.); Judith Crosson, "Waco takes center stage at Oklahoma bombing trial," Reuters (AOL), June 10, 1997; Associated Press, "McVeigh explains courtroom remarks," *Dallas Morning News,* August 18, 1997.
26. Utilizing undercover agents and wiretaps, FBI agents were well informed of the Freemen's activities inside Justus Township. Clair Johnson, "First prosecution

witness describes wiretaps leading to Freemen arrests," *Billings Gazette Online,*
March 17, 1998; Clair Johnson, "Freemen classes helped infiltrators gain trust,"
Billings Gazette Online, March 24, 1998; Tom Laceky, Associated Press, "Hus-
band-wife team tell tale of infiltrating Freemen for FBI," *Billings Gazette
Online,* May 12, 1998; Clair Johnson, "Juror hears threat against judge," *Billings
Gazette Online,* June 16, 1998.

27. Pitcavage, "Every Man a King," [18].
28. Pitcavage, "Every Man a King," [18]; Kathleen McLaughlin, "Montana's
    Freemen have a love-hate relationship with Secretary of State Mike Cooney,"
    Billings Gazette Online, June 9, 1996; Devin Burghart and Robert Crawford,
    Guns & Gavels: Common Law Courts, Militias & White Supremacy (Portland,
    Ore.: Coalition for Human Dignity, 1996), 21. I thank Jean Rosenfeld for kindly
    forwarding this document to me.
29. Pitcavage, "Every Man a King," [26].
30. Johnson, "Juror hears threat against judge."
31. Pitcavage, "Every Man a King," [24]; "Freemen Standoff Enters Second Week,"
    Reuters (AOL), April 1, 1996; Johnson, "Juror hears threat against judge."
32. Richard Lacayo, "State of Siege," *Time,* April 8, 1996, 25.
33. "Jordan standoff turns into a big yawn," *Billings Gazette Online,* April 5, 1996.
        James Pate, editor and writer for *Soldier of Fortune,* was the only reporter
    admitted to Justus Township by the Freemen. See James Brooke, "Freemen
    Farm Attracts the Fringe," *New York Times* (AOL), April 28, 1996.
        On March 27, two days after the standoff began, the Freemen stopped an
    NBC crew that had entered Justus Township land, pointed their guns at them,
    took their video equipment, and ordered them to leave. A CBS crew had been
    threatened at gunpoint earlier that day. Earlier on October 2, 1995, the Freemen
    similarly had confiscated the equipment of an ABC crew. Clair Johnson, "TV
    crews describe armed robberies," *Billings Gazette Online,* June 12, 1998.
        On April 4, 1996, Dick Reavis, author of *The Ashes of Waco* (New York:
    Simon & Schuster, 1995), walked onto the Justus property and delivered a copy
    of his book to a Freeman. Reavis wanted to write an account of the Freemen's
    views, but he was sent away. See David Crisp, "Freemen, negotiators meet in
    ranchland talks," *Billings Gazette Online,* April 5, 1996.
34. Pitcavage, "Every Man a King," [33].
        Stewart Waterhouse walked out of Justus Township on April 27, 1996, and
    was taken into custody. In early September 1997, Waterhouse reached a plea
    bargain agreement with federal prosecutors that was negotiated by his court-
    appointed attorney. Waterhouse (39) pleaded guilty to being an accessory after
    the fact for assisting the Freemen's resistance to being arrested. He agreed to
    cooperate with federal agents in the investigation of the Freemen and to testify
    at their trials. In return, the government promised to seek to dismiss a second
    charge against him of being a fugitive possessing a firearm. Waterhouse was
    accused of sending a threatening letter and attempting to intimidate an officer in
    Oklahoma, and then fleeing Oklahoma with an SKS assault rifle. Waterhouse,
    wearing camouflage clothing, initially presented himself in court as a militia-
    man, and he attempted to utilize Freemen Common Law in his defense. When
    he agreed to the plea bargain, Waterhouse appeared in court dressed in a con-
    ventional suit, spoke respectfully to the judge, and let his court-appointed attor-
    ney conduct his case. "Plea bargain reached in Freemen standoff case," *Billings
    Gazette Online,* September 5, 1997.
35. Lacayo, "State of Siege," 26.
36. Shannan, *Montana Freemen,* 68.
37. Associated Press, "Taped Conversations," *Billings Gazette Online,* June 17, 1996.

38. Pitcavage, "Every Man a King," [36-37].
39. Associated Press, "Thumbnail sketches of some of the principals in the Freemen standoff," Reuters (AOL), June 14, 1996; Pitcavage, "Every Man a King," [6-7]; Joe Kolman, "Legislator sympathetic to Freeman Schweitzer," *Billings Gazette Online,* July 25, 1998.
40. Burghart and Crawford, *Guns & Gavels,* 2; Shannan, *Montana Freemen,* 32-33.
41. Quoted in Burghart and Crawford, *Guns & Gavels,* 12. Appendix C, pp. 46-49, consists of a "True Bill" filed by Schweitzer against former Secretary of the Treasury Lloyd Bentsen. Appendix D, p. 50, is the common law lien filed by Schweitzer against Lloyd Bentsen and his wife. Appendix E, p. 51, is a certified banker's check issued by Schweitzer.
42. Shannan, *Montana Freemen,* 30-34, 40, 62.
43. In the first Freemen trial, Schweitzer was convicted of bank fraud, wire fraud, mail fraud, making false claims to the IRS, interstate transportation of stolen property, threatening a federal official, and being a fugitive possessing a firearm. In the second Freemen trial, Schweitzer was convicted of armed robbery of an ABC crew on October 1, 1995, interference with interstate commerce by threats of violence, and using a firearm. Johnson, "Partial verdict," *Billings Gazette Online,* July 3, 1998; Johnson, "10 Freemen guilty of bank fraud," *Billings Gazette Online,* November 19, 1998.
44. In the first Freemen trial, Daniel Petersen was convicted of bank fraud, making false claims to the IRS, and threatening a federal official. In the second Freemen trial, Petersen was convicted of armed robbery of an ABC crew, bank fraud, and mail fraud. Johnson, "Partial verdicts"; Johnson, "10 Freemen guilty of bank fraud."
45. Clair Johnson, "6 Freemen get acquainted with judge," *Billings Gazette Online,* July 19, 1996. In the second Freemen trial, Cherlyn Petersen was convicted of bank fraud and mail fraud. Johnson, "10 Freemen guilty of mail fraud."
46. Associated Press, "Thumbnail sketches." In the first Freemen trial, Skurdal was convicted of two counts of threatening a federal official. In the second Freemen trial, Skurdal was convicted of bank fraud and armed robbery of an NBC crew. Johnson, "Partial verdicts"; Johnson, "10 Freemen guilty of bank fraud."
47. Associated Press, "Thumbnail sketches." In the first Freemen trial, Jacobi was convicted of making a false claim to the IRS and of two firearms violations. In the second Freemen trial, Jacobi was convicted of armed robbery of an NBC crew. Johnson, "Partial verdicts"; Johnson, "10 Freemen guilty of bank fraud."
48. Pitcavage, "Every Man a King," [21]; Associated Press, "2 Freemen wanted in Colorado," *Billings Gazette Online,* June 15, 1996.
49. Personal communication from Phillip Arnold, June 1996.
50. Johnson, "6 Freemen get acquainted with judge"; Associated Press, "Freemen expected to give up," *Billings Gazette Online,* June 13, 1996.
    In the first Freemen trial, Russell Landers was convicted of threatening federal officials and of a firearms violation. Clair Johnson, "Partial verdict." In May 1998, Dana Dudley Landers pleaded guilty to unlawful transportation in interstate commerce of stolen property obtained through fraud. Clair Johnson, "2 Freemen plead guilty; jury seated," *Billings Gazette Online,* May 28, 1998. In November 1998, Dana Dudley Landers was sentenced to 21 months in prison, but she also faced sentencing in Colorado for illegal activity there. Russell Landers was sentenced to 60 months on the conspiracy count, 135 months for the bank fraud count, 36 months on the threats count, and 41 months on the firearms conviction. These sentences were to be served concurrently with each other and a 30-year sentence for using fraudulent checks to buy vehicles in North Carolina. Clair Johnson, "Freeman receives

longer sentence," *Billings Gazette Online,* November 7, 1998.

51. David Crisp, "Sheriff's dispatcher is a sister to Freeman wife," *Billings Gazette Online,* April 6, 1996. William Stanton was convicted in the second Freemen trial of bank fraud and mail fraud. Agnes Stanton was convicted of bank fraud and mail fraud. Johnson, "10 Freemen guilty of bank fraud."

Ebert Stanton was released from custody on bond in May 1997. In May 1998, Ebert Stanton pleaded guilty in federal court to one count of bank fraud and to being an accessory after the fact in helping federal fugitives (the Freemen) avoid arrest. Stanton was represented in court by his court-appointed attorney. In a plea bargain arrangement, Stanton agreed to give a statement about the Freemen's activities and to testify in their trial in exchange for the possibility of a reduction in his sentence. Clair Johnson, "Freeman's bargain OK'd by trial judge," *Billings Gazette Online,* May 13, 1998.

52. Nick Ehli, "Outbursts don't stop court proceedings for 14," *Billings Gazette Online,* June 15, 1996; Jan Falstad, "Freemen disrupt court arraignments," Reuters (AOL), June 25, 1996.

In March 1998, a federal court convicted Steven Hance, James Hance, and John Hance of weapons charges, of being fugitives in possession of firearms, and of being accessories after the fact to an armed robbery of an NBC news crew. Tom Lacey, Associated Press, "Five Montana Freemen Found Guilty," America Online News, April 1, 1998. A federal judge sentenced Steven Hance to 78 months in prison, James Hance to 67 months, and John Hance to 63 months. Clair Johnson, "Freemen in March trial sentenced," *Billings Gazette Online,* June 6, 1998.

53. In March 1998, Jon Barry Nelson was convicted of weapons charges and of being an accessory after the fact to the armed robbery of the NBC news crew. Tom Lacey, Associated Press, "Five Montana Freemen Found Guilty," America Online News, April 1, 1998. Nelson was sentenced to 71 months. Johnson, "Freemen in March trial sentenced."

54. In the second Freemen trial, Veldhuizen was acquitted of armed robbery of the NBC crew. Johnson, "10 Freemen guilty of bank fraud."

55. In March 1998, Elwin Ward was found innocent of being an accessory to any crimes committed by the Freemen, but he was convicted of submitting a false claim to the Internal Revenue Service. Tom Lacey, Associated Press, "Five Montana Freemen Found Guilty," America Online News, April 1, 1998. Elwin Ward was sentenced to 24 months in prison, which was equivalent to the time he had already served. Johnson, "Freemen in March trial sentenced."

56. Associated Press, "Freemen girls' fathers express joy they are safe," *Billings Gazette Online,* June 7, 1996; Associated Press, "Freemen standoff update: Family leave Freemen compound after getting letter from cult leader," *Billings Gazette Online,* June 7, 1996; "Two young girls leave Montana ranch with family," Reuters (AOL), June 7, 1996; Associated Press, "State will drop charges against woman who left Freemen—for now," *Billings Gazette Online,* June 10, 1996.

57. Personal communication from J. Phillip Arnold, June 1996.

58. In May 1998, Emmett Clark pleaded guilty to making threats against federal officials and to mailing threatening communications. In April 1998, Emmett Clark was released from jail for health reasons. In November 1998, Emmett Clark was sentenced to 22 months he had already served. Johnson, "2 Freemen plead guilty; jury seated," *Billings Gazette Online,* May 28, 1998; Johnson, "Freeman receives longer sentence," *Billings Gazette Online,* November 7, 1998.

59. In March 1998, Edwin Clark was acquitted of accessory charges but was convicted of filing a false claim with the government. Because of Clark's testimony in court, he was released. He also benefited from being willing to let his court-

appointed attorney represent him. Clair Johnson, "'Mr. Clark you are a free man': Federal jury convicts 5, acquits Brusett farmer," *Billings Gazette Online,* April 1, 1998.

60. After spending 438 days in jail after the standoff, Casey Clark was released into the custody of his mother, Janet Clark. Casey Clark accepted his court-appointed attorney, and he agreed to cooperate with his probation officer and obey court orders. But the motion seeking Casey Clark's release from jail also said that he "does specifically reserve his rights to challenge the jurisdiction and venue that issues in this proceeding," indicating that Casey Clark continued to hold Freemen beliefs about the illegitimacy of the federal government. Casey Clark pleaded guilty on September 4, 1997, to helping the other Freemen avoid arrest. The sentence agreed upon in the plea bargain was the jail time he had already served plus two years probation. Casey Clark agreed to cooperate with the investigation of the Freemen and to testify at their trials, although he would not have to testify against his relatives or neighbors, the Stantons. U.S. Attorney Sherry Matteuci said that Casey Clark's "accepting counsel was a key factor in being able to resolve this case. I believe it was a just result." Clair Johnson, "Freeman released to custody of mother," *Billings Gazette Online,* September 3, 1997; Johnson, "Another Freemen pleads guilty," *Billings Gazette Online,* September 6, 1997.

61. In the first Freemen trial, Richard Clark was convicted of threatening a federal official and firearms charges. In the second Freemen trial, Richard Clark was convicted of bank fraud and armed robbery of the ABC crew. Johnson, "Partial verdicts"; Johnson, "10 Freemen guilty of bank fraud."

62. Personal communication from Jean Rosenfeld, May 1996. Rosenfeld based her analysis on an "Edict" written by Skurdal.

63. Dirk Johnson, "Lost in Freemen Standoff: First a Father, Now a Farm," *New York Times* (AOL), June 10, 1996.

    The *Billings Gazette* reported in November 1996 that the Clark farm had been sold by the Farm Service Agency to Alfred Bassett, Dean Clark's father-in-law. Clair Johnson, "Freemen ranch sold through federal drawing," *Billings Gazette Online,* November 16, 1996; Robert Struckman, "Rancher improves site of Freemen standoff," *Billings Gazette Online,* July 13, 1998.

64. In this chapter, I will not cite documents provided to scholars by the FBI during the Freemen standoff.

65. Lanternari, *Religions of the Opressed.*

66. This is my reading of the data contained in Jean E. Rosenfeld, "Pai Marire: Peace and Violence in a New Zealand Millenarian Tradition" (Special issue on Millennialism and Violence, ed. Michael Barkun) *Terrorism and Political Violence* 7, no. 3 (Autumn 1995): 83-108.

67. Lanternari, *Religions of the Oppressed,* 243. Christine Steyn discusses Africans who identified themselves as Israelites in "Millenarian Tragedies in South Africa."

68. Lanternari, *Religions of the Oppressed,* 116, 160, 239.

69. James A. Aho, *The Politics of Righteousness: Idaho Christian Patriotism* (Seattle: University of Washington Press, 1990), 138-46.

70. Examples are William Pierce (leader of National Alliance and Cosmotheist Church), the author of the influential novels, *The Turner Diaries* and *Hunter,* and Robert Mathews, who founded the Order modeled after "the Organization" in *The Turner Diaries.* Some members of the Order had Christian Identity affiliations, but Robert Mathews was an Odinist. *The Turner Diaries* advocates a revolution by mass uprising against the federal government and the cleansing of the Earth of all non-Aryan peoples. *Hunter* encourages the solitary terrorist to take

violent action. See Kaplan, *Radical Religion in America,* 34-55, 61-69, 92, 155.

71. Kaplan, *Radical Religion in America.*

72. Aho, *Politics of Righteousness,* 51, 127-31, 161.

73. Burghart and Crawford, *Guns & Gavels,* 1, 4, 7; Jim Nesbitt (Newhouse News Service), "Extremists use Old Testament to justify violence," *New Orleans Times-Picayune,* September 29, 1996, A-10.

74. Aho, *Politics of Righteousness,* 25, 62-66; Kaplan, *Radical Religion in America,* 5, 61-67; Walter, *Every Knee Shall Bow,* 82-84. Robert Mathews' last letter (given in Aho, 246-50) is a classic example of the thinking found among the revolutionary participants of this Euro-American nativist millennial movement. Mathews expressed that he just wanted to "be left alone" to carve out his desired lifestyle for his family, but instead, he reported that FBI agents attempted to have him fired from his job because of his participation in the "tax-rebellion movement." Mathews expressed his fear that the white race was facing extinction in America.

> The stronger my love for my people grew, the deeper became my hatred for those who would destroy my race, my heritage and darken the future of my children.
>
> By the time my son had arrived I realized that white America, indeed my entire race, was headed for oblivion unless white men rose and turned the tide. The more I came to love my son the more I realized that unless things changed radically, by the time he was my age, he would be a stranger in his own land, a blond-haired, blue-eyed Aryan in a country populated mainly by Mexicans, mulattoes, blacks and Asians. His future was growing darker by the day.
>
> I came to learn that this was not by accident, that there is a small, cohesive alien group [Jews] within this nation working day and night to make this happen. I learned that these culture disorders have an iron grip on both major political parties, on Congress, on the media, on the publishing houses, and on most of the major Christian denominations in this nation, even though these aliens subscribe to a religion which is diametrically opposed to Christianity.

Writing in 1984, Mathews referred to a "secret war" between some American citizens and the FBI that was just beginning.

> A secret war has been developing for the last year between the regime in Washington and an ever growing number of white people who are determined to regain what our forefathers discovered, explored, conquered, settled, built and died for [America].
>
> The FBI has been able to keep this war secret only because up until now we have been doing nothing more than growing and preparing. The government, however, seems determined to force the issue, so we have no choice left but to stand up and fight back. Hail victory!

After describing various conflicts with FBI agents and stating that "to be an FBI agent is to be nothing more than a mercenary for the ADL [Anti-Defamation League] and Tel Aviv," Mathews alleged incidents in which FBI agents threatened members of his family. Mathews concluded his last letter by affirming his willingness to die for his ultimate concern.

> I am not going into hiding: rather I will press the FBI and let them know what it is like to become the hunted. Doing so it is only logical

to assume that my days on this planet are rapidly drawing to a close. Even so, I have no fear. For the reality of life is death, and the worst the enemy can do to me is shorten my tour of duty in this world. I will leave knowing that my family and friends love me and support me. I will leave knowing I have made the ultimate sacrifice to secure the future of my children.

75. Paul de Armond, "Christian Patriots at War with the State, 1996," [9-10]. Available at <http://www.nwcitizen.com/publicgood> or paulf@henson.cc.wwu.edu. This was kindly forwarded to me via email by Jean Rosenfeld. Personal communication from J. Phillip Arnold, September 1996.
76. Freemen, "Argument," 104.
77. Pitcavage, "Every Man a King," [4-5]; Burghart and Crawford, *Guns & Gavels*, 2; Aho, *Politics of Righteousness*, 45; letter from Michael Barkun, July 6, 1997.
78. Pitcavage, "Every Man a King," [6].
79. Eugene V. Gallagher, "God and Country: Revolution as a Religious Imperative on the Radical Right," *Terrorism and Political Violence* 9, no. 3 (Autumn 1997): 63-79.
80. Pitcavage, "Every Man a King," [4-5].
81. David Neiwert, "Priesthood of hate: Out of the radical right, a 'destroying wind' commits mayhem, murder in the name of God's laws," Pacific Rim News Service. This article was kindly forwarded to me by Jean Rosenfeld.
82. Jean E. Rosenfeld, "The Importance of the Analysis of Religion in Avoiding Violent Outcomes: The Justus Freemen Crisis," *Nova Religio: The Journal of Alternative and Emergent Religions* 1, no. 1 (October 1997): 72.
83. Gallagher, "God and Country"; Andrew Macdonald [William Pierce], *The Turner Diaries*, 2d ed. (Hillsboro, W. Va.: National Vanguard Books, 1980). The front piece of this edition of *The Turner Diaries* states that as of February 1995, 198,000 copies of the book had been distributed.
84. Philip Lamy, "Secularizing the Millennium: Survivalists, Militias, and the New World Order," in *Millennium, Messiahs, and Mayhem: Contemporary Apocalyptic Movements,* ed. Thomas Robbins and Susan J. Palmer (New York: Routledge, 1997), 93-117.
85. De Armond, "Christian Patriots at War with the State" [7]; Minges, "Apocalypse Now!"
86. De Armond, "Christian Patriots at War with the State" [7].
87. Freemen, "Argument," 102-3.
88. Freemen, "Argument," 103.
89. Laurie Goodstein, "'Freemen's' Theological Agenda: Group Embraces Racist 'Christian Identity,'" *Washington Post*, April 9, 1996.
90. Personal communication from J. Phillip Arnold, June 1996.
91. Rosenfeld, "Pai Marire," 96.
92. Matt Bender, "Freemen speak of 'invisible barrier': Gritz gives up on talks," *Billings Gazette Online*, May 2, 1996.
93. Adas, *Prophets of Rebellion*, 18, 31, 40, 139, 148-54, 164.
94. Personal communication from Jean Rosenfeld, May 1996.
95. Edward C. Lehman Jr., "Letter from Edward C. Lehman, Jr., to Janet Reno," in *From the Ashes: Making Sense of Waco,* ed. James R. Lewis (Lanham, Md.: Rowman & Littlefield, 1994), 247-50.
96. This was not the first time I wrote to Reno. As chair of the New Religious Movements Group, a program unit in the American Academy of Religion, I organized a Special Topics Forum on "David Koresh and the Branch Davidians: The Academy, the Government, and Non-Traditional Religions" for the 1993 meeting of the AAR in Washington, D.C. I wrote letters inviting Attorney Gen-

eral Janet Reno, President Bill Clinton, and Vice-President Al Gore to attend the session. I received form letters declining from Clinton and Gore. I received two telephone calls from the Justice Department declining for Janet Reno (apparently the bureaucrat forgot that she had already called, because the substance of the message was the same). I was told that Reno could not attend the AAR forum on the Branch Davidian case, because there would be a conflict of interest due to the pending trial of eleven Davidians. When I suggested that other persons in the Justice Department attend the forum, saying, "You might learn something," I was answered with a stony silence. If any federal employees attended the 1993 AAR panel on the Branch Davidian tragedy in Washington, D.C., they did not sign the attendance sheet that was circulated.

97. My letter to Janet Reno, October 20, 1995; letter from Robin L. Montgomery, November 29, 1995.

98. Telephone call, January 26, 1996, from John Hogan, Justice Department.
  Clint Van Zandt, an FBI negotiator during the Branch Davidian siege, testified to the Senate Judiciary Committee hearings (October 31-November 1, 1995) that the tactical strategies such as blaring loud music and unpleasant sounds over loudspeakers counteracted the negotiators' efforts to gain the Davidians' trust. FBI Director Louis Freeh assured the committee that the FBI "would never again use tactics that lack a 'legitimate basis.'" William Esposito, assistant director of the FBI's criminal investigation division, acknowledged that in the Branch Davidian siege, "There certainly was a disconnect between the negotiations and the tactical people." Esposito reported to the committee that the FBI had expanded its crisis management teams and was taking steps to enhance cooperation between negotiators and tacticians. See Marcy Gordon (Associated Press), "Waco forced FBI change, official said," *New Orleans Times-Picayune*, November 2, 1995, A-3. Nancy Ammerman, professor of Sociology of Religion at Hartford Seminary, recommended that agents receive training in behavioral science, and political and religious groups. See Lauri Kellman, "Waco lessons learned, feds say," *Washington Times* (CompuServe), November 1, 1995.

99. At that time, the FBI did not follow through on these arrangements.

100. Fax to Robin Montgomery and Alanna Lavelle, FBI Academy, April 2, 1996, with copies by mail to Michael Barkun, and Janet Reno and John Hogan in the Justice Department. By mail I sent to all of these individuals a copy of my theoretical article, "Millennialism With and Without the Mayhem," which was subsequently published in Robbins and Palmer, *Millennium, Messiahs, and Mayhem*, 47-59.

101. Letter from Michael Barkun, July 6, 1997.

102. Goodstein, "'Freemen's' Theological Agenda."

103. "FBI Declines Comment on Freemen Standoff," Reuters (AOL), April 4, 1996; "Jordan standoff turns into a big yawn," *Billings Gazette Online*, April 6, 1996; David Crisp, "Freemen negotiators meet in ranchland talks," *Billings Gazette Online*, April 5, 1996; David Crisp, "Daughter, mom leave compound," *Billings Gazette Online*, April 7, 1996; Clair Johnson, "Stanton denies guilt in court," *Billings Gazette Online*, June 5, 1996.

104. Joe Kolman, "Legislator looks for way out of Freemen standoff," *Billings Gazette Online*, June 2, 1996.

105. "Former Green Beret Gritz enters Freemen compound," Reuters (AOL), April 27, 1996; "Ex-colonel visits ranch," *Billings Gazette Online*, April 28, 1996; "Freeman surrenders in Montana, says prosecutor," Reuters (AOL), April 28, 1996; Jim Robbins, "Far-Right Figure Continues Effort to Negotiate with Freemen," *New York Times* (AOL), April 29, 1996.

106. Gene Laverty, "Gritz Says Freemen Want Leader Back in Montana," Reuters

(AOL), April 28, 1996.
107. Matt Bender, "Freemen speak of 'invisible barrier': Gritz gives up on talks," *Billings Gazette Online,* May 2, 1996.
108. Matt Bender, "Freemen talk to press—not FBI," *Billings Gazette Online,* May 3, 1996.
109. Linda Collette was not contacted by the FBI. Collette provided very helpful information to Jean Rosenfeld during the standoff and put Rosenfeld in contact with other important sources of information on the Freemen and the broader Christian Patriot movement.
110. Fax to FBI Academy, May 8, 1996.
111. Personal communication from Phillip Arnold, May 1996.
112. Fax to FBI Negotiation Team, Montana, May 10, 1996.
      In May 1998, Jayne Seminare Docherty explained to me that *mediator* is a technical term in the field of negotiation practice and conflict resolution, referring to the negotiator who facilitates the interaction between the parties in the negotiation process. Being uninformed at that time about negotiators' technical terminology, in this memo I clearly meant *mediator* to refer to an intermediary. In this memo, I was arguing for the need to utilize trained "worldview translators" as intermediaries. I thank Jayne Seminare Docherty for this term, *worldview translator*. Email message from Jayne Seminare Docherty, May 16, 1998.
113. Associated Press, "Oregon militia members vow to declare war on U.S. if Freemen standoff turns sour," *Billings Gazette Online,* May 10, 1996.
114. Personal communication from Jean Rosenfeld, May 1996.
115. Tom Laceky (Associated Press), "Freemen standoff no-win situation for FBI," *Billings Gazette Online,* May 12, 1996.
116. Associated Press, "Jordan standoff lasts longer than Waco," *Billings Gazette Online,* May 15, 1996; David Crisp, "'I may strike out, too': Duke hopes to do better than others did with Freemen," *Billings Gazette Online,* May 16, 1996.
117. Associated Press, "Freemen meet with FBI agents," *Billings Gazette Online,* May 17, 1996.
118. Personal communication from Jean Rosenfeld, May 1996.
119. Gene Laverty, "Mediator holds out hope for end to Montana standoff," *Billings Gazette Online,* May 18, 1996.
120. Associated Press, "Negotiators Seated: Progress seen in Freemen talks: Talks called 'horribly complex,'" *Billings Gazette Online,* May 18, 1996.
121. James Brooke, "Some Freemen Are Called Hostages of the Leaders," *New York Times* (AOL), May 18, 1996.
122. Gene Laverty, "Freemen, FBI agents meet for fourth day," Reuters, May 19, 1996; Gene Laverty, "FBI, Freemen hold heated discussion," Reuters (AOL), May 20, 1996.
123. Jean Rosenfeld, fax to Dwayne Fuselier, FBI, Montana, May 20, 1996.
124. Gene Laverty, "FBI-Freemen talks break down in Montana-mediator," *Billings Gazette Online,* May 21, 1996.
125. This is a reference to Robert D. Baird's definition of "ultimate concern" in *Category Formation and the History of Religions* (The Hague: Mouton, 1971).
126. Fax to Dwayne Fuselier, FBI Negotiation Coordinator, Montana, May 21, 1996, with copies faxed to Hogan and Lavelle.
127. Jean Rosenfeld, fax to Ken Crook, FBI, Montana, May 21, 1996, with copies to Hogan and Lavelle.
128. Gene Laverty, "Freemen defiant after negotiations collapse," Reuters (AOL), May 22, 1996.
129. J. Phillip Arnold, RCTF, fax to Dwayne Fuselier, FBI Negotiation Coordinator, Montana, dated May 22, 1996, with copies to John Hogan, Ken Crook, Robin

Montgomery.
130. Fax to Dwayne Fuselier, FBI Negotiation Coordinator, Montana, dated May 23, 1996, with copies faxed to John Hogan, Justice Department, and FBI Academy.
131. Jean Rosenfeld, fax to John Hogan dated May 23, 1996.
132. "FBI to decide on cutting power to Freemen ranch," Reuters (AOL), May 23, 1996.
133. Gene Laverty, "Mediator rides on horseback to see Montana Freemen," Reuters (AOL), May 24, 1996..
134. Joe Kolman, "Legislator looks for way out of Jordan standoff," *Billings Gazette Online,* June 2, 1996.
135. Gritz made this statement on ABC's *Good Morning America.* See James Brooke, "Freemen Earn Enmity of Once-Sympathetic Mediators," *New York Times* (AOL), May 25, 1996.
136. Letter from Michael Barkun, July 6, 1997.
137. Personal communication from Jean Rosenfeld, June 1996; personal communication from J. Phillip Arnold, June 1996.
138. Personal communication from J. Phillip Arnold, June 1996.
139. Associated Press, "FBI brings in armored vehicles: Government still hopes for a peaceful solution," *Billings Gazette Online,* June 1, 1996.
140. Associated Press, "Petition emphasizes community impatience rising," *Billings Gazette Online,* June 6, 1996.
141. Associated Press, "Freemen's girls' fathers express joy they are safe," *Billings Gazette Online,* June 7, 1996; Associated Press, "Family of 4 leaves Freemen complex," *New Orleans Times-Picayune,* June 7, 1996: A-4; "Two young girls leave Montana ranch with family," Reuters (AOL), June 7, 1996; "Two Freemen meet briefly with FBI on Montana ranch," Reuters (AOL), June 7, 1996; Mike Carter (Associated Press), "Freemen mother loses custody," *New Orleans Times-Picayune,* June 8, 1996, A-10; Dirk Johnson, "Officials See More Hope for End to Montana Standoff," *New York Times* (AOL), June 8, 1996; Associated Press, "Mom says Freemen will see that law has betrayed her," *Billings Gazette Online,* June 8, 1996.
142. "Three mediators hold lengthy talks with Freemen," Reuters (AOL), June 10, 1996; Gene Laverty, "Clark returns to Freemen compound after FBI meeting," Reuters (AOL), June 11, 1996; "Rightist defender holds talks with Freemen," *Billings Gazette Online,* June 11, 1996; Clair Johnson (Associated Press), "Clark visits jail, returns to the ranch," *Billings Gazette Online,* June 12, 1996; Neil H. Payne, "Shades of Waco," 1-3, and "To Our Readers," 4, in *The Balance: A Newsletter of Civil Rights and Current Events* 7, no.2 (Summer 1996). I thank J. Phillip Arnold for forwarding to me this newsletter published by the CAUSE Foundation, P.O. Box 1235, Black Mountain, NC 28711.
143. Carey Goldberg, "Freemen closer to surrender," *New Orleans Times-Picayune,* June 13, 1996, A-10; Clair Johnson, "Farmer tills soil on Freemen-occupied land," *Billings Gazette Online,* June 12, 1996.
144. Len Iwanski (Associated Press), "Freemen surrender peacefully," Reuters (AOL), June 14, 1996; Carey Goldberg, "Freemen Holdouts Give Themselves Up," *New York Times* (AOL), June 14, 1996; Clair Johnson, "81-day standoff ends without bloodshed as Freemen give up," *Billings Gazette Online,* June 14, 1996; "Clinton praises peaceful end to standoff," *Billings Gazette Online,* June 14, 1996; Payne, "Shades of Waco," 2-3.
145. Clair Johnson, "Freemen deal includes 5: Negotiator spells out points in agreement," *Billings Gazette Online,* June 19, 1996.
146. David Johnston, "At the End, the Freemen Realized They Were Alone," *New York Times* (AOL), June 15, 1996.

147. Legal documents functioned as scriptures for the Freemen because they were regarded as sources of knowledge and truth. The Freemen were literalists in reading legal documents just as they were literalists in reading the King James Version of the Bible. In both instances, they lacked formal education in law and Religious Studies that would produce a more nuanced reading of the texts and that would increase sensitivity to ambiguities.

148. Pitcavage, "Every Man a King," [29, 34, 39].

149. Shannan, *Montana Freemen*, 24.

150. Tom Lacey (Associated Press), "Freemen Appear in Court" Reuters (AOL), June 14, 1996; Carey Goldberg, "Freemen in Court, but Not Without a Struggle," *New York Times* (AOL), June 15, 1996; Nick Ehli, "Outbursts don't stop court proceedings for 14," *Billings Gazette Online*, June 15, 1996.

   The fourteen Freemen in court were Rodney Skurdal, Dale Jacobi, Steven Hance, Ralph Clark, Jon Barry Nelson, Emmett Clark, Cherlyn Petersen, Edwin Clark, John Hance, James Hance, Russell Landers, Dana Dudley Landers, Casey Clark, Cornelius John Veldhuizen.

151. Clair Johnson, "Judge boots Jacobi out of court," *Billings Gazette Online*, June 21, 1996.

   Garfield County attorney Nicholas C. Murnion was awarded the John F. Kennedy Profile in Courage Award by the John F. Kennedy Library Foundation in May 1998 for his stand against the Freemen. Johnson, "'A Shining Example,'" *Billings Gazette Online*, May 12, 1998.

152. Jan Falstad, "Freemen disrupt court arraignments," Reuters (AOL), June 25, 1996; Clair Johnson, "Freeman threatens magistrate in court," *Billings Gazette Online*, June 26, 1996.

153. Associated Press, "Woman who was at Freemen ranch with children demands them back," *Billings Gazette Online*, June 26, 1996.

154. Clair Johnson, "Federal prosecutors get more time," *Billings Gazette Online*, June 11, 1996.

155. Clair Johnson, "Freemen, judge show restraint at Wednesday hearing," *Billings Gazette Online*, July 18, 1996; Johnson, "6 Freemen get acquainted with judge," *Billings Gazette Online*, July 19, 1996.

156. LeRoy Michael Schweitzer, "Protective Order of Release," obtained at <http://www.alaska.net/~winter/Jefferson.html>.

157. Item dated July 17, 1996, at <http://www.alaska.net/~winter/Jefferson.html>.

158. Clair Johnson, "Not true! Freemen rumors fly," *Billings Gazette Online*, July 24, 1996.

159. Shannan, *Montana Freemen*, 68-69.

160. "Texas sues secessionist group to block bogus liens," Reuters (AOL), June 25, 1996.

161. "Some Ariz. militia under house arrest, others in jail," Reuters (AOL), July 10, 1996; Don Van Natta Jr., "600 NYC Employees Suspected in Plot to Evade Taxes on Income," *New York Times* (AOL), July 18, 1996.

162. "Alleged pipe-bomb makers arrested near Seattle," Reuters (AOL), July 30, 1996.

163. Clair Johnson, "Judges reject 'bunkum' by Freemen backers," *Billings Gazette Online*, August 14, 1996.

   In June 1997, Warren Stone died and was eulogized in the *Billings Gazette* as a likeable figure and staunch Freeman, who was extremely knowledgeable about Common Law, loyal to LeRoy Schweitzer, and "a heck of a patriot." Stone was a U.S. Navy veteran, and a former high school teacher and career counselor. Joe Kolman, "Warren Stone: Freeman till the end," *Billings Gazette Online*, June 17, 1997.

164. Clair Johnson, "Freemen judge hires data expert," *Billings Gazette Online,* August 14, 1996.
165. Clair Johnson, "Schweitzer found guilty in tax case," *Billings Gazette Online,* September 11, 1996.
166. Associated Press, "Report: Montana Freemen Probed," Reuters (AOL), January 11, 1997; "Calif. men taught by Freemen found guilty of fraud," Reuters (AOL), February 6, 1997.
167. Associated Press, "Militia discussed support for Freemen," *Billings Gazette Online,* January 24, 1997; Associated Press, "Jury selection starts in terrorism trial," *Billings Gazette Online,* March 4, 1997; William Stimson, "U.S. militia members guilty of bombings, robberies," Reuters (AOL), July 23, 1997.
168. Associated Press, "FBI Discusses Atlanta Probes," Reuters (AOL), June 9, 1997; Kevin Sack, "Investigators Increasingly Sure of Link Between Bombing Incidents," *New York Times* (AOL), June 10, 1997; Pierre Thomas (*Washington Post*), "Letter is thread tying bombings together," *New Orleans Times-Picayune,* June 10, 1997, A-10.

In October 1998, Eric Robert Rudolph (32) was charged with the three bombings in Atlanta. Rudolph earlier had been charged with bombing a Birmingham, Alabama, abortion clinic. FBI agents had been searching an area in the North Carolina mountain wilderness for Rudolph, and at this writing, he has remained at large. "Fugitive charged in Olympic, bar bombings," *New Orleans Times-Picayune,* October 15, 1998, A-12.
169. Jo Thomas, "7 Arrests Linked to Militia Plot to Attack Army Bases," *New York Times* (AOL), July 23, 1997; Associated Press, "FBI: Militia Planned Army Attacks," Reuters (AOL), July 23, 1997.
170. Clair Johnson, "Freemen resolute in stand against trial," *Billings Gazette Online,* January 23, 1997.
171. Associated Press, "Trial of Freeman Leader Begins," Reuters (AOL), January 14, 1997.
172. Associated Press, "Schweitzer creates scene in N.C. Freemen trial," *Billings Gazette Online,* February 15, 1997.

In February 1997, Russell Landers and a colleague, James Vincent Wells (58), were convicted of using Freemen financial documents to purchase two vehicles that they took to Justus Township. Landers was sentenced to 30 years in prison and ordered to pay $183,961 in restitution. Wells was sentenced to 12 years in prison, and ordered to pay $214,768 in restitution. Associated Press, "Pair convicted in Freemen financing case," *Billings Gazette Online,* February 22, 1997; Associated Press, "2 Sentenced in Montana Freemen Case," Reuters (AOL), August 27, 1997.
173. Sam Howe Verhovek, "Texas Independence Group Has Serious Face," *New York Times* (AOL), January 24, 1997.
174. "Republic causing stir in W. Texas," *Dallas Morning News* article kindly forwarded to me via email on January 15, 1997, by Jean Rosenfeld.
175. <http://www.republic.net/rot/> January 26, 1997.
176. Gerald A. Carroll, "Cease Fire Will Allow Chance to Argue Texas Sovereignty," Media Bypass Magazine, June 1997, at <http://www.4bypass.com>. This article was kindly forwarded to me by Linda Collette. "Separatists end standoff peacefully," *Dallas Morning News* <http:www.dallasnews.com> (May 4, 1997); "Standoff negotiators find 'determined patience' pays," *Dallas Morning News,* May 5, 1997.

Richard McLaren was convicted in 1997 on state kidnapping charges and sentenced to 99 years in prison. He also faced federal mail-fraud charges. Bill

Lodge, "Separatist tells jury: 'I believed': Group's currency was touted as legal, he says," *Dallas Morning News,* April 3, 1998.

177. Associated Press, "Separatist arrested in Texas," *New Orleans Times-Picayune,* September 20, 1997, A-3; Associated Press, "FBI Arrests Separatist Fugitive," Reuters (AOL), September 20, 1997.

178. "The Freemen influence: Some jail inmates spout anti-government rhetoric," *Billings Gazette Online,* August 19, 1997.

179. Clair Johnson, "Freemen try to serve papers on Maxwell," *Billings Gazette Online,* May 8, 1998.

180. Christian Patriot writer J. Patrick Shannan could not understand why the Freemen suddenly decided "that they would be treated fairly by the judiciary." He theorized that the "generators," brought in by the FBI, may have been CIA machines that emitted microwaves "capable of altering the mind and confusing the individual...." In other words, Shannan resorted to the brainwashing theory to explain why the Freemen inexplicably decided to exit Justus Township. See Shannan, *Montana Freemen,* 51-52.

181. Associated Press, "FBI negotiator explains strategy of Freemen peaceful resolution," *Billings Gazette Online,* June 22, 1996.

182. Personal communication from J. Phillip Arnold, July 1996.

183. Jayne Seminare Docherty has noted in personal communications that in the event of future standoffs, right-wing revolutionaries in the United States will not believe assurances that they will be permitted to argue against the legitimacy of the federal government in federal court. Right-wingers have noted the silencing of the Freemen and Richard McLaren in the federal courts.

184. Personal communication from Jayne Seminare Docherty.

185. The papers presented by Eugene Gallagher, Lonnie Kliever, Jayne Seminare Docherty, Stephen O'Leary, and myself appeared in *Nova Religio: The Journal of Alternative and Emergent Religions* 3, no. 1 (October 1999). My paper was entitled, "Religious Studies Scholars, FBI Agents, and the Montana Freemen Standoff," 36-44.

186. Jayne Seminare Docherty has used this phrase in her conversations with FBI agents, and she has used this phrase in her dissertation. See Jayne Seminare Docherty, "When the Parties Bring Their Gods to the Table: Learning the Lessons from Waco," Ph.D. diss., George Mason University, 1998. Docherty derived this phrase from Phillip Lucas, "How Future Wacos Might Be Avoided: Two Proposals," in James Lewis, *From the Ashes,* 209-12. Docherty also discusses Robert D. Baird's concept of religion as "ultimate concern" in her dissertation.

CHAPTER SEVEN

Other Cases Briefly Considered: Solar Temple and Heaven's Gate

1994, 1995, 1997— SOLAR TEMPLE

THE VIOLENCE

On October 4, 1994, a fire erupted in a condominium complex in Morin Heights, Quebec, near Montreal. Two members of the Solar Temple, Gerry and Colette Genoud, died in the fire. Three more bodies were found hidden in a storage closet. Tony Dutoit had been stabbed fifty times in the back, and his wife, Nicki Dutoit, had been stabbed eight times in the back, four in the throat, and once in each breast. Their three-month-old baby, Christopher Emmanuel, had been stabbed six times in the chest. Police subsequently determined that the murders of the Dutoit family had occurred on September 30.

On October 4, 1994, just before midnight, police were called to investigate a burning barn in Cheiry, Switzerland. Inside they found a hidden room that contained the bodies of eighteen people wearing capes and arranged in a circle like spokes on a wheel. Three more bodies were found in an octagonal room with mirrors, and one body was found in the room of a nearby farmhouse. Twenty-one of these individuals had been shot, and fourteen had plastic bags over their heads. Police later concluded that most of these people were killed on October 3.[1]

About 3:00 A.M. on October 5, 1994, fire broke out in a complex of three chalets owned by the Solar Temple in Granges-sur-Salvan, Switzerland, sixty kilometers from Cheiry. Twenty-five bodies were found scattered around two of the chalets. The number of Solar Temple members dead in Switzerland included four children and three teenagers.[2]

A magistrate in Switzerland concluded that, of the fifty-two Solar Temple deaths in Quebec and Switzerland in 1994, only fifteen were true suicides committed by those who regarded themselves as "the Awakened." Thirty people dubbed the "Immortals" were lured into participating in a ritual in which they ingested tranquilizers and then were shot. Seven members considered "traitors" were executed.[3]

Shortly after the winter solstice of 1995, sixteen Solar Temple members, including three children, were found dead in the woods near Grenoble, France. They had been drugged and shot, and their bodies burned. Fourteen of the dead had been arranged in a circular star formation. The bodies of two others were found nearby and were identified as a French police officer and a French immigration inspector, who apparently shot the fourteen and started the fire that consumed the bodies. Some of the deceased had left behind notes about going to "see another world."[4]

On March 22, 1997, five Solar Temple believers were found dead in a home in Saint-Casimir, Quebec. An elderly woman was suffocated in a plastic bag, while Bruno Klaus and three other adults died in a fire that engulfed the house. All had taken tranquilizers. Three teenagers had been spared from participating in this group suicide.[5]

All of these people were members or former members of the Solar Temple (Ordre du Temple Solaire, OTS). "Transit letters" or "Testaments," received by journalists, government officials, and scholars after the 1994 deaths explained that some of those deaths involved the execution of "traitors," some of the other murders were intended to help weaker Solar Temple members make a transit to a higher world, and the remaining deaths were self-inflicted by those strong enough to make the transit themselves.[6] The transit was to salvation in a higher realm of existence and consciousness. The believers would receive "glorious 'solar bodies' on the star Sirius,"[7] but Jupiter and Venus were also mentioned by Solar Temple believers as their destination.[8]

LUC JOURET AND JOSEPH DI MAMBRO

The leaders of the Solar Temple were Joseph Di Mambro and Luc Jouret. Joseph Di Mambro was the leader who used the attractive and younger Luc Jouret as a front man and proselytizer for the group.

Dr. Luc Jouret (1947–1994) was born in the Belgian Congo (today called Zaire), earned a medical degree at the Free University of Brussels in 1974, served in the Belgian army as a paratrooper, traveled to India where he became interested in homeopathic medicine, and in the 1980s established a thriving homeopathic medical practice in France, Switzerland, and Canada.

Luc Jouret. (Photo courtesy of Simpos)

Jouret and Joseph Di Mambro founded the Ordre International Chevalresque Tradition Solaire in 1984, which was later called the Ordre du Temple Solaire (OTS). The Solar Temple was a secret society with several other organizations, Club Amenta and Club Archédia serving as fronts. Jouret was a popular public speaker on the New Age circuit, giving lectures in Belgium, France, Switzerland, Quebec, and Martinique. In 1984, Jouret was a paid motivational speaker at two district offices of Hydro-Quebec, Quebec's public hydroelectric utility. Persons drawn to his message were first directed into the Clubs Amenta and Archédia, and those deemed ready were funneled into the Solar Temple.[9]

Joseph Di Mambro (1924-1994) was the leader of the Solar Temple, although he preferred to direct the group from behind the scenes. Born in France, he became a watchmaker and jeweler. From 1956 to 1969 he belonged to the Rosicrucian order AMORC, and became the Master of the AMORC Lodge in Nimes, France. During the 1970s, Di Mambro made a full-time career as a New Age teacher. In 1973, he founded the Center for the Preparation of the New Age in Annemasse, France, close to Switzerland. In 1976, he founded a communal group, La Pyramide, near Geneva, Switzerland. In 1978, Di Mambro founded the Golden Way Foundation in Geneva. The Golden Way Foundation became the parent of the Solar Temple. Di Mambro functioned as a prophet speaking the words of the enlightened Masters of the Great White Brotherhood, who were believed to guide evolution on planet Earth. Di Mambro claimed to be the reincarnation of Osiris, Akhnaton, Moses, and Cagliostro, and his followers saw him as a "Cosmic Master."[10] Immediately prior to the transit, the 70-year-old Di Mambro was very ill, suffering from kidney failure and incontinence as well as severe diabetes, and he believed he had cancer.[11]

Jouret and Di Mambro both died in the 1994 transit.

SOLAR TEMPLE

The Solar Temple was a Neo-Templar secret society that participated in the diffuse Western occult tradition, which includes Freemasonry, Rosicrucianism, Neo-Templar, and Theosophical groups.

Contemporary Neo-Templar groups claim to be the heirs to the Order of the Temple founded in 1118–1119, whose members participated in crusades and were persecuted by the French monarch, Philip the Fair, who had all known Templars arrested. The organization was then dissolved by Pope Clement V. Fifty-four Templars were burned at the stake on May 12, 1310, and their Grand Master, Jacques de Molay, was burned four years later.[12]

The Solar Temple leaders were influenced by Jacques Breyer, who founded the Sovereign Order of the Solar Temple (OSTS) after his mystical experiences in 1952 in the castle at Arginy, France, and by Julien Origas (1920–1983), who founded a Renewed Order of the Temple (ORT).[13]

The Solar Temple members were well-to-do, educated people. Those who died in 1994 included a high-ranking official in the Quebec government, a reporter for a Quebec newspaper, a retired sales manager for the Swiss watch corporation Piaget, a mayor of a Quebec town, and a wealthy Geneva businessman.[14] The Solar Temple appealed to French-speaking people of Roman Catholic background. The elaborate Solar Temple liturgies appear to have been an important attraction to the believers, along with the promise that, through participation in rituals, they would achieve the enlightened consciousness necessary for their inclusion in the coming Age of Aquarius. Di Mambro had contrived appearances of the Masters, utilizing electronic and laser technology in the group's Sanctuaire at Salvan. The technology used to facilitate the appearances of the Masters was created by Tony Dutoit.[15]

The community of Solar Temple members was said to be an *egregore,* possessing a "common aura" or "bank of consciousness" that would usher in the New Age.[16]

In the 1980s, a Solar Temple commune was established at St. Anne-de-Perade, Quebec, to be an "ark of safety" during the coming apocalyptic tribulation. Jouret was to govern this commune, but its members resented his high-handed interference in their personal lives. In 1987, the commune's administrative council voted Jouret out of office and elected another person. The European branch of the Solar Temple did not accept this decision, and the episode put Jouret in some disgrace in Di Mambro's eyes.[17]

In general, however, the Solar Temple members permitted their identities and marriages to be rearranged by the leaders. Di Mambro would identify various members as the reincarnations of various famous people and even deities, such as Bernard de Clairvaux, Joseph of Arimathea, Queen Hapshetphout, and Ram. Members often were paired in "cosmic marriages" between partners with significant age differences.[18]

Di Mambro was attracted to the idea that his group would produce exceptional children, important to the world's destiny. Di Mambro's son, Elie (1965–1994), was said to have been conceived on Mount Carmel, a mountain in the Holy Land associated with the prophet Elias. The Solar Temple aimed to conceive and rear nine "cosmic children," who would bring in the New Age. Foremost among these children was Emmanuelle (age 12 when she died in the 1994 transit), who was the daughter of Di Mambro and Dominique Bellaton. Di Mambro and Bellaton staged an "immaculate conception" in the Sanctuaire when a Master pointed his sword, which emitted a laser beam that appeared to illuminate Bellaton's throat. Di Mambro, thus, was raising an *avatar* (in Hinduism, "descent"), the messiah who would bring in the New Age. To keep Emmanuelle pure, she had to wear a helmet and gloves, and no one but family members were permitted to touch her. Her father always referred to Emmanuelle as "he." At age twelve, however, Emmanuelle was becoming unruly and expressing interest in teenage popular culture.[19]

At the height of the Solar Temple's membership in January 1989, there were 442 members: 90 in Switzerland, 187 in France, 53 in Martinique, 16 in the United States, 86 in Canada, and 10 in Spain. The members made considerable financial contributions to the Solar Temple. But in the 1990s, the Solar Temple began losing members, and the former benefactors demanded reimbursements. In 1990, Di Mambro's son, Elie, discovered the technological means by which the Masters and other apparitions were produced and spoke openly of the trickery, thereby increasing the number of defections of members and their demands for the return of funds. Elie separated from his father and the Solar Temple.[20]

A letter written to Di Mambro on December 10, 1993, by a devoted Swiss believer, revealed the problems that beset the Solar Temple and indicated that Di Mambro's credibility as the Masters' prophet was eroding.

> In France, in the south, lots of upheaval caused by suspicious talk and the denigration in opposition to the hierarchy of the Order, its authenticity and the integrity of its representatives are called into doubt.... Rumors about embezzlement and various skull-

duggery are propagated by influential ex-members. Many members of this degree have left or are leaving. They feel their ideals have been betrayed. The three degrees of OTS are still kept out of these grumblings (knock on wood!!!).

The same grumblings are heard [in Aquitaine] as in the Midi. It is even said that you have failed because of money and women, and you're no longer credible. This is very serious for the order's mission.

There are even more serious grumblings, and you know them. Here they are: everything that we saw and heard in certain places has been a trick. I have known this for some time. Tony [Dutoit] has been talking about for years already.... I have always refused to pay attention to these rumors, but the evidence is growing, and questions are being asked. This calls into question many things I've seen, and messages. I would really be annoyed if I thought I was sincerely prostrating myself in front of an illusion!!!.... There is enough stuff here to send less committed people packing. And all the resignations and departures of recent times just confirm it.[21]

Di Mambro had instructed Nicki Dutoit not to bear children, but she became pregnant and the Dutoit couple left Switzerland and moved to Quebec, where they had a son they named Christopher Emmanuel. Di Mambro felt that this child threatened the status of his daughter as the *avatar*, and he concluded that the Dutoit infant was the Antichrist. The sins of the Dutoit family were compounded by Tony Dutoit's revelations to Solar Temple members that he was the engineer who created the apparitions of the Masters in Salvan. The entire Dutoit family thus became regarded as dangerous traitors, and they were ritually executed prior to the transit.[22]

The difficulties internal to the Solar Temple, and the cultural opposition the Solar Temple experienced in the 1990s (see the following section on persecution), appears to have prompted the inner circle in the summer of 1994 to begin working to create a new organization, the Rose+Cross Alliance (ARC), for the dedicated Solar Temple members.[23] This effort was aborted by the transits in October 1994.

CATASTROPHIC MILLENNIALISM

The Solar Temple possessed a cosmology similar to that found in other Western occult groups, including Theosophical groups, in which the evolution of consciousness is described as taking place in recurring cycles on planets. At various points, the advanced seeds of consciousness (the fruit of evolution on a planet) transfer from one planet to another, and the cycles of evolution continue.[24] Whereas optimistic, progressive expectations about the transition from the Age of Pisces to the Age of Aquarius tend to stress the upward movement of a cycle of evolution, the Solar Temple's experience of cultural opposition and internal stresses made committed members focus instead on the downward movement of the cycle, and they concluded that evolution had reached its end on Earth.

A Solar Temple liturgy, called the "Essenian rite," was a mass in which Alice Bailey's "Great Invocation" was recited to invoke the Christ consciousness on Earth.[25] The use of Bailey's Great Invocation is typical of New Age millennialism with progressive, noncatastrophic expectations.[26] But Solar Temple members believed that the transition from the Age of Pisces to the Age of Aquarius would involve cataclysmic destruction, and members were encouraged to finance and move to "life centers" in Canada and Switzerland for safe refuge during the imminent upheaval. A farm established in Quebec was particularly seen as an "ark of safety" in the imminent tribulation. In the 1980s, the Solar Temple's orientation was toward survivalism.[27]

In the 1990s, as a result of the weaknesses internal to the Solar Temple, and the simultaneous experience of cultural opposition, the Solar Temple leaders' views about the evolution of consciousness on Earth became pessimistic, and a theology was developed to justify a transit to escape Earth and the imminent cataclysm.

THE PERSECUTION

The decision made by the inner circle of Solar Temple adepts, to make the transit, occurred about the time the Solar Temple was experiencing cultural opposition on a number of fronts, which they regarded as persecution.[28]

In 1991, a disgruntled defector, Rose-Marie Klaus contacted a Montreal anticult organization, Info-Secte, which then put out a letter warning of the dangers of the Solar Temple to other Quebec organizations. Klaus's husband had left her for a cosmic marriage to another woman, and Klaus wanted to recoup her share of the money she and her husband had donated to the Quebec commune. Klaus pursued a lawsuit to this end, and she spoke against the Solar Temple in Martinique, which in turn prompted some of those members to demand the return of their financial contributions. Klaus incited negative media coverage of the Solar Temple whenever she could.

In 1993, the Canadian police began to investigate whether the Solar Temple was connected to a mysterious "Q-37" group that had threatened to assassinate public officials (police later determined that Q-37 never existed).[29] On March 8, 1993, two Quebec members of the Solar Temple, loyal to Jouret, were arrested for illegally purchasing three handguns with silencers, and Luc Jouret, who was at that time in Europe, also was charged. One of these men was dismissed from his management position at Hydro-Quebec, and an investigation was made into Jouret's activities with that organization. Rose-Marie Klaus's photo was displayed twice in Quebec newspapers in connection with articles in which she denounced the Solar Temple. At trials, the two Solar Temple loyalists and Jouret were each sentenced to one year of unsupervised probation and were ordered to pay $1,000 each to the Red Cross. Despite the light sentences, the incident triggered international police investigations into Solar Temple's financial dealings and into the possibility that its members were trafficking in arms (they were not). Di Mambro's wife, Jocelyne, had difficulty getting her passport renewed.[30]

The siege of the Branch Davidians in the United States was going on at this time, and the Solar Temple adepts felt equally besieged by law enforcement agents. The bad publicity in Quebec prompted even more defections and more demands for refunds of money, especially in Quebec and Martinique. Jouret lost his good reputation, and he was no longer able to pursue his career as a New Age lecturer.[31]

About this time, Jocelyne Di Mambro typed a document on a computer at Salvan, which expressed the group's sense of persecution.

> Our file is the hottest on the planet, the most important of the last ten years, if not of the century.
> However that may be, as it turns out, their concentration of hate against us will give us enough energy to leave.[32]

An audiotape recorded in the spring of 1994 reported Jo Di Mambro saying, "We are rejected by the whole world. First by the people, the people can no longer withstand us. And our earth, happily she rejects us. How would we leave [otherwise]? We also reject this planet. We wait for the day we can leave...life for me is intolerable, intolerable, I can't go on. So think about the dynamic that will get us to go elsewhere."[33]

THE FAILURE OF THE MILLENNIAL GOAL

The members of the Solar Temple were failing to form a nucleus of people who would bring in the Age of Aquarius. The "ark of safety" commune in Quebec had revolted against European hierarchical control. The negative publicity in Quebec ruined Jouret's career as a New Age lecturer, greatly diminishing the chances that the Solar Temple, or any new organizational offspring, would be able to attract new members. Particularly in Quebec and

Martinique, the number of defectors was increasing and these people were demanding the return of their financial contributions. In Quebec and France, revelation of the faked apparitions of the Masters further eroded Di Mambro's credibility. Di Mambro's health was failing, and, furthermore, he had lost control of his children, whom he had raised for exalted roles in the New Age. His 29-year-old son, Elie, was a prominent apostate who spoke openly to members against his father and revealed the secrets of the Sanctuaire. Twelve-year-old Emmanuelle, the *avatar*, was becoming unmanageable, and her messianic role was threatened by the Dutoit child, the Antichrist. The investigations of the Solar Temple by international police, and the highly negative publicity received in Quebec, convinced the members of the Solar Temple inner circle that humanity on Earth was refusing to evolve the higher consciousness necessary to move into the Age of Aquarius.

THE DECISION TO COMMIT VIOLENCE

Four letters or "Testaments" were received by several people after the 1994 transit, and these explained why Solar Temple leaders felt it was no longer possible to effect a transition to the New Age of Aquarius.

The Testament entitled "Transit to the Future" rejected the idea of human progress in earthly evolution: "The blissful illusion of those who believe that the world is improving and that man is progressing cannot see the light of day, because they remain victims of their divisions and of their own illusion."[34] This Testament expressed the belief in irrevocable environmental disaster as well as the concern for purity, which was a hallmark of the Solar Temple.

> The race is heading irreversibly toward its own destruction. All of Nature is turning against those who have abused it, who have corrupted and desecrated it on every level. Man will pay heavy tribute for he remains no less than the only [one] responsible for it.
>
> Awaiting favorable conditions for a possible Return, we will not participate in the annihilation of the human kingdom, no more than we will allow our bodies to be dissolved by the alchemical slowness of Nature, because we don't want to run the risk of their being soiled by madmen and maniacs.[35]

The Testament entitled "To Lovers of Justice" was addressed "to those who in this rotten world remain devoted to Justice and Truth."[36] Referring to the scandal in Quebec, this letter asserted: "This was a great deal, especially for men and women whose actions have only been motivated by a profound desire to help the Beings in search of Justice and Truth, and to awaken in them the Spirit of an Eternal Knighthood through the Order to which

A surveillance photograph of Joseph
Di Mambro arriving in Brisbane,
Australia, late in 1993. (AP Photo)

they belong."[37] In addition to complaining about the manner of the police investigation and intimidation of Solar Temple members, this Testament complained bitterly of biased news reporting.

7. Why were the contents of the teachings of the Solar Temple Order...systematically silenced during the entire scandal, as well as those distributed by Dr. Jouret through conferences, seminars, television and radio broadcasts, press releases, tapes, audiovisual documents, books, etc...?Our detractors know too well that the only objective of these teachings is to ennoble the conscience of man.

8. Why does the mass media, who organized the scandal in collaboration with judicial and political authorities, obstinately refrain from clearly stating the decisions of the Court in regards to the three persons accused?[38]

The "To the Lovers of Justice" Testament mentioned the popular New World Order conspiracy theory and expressed sentiments that are commonly associated with anti-Semitism, but stopped short of naming the identity of those who conspired to dominate the world.

It is sufficient to note all the futile, lying and useless distortions of international authorities concerning current conflicts in the world, in order to convince oneself of the existence of a secret evil organization on a worldwide scale, highly supported financially, and determined to silence or destroy all those who would be likely to interfere with their interests.[39]

The "To the Lovers of Justice" Testament concluded that, in the face of systematic persecution of "Bearers of Light" (John F. Kennedy, Mohandas Gandhi, and Martin Luther King Jr. were mentioned), and in the face of impending ecological, nuclear, and chemical catastrophes, "we have decided to withdraw ourselves from this world, with all lucidity and in full consciousness."[40]

The testament entitled "To All Those Who Can Still Understand the Voice of Wisdom...We Address This Last Message" reported a doctrine—novel in the Western occult tradition—that the Masters, the "last Elder Brothers of the Rose+Croix," left planet Earth on January 6, 1994, at 12:04 A.M. because of humanity's stubborn refusal to evolve the consciousness required for entrance into the New Age. Furthermore, the "Seven Entities of the Great Pyramid of Gizeh left the Secret Chamber during the night of March 31, 1993, taking with them the capital Energy-Conscience of the seven fundamental planets of our solar system."[41] The "Great White Lodge of Sirius" had decreed the transit of the faithful "Servants of the Rose+Croix." According to the decree of the Great White Lodge of Sirius, the Solar Temple adepts arranged for the destruction by fire of each of the Solar Temple residences so that they would not be desecrated by impure human beings. This Testament issued a call to other Solar Temple faithful to join them: "from the Planes where we will work from now on and by a just law of magnetism, we will be in the position of calling back the last Servants capable of hearing this last message."[42]

> Men, cry not over our fate, but rather cry for your own. Ours is more enviable than yours.
>
> To you who are receptive to this last message, may our Love and our Peace accompany you during the terrible tests of the Apocalypse that await you. Know that from where we will be, we will always hold our arms open to receive those who are worthy of joining us.[43]

A fourth Testament entitled "The Rose+Croix" appeared to offer ritual instructions for others to make the transit by promising "IMMORTALITY" to those who did, concluding, "It is into their strange and incredible universe that they invite you to enter...."[44]

A doctrinal grandfather of the Solar Temple, Jacques Breyer (founder of the OSTS in 1966), had calculated in his 1959 book, *The Secrets of the*

Solar Temple (*Arcanes Solaire*), that, since Jesus was born in 4 B.C., the "Grand Monarchy" would leave the earth around 1995–1996, two thousand years after the birth of Jesus Christ.[45] Therefore, the Solar Temple tradition contained within it a theological resource that had the potential to stimulate a group suicide. But Breyer's dates were ambiguous, and he had also proposed 1999, 2147, 2156, and 2666 for the end.[46]

Millennialists typically respond to actual events in developing their doctrines, interpretations, and prophecies. The conviction that they were being persecuted, combined with internal stresses, made the Solar Temple a fragile millennial group. As in the case of other fragile millennial groups, for instance Aum Shinrikyo, the date for the end of the world was brought closer as a result of the group's fragility, and the Solar Temple adepts executed traitors and made their first transit in 1994. If the Solar Temple had not become fragile due to simultaneous internal weaknesses and cultural opposition, the Solar Temple members could just as easily have responded to favorable circumstances by continuing their work to bring about the Age of Aquarius. The Solar Temple, therefore, had the potential to become a noncatastrophic, progressive millennial group. The adverse events experienced by the Solar Temple caused its members to give even greater emphasis to the gnostic dualism found in the Western occult tradition between spirit and matter, and the Solar Temple adepts opted to abandon this contaminated earthly world to its cataclysmic fate, while they carried the fruit of the earthly evolution of consciousness forward into an evolutionary cycle on another world.

1997, 1998— HEAVEN'S GATE

THE VIOLENCE

On Thursday morning, March 27, 1997, I was walking on the treadmill at my health club when the television monitors flashed a story on a group suicide near San Diego. I glimpsed images of corpses dressed in black shirts and pants, wearing black and white Nike sneakers, lying on cots and bunkbeds, and draped with diamond-shaped purple shrouds. The following Sunday was Easter, so I went home to spend my spring break watching the news unfold about Heaven's Gate, giving telephone interviews to news reporters, and studying the Heaven's Gate web page.

Heaven's Gate was a fragile millennial group whose members committed group suicide, the largest to occur in the United States,[47] to preserve their ultimate concern, which was to enter the Kingdom of Heaven. The group's leader, Marshall Herff Applewhite, called "Do" at the time of his death, had feelings of persecution dating back twenty-five to thirty years, but at the time of the suicide, the group was not really persecuted.

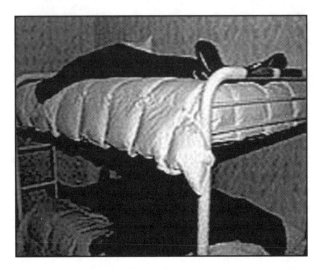

Two of the Heaven's Gate bodies discovered in a mansion in Rancho Santa Fe, California, in 1997. (Video footage courtesy of the San Diego County Sheriff's Department)

The decision to "exit" planet Earth was made in response to internal weaknesses that were caused by Do and the other leader, Bonnie Lu Nettles (called "Ti"), who died in 1985. But the group's uncomfortable relationship with mainstream American society contributed to the Heaven's Gate believers' group suicide. Heaven's Gate was a monastic community with religious goals, methods, and lifestyle not very different from the Hindu and Buddhist monastic traditions.[48] For instance, in India, people who renounce family and work life are honored and supported, and while religious suicide is not unknown, it is rare and involves individuals—usually when they are elderly. The lack of social support in the United States for the Heaven's Gate monastic community exacerbated the members' sense of alienation from society and their sense of persecution, creating a context in which it seemed reasonable for the believers to exit planet Earth to attain salvation.

The Heaven's Gate exit from planet Earth was designed to reunite the members with their other leader, Ti, who they believed was piloting a flying saucer behind the Hale-Bopp comet approaching Earth. The Heaven's Gate exit of thirty-nine believers, including Do, probably began on Saturday, March 22, 1997, when the Hale-Bopp comet was closest to the earth. This was the same day that the residence of Solar Temple believers in St.-Casimir, Quebec, burst into flames, revealing five suicides there.[49]

The exit of thirty-nine members of Heaven's Gate was carried out in a mansion in Rancho Santa Fe, outside San Diego, California. On the first day, fifteen believers consumed pudding or applesauce mixed with phenobarbital, drank vodka, and, with assistance, pulled plastic bags over their heads. The surviving members removed the plastic bags and draped each body with a purple shroud. On the next day, fifteen more died in the same manner. Then seven more committed suicide, assisted by two women. The bodies of the final two were found with the plastic bags still on their heads.

The bodies of the Heaven's Gate thirty-nine members were found lying on individual beds or cots. They were dressed in black pants and shirts. On the left shoulders of the shirts were patches that read "Heaven's Gate Away Team."[50] Overnight bags were found near each body, neatly packed with clothes, spiral notebooks, and lip balm. Each person had a $5 bill and quarters in the front shirt pocket.[51]

Of those thirty-nine who died in the Heaven's Gate group suicide, there were nineteen men and twenty women. Three were in their 20s, two in their 30s, twenty were in their 40s, eight were in their 50s, four were in their 60s, and one woman was 72. Of the thirty-eight followers, thirty had joined the group in the 1970s (although not all had remained in the group continuously), and eight had joined in the 1990s.[52]

After making an appearance on a *60 Minutes* news program, in which he was interviewed by Lesley Stahl, Wayne "Nick" Cooke (56) (also called Justin in the group) committed suicide in a hotel room in Encinitas on May 6, 1997, along with Chuck Humphrey (called Rkkody in the group). They both consumed phenobarbital and vodka or whiskey and pulled plastic bags over their heads. They were dressed as the other members had been, including the $5 bills and three quarters in their pockets. When San Diego County sheriff's deputies arrived, they found that Cooke was dead, but Humphrey was still alive. Humphrey was taken to a hospital and revived.[53]

Chuck Humphrey concluded that he had been turned back temporarily from Heaven's Gate to carry out a mission of distributing accurate information about the group and its theology. Humphrey created a web page and replicated the original Heaven's Gate web page, sold copies of the Heaven's Gate desktop-published book for cost, gave interviews to reporters, made a brief attempt at proselytizing by showing a video, at the Berkeley Conference Center, of Do speaking (the presentation was poorly received), and distributed audiotapes of the lessons given by Ti and Do, videotapes, and CD-ROMs to libraries. Feeling he had completed his task, Chuck Humphrey (55) exited Earth from the Arizona desert in February 1998. Humphrey put a plastic bag over his head and filled it with carbon monoxide from his car's exhaust. Humphrey wore black pants and a black shirt with a patch saying "Heaven's Gate Away Team," and he had a $5 bill and quarters in his pocket. The purple shroud was nearby, as was a note reading, "Do not revive."[54]

Compared to other groups discussed in this book, it is remarkable that Heaven's Gate's violence involved only consenting adults who wanted to exit Earth. Heaven's Gate believers did not drag children into their violence. They felt that only adults could prepare themselves and make the decision to leave Earth for the Next Level (the Kingdom of Heaven). Furthermore, Heaven's Gate disciples did not attempt to kill any perceived enemies. The group had dealt with cultural opposition in the 1970s by becoming extremely secretive about their identities and location.

BONNIE LU NETTLES AND MARSHALL HERFF APPLEWHITE

Bonnie Lu Truesdale Nettles was born in 1924 and was raised in Houston as a Baptist. She married and had four children. Nettles worked as a registered nurse. She became interested in astrology, Spiritualism, and Theosophy. Nettles was a member of the Houston Lodge of the Theosophical Society in America from February 3, 1966, to June 1, 1973 (with a temporary lapse in payment of her dues). Nettles's marriage was ending in 1972, when she met Marshall Herff Applewhite.[55]

Applewhite was the son of a Texas Presbyterian minister, and he had briefly attended seminary. Applewhite became a music professor, who directed choral groups and choirs and sang baritone in operas. Around 1965, Applewhite was dismissed from his position in the University of Alabama School of Music in Tuscaloosa for having an affair with a male student. Applewhite's wife left him, taking their two children. In 1970, he lost his job at the University of St. Thomas in Houston, reportedly because of an affair with a young woman. Applewhite may have experienced additional stress when his father died in 1971.[56]

After meeting in March 1972, Nettles and Applewhite briefly operated a Christian Art Center in Houston that offered classes on religion, art, and music. They then opened a center called Know Place for the study of metaphysics. During this time, Applewhite began studying *The Secret Doctrine* (1888) by Helena P. Blavatsky, the philosopher and cofounder of the Theosophical Society.[57]

In January 1973, Nettles and Applewhite left behind their lives in Houston and began traveling together. On one occasion, in their early travels, their car died in front of a house belonging to an Ananda Marga group in Portland, Oregon, and they were given shelter. This may have been one of the sources of their familiarity with Hinduism. While camping in Oregon, they realized they were the "Two Lampstands" or "Two Witnesses" mentioned in chapter 11 of the book of Revelation, who have come to spread the word of God's impending judgment and salvation. This biblical passage predicted the Two would be assassinated, their bodies would lie in the street for three-and-a-half days, and that they would be resurrected and ascend to heaven in a cloud, which Nettles and Applewhite believed would be a flying saucer. They began proselytizing at New

Age bookstores and to friends and strangers. One woman from Houston became their follower briefly in the spring of 1974.[58]

The message of the Two was a literalist interpretation of the Bible (reflecting the fundamentalism of the Bible Belt in the southern United States) as well as of Theosophical doctrines. They combined Christian and some Theosophical doctrines with belief in UFOs, extraterrestrials, and space aliens.[59] When the Bible spoke of Jesus's resurrection and his ascension in a cloud of light into the kingdom of Heaven, Nettles and Applewhite understood that to mean that Jesus had transformed his human body into a divinized body and that Jesus had been picked up by a flying saucer and taken to the Next Level (the Kingdom of Heaven). Nettles and Applewhite concluded that they, and their followers, would likewise transform their bodies into extraterrestrial bodies, described as being genderless and eternal, just as a caterpillar metamorphoses into a butterfly. They would be picked up by flying saucers,[60] and then spend eternity traveling in outer space guiding evolution on various planets (as the Masters in Theosophy are said to do—without the technological trappings). Nettles and Applewhite taught that Applewhite had come to Earth from The Level Above Human (T.E.L.A.H.), also called the Kingdom of Heaven or the Next Level, about 2,000 years ago as Jesus, but on this current visit—the Second Coming—he had brought with him his heavenly Father, Nettles. One day in Next Level time equaled 1,000 years in Earth time. T.E.L.A.H. inhabitants sent "Representatives" to harvest the worthy into the Next Level every other day.[61]

On August 28, 1974, in Harlingen, Texas, Nettles and Applewhite were arrested. Nettles was charged with credit card fraud (the husband of their one follower did not appreciate the charges on his credit card), but the charges were dropped and Nettles was released. Applewhite was moved to the St. Louis County jail and sentenced to four months for stealing a rental car. Upon Applewhite's release in early 1975, they went to southern California where they attracted a number of converts from a New Age group in Los Angeles.[62]

HEAVEN'S GATE

Out of the Los Angeles group, Nettles and Applewhite, who at that time called themselves Guinea and Pig, gained twenty-four followers.[63] Guinea and Pig taught that followers had to abandon their families and previous lives, overcome all human attachments and desires, live a celibate lifestyle, and discipline themselves to overcome their human nature. The believers were promised that they would transform their human bodies into eternal, genderless, extraterrestrial bodies, and that soon the flying saucers would pick them up.

In September 1975, the Two, calling themselves Bo and Peep, attracted over thirty converts after giving a public lecture in Waldport, Oregon. These individuals left their families and jobs, and the incident was given sensationalized media coverage nationwide for the next two months. At this time, the Two called their group HIM, for human individual metamorphosis.[64]

Shortly after the Waldport meeting, two sociologists, Robert Balch and David Taylor, infiltrated the group, posing as new members. Balch and Taylor reported that, at that time, there was minimal indoctrination and socialization of new members. Bo and Peep were in hiding, apparently in response to the negative news coverage. New recruits gathered at camp sites where they were paired into celibate couples and told to travel about while trying to overcome their humanness and listening for guidance from The Level Above Human. Needless to say, many converts dropped out, and various individuals began receiving revelations that contradicted the teachings of the Two. The converts at that time typically were young people in their 20s who were already involved in the counterculture, with few attachments. The converts had been spiritual seekers for some time before being attracted to Bo and Peep's message. Balch and Taylor left the amorphous movement at the end of 1975.[65]

At a public meeting in Kansas on April 21, 1976, Bo and Peep were interrupted by hecklers. Peep then stood up and announced, "the doors to the next level are closed." She declared, "The harvest is closed," and the group did not proselytize for the next seventeen years.[66]

In the summer of 1976, the Two took their followers (less than 100) to camp in Wyoming. At that time, the Two announced that "the demonstration," in which they would be assassinated and then resurrected, was called off. They said that their assassination by the press had fulfilled that prophecy.[67]

At the Wyoming camp, the Two instituted more rigorous socialization processes. To prevent revelations from other individuals, they explained that information from the Next Level came through a "chain of mind" that was channeled through the Two. They imposed monastic disciplines involving structured daily work, listening to a vibrating tuning fork, working with different partners, observing times of silence, wearing uniforms such as hooded windbreakers and loose clothing to conceal sexual characteristics. The Two minimized dissent by asking doubters to leave and by giving them financial help to do so. The group had become a "class" preparing for graduation into The Level Above Human. Class members were given new names ending in "ody" and the Two began calling themselves Ti and Do. The group's membership dropped to about eighty.[68]

Bo and Peep (on right) make a public presentation flanked by two of their followers. (Corbis)

The students regarded the monastic disciplines of the class as purifying their minds of the influences of discarnate entities and evil space aliens, which strove to cause humans to be attached to their human bodies ("their vehicles"), families, and traditional social roles. The students were training to realize that they were not their human bodies and they tried to overcome all human desires in order to become worthy of entering into The Level Above Human. Until one entered T.E.L.A.H.,[69] there was constant transmigration in the earthly realm. The goal was to be released from earthly transmigration to enter into the Kingdom of Heaven. This is very similar to the Hindu ultimate goal of liberation from the cycle of rebirth, and the class's monastic discipline and constant travel were similar to those of Hindu renunciants who aim to eliminate all desires. The identification of the body as a vehicle or a "suit of clothes," which is discarded at death to put on a new suit of clothes, is found in the Hindu text, the Bhagavad Gita, which Applewhite and Nettles could have learned about through Theosophy, through their reading about world religions, or through encountering Hindu-derived new religious movements in their travels.

The evil space aliens were called Luciferians, and they were described as being humans from other worlds who possessed greatly advanced technology. The Luciferians had turned against the Next Level and strove to manipulate humans on Earth and prevent them from evolving to T.E.L.A.H. Ti and Do connected the Luciferians to popular conspiracy theories of a One World Government. Luciferians held humans in slavery

with social norms that promote conventional family life, sexual repro-
duction, and holding steady jobs. Luciferians were identified as "humans'
GREATEST ENEMY."[70]

Ti and Do taught that individuals who accepted their message and recognized them as Representatives from the Next Level had earlier received
a "deposit" of a soul containing life from the Next Level. All other human
beings were simply mammalian "plants" who possessed spirits, not living
souls. The seed of life contained in the deposit had to be nurtured by contact with a Representative from the Next Level in order to prepare that
individual for entrance into The Level Above Human. The disciple should
aim to "graft" onto the Representative from the Next Level, who was the
"vine" who connected the disciple to the Kingdom of Heaven. This meant
that Do was the Father of the class's students. In a previous age, Do had
grafted onto Ti as his Father; this meant that Ti was the Grandfather of the
group. Since the members of the Next Level did not reproduce by sexual
intercourse, they gained new members in the Kingdom of Heaven by this
method, which involved metamorphosis and grafting. The "chain of mind"
was the vine that led all the way up a hierarchy to the Chief of Chiefs, the
ultimate Creator. By being devoted to serving their Representative, their
Older Member, who was their sole means of entering the Kingdom of
Heaven, the disciples aimed to become instruments of the mind of their
Older Member. In this manner, they cultivated the advanced thinking and
consciousness of The Level Above Human.[71]

This notion of grafting onto an Older Member to enter the Kingdom
of Heaven came from a literalistic reading of the biblical passage stating,
"I am the vine, ye are the branches."[72] In the New Revised Standard Version,
this passage in John 15: 5-11 reads:

> I am the vine, you are the branches. Those who abide in me and I
> in them bear much fruit, because apart from me you can do noth-
> ing. Whoever does not abide in me is thrown away like a branch
> and withers; such branches are gathered, thrown into the fire, and
> burned. If you abide in me, and my words abide in you, ask for
> whatever you wish, and it will be done for you. My Father is glo-
> rified by this, that you bear much fruit and become my disciples.
> As the Father has loved me, so I have loved you; abide in my love.
> If you keep my commandments, you will abide in my love, just
> as I have kept my Father's commandments and abide in his love.
> I have said these things to you so that my joy may be in you, and
> that your joy may be complete.

When people decided to leave after going through the socialization
processes of the class's monastic discipline, it was usually not because they

did not believe the teachings, but because they doubted their ability to adhere to the monastic discipline. Usually when people left the class, they remained believers,[73] and some returned later.

Ti and Do continued to assert that the group would be picked up in flying saucers to be transported into the Kingdom of Heaven. One time, while camping in south Texas, Nettles received a message from the Next Level that the flying saucer would land that evening. The next day, she apologized, "Well, I feel like I have egg on my face."[74]

When two members inherited about $300,000 in 1977, the group began renting houses, but they moved periodically to avoid developing attachments to one place and to prevent family members from finding them. Each house was a "craft" and activities were highly scheduled to develop crew-mindedness and the impeccable attention to detail that was said to characterize Next Level existence. Balch estimates that by the end of 1978, the group had forty-eight members. Members of the group took turns standing "on watch" at night looking for the arrival of the flying saucer.[75] Once, while staying in a house in Canyon Lake, Texas, their neighbors vandalized their home, thinking they were Satanists.[76]

The movie *Cocoon* about extraterrestrials picking up humans motivated the class to rent a houseboat in the Gulf of Mexico in hope of being picked up there.[77]

In 1983, on Mother's Day, many of the students unexpectedly returned to their homes to visit their parents. Their parents found them to be pleasant, polite, and helpful, but they all disappeared again after a two-week visit.[78]

In 1983, Nettles had to have an eye removed because of cancer. The cancer spread to her liver, and Nettles died in a Dallas hospital in June of 1985. Nettles's death disconfirmed the Two's teaching that the group's members were transforming their human bodies into Next Level extraterrestrial bodies. Do began teaching that, as the class's students engaged in ascetic discipline, they were creating "a parallel body with a different molecular structure—grown as a human mastered Next Level knowledge...."[79]

Some of the class's students decided to leave. Michael Conyers left in 1988, Dick Joslyn in 1990, Lee Ann Fenton in 1991, and Michael Fiester in 1992. Joslyn subsequently told reporters that he left because he was convinced the flying saucers were not going to come. By 1993, there were only about twenty-five disciples left.[80]

Some of the group's male members wanted to be castrated to remove their sexual drives. The first castration was performed in Mexico in 1993. Subsequently, Do and seven other men were castrated.[81]

In the 1990s, the group began proselytizing again. Calling themselves Total Overcomers Anonymous, they produced a video series entitled "Beyond Human—The Last Call" and had it transmitted in 1991 and 1992 via satellite TV.[82]

In 1993, Total Overcomers Anonymous ran an ad in *USA Today* entitled "'UFO Cult' Resurfaces with Final Offer," announcing that "The Earth's present 'civilization' is about to be recycled—'spaded under.' Its inhabitants are refusing to evolve. The 'weeds' have taken over the garden and disturbed its usefulness beyond repair."[83] The *USA Today* ad was written in "*Star Trek* vernacular" because the class constantly searched for "contemporary ways to express our information that could potentially override traditional religious, as well as 'New Age,' preconceptions and stereotyping."[84] Similar ads were placed in over twenty alternative newspapers and magazines in the United States, Canada, and Australia. In 1994, the students began holding public recruiting meetings all over the United States.[85] While proselytizing in public lectures offering the "last chance," group members again experienced some heckling. Do, once again, concluded that they might be assaulted and martyred, and in 1995 class members bought two rifles, three revolvers, and two semiautomatic pistols, perhaps thinking to provoke a government attack, but the students were not comfortable with the weapons and put them in storage.[86]

The class gained some new members as a result of the 1990s proselytizing, including Richard Ford, who took the name Rio DiAngelo, and who first discovered the group suicide and alerted authorities.[87]

In 1994, the class gathered on a Santa Monica pier, expecting the saucer to pick them up. Also in 1994, Do discussed with his disciples the possibility that they might need to kill their earthly bodies to be transported to the Next Level to determine what they thought of that idea.[88]

On September 25-26, 1995, the class posted a statement entitled "Undercover Jesus Surfaces Before Departure" on the World Wide Web and to ninety-five UseNET groups on the Internet. On October 11, 1995, they posted another statement, "'95 Statement by an E.T. Presently Incarnate." The responses they received by email expressed "ridicule, hostility, or both...." They concluded: "This was the signal to us to begin our preparations to return 'home.'"[89]

By the fall of 1996, the class was living in a mansion in Rancho Santa Fe, and the students were earning a substantial income as computer experts and as designers of World Wide Web pages. Their computer business was called the Higher Source. They liked watching science fiction movies and television shows, such as *Star Wars*, *Star Trek*, and *The X-Files*. At age 65, Do was suffering from severe constrictive coronary arteriosclerosis. The Hale-Bopp comet had been spotted by astronomers,[90] and rumors that a flying saucer was following behind the comet prompted the Heaven's Gate members to conclude that Ti was coming in the mothership to pick them up.

CATASTROPHIC MILLENNIALISM

Ti and Do utilized plant and gardening metaphors in their teachings. These metaphors were derived from a literalistic reading of the parables of Jesus, such as the parable of the sower who sows seed on good soil and on rocky ground (Matthew 13:18-23; Mark 4:3-9), the parable of the weeds of the field that will be burned up at the end of time while the good plants will be harvested into the Kingdom of Heaven (Matthew 13:37-43), and Jesus's statement that "Every plant that my heavenly Father has not planted will be uprooted" (Matthew 15:12). Ti and Do also took literally New Testament passages such as "For in the resurrection they neither marry nor are given in marriage, but are like angels in heaven" (Matthew 22:29-30), Jesus's praise for those who have "made themselves eunuchs for the sake of heaven" (Matthew 19:12), Jesus's praise for those who abandon their families for the sake of the Kingdom of Heaven (Matthew 10:37-39; Matthew 19:29-30; Luke 14:26-27), and Jesus's statement that one's true parents and family are "whoever does the will of God...." (Mark 3:35).

Ti and Do rejected the monism (belief in the unity of all levels of existence) of Theosophy that they had studied in Blavatsky's *The Secret Doctrine*. But Ti and Do also made a literalistic interpretation of such Theosophical doctrines as that there are graduated levels of existence/consciousness in the universe and that these consist of very fine, divinized matter at the highest levels and gross, dense matter on the earthly level. According to Theosophical doctrines, a human possesses subtle bodies that operate on the subtle levels of existence, but these subtle bodies are unified with the gross physical body, and someone possessing enlightened wisdom can function consciously in all the bodies simultaneously. In Theosophical teachings, the subtle bodies are asserted to be manifested in auras perceived by some psychics. Ti and Do taught that The Level Above Human inhabitants possess eternal, genderless bodies. Initially, they taught that by practicing the group's monastic discipline members were transforming their human bodies into these eternal T.E.L.A.H. bodies. This was disconfirmed in 1985 by Ti's death. By the time of the exit in 1997, Do taught that the mammalian vehicles had to be shed in order to obtain T.E.L.A.H. bodies aboard Ti's mothership.

Ti and Do taught that since Next Level inhabitants were not mammalians and were therefore genderless, they reproduced by harvesting "plants" possessing souls from "gardens" on various planets. They did this by periodically sending Representatives from the Kingdom of Heaven to the gardens so that those souls, who recognized the truth of their message, might "graft" onto that Representative and be harvested into the Kingdom of Heaven.

Do claimed to be the Second Coming of Jesus, the Representative who came 2,000 years ago, but who found then that his disciples were not yet ready to enter into the Kingdom of Heaven. This time he had come to Earth with his "Older Member" or "Father" on whom he was grafted, by which means he had entered the Kingdom of Heaven. Together they were harvesting souls into T.E.L.A.H. Their mission was urgent, because the Earth was to be "spaded under" in an imminent cataclysm caused by the Luciferians, but which would serve the Next Level's purpose of giving the Earth a rest. The "weeds" on Earth were the children of Lucifer. The Luciferians or "fallen angels" were evil space aliens. The Luciferian influence "programmed" humans to conform passively to conventional social norms.[91] Luciferians were disobedient to the will of The Level Above Human, the source of all creation, and sought to inhibit the evolution of others toward the Next Level. The Earth was currently overgrown with weeds and since evolution could no longer progress, the elect were being harvested, and then the Earth would be spaded under.

Do defined the Antichrist as "those propagators of sustained faithfulness to mammalian humanism."[92] The Antichrist consisted of the Luciferians, or anyone who turned against the Next Level and strove to inhibit the evolution of others into the Next Level. Do was adamant in his dualistic perspective, which pitted evil earthly matter against divinized matter and consciousness in the Kingdom of Heaven. Any doctrine that stressed unity between the various levels of existence in the universe was the Antichrist. The Antichrist was any doctrine that brought the divine into everyday life. Therefore, Do wrote:

> They [the Two] also came to know that the true antichrist is now here and has taken several faces, one of which is the New Age "Ye are Gods" concept, or "I have only to become aware of my own 'Christ consciousness within'" while continuing to practice the ways of the world.[93]

Do further wrote that the Theosophical tradition was the Antichrist, probably due to its monism. His statement reveals familiarity not only with the literature of the parent Theosophical Society (Blavatsky's works and the Mahatma Letters) and most likely with the literature of the Church Universal and Triumphant and its doctrine of Ascended Masters. (For the most part, the Masters of the parent Theosophical Society are said to be human beings, not ascended.) According to Do, the Two were "tempted by the forces of Lucifer, when in the early stages of their awakening, they were drawn into the study of Theosophy, with its teachings of the Ascended Masters, Blavatsky's materials, and the Mahatma's [sic] Letters."[94]

THE PERSECUTION

Applewhite's sense of persecution probably dated back to his struggles over his sexual identity in the culturally conservative South and to his related losses of employment, family, and good name.

Applewhite was mortified by his arrest and imprisonment in 1974-1975. In 1988, Do described his first brush with law enforcement agents, and also, ironically, his first encounter with a news reporter:

> Sometime later, while in Brownsville, Texas, they made an appointment with a news reporter to share what they had come to know, telling him that this would be the biggest story he had ever received. He believed them, but thought that their story was about drug trafficking and brought hoards of authorities with him to the interview. This frightened *the two*, who were pretty paranoid by now anyhow, and when they saw the authorities, they left abruptly, which made the authorities follow them. In the process of following them, though the police didn't know why *the two* were running, they checked out the license of the rented car which had been reported stolen.[95]

Nettles spent a brief time in jail for using credit cards that belonged to their sole follower's husband (the charges were dropped), and Applewhite was extradited to St. Louis for a trial for car theft. After he had served six months in jail, the case came to trial. He was sentenced to four months in prison, and was released. Do reported the reaction of Applewhite and Nettles to their encounter with law enforcement:

> They were at first horrified at what had happened, thinking that a jail record had ruined their mission, that no one would listen to them if their credibility was questionable. However, they could see that even prior to the jail incident their stability and credibility was by now unquestionably questionable.[96]

Do frankly reported, "It might be interesting to note that during Do's trial, because of the judge's awareness of the peculiar circumstances surrounding the arrest, the judge ordered a psychiatric examination. Although Do passed it with flying colors, not a 24-hour period slipped by that he didn't question his own sanity."[97]

After this episode, the Two resumed their travels, but "with a new 'down to earth' modus operandi: take no chances." They also resolved never to use credit cards. "This too reminded them that credit and credit cards are not the ways of the Next Level, but rather some of 'Lucy's' (Lucifer's) ways of guaranteeing your service to this world."[98]

Writing in 1988, Do described the distress of the Two at the sensationalized media coverage they received in 1975, after their conversion of people at Waldport.

> Ti and Do were in Las Vegas when the TV network news programs all broke the story about *the two*. Now because of the kind of publicity that had come out across the country, climaxed by the networks, Ti and Do felt that further meetings were pretty hopeless and people had already made up their minds about how ridiculous this all was. Ti and Do felt that the demonstration was still the one thing that could change that. However, they grieved literally for days, feeling like they had been shot down by the media and the mission was dead.
>   They received instruction to not walk into a physical demonstration but rather to know that the "killing in the street" of the two witnesses had occurred at the hands of the media. However, they felt like this was a cop-out or a "chickening out" interpretation of the one act that was the basis of their own following. So with much embarassment, they called their students together, convinced that without a physical demonstration, their students would have every right to call them charlatans. Much to their surprise the students, almost without exception, accepted the interpretation and said, "OK then, where do we go from here?"[99]

Do criticized the inaccurate news reporting of their teachings in 1975–1976.

> We had become a national media item. Their unrelenting spotlight glared upon us for over half a year. And by and large, almost every report either written or aired about us was either riddled with inaccuracies or outright lies, that is, with one noteworthy exception. On Sunday, February 29, 1976, the *New York Times* published the best researched article to date. As the cover story of *The New York Times Magazine*, free-lance writer James S. Phelan, who actually had a lengthy interview with Ti and Do, wrote a generally quite objective article (though certainly not the way we would have written it) despite the "journalistic tide" against his doing so.[100]

The Two reacted by becoming extremely secretive about the group's whereabouts, and, shortly thereafter, ceased proselytizing after being heckled by a Kansas audience. The Two taught a dualistic view of the world: materialistic and mammalian society is evil and controlled by sinister Luciferians; the Kingdom of Heaven and its inhabitants and way of life are good. When they received negative feedback to their proselytizing efforts in the 1990s, it simply confirmed their belief that the earthly garden was overgrown with weeds and would soon be spaded under.

The Failure of the Millennial Goal

In 1988, Do wrote:

> One of the greatest temptations that Do and members of the class as individuals have had to deal with is the feeling of failure or not measuring up to the best potential of their task. However, they repeatedly recovered on the basis that whatever they might have appraised as a mistake can be reappraised as a lesson, hopefully learned, not needing to be repeated. They know that the Next Level, the Kingdom of God, always knows how to use what might have appeared as a major negative or a mistake, and change it into a positive, or a forward step of even greater magnitude.[101]

The Two had promised that flying saucers would pick up the class and carry them to the Next Level. Dates were set from time to time, and the saucers inevitably failed to show up. The Two had promised their disciples that they were transforming their human bodies into eternal extraterrestrial bodies, just like a caterpillar turns into a butterfly. In 1985, this was disconfirmed by Ti's death.

Ti and Do had set an impossible goal for the class, their physical transformation and ascension into the Kingdom of Heaven. The failure of the saucers to appear and Ti's death called the class's ultimate concern into question. The students had been taught to depend on their Older Member as the sole means to enter the Kingdom of Heaven, but Do was getting old and would certainly die. To preserve their ultimate concern, the class decided to take violent action.

THE DECISION TO COMMIT VIOLENCE

In some of his last statements to the public, Do asserted: "As true today as it was 2000 years ago, no one gets to my Father or enters the Kingdom of Heaven except through me. There is no other Son of His or Representative from His Kingdom incarnate. Connecting with that Kingdom occurs only while a Member is incarnate, as I am today."[102] Do further asserted: "The only way an individual can grow in the Next Level is to learn to be dependent on his Older Member as that source of unlimited growth and knowledge. So, any younger member in good standing, forever remains totally dependent upon (and looks to) his Older Member for all things."[103]

Do was confronting the dilemma of what happens after the death of the founder of a new religious movement. He had taught his disciples that dependence upon him was their only means to enter the Kingdom of Heaven. What would happen to the students after his death?

The reliance on the teacher or guru as the means to salvation is found particularly in the *siddha* (perfected saint) tradition of Hinduism. The disciple is taught to surrender totally to the guru, and that salvation comes through the guru's grace. But in India, gurus are highly respected, and renunciants living a disciplined monastic lifestyle are supported by society. In America, the Heaven's Gate group received ridicule, although their goal of escaping the trap of constant transmigration is similar to the religious goal of Hinduism. This situation exacerbated the students' feelings of alienation from American society. In the Hindu *siddha* tradition, the problem of what happens after the death of the guru is solved by the guru's designation of a successor. Before he dies, the guru passes his enlightened consciousness to his successor. This lineage of gurus is termed a *parampara*. The theology taught by Do did not provide for the establishment of a lineage of leaders to succeed him. Do had stressed to his disciples that *he* was the only means by which they could enter the Kingdom of Heaven.

Although Ti and Do taught that their disciples should overcome their humanness and their longing for family and human connections, the Heaven's Gate class became a surrogate family for its members. The students cultivated such strong feelings of dependency on Ti (their Grandfather) and Do (their Father) that they could not imagine carrying on in this world after Do's death. It would be better to exit with Do and be assured of their entrance into the Kingdom of Heaven. This view was expressed in many of the exit statements given by the Heaven's Gate disciples.

Chkody wrote about the sense of alienation the students experienced when their efforts to proselytize resulted only in their being considered "looney tunes." Chkody concluded that the One World Government conspiracy was true; the world was controlled by powerful evil ones who disseminated misinformation. Chkody believed that the existence of militia groups, who resisted the control of the evil American government, was an indication that these were indeed the "end times." Chkody chose to follow Ti and Do into the Next Level because they were the true parents. "There is only one real family and it is not determined by the flesh but by the mind that occupies the soul."[104]

Glnody wrote that, "We value our Next Level family over any human family these vehicles might have issued from." According to Glnody:

> I know who my Older Members, Ti and Do, are. I believe in, cleave to, trust in, and rely totally upon them. I know my Older

Member, Do, is going to his Older Member, Ti, at this time. Once He is gone, there is nothing left here on the face of the Earth for me, no reason to stay a moment longer. Furthermore, I know that my graft to Them would be jeopardized if I linger here once They have departed. I know that my classmates/siblings feel the same as I do and will be choosing to go when Do goes. I want to stay with my Next Level family. Choosing to exit this borrowed human vehicle or body and go home to the Next Level is an opportunity for me to demonstrate my loyalty, commitment, love, trust, and faith in Ti and Do and the Next Level. It is my chance to prove to the Next Level that there is nothing here in this world that I want and that I clearly know that I am the soul and the Next Level Mind which occupies it and not this biological outer garment that I am currently occupying. It is my chance to go to God, to prove that I love His World. How could I honestly say I love Him more than anything if I cling to this world at all costs and only leave here when I am forced to go when this vehicle ceases to function?[105]

The Two's teaching, that ordinary human beings were merely plants without life, made it easy to exit Earth. According to Glnody, "There is no life here in the human world. This planet has become the planet of the living dead. The human plants walk, talk, take careers, procreate, and so forth, but there is no life in them. It is all just a counterfeit illusion crafted by the forces in opposition to the Next Level." Glnody concluded that true suicide would be "to turn away from this incredible opportunity I've been given, to turn my back on the Next Level and the life they are offering after all the care and nurturing I've been given."[106] The class's exit was an option for life in the Kingdom of Heaven.

Glnody reported that the class had successfully cultivated the crew-mindedness that was required for existence in the Next Level.

We have grown to realize the value of not trusting our own individual judgment and rely upon the higher judgment that comes when we approach a situation together as partners with teams looking to a senior member. Some humans assume that we must be weak-minded or incapable of individual thought since we do not make snap decisions, when in reality we are each stronger than any single human could ever be because of our looking beyond ourselves for answers.[107]

Quite a few of the students wrote of experiencing a sense of recognition when they first met Ti and Do. Srrody wrote of growing "to love this individual [Do], His Father, and His Family with all that I am. All I wanted to do was be close to Them, to be part of Them." Srrody wrote of being shaken by Ti's death in 1985. "When my Grandfather's vehicle finally gave out, it was a real wake-up call for me—the realization that my teachers may not be able to teach me all I needed to know and apply before their vehicles gave out from the intolerable conditions here." Srrody's statement concluded by inviting others to follow them into the Kingdom of Heaven. "Some could even be accelerated by our exit, even as we were accelerated by Ti's, and use this opportunity to join us. If so, we will be watching and waiting to assist for as long as we can. Good luck."[108]

Do's assertion was captured in the titles of two of the group's exit videos, "Planet about to Be Recycled: Your Only Chance to Survive— Leave with Us" and "Last Chance to Evacuate Earth before It's Recycled,"[109] and provided a sense that it was urgent that the class and others commit the extreme act of killing their mammalian vehicles to enter into the Kingdom of Heaven. As with some of the other millennial groups considered in this book, catastrophic millennialism had the effect of radically devaluing earthly existence. If the Earth is to be destroyed imminently, why stay? The Heaven's Gate web page[110] stressed that there was only a small window of opportunity to enter into the Next Level, and that was associated with the presence of the Hale-Bopp comet.

One hopes that Heaven's Gate is now closed and will not be reopened until the next Representative from The Level Above Human comes, which by Heaven's Gate reckoning should be about 2000 years from now.

Notes

1. Personal communication from Jean-François Mayer. I thank Jean-François Mayer for information he has provided to me. He was involved in the Swiss police investigation of the Solar Temple deaths.
2. John R. Hall and Philip Schuyler, "The Mystical Apocalypse of the Solar Temple," in *Millennium, Messiahs, and Mayhem: Contemporary Apocalyptic Movements*, ed. Thomas Robbins and Susan J. Palmer (New York: Routledge, 1997), 285-87, 306; Jean-François Mayer, "Myths of the Solar Temple," translated by Elijah Siegler. Paper presented to the ISAR/CESNUR Symposium on "Violence and the New Religions," Nashville, Tennessee, March 10, 1996.
3. Susan J. Palmer, "Purity and Danger in the Solar Temple," *Journal of Contemporary Religion* 3 (October 1996): 303-4.
4. Palmer, "Purity and Danger in the Solar Temple," 303-18; Hall and Schuyler, "Mystical Apocalypse," 309.
5. Massimo Introvigne, "The Magic of Death: The Suicides of the Solar Temple," in *Millennialism, Persecution, and Violence: Historical Cases*, ed. Catherine Wessinger (Syracuse: Syracuse University Press, 2000), 138–57.
6. Another letter was written by Joseph Di Mambro deploring that what should have been a glorious transit at Cheiry was turned into a "veritable carnage"

perpetrated by "the barbarous, incompetent" Dr. Luc Jouret. See Introvigne, "Magic of Death."

7. Palmer, "Purity and Danger in the Solar Temple," 303.

8. Mayer, "Myths of the Solar Temple," 13, 15; Hall and Schuyler, "Mystical Apocalypse," 307; Introvigne, "Magic of Death."

9. Hall and Schuyler, "Mystical Apocalypse," 292-93; Massimo Introvigne, "Ordeal by Fire: The Tragedy of the Solar Temple," *Religion* 25 (1995): 273-74.

10. Hall and Schuyler, "Mystical Apocalypse," 291, 296; Mayer, "Myths of the Solar Temple," 2-4; Introvigne, "Magic of Death"; personal communication from Jean-François Mayer. Mayer points out that Di Mambro's followers probably did not call him a prophet. One woman, who subsequently died in the 1995 transit, told Mayer that she saw Di Mambro as a "Cosmic Master." Nevertheless, Di Mambro functioned as a prophet since he presented revelations from the Masters. See the definition of the term *prophet* in chapter 2.

11. Palmer, "Purity and Danger in the Solar Temple," 315.

12. Hall and Schuyler, "Mystical Apocalypse," 290; Introvigne, "Ordeal by Fire," 267.

13. Introvigne, "Ordeal by Fire," 271-72; Introvigne, "Magic of Death."

14. Introvigne, "Ordeal by Fire," 280.

15. Introvigne, "Ordeal by Fire," 275; Palmer, "Purity and Danger in the Solar Temple," 306, 313; Hall and Schuyler, "Mystical Apocalypse," 294-95. Jean-François Mayer reports that the Swiss police found no holographic technology at the Sanctuaire in Salvan.

16. Palmer, "Purity and Danger in the Solar Temple," 311.

17. Hall and Schuyler, "Mystical Apocalypse," 294; Palmer, "Purity and Danger in the Solar Temple," 308.

18. Palmer, "Purity and Danger in the Solar Temple," 309.

19. Introvigne, "Magic of Death"; Palmer, "Purity and Danger in the Solar Temple," 310-11, 315.

20. Mayer, "Myths of the Solar Temple," 9; Palmer, "Purity and Danger in the Solar Temple," 315.

21. Mayer, "Myths of the Solar Temple," 10.

22. The Dutoits were murdered by Joel Egger, Dominique Bellaton, and the Genouds. Egger and Bellaton then returned to Switzerland to join the others for the transit. The Genouds committed suicide by setting the Quebec residence on fire. See Palmer, "Purity and Danger in the Solar Temple," 312-13.

23. Mayer, "Myths of the Solar Temple," 16-17.

24. See Catherine Wessinger, "Millennialism With and Without the Mayhem," in Robbins and Palmer, *Millennium, Messiahs, and Mayhem*, 54-55, in which I point out that a cyclical view of time is fully compatible with millennialism.

25. Mayer, "Myths of the Solar Temple," 8.

26. Alice Bailey left the Theosophical Society in America in 1920. Bailey, who claimed to speak for the Masters, founded the Arcane School to disseminate the Masters' teachings. Bailey's millennial thought was influenced by that of Annie Besant, who at that time was the president of the international Theosophical Society headquartered at Adyar, Madras, India. Bailey's corpus may have been the first to use the term *Age of Aquarius*. Bailey's Great Invocation is utilized by many in the New Age movement, including those not directly affiliated with one of the organizations in the Theosophical movement. It reads:

> From the point of Light within the Mind of God
> Let light stream forth into the minds of men.
> Let Light descend on Earth.
> From the point of Love within the Heart of God

Let love stream forth into the hearts of men.
May Christ return to Earth.
From the center where the Will of God is known
Let purpose guide the little wills of men—
The purpose which the Masters know and serve.
From the center which we call the race of men
Let the Plan of Love and Light work out
And may it seal the door where evil dwells.
Let Light and Love and Power restore the Plan on Earth.

See Catherine Lowman Wessinger, *Annie Besant and Progressive Messianism* (Lewiston: N.Y.: Edwin Mellen Press, 1988), 326-30.

27. Mayer, "Myths of the Solar Temple," 9, 12.
28. This is suggested by the dates of documents discussing the transit saved on a computer at Salvan. See Introvigne, "Magic of Death."
29. Personal communication from Jean-François Mayer.
30. Hall and Schuyler, "Mystical Apocalypse," 301-3.
31. Hall and Schuyler, "Mystical Apocalypse," 305-6.
32. Mayer, "Myths of the Solar Temple," 19.
33. Mayer, "Myths of the Solar Temple," 17-18.
34. "Transit to the Future," *Gnosis Magazine,* Winter 1995, 92. I thank Timothy Miller for sending me the *Gnosis* articles on the Solar Temple.
35. "Transit to the Future," 93.
36. "To Lovers of Justice," *Gnosis Magazine,* Winter 1995, 93.
37. "To Lovers of Justice," 94.
38. "To Lovers of Justice," 94.
39. "To Lovers of Justice," 95.
40. "To Lovers of Justice," 95.
41. "To All Those Who Can Still Understand the Voice of Wisdom...We Address This Last Message," *Gnosis Magazine,* Winter 1995, 90.
42. "To All Those Who Can Still Understand," 90.
43. "To All Those Who Can Still Understand," 90.
44. "The Rose+Croix," *Gnosis Magazine,* Winter 1995, 91.
45. Hall and Schuyler, "Mystical Apocalypse," 304.
46. Introvigne, "Magic of Death."
47. Anne Krueger and Susan Gembrowski, "Strange odyssey of Heaven's Gate," *San Diego Union-Tribune,* April 13, 1997. Articles from the *San Diego Union-Tribune* were obtained at <http://www.uniontrib.com>.
48. The July 1997 issue of *Hinduism Today* rightly criticized the American news media for blaming Hinduism for the Heaven's Gate group suicide, by pointing out that the primary theological influences on Marshall Herff Applewhite were the Bible and Christianity. The editorial in *Hinduism Today* concluded that Christians did not want to acknowledge that Christianity produced the Heaven's Gate group suicide, but instead they were casting about for strange and exotic religious traditions to blame. See "Cults: The Spaceship Suicide," *Hinduism Today,* July 1997, 22-25.
49. There may have been astrological considerations for the timing of both group suicides. The vernal equinox was on March 21, the Hale-Bopp comet was closest to the Earth on March 22, and on Sunday, March 23, an eclipse of the full moon occurred in the sign of Libra. I thank Pat Eddishaw for the astrological information.
50. The "Away Team" was a term popularized in the television series, *Star Trek: The Next Generation.* It referred to a small group of crew members sent away

from the starship on a planetary mission. The Away Team always aims to return to the spaceship and rejoin the crew there.

51. "'The Next Level,'" *Newsweek*, April 7, 1997, 28-30; "Trek toward destruction: When and where members joined Heaven's Gate," *San Diego Union-Tribune*, April 13, 1997.

    Robert W. Balch explains that Heaven's Gate members always carried a $5 bill and a few quarters when they left the residence in case they needed cab fare or to make a call. See Robert W. Balch, "Heaven's Gate: Implications for the Study of Commitment to New Religions," in *The Gods Have Landed*, ed. James R. Lewis, 2d ed. (Albany: State University of New York Press, forthcoming), note 2. The travel bags and supplies, the "Away Team" patches, and the Nike shoes (Nike at that time used the slogan "Just Do It!") suggest a humorous approach to the exit. Ti and Do encouraged the cultivation of Next Level (Kingdom of God) humor among the group. The Heaven's Gate members believed that on Ti's mothership they would acquire new bodies that would not need fresh clothing and lip balm. Having the familiar articles close by while committing suicide may have provided a comforting context in which to take that important step.

52. "Trek toward destruction."

53. Kelly Thornton and Susan Gembrowski, "Cult claims 2 new victims," *San Diego Union-Tribune*, May 7, 1997.

54. Sandi Dolbee, "Believers keep Heaven's Gate alive: 4 ex-members sponsor session to gauge interest," *San Diego Union-Tribune*, August 25, 1997; Associated Press, "Ex-Heaven's Gater Is Found Dead," America Online News, February 21, 1998.

55. Barry Bearak, "Eyes on the Glory: Pied Pipers of Heaven's Gate," *New York Times* (AOL), April 28, 1997; letter from John Algeo, president of the Theosophical Society in America, dated July 13, 1997; Robert W. Balch, "Bo and Peep: A Case Study of the Origins of Messianic Leadership," in *Millennialism and Charisma*, ed. Roy Wallis (Belfast: The Queen's University, 1982), 28.

56. Bearak, "Eyes on the Glory"; David Daniel, "The Beginning of the Journey," *Newsweek*, April 14, 1997, 36-37; Balch, "Bo and Peep," 30, 32.

57. Balch, "Bo and Peep," 34-38.

58. Balch, "Bo and Peep," 38-42; [Do], "'88 Update—The UFO Two and Their Crew: A Brief Synopsis," in *How and When "Heaven's Gate" (The Door to the Physical Kingdom Level Above Human) May Be Entered*, by Representatives from the Kingdom of Heaven (New Mexico Republic, the united States of America: Heaven's Gate Representatives, Common Law Copyright 1996), section 3, p. 3. The format of this copyright statement for this desktop-published book indicates influence from the Freemen/Common Law movement. I am grateful to the late Chuck Humphrey for distributing this book.

59. In Heaven's Gate terminology, *extraterrestrials* were the benevolent inhabitants of The Level Above Human (T.E.L.A.H.) the believers aimed at becoming. *Space aliens* was a term they used for evil "Luciferians" who work to retard evolution of others toward the Next Level (T.E.L.A.H. or the Kingdom of Heaven).

60. Ti and Do, "First Statement of Ti and Do, Sent Out from Ojai, California, March 1975," in *How and When "Heaven's Gate" May Be Entered*, section 2, p. 2.

61. Jwnody, "'Away Team' from Deep Space Surfaces Before Departure," in *How and When "Heaven's Gate" May Be Entered*, Appendix A, p. 17.

    Lvvody reported that Jesus departed Earth without his disciples because he knew they were not adequately prepared to enter the Kingdom of Heaven. He left with the intention of returning at the end of the age, only two days later in T.E.L.A.H. time. See Lvvody, "Ingredients of a Deposit—Becoming a New Creature," in *How and When "Heaven's Gate" May Be Entered*, Appendix A, p. 2.

62. Balch, "Bo and Peep," 49-51; Bearak, "Eyes on the Glory." Robert W. Balch, "Waiting for the Ships: Disillusionment and the Revitalization of Faith of Bo and Peep's UFO Cult," in *The Gods Have Landed: New Religions from Other Worlds*, ed. James R. Lewis (Albany: State University of New York Press, 1995), 142.

63. Balch, "Bo and Peep," 51-53.

64. Balch, "Waiting for the Ships," 137.

65. Balch, "Waiting for the Ships," 137-53.

66. Balch, "Waiting for the Ships," 154; Susan Gembrowski and Anne Krueger, "Doubts, discipline led many members to quit," *San Diego Union-Tribune*, April 14, 1997.

67. Bearak, "Eyes on the Glory."

68. Balch, "Waiting for the Ships," 153-57; Gembrowski and Krueger, "Doubts, discipline led many to quit." The suffix "ody" was supposed to be a diminutive for "od" in "God." See Balch, "Heaven's Gate." The suffix "ody" also recalled the names "Ti" and "Do" and indicated that the students were the children of Ti and Do to be taken to their heavenly home.

69. Chkody, "The Hidden Facts of Ti and Do," in *How and When "Heaven's Gate" May Be Entered*, Appendix A, p. 15.

70. "'UFO Cult' Resurfaces With Final Offer," in *How and When "Heaven's Gate" May Be Entered*, section 5, p. 4.

71. Lvvody, "Ingredients of a Deposit—Becoming a New Creature," in *How and When "Heaven's Gate" May Be Entered*, Appendix A, p. 3; Nrrody, "The Truth Is...," in *How and When "Heaven's Gate" May Be Entered*, Appendix A, p. 5.

72. [Do], "'88 Update," in *How and When "Heaven's Gate" May Be Entered*, section 3, p. 12.

73. Balch, "Heaven's Gate."

74. Bearak, "Eyes on the Glory."

75. Balch, "Waiting for the Ships," 157-59; Balch, "Heaven's Gate."

76. Gembrowski and Krueger, "Doubts, discipline led many members to quit."

77. Balch, "Heaven's Gate."

78. Balch, "Waiting for the Ships," 162-63; Gembrowski and Krueger, "Doubts, discipline led many members to quit.".

79. Bearak, "Eyes on the Glory"; Gembrowski and Krueger, "Doubts, discipline led many members to quit."

80. Bearak, "Eyes on the Glory"; Gembrowski and Krueger, "Doubts, discipline led many members to quit."

81. Bearak, "Eyes on the Glory."

82. "Beyond Human—The Last Call: Late 1991–Early 1992: Transcripts of Video Tape Series," in *How and When "Heaven's Gate" May Be Entered*, section 4, pp. 1-87.

83. "'UFO Cult' Resurfaces with Final Offer," in *How and When "Heaven's Gate" May Be Entered*, section 5, p. 4.

84. "*USA Today* Ad/Statement and Misc. Documents—1993," in *How and When "Heaven's Gate" May be Entered*, section 5, p. 1.

85. "*USA Today* Ad/Statement and Misc. Documents—1993," section 5, pp. 1, 5, and "Public Meetings 1994," section 6, pp. 1-2, in *How and When "Heaven's Gate" May Be Entered*.

86. Bearak, "Eyes on the Glory."

87. Balch, "Heaven's Gate."

88. Balch, "Heaven's Gate"; Bearak, "Eyes on the Glory."

89. "Preface," in *How and When "Heaven's Gate" May Be Entered*, vii.
90. Bearak, "Eyes on the Glory"; Gembrowski and Krueger, "Doubts, discipline led many members to quit"; Cheryl Clark, "Cultist Applewhite had a severe heart disease," *San Diego Union-Tribune*, April 12, 1997.
91. Helena P. Blavatsky named her journal published in London, *Lucifer*, but for her name had the positive connotation of "light bearer." Ti and Do's belief in space aliens who were evil fallen angels suggests that they had read the materials produced by the Church Universal and Triumphant, which is part of the broad Theosophical movement.
92. Do, The Present Representative, "Aids in Approaching This Material," in *How and When "Heaven's Gate" May Be Entered*, iv.
93. Do, "'88 Update," in *How and When "Heaven's Gate" May Be Entered*, section 3, p. 4.
94. Do, "'88 Update," in *How and When "Heaven's Gate" May Be Entered*, section 3, p. 13.
95. Do, "'88 Update," in *How and When "Heaven's Gate" May Be Entered*, section 3, p. 5.
96. Do, "'88 Update," in *How and When "Heaven's Gate" May Be Entered*, section 3, p. 5.
97. Do, "'88 Update," in *How and When "Heaven's Gate" May Be Entered*, section 3, p. 5.
98. Do, "'88 Update," in *How and When "Heaven's Gate" May Be Entered*, section 3, p. 6.
99. Do, "'88 Update," in *How and When "Heaven's Gate" May Be Entered*, section 3, p. 8.
100. [Do], "Early Classroom Materials: 1975–1988," in *How and When "Heaven's Gate" May Be Entered*, section 2, p. 1.
101. Do, "'88 Update," in *How and When "Heaven's Gate" May Be Entered*, section 3, p. 13.
102. Do, "Undercover 'Jesus' Surfaces Before Departure," in *How and When "Heaven's Gate" May Be Entered*, section 1, p. 4.
103. [Do], "'95 Statement by an E.T. Presently Incarnate," in *How and When "Heaven's Gate" May Be Entered*, section 1, p. 7.
104. Chkody, "Earth Exit Statement," in *How and When "Heaven's Gate" May Be Entered*, Appendix C, pp. 2-3. Chuck Humphrey, from whom I purchased this book, noted that the pages in Appendix C were added by him. He reported that these final exit statements by students were supposed to have been added to the book by unnamed others who were at that time outside the group. Therefore, Appendix C is likely to be available only in the edition of in *How and When "Heaven's Gate" May Be Entered* produced by Chuck Humphrey (Rkkody). See page 1 of Appendix C.
105. Glnody, "Earth Exit Statement," in *How and When "Heaven's Gate" May Be Entered*, Appendix C, p. 5.
    Glnody reported that the Heaven's Gate group was aware that their monasticism was similar to that of Hinduism and Buddhism. They had considered moving to another country—as opposed to committing group suicide. They did not want to move to another Christian nation because "Christians have been the quickest to condemn us even though we are the return they say they are anxiously awaiting." They decided not to go to a Muslim nation, because they wanted to avoid discrimination against the class's women. They considered moving to either India, Thailand, or somewhere in the Buddhist world, but decided against it because they would have gained converts in one of those nations. They no longer wanted converts. They were confident they had

attracted those who were ready to graduate to the Next Level. They were ready to exit. Glnody, p. 5.

106. Glnody, "Earth Exit Statement," p. 5.

107. Glnody, "Earth Exit Statement," p. 4.

108. Srrody, "Earth Exit Statement," in *How and When "Heaven's Gate" May Be Entered*, Appendix C, pp. 7-8.

109. I am grateful to the Telah Foundation for sending me these two videotapes and two others containing the exit statements of Do and the students.

110. The original Heaven's Gate web page was at <http://www.heavensgate.com>. There are now several web sites that replicate this original Heaven's Gate web site. See <http://cti.itc.virginia.edu/~jkh8x/soc257/heavensgate/>, and <http://www.clas.ufl.edu/users/gthursby/rel/gate/>. Note that Gene Thursby's web page provides a mirror of the web page maintained by Chuck Humphrey (Rkkody), and Humphrey did make some changes to the original Heaven's Gate web page.

CHAPTER EIGHT

1998—Chen Tao: Assessing the Potential for Violence

IN MARCH 1998, CHEN TAO (the name means "True Way"), a group of Taiwanese living in Garland, Texas, near Dallas, captured the attention of news reporters and law enforcement agents. The concern was whether the Chen Tao believers would commit group suicide when their leader's prophecies were disconfirmed. In 1998, Chen Tao members were not involved in violence or a confrontation with law enforcement agents, so my presentation of the data in this chapter differs from the treatment of the other groups in this book.

Hon-Ming Chen (42), reportedly a former social sciences professor, lived with about 150 followers, including children, in houses they purchased in Garland, Texas. Teacher Chen told reporters that they had moved to Garland because Garland sounded like "God's land." Teacher Chen predicted that God would make a promotional announcement on Channel 18 on television sets worldwide on March 25, 1998, at 12:01 A.M. U.S. Central Standard Time. In his television advertisement, God would announce his forthcoming arrival at Teacher Chen's address in Garland at 10:00 A.M. on March 31. Teacher Chen said that when God appeared on March 31, at 3513 Ridgedale Drive, God would appear in a form that would look exactly like Teacher Chen. To show that it was not Teacher Chen impersonating God, God would demonstrate his ability to appear and disappear at will, replicate his body to shake hands simultaneously with all who came to greet him, and speak the languages of everyone present there. (Teacher Chen spoke only Taiwanese Mandarin.) Teacher Chen said that God would come at that time to offer salvation from the apocalyptic destruction that would occur in 1999, by taking the faithful up from Earth in flying saucers. Teacher Chen said that if his prophecies about God's appearance in Garland proved wrong, his followers could stone or crucify him.[1]

Sign in Teacher Chen's yard advertising God's appearance on Channel 18 on March 25, 1998, and in Teacher Chen's front yard on March 31, 1998. (Photo courtesy of Lieutenant Rod Gregg)

Obviously Teacher Chen had set impossible goals for his group: the appearance of God and being carried away in flying saucers, not to mention God's promotional message on Channel 18. What would the Chen Tao believers do when the prophecies failed? The similarity to Heaven's Gate's belief in flying saucers drew the attention of news reporters, who expected to cover a group suicide. The Garland police had to control the crowds gathering in the neighborhood where the Chen Tao believers lived, and the police had to consider whether some sort of intervention was necessary to save lives. Fortunately, both news reporters and the Garland police consulted Religious Studies scholars about Chen Tao. Dr. Lonnie Kliever of Southern Methodist University in Dallas worked closely with the Garland police and did a magnificent job of interfacing with the local, national, and international news media. Kliever's work helped prevent the police and news reporters from overreacting to the Chen Tao case.

In Taiwan, Chen Tao had attracted thoughtful and educated people who were financially well off. The group included doctors, engineers, and teachers. Their spokesman and translator was Richard Liu, formerly a professor of American Literature. Their desktop published book, *God's Descending in Clouds (Flying Saucers) on Earth to Save People* purported to have been written by God—The Supreme Being speaking through Teacher Chen. *God's Descending in Clouds* revealed that Teacher Chen was a person dismayed at the exploitation and suffering that he observed in Taiwan.

God's Descending in Clouds expressed a sense of extreme alienation from Taiwanese society, saying that at least 85 percent of the people in Taiwan and East Asia were possessed by devils, "outside spirits," similar to the "hungry ghosts" of Chinese popular religion. On the other hand, only 15 percent of the population in the United States was said to be devil-possessed. The United States was a place of safe refuge from the nuclear war that would originate in East Asia in 1999. God would come in flying saucers to America to pick up the faithful and carry them away to escape the nuclear fallout and other terrors of the tribulation. Relatives in Taiwan, who opposed the believers' move to the United States, most certainly were devil-possessed.[2]

Chen Tao theology was a syncretistic blend of Buddhism, Christianity, Taoism, traditional Chinese beliefs, and faith in UFOs. Chen Tao teachings were presented in scientific language. Buddhas and bodhisattvas were described as traveling in flying saucers to various planets to educate the inhabitants there.[3] Teacher Chen, as the prophet, identified two boys in the group as being the reincarnations of the Buddha and Jesus. Perhaps these boys are being groomed to be messiahs, but more information is needed. The Chen Tao followers demonstrated a concern for purity by wearing white. They typically wore hats for protection against the Texas sun, and many of them opted to wear white cowboy hats.

Religion scholars cannot make predictions about what members of a religious group may do. Human free will and undetermined social factors always come into play. The comparative study of the groups in this book, however, suggests that certain factors may be identified to indicate whether or not there may be cause for concern. After studying the news reports about Chen Tao and reading *God's Descending in Clouds*, I made

Chen Tao members performing a purification ritual. (Photo courtesy of Lieutenant Rod Gregg)

a list of the features that caused me to worry about what Chen Tao believers might choose to do. I made another list of Chen Tao's characteristics that I found reassuring.

The worrying characteristics of Chen Tao that I listed in the "minus column" were numerous.

1. Teacher Chen took a literalistic approach to interpreting the Bible.

Although Teacher Chen taught that parts of the Bible were written by devils, for instance that the book of Revelation was composed by King Satan, he taught that the Bible's prophecies would come true and that devils and devil-possessed humans in East Asia would cause nuclear armageddon in 1999.[4]

Heaven's Gate was noteworthy for its literalistic interpretation of the Bible, and arguably some of the other groups treated in this book could be considered to have taken such an approach to the Bible.

2. Teacher Chen taught a radically dualistic view of good vs. evil.

Devils or "outside souls"[5] were dominating humanity and driving humans to self-destruction. God would not destroy the world. God would rescue some humans by coming in flying saucers to remove the faithful and pure from the Earth to save them from the nuclear fallout and other perils of the tribulation.

All of the other groups treated in this book—Peoples Temple, the Branch Davidians, Aum Shinrikyo, the Montana Freemen, the Solar Temple, and Heaven's Gate—possessed a radical dualistic view of good locked in battle with evil.

3. Teacher Chen's dualism negated the humanity of most of the people on Earth by attributing a devilish nature to them.[6]

God speaking through Teacher Chen asserted that devil possession was particularly rampant in East Asia, where 85 to 90 percent of the people were devil-possessed.

The dehumanization of other human beings was characteristic of the members of Peoples Temple, Aum Shinrikyo, the Montana Freemen and related racist groups, the Solar Temple, and Heaven's Gate.

The Branch Davidians appear to be the exception here because they were so committed to their proselytization efforts. In his last recorded conversation, David Koresh told a negotiator to tell the tactical agents surrounding his residence and their commanders, "we love 'em" (see transcript at the end of chapter 4).

4. Teacher Chen predicted that nuclear armageddon would originate in East Asia in 1999 without fail.

Teacher Chen's predicted nuclear scenario focused on Taiwan, the People's Republic of China, North and South Korea, and Japan. This was before India and Pakistan tested nuclear bombs in May 1998. These developments in South Asia may well be incorporated into Teacher Chen's future teachings about the apocalypse.

All of the groups studied in this volume believed in imminent catastrophic destruction.

5. The Chen Tao group had reacted to perceived social threats by withdrawing to a safe haven in America.

This pattern of withdrawal from enemies was observed in the relocation of Peoples Temple to Jonestown, Guyana, the building of communes by Aum Shinrikyo, the Montana Freemen's withdrawal into Justus Township, the establishment of "life centers" by the Solar Temple to be "arks of safety," and the secrecy of the Heaven's Gate class concerning their whereabouts.

The Branch Davidians lived in community but they did not initiate violence. They were assaulted.

6. Teacher Chen had set an impossible goal for the group, the appearance of God in his front yard on March 31, 1998. This predicted event was related to Teacher Chen's prediction that God would arrive with flying saucers in 1999 to rescue the faithful from the apocalyptic destruction of the Earth and its population.

Jim Jones, Shoko Asahara, Joseph Di Mambro, and Ti and Do all set impossible goals for their respective groups.[7]

The glare of the media spotlight in March 1998 removed the much needed privacy of the Chen Tao group to work out how they would respond to the disconfirmation of Teacher Chen's prophecies.[8]

7. News reporters were flocking to Garland to cover Chen Tao, and the scene threatened to become a media circus.

Sensationalized news reporting had convinced members of Peoples Temple, Aum Shinrikyo, Solar Temple, Heaven's Gate, and the Branch Davidians that they were being persecuted.

8. Chen Tao theology combined belief in reincarnation with biblical apocalypticism (catastrophic millennialism).

Taken individually, each of these beliefs has the potential to relativize the value of earthly existence. Putting these two doctrines together in a single worldview appears to have the potential to radically devalue earthly life, especially if the group experiences cultural opposition in conjunction with stresses internal to the group.

The groups treated in this book that combined belief in reincarnation with apocalypticism are Peoples Temple, Aum Shinrikyo, the Solar Temple, and Heaven's Gate.

9. Chen Tao was a small, new, and uninstitutionalized group that had not yet routinized the charisma of its prophet, Teacher Chen, into organizational structures.

An over-reliance on the charismatic authority of a prophet or messiah could lead to disaster if the prophet's credibility was endangered as was the case with Jim Jones, Shoko Asahara, Joseph Di Mambro, and Ti and Do. Furthermore, over-dependence on a prophet or messiah could lead to unquestioning obedience of orders given by the charismatic leader.

10. Teacher Chen had staked his life on his prophecies coming true, indicating the importance of the March 31 prediction to his credibility.

I worried that Teacher Chen might be motivated to take extreme actions to preserve his credibility concerning the group's ultimate concern, as had Jim Jones, Shoko Asahara, Joseph Di Mambro, and Do.

While there is no clearcut evidence that David Koresh had his residence set on fire, he may have done so to fulfill biblical prophecies. It is clear that David Koresh refused to come out of Mount Carmel unless doing so validated his authority as a messiah by conforming to interpretation of biblical prophecies.

In the "plus column," Chen Tao had a few very important positive characteristics.

1. The Chen Tao believers, despite their dualistic catastrophic millennialism, which seemed rather paranoid to nonbelievers, responded openly and constructively to questions about themselves, their activities, and their theology.

I observed this open and constructive response to the media and law enforcement investigation in 1993, on the part of the members of the Church Universal and Triumphant. I regard this response as a positive sign as opposed to the withdrawal and/or combative response of the members of Peoples Temple, Aum Shinrikyo, the Montana Freemen, the Solar Temple, and Heaven's Gate. The Branch Davidians, likewise, manifested a relatively open and constructive response to investigators, but they also armed themselves and used those arms when they were assaulted.

Although Chen Tao members had withdrawn from the evil and impure Taiwanese society, they regarded America as the place of safe refuge and they believed that most Americans were not devil-possessed.

The fact that Teacher Chen had designated a follower to be the public relations person (and translator) was a good sign, one that I regard as a positive response on the part of new religious movements to criticism and inquiry. Richard Liu explained Chen Tao's beliefs to reporters, police, and to Dr. Lonnie Kliever.

2. *God's Descending in Clouds* had a statement against suicide on page 38.

At first reading, I did not trust this statement against suicide. Heaven's Gate had posted a statement against suicide on its web page, but it simply redefined suicide as turning against the Kingdom of Heaven and asserted that movement toward the Kingdom of Heaven was life-affirming.[9] But after reading *God's Descending in Clouds* in its entirety and thus learning how much the Chen Tao believers were concerned to avoid devil possession, I decided to trust this statement against suicide. Religious leaders certainly change doctrines in response to circumstances, but I hoped that if Teacher Chen tried to incite the group to commit suicide, the members would remind him that God had taught them that suicide was always motivated by devil-possession and produced extremely detrimental karma.

The relevant passage in *God's Descending in Clouds* reads:

(9). Suicide: The ostensible reasons for suicide, whether on grounds of emotion, career failure, or religious faith, may seem to be related to personal background or personality, but through deeper understanding, we find that most of the suicides are annoyed or possessed by outside souls. It is further related with the causality in previous life. Especially in the circle of religious faith, if a person is introduced into a sect by the priest and enticed to commit suicide in the name of "liberation" or "entering into the paradise," the outcome is always formidable. In most cases, it is always the great heavenly devil which pulls strings in the back. As for the priest, the sin that he commits is so deep-rooted that the suicide will track down on him for many generations, and in the future life, he is going to suffer the same consequence. In the ending period of the world, this kind of events (sic) will come about from time to time.

God gives us life and physical body in the hope that we can cultivate the "true" by means of the "false." That is why it is said that "physical body is hard to acquire." It is only when the three souls co-exist in a physical body that the level of spiritual cultivation can be promoted in the fastest way.[10]

Suicide! Whether in the manner of taking drugs, drowning, burning, hanging, or the like, the way of suicide will be repeated again in the coming life because it is recorded in the soul. Besides, it is an impediment to one's cultivation and going back to the origin.

3. *God's Descending in Clouds* contained only the prediction about God's appearance in Garland on March 31, and said nothing about God's predicted television announcement on March 25.

I wondered if by adding the television prediction for March 25, which would be disconfirmed, Teacher Chen was giving himself a way out of his prediction of God's appearance on March 31. This was exactly how it worked out.

Prior to March 25, Teacher Chen told news reporters that if God did not make his television announcement at midnight that evening, his prediction for March 31 should be regarded as nonsense.[11] Sure enough, when God's announcement did not occur on Channel 18 at midnight on March 25, Teacher Chen promptly told reporters that they should consider his prediction for March 31 nonsense. But Chen Tao believers, news reporters, anticultists, and curious onlookers and scholars gathered at 3513 Ridgedale Drive on March 31, just in case God decided to appear.

On March 31, Teacher Chen explained to the limited crowd, which had been permitted into the neighborhood by the police, that God was indeed present among them and that "since they are all God, they can use their own right hands to shake their own left hands, and they can ask themselves any question. Since people speak many different languages, so does God, he said." Dr. Kliever explained to a reporter that Teacher Chen was shifting from a literalistic interpretation of prophecies to a symbolic interpretation, and that many religions have done the same in order to survive. Dr. Kliever said, "He, like every religious leader develops his message in response to changing circumstances and human needs."[12] Since God did not appear in the manner predicted, Teacher Chen offered himself to his followers to be stoned or crucified, but they declined.

Teacher Chen reiterated the truth of his predictions of nuclear armageddon in 1999, and that God would come in flying saucers to pick up the believers. Furthermore, Teacher Chen asserted that the presence of so many reporters to help him spread God's message was proof that God was carrying out his plan for salvation. The reporters like everyone else there were God.[13]

The fact that Teacher Chen did not speak English may have helped him avoid any sense of being persecuted by the American and international press, but generally the reporters were polite when interviewing Teacher Chen and Richard Liu.[14] Christine Wicker, the religion newswriter for the *Dallas Morning News* did an exceptionally thorough and careful job of reporting about Chen Tao. She interviewed Chen Tao believers and scholars of religion, and she did not sensationalize the story. Therefore, careful reporting contributed to a situation in which the Chen Tao believers did not experience persecution from the press.

The Garland police consulted a Religious Studies scholar, Dr. Lonnie Kliever, about Chen Tao. The police facilitated Dr. Kliever's access to the group for observation and interviews. Having immediate access to the group and the pertinent data enabled Dr. Kliever to provide informed advice to the police. Having received sound advice from a *bona fide* religion expert, the Garland police did not overreact to the situation. The police took normal measures to observe the group and maintain the peace.

It remains to be seen how Chen Tao will develop in the future. By May 1998, about half of the followers had returned to Taiwan because of

Teacher Chen (left) with Richard Liu (right). (Photo courtesy of Lieutenant Rod Gregg)

visa problems. The other half moved with Teacher Chen to Olcott, New York. They waited for God's flying saucers to come when the nuclear armageddon occurred in 1999.[15]

What will happen if Teacher Chen's prophecies about 1999 are disconfirmed remains to be seen. Teacher Chen may be able to reinterpret his prophecies again, especially if he does not feel persecuted and if there are no stresses internal to the group that threaten his status as prophet or threaten the group's ultimate concern of salvation. If there are no persecution or internal stresses, perhaps the Chen Tao members will reinterpret their ultimate concern in some manner, by constructing their millennial kingdom on Earth and/or expecting salvation after death. Greater emphasis may be put on Chen Tao's expressed ultimate concern of "perfect souls" attaining "everlasting life in God's magnetic field of the Void."[16] Recall that ultimate concerns are about achieving well-being, and this ultimate concern is not inconsistent with hoping for salvation from armageddon. The Chen Tao believers may be able to conclude that their rituals and religious practices averted armageddon. Or they may conclude that armageddon will occur at some unknown date in the future.

On the minus side in the future, the boys (ages 10 and 9 in 1998) who were identified as Jesus and Buddha may not cooperate with Teacher Chen's plan for them. Repeated disappointment when God's flying saucers fail to appear *could* lead Chen Tao believers to take extreme actions to preserve their ultimate concern.

The saga of Chen Tao is not over, and only time will tell how it will turn out.

Notes

1. CESNUR, "Apocalypse Delayed: Group Leaves Texas and Relocates in Olcott, New York," CESNUR's Watch Page of Chen Tao, <http://www.cesnur.org/Chen.htm>, downloaded May 9, 1998; Charles Zewe, "Cult claims God will appear in flying saucer—and on TV," *CNN Interactive* (March 19, 1998), at <http://cnn.com>; God—The Supreme Being, *God's Descending in Clouds (Flying Saucers) on Earth to Save People* (Garland, Tex.: Kingdom of God, 1997). I thank both Massimo Introvigne and Forrest Jackson for making arrangements to provide me with this book.
2. Teacher Chen's complicated apocalyptic scenario for 1999 is described in God, *God's Descending in Clouds*, 92-119, 133-38. According to God, the coming retribution, World War III, "is an unavoidable and uncompromising war." See God, 174. On the percentages of devil-possessed human populations, see God, 105.
3. God, *God's Descending in Clouds*, 54-55.
4. On King Satan and the book of Revelation, see God, *God's Descending in Clouds*, 81, 122-38.
   Interestingly, Jesus's parable of the good seed being harvested and the weeds being burned was important to Teacher Chen as with Do. See God, *God's Descending in Clouds*, 22-23.

5. The origins of outside souls are explained in God, *God's Descending in Clouds*, 34-41.
6. God asserted that "When people are in the condition of being combined with devils, they cannot be taken as human beings." God, *God's Descending in Clouds*, 90.
7. Hitler and Mao Zedong, also, set impossible goals for the nations they governed. See Robert Ellwood, "Nazism as a Millennialist Movement," 241–60, and Scott Lowe, "Western Millennial Ideology Goes East: The Taiping Revolution and Mao's Great Leap Forward," 220–40, in *Millennialism, Persecution, and Violence: Historical Cases*, ed. Catherine Wessinger (Syracuse: Syracuse University Press, 2000).
8. Dr. Scott Lowe, an expert on Chinese religions, told a reporter that it would be better if reporters would leave Chen Tao alone so the group would not lose face and be able to deal with the disconfirmation of their prophecies in private. Christine Wicker, "Garland sect prepares for God's arrival," *Dallas Morning News*, March 22, 1998, A-32. Many of the stories about Chen Tao were not posted on the *Dallas Morning News* web page. I thank Christine Wicker for kindly forwarding these newspaper articles to me.
9. "Our Position Against Suicide," at <http://www.clas.ufl.edu/users/gthursby/rel/gate/letter.htm.
   Dr. Gene Thursby has reproduced on his web page the Heaven's Gate web page as it was preserved on the web page formerly operated by Chuck Humphrey (Rkkody).
10. The Buddhist tradition teaches that the human body and life is a precious gift that provides the best context for the achievement of *nirvana*. Chinese traditional religion has taught that a person has multiple souls. According to Teacher Chen, the three souls are the "main soul light," the "conscious soul," and the "physical soul." See God, *God's Descending in Clouds*, 17. These tend to correspond to the Buddhist idea that in addition to the physical body, the individual possesses vehicles for operation in the spiritual realms. This idea is also found in Hinduism and was picked up by Theosophy.
11. Christine Wicker, "Garland sect prepares for God's arrival," *Dallas Morning News*, March 22, 1998, A-32.
12. Christine Wicker, "Apparent Appearances," *Dallas Morning News*, April 1, 1998, A-28.
13. Wicker, "Apparent Appearances," A-23.
14. Personal communication from Christine Wicker.
15. CESNUR, "Apocalypse Delayed."
16. God, *God's Descending in Clouds*, 27. Expressing a belief similar to those of the Solar Temple and Heaven's Gate, *God's Descending in Clouds* states that the "final goal of human evolution is to make people elevated to the level of transcending the physical bondage and being able to travel freely across different time and space in the universe." I suggest that the manner in which the accomplishment of this ultimate goal will be interpreted will be determined by whether or not Chen Tao can become comfortably accommodated to society.

CHAPTER NINE

Comparative Conclusions

IN COMPARING JONESTOWN, the Branch Davidians, Aum Shin-rikyo, the Montana Freemen, the Solar Temple, Heaven's Gate, and Chen Tao, all of which were catastrophic millennial groups that expected a cataclysmic transition to the collective salvation, and the majority of which were involved in violence,[1] there is a great deal to be learned.

Categories of Catastrophic Millennial Groups Involved in Violence

Every millennial group or movement has an ultimate concern because it is a religion. The ultimate concern of a religion is the goal that is the most important thing in the world for an individual or group.[2] When placed under pressure or faced with disconfirming evidence, people may change their ultimate concerns. However, the millennial groups studied here, which were caught up in violence, involved people who clung to their ultimate concerns so tightly that they were willing to kill or to die for them.

The categories used in this book—assaulted millennial groups, fragile millennial groups, and revolutionary millennial movements—are not rigidly distinct. An assaulted millennial group is attacked by law enforcement agents and/or concerned citizens because the religious group is viewed as dangerous to society. A fragile millennial group is suffering from internal stresses as well as opposition from the outside culture that endanger the group's ultimate concern. Members of fragile millennial groups initiate violence in order to preserve their religious goal. The violence of a fragile millennial group may be directed inwardly against members or outwardly against enemies, or both. The ideology of a revolutionary millennial movement prompts believers to commit violent acts to overthrow what they view as a persecuting regime in order to establish the millennial kingdom. These categories can be considered specific moments on a continuum relating to the possibility of millennial groups becoming involved in violence. Catastrophic millennial groups that become involved in violence may belong to more than one of these categories, or they may shift from one category to the another.[3]

I find it useful to determine if a millennial group involved in violence has been assaulted by outsiders, or if the members have committed violent acts due to the group's fragility, or if believers carry out violent acts according to a revolutionary ideology, because that illuminates which party, the millennialists or outsiders, is responsible for initiating the violence and why the violence occurred. In all cases, the quality of the interactions between members of mainstream society and the believers is a crucial element in determining a group's potential volatility. Law enforcement agents, news reporters, concerned family members, and anticultists should become aware that their activities can contribute to an undesired, tragic outcome.

Radical dualism on both sides of a conflict increases the potential for violence. It would be good if catastrophic millennialists became more sensitive to the manner in which their dualistic worldview increases the possibility of overreacting to any expression of opposition from society. A radical dualistic worldview that sees reality in terms of clear-cut good versus evil, us verses them, can be found among the various opponents of new religious movements as well as among members of catastrophic millennial groups.

The religions studied in this book demonstrate the fluidity of the categories I have highlighted for millennial groups involved in violence: assaulted millennial groups; fragile millennial groups; and revolutionary millennial movements.

The Jonestown murders and mass suicide occurred because of Jonestown's fragility, although there was a revolutionary dimension to Peoples Temple ideology, and there was a real sense in which Jonestown was under assault. Peoples Temple identified with a revolutionary millennial tradition, communism, but Peoples Temple members relied on social and political work, not revolution, to build their millennial utopia. The majority of Peoples Temple members withdrew to Jonestown in the Guyanese jungle as their place of refuge from opponents. Jonestown was fragile because of the physical and financial circumstances of the collective, the defection of key members and leaders, and the erratic actions of Jim Jones. Jonestown's fragility was heightened by cumulative opposition from anticultist apostates, concerned family members, news reporters, and American federal agents and agencies. The group suicide and murders were initiated because Jonestown was fragile and its residents perceived the need to take violent actions to preserve their ultimate concern—maintaining the cohesiveness of their community.

The Branch Davidians near Waco, Texas, were assaulted by federal agents. In 1993, the Branch Davidians were not a revolutionary millennial group, although they possessed the theological potential to become revolutionary at a future time. The Branch Davidians *appeared* to be a revolutionary millennial group to the ATF agents investigating them because they were armed. David Koresh had predicted that in 1995 they would move to Israel and fight on the side of Israel against the United States in armageddon. However, the Davidians of Mount Carmel had been expecting to move to the Holy Land for the endtime events and the establishment of God's kingdom since 1935. As of 1993, the Davidians showed no signs of preparing to move to Israel. Financial realities may have prevented those preparations, and Koresh would have had to reinterpret his prophecies. Eugene V. Gallagher's in-depth study of Koresh's audiotaped Bible study sessions and the negotiation transcripts indicate that Koresh did not incite the Davidians to initiate violence. Koresh reserved the initiation of apocalyptic violence to God, although he taught that the Davidians would fight on God's side when armageddon occurred.[4] David Koresh and Paul Fatta bought and sold arms in the profitable gun trade in Texas, and these funds helped support the community. It was never demonstrated by federal agents that the Davidians' weapons were illegal. Koresh had the Davidian residence fortified and stored supplies and arms in case they were attacked by "Babylon." The Branch Davidians were prepared to defend themselves, but they were not revolutionary in 1993. David Koresh had a history of cooperating with the investigations of law enforcement agents and social workers. The Branch Davidians were assaulted twice by federal law enforcement agents because they were viewed as dangerous, brainwashed cultists.

The leaders of Aum Shinrikyo had revolutionary plans, but the violent acts committed by Aum devotees were related to the fragility of Aum Shinrikyo. Aum Shinrikyo leaders had the revolutionary goal of overthrowing and destroying the Japanese government and conventional Japanese society. Aum's guru, Shoka Asahara, had the goal of dominating Japan and the world. To that end, Aum Shinrikyo's leaders and scientists spent a great deal of time, energy, and money in researching, acquiring, and testing weapons of mass destruction. Shoko Asahara himself endangered the ultimate concern and caused the fragility of the group by setting an impossible recruitment goal to prevent armageddon, and then by predicting imminent armageddon. The violent acts committed by devotees were aimed at preserving the Aum Shinrikyo ultimate concern—the establishment of the Buddhist millennial kingdom by the Buddha, Shoko Asahara. Even the planned revolutionary violence had the goal of protecting the ultimate concern and maintaining the credibility of the guru. Shoko

Asahara claimed to be a Buddha with infallible powers of prophecy, so when he predicted armageddon, armageddon *had* to occur. Salvation came only through the grace of Asahara, the infallible Buddha, and if he was proved to be fallible, then the whole basis of Aum Shinrikyo as a religion would have crumbled. Therefore, Aum Shinrikyo was a fragile millennial group when its members committed violent acts, although revolutionary ideology and preparations were a significant aspect of this religion.

The Montana Freemen were a revolutionary millennial group that had the potential to become either assaulted or fragile. The Freemen were waging "paper warfare" against the "satanic" federal government. The Freemen were armed, and during the standoff they professed a willingness to fight the FBI agents surrounding them. The Freemen hoped that their violent conflict with federal agents would spark the "second American Revolution," in which other Patriots would join them in the battle to overthrow the government. As an isolated community cordoned off by FBI agents, the Freemen could have been assaulted by the agents, which would have resulted in the loss of life among the innocent adults and children inside Justus Township, the federal agents, and the ideologically-committed Freemen. Due to the new post-Waco FBI policy of patience, negotiation, and consultation with outside experts on religion, the Freemen were not assaulted. But the Freemen also had the potential to become a fragile millennial group. If FBI agents had applied so much tactical pressure on the Freemen as to make them despair of achieving their ultimate concern—the elimination of the federal government—the committed Freemen might have initiated violence in an effort to achieve their goal. The Freemen might have begun a gun battle with FBI agents with the intention of sparking the second American Revolution. The Freemen could have chosen to commit group suicide in order to protest the satanic government, which would have meant killing the children and less-committed adults inside Justus Township. The FBI's policy of patience and nonconfrontation avoided exacerbating the Freemen's sense of being persecuted, and permitted negotiation to continue until a way was found for the Freemen to be taken into custody, while maintaining allegiance to their ultimate concern. The Freemen were a revolutionary millennial group whose potential for violence was contained successfully by law enforcement agents with no loss of life.

The members of Solar Temple and Heaven's Gate initiated violence because of the fragility of their respective groups. Due to stresses present within the Solar Temple, which included vocal critics who caused the loss of faith of members, former members demanding the return of their financial resources, and the severe illness of the leader, Joseph Di Mambro, the adepts concluded that the cultural opposition that they experienced was persecution. Weaknesses internal to the group were also the primary fac-tors in Heaven's Gate. Ti and Do had set an impossible goal for their stu-dents, and the Heaven's Gate class decided to commit group suicide to preserve their ultimate concern—obtaining eternal extraterrestrial bodies that would travel in flying saucers—a literal entering of the Kingdom of Heaven. In both the Solar Temple and Heaven's Gate, the radical dualism of their catastrophic millennial worldviews contributed to the overreac-tions of the believers to any sign of opposition or disagreement from out-side society.

It remains to be seen if Chen Tao can avoid becoming a fragile mil-lennial group, and if Chen Tao believers can continue to respond con-structively if they simultaneously experience internal stresses and cultural opposition. If more of Teacher Chen's prophecies are disconfirmed, the Chen Tao believers may be able to reinterpret the prophecies and shift the emphasis of their ultimate concern, especially if they continue to regard America as their place of safe haven.[5]

What to Do?

In several of the catastrophic millennial groups studied in this book—Jonestown, Aum Shinrikyo, Solar Temple, and Heaven's Gate—weak-nesses internal to the group were crucial in motivating members to commit violent acts, but the manner in which outsiders interacted with these believers was also important.

Law enforcement agents and news reporters, with no knowledge of how catastrophic millennialists might react to cultural opposition, may engage in aggressive tactics that make the millennialists feel persecuted, and thus contribute to a situation in which the millennialists may decide to take violent actions. I suggest that avoiding labeling unconventional groups "cults" and treating the believers as religious people worthy of respect will go far in reducing the sense of antagonism between catastrophic millennial groups and society. Whenever it is possible, the believers should be interviewed respectfully and asked to cooperate in the investi-gation. Care should be taken to make accurate reports about the religious group that avoid sensationalism and exaggeration. Excessive force should not be used against a group because it is labeled with the pejorative term *cult.* Because the word *cult* has become so pejorative, I recommend that people avoid using this term and instead recognize that these groups are religions. Law enforcement agents should avoid precipitating a siege of a millennial group whose members have a commitment to a higher author-ity than civil law.

Religious groups suspected of criminal activities should be investigated—but according to normal law enforcement and news reporting procedures. It is important to interview the believers to get their side of the story and to humanize them. If members of a religious group have committed crimes, then ordinary, not excessive, law enforcement measures should be taken.

When there are questions about a religious group, *bona fide* scholars of religion should be consulted to get accurate, nonbiased information and informed advice. In the United States, the American Academy of Religion and the Society for the Scientific Study of Religion are two professional organizations that can provide religion experts possessing academic credentials.[6]

Law enforcement agents, news reporters, anticultists, apostates, and concerned family members and friends should be aware that if their activities are perceived by members of a catastrophic millennial group as threatening their ultimate concern, this could motivate the believers to seek to destroy their enemies. This was the case with the Jonestown residents, Aum Shinrikyo devotees, and the Solar Temple adepts. Opposing, or even investigating, a group that feels beleaguered occasionally can become life-threatening. When believers feel that their ultimate concern is threatened, they sometimes choose to resort to violent actions.

Individuals who are members of a millennial group, or persons who are considering joining a millennial religion should give careful consideration to what the "exit costs" might be if the situation turns out to be less than satisfactory. If one has assumed a new identity, perhaps a new name, cut off all contact with one's birth family, made the group one's surrogate family, handed over financial assets, and allowed the group to provide one's sole means of livelihood, there will be heavy costs to leaving. Some women have found that having children with the charismatic leader bound them to a group that they otherwise would have preferred to leave. Most, but not all, of the Jonestown residents, and the Heaven's Gate class members decided it was better to die with their surrogate families than to pay the exit costs. Aum Shinrikyo became such a totalitarian organization that people who wanted to leave were confined, drugged, tortured, and murdered—obviously very high exit costs. Some Jonestown residents were also confined and drugged, and these people obviously did not choose to die in the mass suicide. Therefore, it is worth considering in advance of joining a group the types of costs that might have to be paid later if one wants to leave.

For concerned family members, there are no easy answers. The right of adults to exercise freedom of religion has to be respected. It is best to keep the lines of communication open as much as possible, so that a loved one will feel free to come home or ask for help when he or she wants to leave a religious group. Keeping the lines of communication open, however, is no guarantee that things will turn out well. Sometimes millennial groups are assaulted, or believers commit violent acts because of the fragility of their group, or the members act on revolutionary ideologies; these dynamics are outside the control of concerned family members who are trying to maintain positive communication with their loved ones. But concerned family members who become vocal anticultists and promote sensationalized news reporting and aggressive government investigations can intensify a group's fragility, or perhaps prompt an assault by law enforcement agents who are concerned about the leader's intentions. There are no guaranteed outcomes, but the best thing to do, if possible, is to keep the lines of communication open with loved ones who have joined alternative religions, gain accurate, nonbiased information on the new religion, and resist being panicked by anticult propaganda and activists.

General Observations

A number of general observations can be drawn from comparison of the millennial groups studied in this book. I will highlight these general observations before describing religious characteristics that cause me to become concerned about a catastrophic millennial group as well as those characteristics that I find reassuring.

1. The project of raising "messianic children" can backfire. The teenaged or grown children of a group's prophet or messiah can destabilize a group and call into question the charismatic leader's authority.

Messianic children can grow up to reject the role attributed to them.[7] I suggest that raising a child to be a messiah is a heavy burden to place on a child and is psychologically unhealthy.

Jim Jones's grown sons were a serious challenge to his authority, especially because Jones's mental and physical health was debilitated. Joseph Di Mambro's grown son, Elie, weakened the Solar Temple by disclosing that the apparitions of the Masters were caused by technological tricks. Immediately prior to the executions committed by Solar Temple adepts and then their transit from Earth by murder and suicide, Di Mambro's twelve-year-old messianic daughter, Emmanuelle, was rebelling. Most of David Koresh's children were very young (his eldest son, Cyrus, was eight), but David Koresh had fathered over a dozen children for rulership in God's kingdom. If Koresh's children residing at Mount Carmel had lived, they might have challenged his authority later and rejected the roles he had designated for them.

2. While the psychological health or dysfunction of a religious leader is pertinent, it is a *serious* mistake to rely solely on psychological diagnosis of the leader when attempting to understand a religious group and the actions it might take.

Analysis of the group's theology and social dynamics are crucially important. The teachings of the leader constitute a coherent worldview that makes sense to the believers, and credentialed Religious Studies scholars are trained to analyze worldviews. Religious Studies scholars and sociologists of religion are trained to pay attention to the social dynamics internal to the group and to the group's interactions with outside society. Religious worldview and sociological factors were discounted by federal agents dealing with the Branch Davidians with obviously tragic results. The psychotherapists who diagnosed David Koresh had no understanding of the biblical worldview that informed the statements and actions of Koresh and the Branch Davidians. *Solely applying a psychological diagnostic label to a charismatic religious leader is not conducive to the broad interdisciplinary understanding that can assist in resolving crisis situations peacefully.*

3. Persecution may either strengthen a group by confirming prophecies, or weaken it by endangering the group's ultimate concern.

If persecution confirms prophecies, the group and the status of the charismatic leader in the group will be strengthened. This was the case with the Branch Davidians, and also with the Mormons in the nineteenth century.[8]

Persecution—real or imagined—in other words, if there is any cultural opposition at all—can endanger a group's ultimate concern and motivate the members to commit violent acts to preserve their religious goal. As discussed in the previous chapters, this was the case with Jonestown, Aum Shinrikyo, the Solar Temple, and Heaven's Gate.

4. Factors internal to the group, such as having an already endangered ultimate concern, possessing a radical dualistic worldview, and hiding criminal secrets, can make members of a catastrophic millennial group extremely sensitive, so that even minimal cultural opposition will be viewed as persecution.

The dualism of a catastrophic millennial worldview, which promotes the stark perspective of "good versus evil," "us versus them," heightens the possibility that group members will conclude they are being persecuted in response to the activities of law enforcement agents, news reporters, and others.

Aum Shinrikyo's ultimate concern was endangered by Shoko Asahara who had set impossible goals for the group and who taught a radical dualistic worldview. Aum Shinrikyo leaders were especially nervous about being investigated, because they were hiding criminal secrets.

Heaven's Gate was not hiding criminal secrets, but the class's ultimate concern was endangered because of its leaders' setting an impossible goal. The radical dualistic worldview of Heaven's Gate members caused them to interpret any sort of negative feedback from the outside society as persecution.

Likewise the Solar Temple adepts' perception of being persecuted by law enforcement agents, anticultists, and vocal apostates was heightened by their radical dualistic worldview that was related to their catastrophic millennialism.

5. A catastrophic millennial group that feels it is persecuted may bring the date for the end closer.

This was done by the Branch Davidians, Aum Shinrikyo, and the Solar Temple. Bringing the date for the end closer appears to be a barometer indicating the extent to which the members and leaders of a catastrophic millennial group feel persecuted.

6. Millennial groups and their leaders make adjustments in their theologies and actions in response to events.

If a catastrophic millennial group has some success in building the millennial kingdom, it can shift to noncatastrophic, progressive millennial expectations about the nature of the transition to the collective salvation. Or the catastrophic expectations may become less urgent and be put off into the indefinite future. If the catastrophic millennial group experiences persecution, the date for the end may be brought closer.

The "pragmatics of failure" means that if methods to achieve the ultimate concern are failing, believers may shift to using other methods, which may be either peaceful or violent.[9]

Catastrophic millennialists will respond to political events and natural disasters by incorporating them into their apocalyptic scenarios by interpreting them as signs that the endtime has arrived and as confirmation of prophecies.

7. Popular media express mythic themes and values that may resonate with the hopes and values of religious people and may be incorporated into their theologies.

The depictions of violent battles between good and evil in Japanese *anime* (animated videos) appear to have influenced Aum Shinrikyo leaders and members. The American television series *Star Trek* is not apocalyptic science fiction, but its depiction of the "crew" as an alternative family was appealing to the Heaven's Gate class.

8. Social indoctrination processes are more effective when they are undertaken voluntarily, and coercive indoctrination procedures do not produce believers.

Most of the groups studied in this book regarded the socialization of mainstream society to be negative conditioning or "programming" that had to be counteracted by indoctrination into the truth offered by their respective groups. For instance, Heaven's Gate members wanted to have their minds cleansed by means of monastic discipline of the impurities they believed were put there by conventional society, as did the voluntary Aum Shinrikyo devotees.

While the coercive indoctrination practices of Aum Shinrikyo injured numerous people, they did not produce any true believers.

9. There is no need to have a charismatic leader for a group to be potentially violent.

The Freemen and the broad Euro-American revolutionary millennial movement of which they are a part do not have a single charismatic leader. The term *charisma* is used here in the Religious Studies sense of indicating a person who is believed to receive divine revelation.

10. The charismatic leader of a group may not be as all-powerful as outsiders assume.

The "myth of the omnipotent leader" is part of the anticult stereotype of unconventional religions, but the leader often is not as powerful as outsiders imagine. For instance, David Koresh's authority was contingent on whether he could present to his followers plausible interpretations of the Bible that appeared to be divinely inspired. The Branch Davidians checked Koresh's assertions of truth against the Bible. Unfortunately, this fact, which was explained to the negotiators by the Davidians, was overlooked by FBI agents because they believed in the "myth of the omnipotent leader" of a "cult."[10]

11. A charismatic leader cannot become a totalitarian leader without the agency and complicity of willing followers.

Related to the "myth of the omnipotent leader" is the anticult "myth of the passive, brainwashed follower."[11] Turnover in the membership of unconventional religious groups indicates that people think for themselves in deciding to join a group, in participating in its activities, and in leaving. No leader can become a totalitarian leader without the agency and complicity of followers. Aum Shinrikyo demonstrates that once a group becomes truly totalitarian, it can be virtually impossible to leave, but Asahara could not have exercised control of life and death over members and outsiders without the willing and active support of a critical mass of his followers.

12. Repeated acts of violence take on a ritualistic nature, and continually enacted rituals of violence tend to escalate the level of violence that participants find acceptable. This is true for law enforcement agents as well as for members of unconventional religious groups.

The violence within Peoples Temple began as punishments meted out to misbehaving members, such as having to endure humiliating boxing matches before the other members. In Jonestown, the rituals of violence escalated to the capture, confining, and drugging of people who wanted to leave. The private suicide rituals to test loyalty within Jim Jones's inner circle escalated to the "white night" rehearsals within Jonestown of their eventual mass suicide. The mass suicide was carried out along with the murder of people in Congressman Ryan's party who were identified as being enemies of Peoples Temple and the murder of Jonestown's children as well as any adults, who because they were drugged, confined, or incapacitated were unable to leave.

The activities of federal agents outside Mount Carmel Center, the residence of the Branch Davidians, amounted to ritual acts of violence that culminated in the final assault against the Davidians. Tanks were used to demolish the cars and property belonging to the Davidians. The drivers of the tanks cursed the Davidians and made obscene gestures at them. Cutting off the electricity and telephone wires, shining bright spotlights at the building during the night, blasting high decibel sounds at the residence were all rituals of violence that culminated in the assault against the Davidians by firing canisters of CS gas into the residence and the demolition of parts of the building by tanks. The fire that destroyed the residence, that took the lives of seventy-four Davidians including twenty-three children, occurred because of this final assault.

In Aum Shinrikyo, the rituals of violence began as acts of extreme asceticism by devotees. If an Aum devotee was unwilling to be immersed in either very hot or cold water, he or she was forced to undergo that austerity. The first death within Aum Shinrikyo was probably the accidental death of a devotee due to extreme ascetic practice. Subsequently a member who wanted to defect was killed. These rituals of violence escalated to include the confinement, torture, and coercion of people who wanted to leave or who had helped others to leave. Many of these people were killed. These rituals escalated to murder and murder attempts against people in society outside of Aum Shinrikyo who were identified as enemies. These rituals of violence culminated in the sarin gas attack on the Tokyo subway.

13. Dualistic or dichotomous thinking is not confined to catastrophic millennialists, but is found also among law enforcement agents, anticultists, and people generally.

Dualistic thinking is a pervasive and common feature of human nature. It is expressed in cartoons, movies, novels, television shows, video games, news reporting, and in religious doctrines. Radical dualistic thinking attributes a battle between good and evil to human beings who are divided into "us" and "them." Radical dualistic thinking dehumanizes and demonizes those identified as the "other." Dualistic thinking is probably as common among law enforcement agents, soldiers and military officers, and anticultists as it is among catastrophic millennialists. Not surprisingly, these individuals can become locked in pitched battles against each other. Radical dualistic thinking is overcome by learning to view the group designated "the other" as valued human beings like ourselves. Face-to-face dialogue is the obvious way to humanize the demonized "other."

Characteristics That Cause Concern

Based on my study of the millennial religions in this book, there are characteristics that concern me when I observe them in a group. The more such characteristics a group has, the more cause for concern. But a group's possession of many of the characteristics listed in the text to follow DOES NOT constitute a prediction that violence will occur. A group may have other characteristics that offset the ones that I regard as problematic. A group's possession of a number of these characteristics should never be used as an excuse by law enforcement agents to take unnecessary aggressive action against a religious group. Nor should this list of characteristics be used by news reporters to produce sensationalized and dehumanizing stories about a group. The manner in which outsiders interact with members of catastrophic millennial groups is crucial in determining the potential for volatility.

Having stated this caution, I will list the characteristics of some catastrophic millennial groups that cause me concern.

1. Catastrophic millennial beliefs combined with belief in reincarnation and with the members' conviction that the group is being persecuted.

Catastrophic millennial beliefs and belief in reincarnation taken separately have no necessary relation to violence. But the combination of these beliefs can radically devalue earthly existence, especially if group members feel that they are being persecuted.

The Jonestown residents, the Solar Temple adepts, and the Heaven's Gate class members all combined catastrophic millennial beliefs with belief in reincarnation, and they all were convinced that their respective groups were being persecuted. If group members feel they are being persecuted, and furthermore, believe that the Earth will be violently destroyed soon, and that reincarnation means that their true home is not on this planet and that their true identities are not tied to their bodies, then why not leave earthly life?

The Aum Shinrikyo devotees are unique, in that their belief in catastrophic millennialism, reincarnation, and their sense of persecution led them to devalue not their own lives but the lives of those who were identified as not being true Aum believers.

It remains to be seen if the combination of catastrophic millennialism and reincarnation in Chen Tao will become problematic. If the Chen Tao members do not feel themselves to be persecuted, the chance is lessened that this theological combination will become lethal.

2. The theological conviction that one's home is not on this planet, combined with social alienation due to a sense of persecution and lack of social acceptance.

Jim Jones's conviction that he had come from another planet and that he was a man far ahead of his time here on Earth was an expression of his social alienation that was increased by his belief (shared by his followers) that outsiders were engaged in a conspiracy to destroy Jonestown. The Solar Temple adepts' belief that their true home was another planet was reinforced by their conviction that they were being persecuted by law enforcement agents, reporters, apostates, and anticultists. Heaven's Gate members' alienation was expressed in their belief that they were overcoming their despised gendered humanness to be admitted to the Kingdom of God in neuter, extraterrestrial bodies. American society did not support the monastic and ascetic lifestyle of the Heaven's Gate class, whereas Hindu and Buddhist societies do give support to renunciants, who seldom commit religious suicide.

3. A sense of persecution that is expressed in a belief in conspiracy theories.

It does not matter whether or not the alleged conspiracies against the group have any basis in fact. As Jeffrey Kaplan has stated eloquently, "Real Paranoids Have Real Enemies."[12] There may indeed be factual reasons for the believers to be convinced that they are being persecuted.

The Jonestown residents, the Aum Shinrikyo devotees, the Montana Freemen, the Solar Temple adepts, and the Heaven's Gate class members were avid consumers and advocates of conspiracy theories.

4. Catastrophic millennial beliefs that are related to a radical dualistic view of good versus evil that dehumanizes other people.

Peoples Temple's dualism was between good communists and evil capitalists. The Branch Davidians believed in imminent armageddon, in which those standing with God would fight against evil "Babylon." Aum Shinrikyo's dualism was between spirituality and materialism, and anyone who did not accept Asahara as the guru deserved to die. The Freemen, as Identity Christians, believe that white people are the true Israelites and that only white people can be Christians. The Freemen are among the Identity Christians who believe that Jews are the children of Satan (who control the government, media, and the economy) and that people of color are animals. They also believe that Jews and people of color will be eradicated in the coming war between good and evil that will create God's kingdom on Earth. The Solar Temple's dualism was between light and dark, spirituality and matter. Heaven's Gate's dualism was between the good existence in the Kingdom of Heaven versus evil mammalian existence here on Earth. They regarded most human beings as "plants" who did not possess souls. Chen Tao believers regard 90 percent of humans in East Asia as being possessed by devils.

5. Catastrophic millennial and dualistic beliefs that expect and perhaps promote conflict.

The Freemen's dualistic and catastrophic millennial beliefs motivated them to wage a war against the American government. The Branch Davidians were not revolutionary in 1993, but the assaults against their residence confirmed Koresh's apocalyptic prophecies, and they were prepared to fight and die for their faith. Aum Shinrikyo's dualism resulted in a doctrine that justified killing enemies. The dualism of the Jonestown residents justified killing enemies and commiting group suicide and murder, as did the dualism of the Solar Temple adepts. Heaven's Gate's dualism prompted the class members to interpret minimal cultural opposition as persecution, and motivated them to commit group suicide to leave this evil world.

6. The group's resistance to investigation and withdrawal to an isolated refuge, and/or a very aggressive battle against its enemies.

Peoples Temple, Aum Shinrikyo, and the Montana Freemen simultaneously withdrew to refuges and took overly aggressive measures to battle their enemies. Heaven's Gate members relied on withdrawal alone to protect themselves from opposition.

The Branch Davidians, although living in community and possessing arms to defend themselves against "Babylon," were not resistant to investigation and cooperated with investigators on a number of occasions.

7. Followers dependent on a charismatic leader as the sole means to achieve the ultimate concern.

In Aum Shinrikyo, Shoko Asahara was the sole means to obtain salvation, as was Do in Heaven's Gate. A sense of dependence on Jim Jones was expressed by a number of members of Peoples Temple as they committed group suicide. A similar sense of dependence on Do was expressed by some of the Heaven's Gate class members in their statements before exiting.

If dependence on the group's leader is the sole means to obtain salvation (admission to the millennial kingdom), then the leader cannot be demonstrated to be fallible or limited in any way. If such a leader errs or sins, or if the leader dies without providing for a successor, then the followers cannot achieve the ultimate concern. The members may resort to violent acts to preserve their ultimate concern, which is threatened because of their overdependence on the charismatic leader.

8. The charismatic leader who sets impossible goals for the group.

This occurred with Jonestown, Aum Shinrikyo, Heaven's Gate, and arguably with the Solar Temple. Jim Jones set the goal of creating a perfectly harmonious and economically viable collective in the Guyanese jungle. Shoko Asahara set a goal of gaining an excessive number of renunciants to avoid armageddon and establish the Buddhist millennial kingdom. Ti and Do told the Heaven's Gate class members that they were transforming their human bodies into eternal, extraterrestrial bodies and that the flying saucer would land to pick them up. The Solar Temple adepts had the goal of advancing the world's population into the idealized Age of Aquarius. These are all impossible goals that were disconfirmed by physical events, thereby producing stress within these groups.

The setting of impossible goals can lead to a "pragmatics of failure" phenomenon in which the believers might choose to resort to violence to achieve their ultimate concern.

9. A catastrophic millennial group that gives up on proselytizing to gain converts, and turns inwards to preserve salvation for its members alone.

This was observed in Jonestown, Aum Shinrikyo, the Solar Temple, and Heaven's Gate. When a cohesive millennial group stops proselytizing, it is expressing pessimism about the worthiness of persons outside the group to achieve salvation. Drastic and violent actions may then be taken to secure salvation for the millennial group's members alone.

10. The above characteristics, combined with membership in a group that demands high exit costs in terms of personal identity, associations, and livelihood.

Groups with high exit costs do not necessarily become violent, but when the characteristics described above are found in a group that makes excessive demands on members, the high exit costs make it more likely that believers might resort to violent actions to preserve their threatened ultimate concern. As seen in the previous chapters, this was definitely the case with Jonestown, Aum Shinrikyo, Solar Temple, Heaven's Gate, and also the Branch Davidians.

11. The group's leader giving new identities to the followers, perhaps including new names, and drastically rearranging the members' family and marriage relationships.

In Peoples Temple, it was preferred that married couples not be very bonded to each other; to effect the lessening of bonding between couples and to encourage bonding with him, Jim Jones had sexual relations with many of his followers. David Koresh taught that all the men should be celibate and that all the women at Mount Carmel were his wives. In Aum Shinrikyo, the monastic members were celibate (although the leaders were not) and were given religious names. In the Solar Temple, Joseph Di Mambro informed believers they were the reincarnations of various famous people, and believers were paired in "cosmic marriages," regardless of whether they were already married to other people. In Heaven's Gate, the students were celibate and given new names.

I regard the endowment of new identities and disruption of previously existing family and marital ties to be excessive control exercised by religious leaders. It should be noted that this control is not possible unless followers permit and facilitate it. These new identities indicate a high level of commitment that can involve extremely high exit costs if a member wishes to defect later, but they do not necessarily mean that violence will occur.

12. The group's living in an isolated situation where information about the outside world is controlled by the leader, so that the members are not exposed to alternative interpretations of reality.

This was the case in Jonestown, which was located in the Guyanese jungle, the Aum Shinrikyo communes, and the reclusive Heaven's Gate class.

The Freemen were in constant touch with the outside world via electronic media; they imposed on themselves a worldview as a lens through which they interpreted events.

Prior to the siege, the Branch Davidians did have contact with the outside world by holding jobs and operating businesses, attending gun shows, proselytizing, and having other interactions with the surrounding community. The isolation of the Branch Davidians was imposed on them by federal agents, who placed them under siege and cut off their electricity and telephone contact with the outside world.

13. Relatively small acts of violence repeated in a ritualistic manner so that the scale and intensity of the violence increases.

It was noted above that the rituals of violence in Peoples Temple culminated in the mass suicide and murders in Jonestown, and that the ritualistic violence and murders committed by Aum Shinrikyo devotees culminated in the sarin gas attack on the Tokyo subway. Members of an unconventional religion are not likely to let outsiders become aware of the rituals of violence occurring within their group. Therefore, insiders will be wise to be diligent in noting whether or not they are participating in and abetting rituals of violence.

The rituals of violence carried out by federal agents against the Branch Davidians were depicted on television, but, unfortunately, the prejudiced stereotype of "cults" shared by the agents and the majority of the American public made those actions appear to be reasonable. Law enforcement agents also will be wise to be diligent in noting whether or not they are participating in and abetting rituals of violence that are likely to escalate. Citizens have the duty of noting when law enforcement agents are engaging in rituals of violence and taking appropriate nonviolent actions to halt the excessive activities of law enforcement agents.

Reassuring Characteristics

In highlighting the characteristics that I find to be reassuring, it is important to note first that religious groups change over time. An unconventional religion can become "domesticated" as its members have children and, therefore, the group will tend to become less radical in relation to the norms of mainstream society. Unconventional religious groups evolve and make changes in response to internal stresses and pressures from outside society.[13] The nature of the unconventional group's responses to the outside society is crucial and is related to the following characteristics that I find to be reassuring:

1. The group is not being attacked by hostile opponents, such as reporters, government agents, law enforcement agents, concerned relatives, and former members.

2. The group openly addresses queries about its beliefs and practices, and cooperates with investigations by social workers, law enforcement agents, news reporters, concerned family members, and scholars.

3. The group reaches out to its community, and the members strives to be good citizens and neighbors by participating in the activities of society outside its boundaries.

4. The group is active proselytizing to extend salvation to others, but is not preaching a revolutionary or hate-filled ideology.[14]

Even though these positive characteristics are few in number, they can have an extremely important effect in counteracting the characteristics that I identify above as cause for concern. These reassuring characteristics are related to whether religious believers are willing to consider that they might not possess the absolute truth and are willing to consider other perspectives.[15] These characteristics are indicative also of a sense of connection the believers have to people outside their religious community.

282 HOW THE MILLENNIUM COMES VIOLENTLY

The Future

My purpose in writing this book is not to demonize or dehumanize people who participate in unconventional and millennial religious groups. My purpose is to make a comparative study from which lessons can be drawn so that we all will be wiser about religious characteristics that have the potential to contribute to violence.

I will be very happy if we see no more violent episodes related to millennialism, but since millennialism, in all of its varieties, expresses the hopes, fears, and flaws of the human condition, I am not confident that this will be the case.

The New Millennium: It Is Just an Arbitrary Date

The year 2000 and the new millennium appear to have the power to excite the hopes and fears of people about what the future has in store. Many hope that the new millennium will be a new era in which the limitations of the human condition will be overcome to a great extent. Many believe that the transition into this new era will take place through catastrophic destruction of the world as we know it. More optimistic millennialists believe that we will make this transition noncatastrophically and progressively. People who are fatalistic believe that destruction is inevitable and that it holds no promise for a better world.[16]

Those millennial groups whose members believe in imminent catastrophic destruction appear to hold the greatest potential for becoming involved in violence as either assaulted millennial groups, fragile millennial groups, or revolutionary millennial movements. However, there have been revolutionary progressive millennial movements that have produced massive violence in efforts to speed up the rate of progress. Examples of revolutionary progressive millennial movements include the German Nazis, the Maoists in China, the Khmer Rouge in Cambodia, to name only a few.[17] The worldview of revolutionary progressive millennialism involves a radical dualism, as does catastrophic millennialism.[18] Acting upon radical dualistic beliefs that divide humans into "us" versus dehumanized and demonized "them" causes suffering.

Millennial beliefs have great power to motivate people to take actions, sometimes violent actions, to create new societies and religions and to try to change the world. We need to evaluate critically the types of groups that we may join and the types of movements that we may support.

For those who think that the years 2000 and 2001 are significant dates, it is well to remember that these are just arbitrary dates. The Gregorian calendar did not accurately determine the years of Jesus's birth and death. Scholars believe that Jesus was born in 4 B.C. or earlier. If Jesus was born in 4 B.C., then 1996 was the year marking the 2,000th anniversary of his birth.

When tempted to attribute significance to the years 2000 or 2001, it is useful to remember that the Christian Gregorian calendar is not the only calendar in use.[19] There are Zoroastrian, Hebrew, Muslim, and Baha'i calendars. There are numerous Hindu and Buddhist calendars. The Egyptians, Mayans, Aztecs, Greeks, and Romans all had various calendars.[20]

The year 2000 is a very arbitrary date.

The Responsibility of the Media

As we approach New Year's Eve of 2000 and 2001, it will be wise not to become overly influenced by media hype. For instance, on New Year's Eve of 1997, the Learning Channel in the United States played a series all evening on "Ancient Prophecies," dramatizing frightening prophecies from various sources about the imminent end of the world.

The media play both sides of the game. The media contribute to public fears about the new millennium by airing shows on frightening prophecies that have no verifiable basis. The media also present sensationalized news coverage of millennial "cults" whose members commit drastic actions because they believe it is the endtime.[21]

We need to be critical media consumers.

Millennialism in the Next Millennium

Millennial expectations may be especially heightened through 2033, the 2,000th anniversary of the purported year of Jesus's death (see discussion in chapter 1), but millennial beliefs will always be present, because they address the human desire to overcome finitude. Therefore, it is important to understand the characteristics and the social dynamics that can cause millennial groups to become caught up in violence. Millennialism—either progressive millennialism or catastrophic millennialism—does not necessarily produce violence. Millennial groups, including those involved in violence, are not all the same. Those millennial groups that become involved in violence may be assaulted, fragile, or revolutionary. The quality of the interactions between millennialists and outsiders is a critical component in determining the potential for volatility. Extreme radical dualism—a heightened sense of good versus evil—can contribute to the conviction of believers that their group is being persecuted, and, thereby intensify the conflict between millennialists and cultural opponents. A crucial issue is whether or not the success of the millennial group's ultimate concern is threatened by stresses internal to the group combined with the group's experience of cultural opposition.

Millennialism will always exist because it addresses the perennial human hope to overcome finitude and achieve permanent well-being. Millennialism as a religious pattern offers this salvation to collectivities of people as opposed to individuals. In offering the hope of accomplishing an idealized millennial kingdom, millennial religions will always be in tension with the established social order. The unconventional lifestyle of millennial communities and the activities of their members will continue to attract the attention of concerned family members and citizens, news reporters, and law enforcement agents. It is essential that we learn the lessons of past cases of violence involving millennial groups to prevent tragedies from occurring in the future.

Notes

1. The Freemen threatened violence, and there was no violence involving Chen Tao.
2. Robert D. Baird, *Category Formation and the History of Religions* (The Hague: Mouton, 1971).
3. I thank Thomas Robbins, Eugene V. Gallagher, and Rebecca Moore for stressing this point to me in personal communications.
4. Eugene V. Gallagher, "'Theology is Life and Death': David Koresh on Violence, Persecution, and the Millennium," in *Millennialism, Persecution, and Violence: Historical Cases*, ed. Catherine Wessinger (Syracuse: Syracuse University Press, 2000), 82–100.
5. Reinterpretation, or rationalization, is the most common response to failed prophecy. In summarizing the current literature on the subject, Lorne L. Dawson states that there are at least four types of rationalization: spiritualization (the event occurred in a spiritual manner), (the failure was) a test of faith, the attribution of error to followers, and blaming others for the failure. It is likely that the rationalization will involve a blending of two or more of these approaches. Lorne L. Dawson, "When Prophecy Fails and Faith Persists: A Theoretical Overview," *Nova Religio: The Journal of Alternative and Emergent Religions* 3, no. 1 (October 1999):60-82.
6. The executive office of the American Academy of Religion is located in Atlanta. Its telephone number is 404-727-7920. The web page for the AAR is found at <http://www.aar-site.org/>.
   As of this writing in 1999, Dr. Marie Cornwall is the Executive Officer of the Society for the Scientific Study of Religion. Her telephone number is 801-378-3413. The web address for the Society for the Scientific Study of Religion is <http://fhss.byu.edu/soc/sssr/index.html>. Dr. Stuart Wright, Lamar University, Beaumont, Texas, is the press liaison for the Society for the Scientific Study of Religion. His office telephone number is 409-880-8547.
7. As a twelve-year-old boy, J. Krishnamurti was adopted by Annie Besant, the second president of the Theosophical Society, and was groomed by her to be the "World-Teacher." Besant built up an international organization around Krishnamurti, the Order of the Star in the East, that awaited the coming of the World-Teacher. In his late 20s, Krishnamurti began speaking as the World-Teacher, but in 1929 at age 33, Krishnamurti dissolved the Order of the Star and distanced

himself from the Theosophical Society, although he never denied being the World-Teacher. Krishnamurti continued his career as a public philosopher until his death. See Catherine Lowman Wessinger, *Annie Besant and Progressive Messianism* (Lewiston, N.Y.: Edwin Mellen Press, 1988).

8. See Grant Underwood, "Millennialism, Persecution, and Violence: The Mormons," in Wessinger, *Millennialism, Persecution, and Violence*, 43–61.

9. Ian Reader coined the phrase "the pragmatics of failure." See Catherine Wessinger, "The Interacting Dynamics of Millennial Beliefs, Persecution, and Violence," 3–39; Ian Reader, "Imagined Persecution: Aum Shinrikyo, Millennialism, and the Legitimation of Violence," 158–82; and Jacqueline Stone, "Japanese *Lotus* Millennialism: From Militant Japanese Nationalism to Contemporary Peace Movements," 261–80; all in Wessinger, *Millennialism, Persecution, and Violence*.

10. James T. Richardson and I have discussed the "myth of the omnipotent leader" in personal communications.

When Religious Studies scholars use the term *myth* to refer to a story about personal beings that conveys values important to a culture, we use the term in an objective manner that does not comment on the truth or falsity of the narrative. Here I am using the term in the popular sense of a belief that is untrue or misguided—a misconception.

11. Personal communication from James T. Richardson.

12. Jeffrey Kaplan, "Real Paranoids Have Real Enemies: The Genesis of the ZOG Discourse in the American National Socialist Subculture," in Wessinger, *Millennialism, Persecution, and Violence*, 299–322.

13. James T. Richardson, "Update on 'The Family': Organizational Change and Development in a Controversial New Religious Group," in *Sex, Slander, and Salvation: Investigating The Family/Children of God*, ed. James R. Lewis and J. Gordon Melton (Stanford, Calif.: Center for Academic Publications, 1994), 27-39; James T. Richardson, "The 'Deformation' of New Religions: Impacts of Societal and Organizational Factors," in *Cults, Culture, and the Law: Perspectives on New Religious Movements*, ed. Thomas Robbins, William C. Shepherd, and James McBride (Chico, Calif.: Scholars Press, 1985), 163-75.

14. The first characteristic was a very important factor in the peaceful resolution of the Montana Freemen standoff. I have observed 2, 3, and 4 in the Church Universal and Triumphant, which has its headquarters in Montana. The fourth characteristic was seen in the Branch Davidians.

15. I am grateful to Timothy Miller for making this observation to me in a personal communication.

16. For a description and discussion of apocalyptic fatalism as well as catastrophic and progressive millennialism, see Daniel Wojcik, *The End of the World As We Know It: Faith, Fatalism, and Apocalypse in America* (New York: New York University Press, 1997).

17. See Robert Ellwood, "Nazism as a Millennialist Movement," 241–60; Scott Lowe, "Western Millennial Ideology Goes East: The Taiping Revolution and Mao's Great Leap Forward," 220–40; and Richard C. Salter, "Time, Authority, and Ethics in the Khmer Rouge: Elements of the Millennial Vision in Year Zero," 281–98; all in Wessinger, *Millennialism, Persecution, and Violence*. See my introduction to this volume, "The Interacting Dynamics of Millennial Beliefs, Persecution, and Violence," 3–39, for a general discussion of revolutionary progressive millennialism.

18. The dominant emphasis of the progressive millennialism that I studied in the thought of Annie Besant was monistic—stressing oneness and interconnection—not dualism, although dualism was not absent in Besant's thought or in that of

her contemporaries in the Theosophical Society. See Wessinger, *Annie Besant and Progressive Messianism*. There need to be more scholarly studies of progressive millennialism.

19. The Julian calendar was the precursor of the Gregorian calendar, which was adopted in Roman Catholic countries beginning in 1582. The Julian calendar is still used by Eastern Orthodox Churches and is the calendar "used by scientists and historians for referring to dates prior to A.D. 1582." Margo Westrheim, *Calendars of the World: A Look at Calendars & the Ways We Celebrate* (Oxford: Oneworld Publications, 1993), 70.

20. See Westrheim, *Calendars of the World*.

21. In the United States, media coverage of millennial groups became noticeably more moderate and objective after the Waco fiasco, but it is still far from perfect.

Bibliography

Adas, Michael. 1979. *Prophets of Rebellion: Millenarian Protest Movements against the European Colonial Order*. Chapel Hill: University of North Carolina Press.

Aho, James A. 1990. *The Politics of Righteousness: Idaho Christian Patriotism*. Seattle: University of Washington Press.

Ammerman, Nancy T. 1995. "Waco, Federal Law Enforcement, and Scholars of Religion." In *Armageddon in Waco: Critical Perspectives on the Branch Davidian Conflict*, ed. Stuart A. Wright. Chicago: University of Chicago Press, 282-96.

Anonymous. 1995. "The Rose+Croix," *Gnosis Magazine* (Winter): 91.

Anonymous. 1995. "To All Those Who Can Still Understand the Voice of Wisdom... We Address This Last Message." *Gnosis Magazine* (Winter): 90.

Anonymous. 1995. "To Lovers of Justice." *Gnosis Magazine* (Winter): 93.

Anonymous. 1995. "Transit to the Future." *Gnosis Magazine* (Winter): 92.

Arnold, J. Phillip. 1994. "The Davidian Dilemma—To Obey God or Man?" In *From the Ashes: Making Sense of Waco*, ed. James R. Lewis. Lanham, Md.: Rowman & Littlefield, 23-31.

Baird, Robert D. 1971. *Category Formation and the History of Religions*. The Hague: Mouton.

Balch, Robert W. 1982. "Bo and Peep: A Case Study of the Origins of Messianic Leadership." In *Millennialism and Charisma*, ed. Roy Wallis. Belfast: The Queen's University, 13-72.

———. 1995. "Waiting for the Ships: Disillusionment and the Revitalization of Faith in Bo and Peep's UFO Cult." In *The Gods Have Landed: New Religions from Other Worlds*, ed. James R. Lewis. Albany: State University of New York Press, 137-66.

———. Forthcoming. "Heaven's Gate: Implications for the Study of Commitment to New Religions." In *The Gods Have Landed*, ed. James R. Lewis. 2d ed. Albany: State University of New York Press.

Barkun, Michael. 1997. *Religion and the Racist Right: The Origins of the Christian Identity Movement*. Rev. ed. Chapel Hill: University of North Carolina Press.

Bates, Albert. 1994. "What Happened at Waco?" *Natural Rights: News of the Natural Rights Center* 9, no.1 (Spring): 1-5, 8.

———.1994. "Waco: Trial By Fire." *Natural Rights: News of the Natural Rights Center* 9, no.3 (Fall): 1-7.

Blacker, Carmen. 1975. *The Catalpa Bow: A Study of Shamanistic Practices in Japan*. London: George Allen & Unwin Ltd.

Breault, Marc A. 1992. "Vernon Howell and the 1995 Deadline." <http://www.ime.net/~mswett>.

Breault, Marc, and Martin King. 1993. *Inside the Cult: A Member's Chilling, Exclusive Account of Madness and Depravity in David Koresh's Compound.* New York: Signet Books.

Bromley, David G., and Edward D. Silver. 1995. "The Davidian Tradition: From Patronal Clan to Prophetic Movement." In *Armageddon in Waco: Critical Perspectives on the Branch Davidian Conflict*, ed. Stuart A. Wright. Chicago: University of Chicago Press, 43-72.

Burghart, Devin, and Robert Crawford. 1996. *Guns & Gavels: Common Law Courts, Militias & White Supremacy.* Portland, Ore.: Coalition for Human Dignity.

Buruma, Ian. 1995. "Lost Without a Faith: In the Spiritual Vacuum of the Postwar Years, Some Japanese Seek New Gods." *Time* 145, no.14 (April 3): 34.

Carroll, Gerald A. 1997. "Cease Fire Will Allow Chance to Argue Texas Sovereignty." Media Bypass Magazine (June). <http://www.4bypass.com>.

Carstarphen, Nike. 1995. "Third Party Efforts at Waco: Phillip Arnold and James Tabor." Unpublished paper. Institute for Conflict Analysis and Resolution, George Mason University.

CESNUR. 1998. "Apocalypse Delayed: Group Leaves Texas and Relocates in Olcott, New York." CESNUR's Watch Page of Chen Tao, <http://www.cesnur.org/Chen.htm>, downloaded on May 9.

Chidester, David. 1991. *Salvation and Suicide: An Interpretation of Jim Jones, the Peoples Temple, and Jonestown.* Bloomington: Indiana University Press.

"Cults: The Spaceship Suicide." 1997. *Hinduism Today* (July): 22-25.

Daniel, David. 1997. "The Beginning of the Journey." *Newsweek* (April 14): 36-37.

Dawson, Lorne L. 1999. "When Prophecy Fails and Faith Persists: A Theoretical Overview." *Nova Religio: The Journal of Alternative and Emergent Religions* 3, no. 1 (October): 60-82.

de Armond, Paul. 1996. "Christian Patriots at War with the State." <http://www.nwcitizen.com/publicgood>.

Docherty, Jayne Seminare. 1998. "When the Parties Bring Their Gods to the Table: Learning Lessons from Waco." Ph.D. diss., George Mason University.

Dyer, Joel. 1997. *Harvest of Rage: Why Oklahoma City Is Only the Beginning.* Boulder, Colo.: Westview Press.

Ellison, Christopher G., and John P. Bartkowski. 1995. "'Babies Were Being Beaten': Exploring Child Abuse Allegations at Ranch Apocalypse." In *Armageddon in Waco: Critical Perspectives on the Branch Davidian Conflict*, ed. Stuart A. Wright. Chicago: University of Chicago Press, 111-49.

Ellwood, Robert. 2000. "Nazism as a Millennialist Movement." In *Millennialism, Persecution, and Violence: Historical Cases*, ed. Catherine Wessinger. Syracuse: Syracuse University Press, 241-60.

Gallagher, Eugene V. 1997. "God and Country: Revolution as a Religious Imperative on the Radical Right." *Terrorism and Political Violence* 9, no.3 (Autumn): 63-79.

———. 2000. "'Theology is Life and Death': David Koresh on Violence, Persecution, and the Millennium." In *Millennialism, Persecution, and Violence: Historical Cases*, ed. Catherine Wessinger. Syracuse: Syracuse University Press, 82-100.

Gardner, Richard. 1997. "Aum Shinrikyo's Use of Animated Scriptures and a Panic about Popular Culture." Paper presented at the American Academy of Religion meeting in San Francisco, November 18.

God—The Supreme Being. 1997. *God's Descending in Clouds (Flying Saucers) on Earth to Save People.* Garland, Tex.: Kingdom of God.

Goodman, David G., and Masanori Miyaza. 1995. *Jews in the Japanese Mind: The History and Uses of a Cultural Stereotype.* New York: The Free Press.

Hall, John R. 1987. *Gone From the Promised Land: Jonestown in American Cultural History.* New Brunswick, N.J.: Transaction Books.

— — —. 1995. "Public Narratives and the Apocalyptic Sect: From Jonestown to Mt. Carmel." In *Armageddon in Waco: Critical Perspectives on the Branch Davidian Conflict*, ed. Stuart A. Wright. Chicago: University of Chicago Press, 205-35.

Hall, John R., and Philip Schuyler. 1997. "The Mystical Apocalypse of the Solar Temple." In *Millennium, Messiahs, and Mayhem: Contemporary Apocalyptic Movements*, ed. Thomas Robbins and Susan J. Palmer. New York: Routledge, 285-311.

Hardacre, Helen. 1995. "Aum Shinrikyo and the Japanese Media: The Pied Piper Meets the Lamb of God." Columbia University, East Asian Institute.

Hirsh, Michael, and Hideko Takayama. 1997. "Big Bang or Bust? Mobsters slow Tokyo's plan to join world markets." *Newsweek* (September 1): 44-45.

Homer, Michael W. 1996. "Violence in Nineteenth-Century New Religion: The Mormon Case." Paper presented at the Society for the Scientific Study of Religion in Nashville, November 10.

House of Representatives. 1996. *Investigation into the Activities of Federal Law Enforcement Agencies toward the Branch Davidians: Thirteenth Report by the Committee on Government Reform and Oversight Prepared in Conjunction with the Committee on the Judiciary together with Additional and Dissenting Views*. Report 104-749. Washington, D.C.: U.S. Government Printing Office.

Introvigne, Massimo. 1995. "Ordeal by Fire: The Tragedy of the Solar Temple." *Religion* 25: 267-83.

— — —. 2000. "The Magic of Death: The Suicides of the Solar Temple." In *Millennialism, Persecution, and Violence: Historical Cases*, ed. Catherine Wessinger. Syracuse: Syracuse University Press, 138-57.

Irish, Mike, ed. N.d. *Heroes of the Heartland*. Boca Raton, Fla.: Globe International, Inc.

Kahalas, Laurie Efrein. 1998. *Snake Dance: Unravelling the Mysteries of Jonestown*. New York: Red Robin Press.

Kaplan, David E., and Andrew Marshall. 1996. *The Cult at the End of the World: The Terrifying Story of the Aum Doomsday Cult, from the Subways of Tokyo to the Nuclear Arsenals of Russia*. New York: Crown Publishers.

Kaplan, Jeffrey. 1997. *Radical Religion in America: Millenarian Movements from the Far Right to the Children of Noah*. Syracuse: Syracuse University Press.

— — —. 2000. "Real Paranoids Have Real Enemies: The Genesis of the ZOG Discourse in the American National Socialist Subculture." In *Millennialism, Persecution, and Violence: Historical Cases*, ed. Catherine Wessinger. Syracuse: Syracuse University Press, 299-322.

Kisala, Robert. 1997. "1999 and Beyond: Use of the Nostradamus Prophecies by Japanese Religions." Paper presented at the Society for the Scientific Study of Religion meeting in San Diego, November 8.

— — —. 1998. "The AUM Spiritual Truth Church in Japan." In *Wolves Within the Fold: Religious Leadership and Abuses of Power*, ed. Anson Shupe. New Brunswick, N.J.: Rutgers University Press, 33-48.

Lacayo, Richard. 1996. "State of Siege." *Time* (April 8): 25.

Lamy, Philip. 1997. "Secularizing the Millennium: Survivalists, Militias, and the New World Order." In *Millennium, Messiahs, and Mayhem: Contemporary Apocalyptic Movements*, ed. Thomas Robbins and Susan J. Palmer. New York: Routledge, 93-117.

Lanternari, Vittorio. 1963. *The Religions of the Oppressed: A Study of Modern Messianic Cults*, trans. Lisa Sergio. New York: Alfred A. Knopf.

Lehman, Edward C., Jr. 1994. "Letter from Edward C. Lehman, Jr., to Janet Reno." In *From the Ashes: Making Sense of Waco*, ed. James R. Lewis. Lanham, Md.: Rowman & Littlefield, 247-50.

Lewis, James R., ed. 1994. *From the Ashes: Making Sense of Waco*. Lanham, Md.: Rowman & Littlefield.

Lilliston, Larry. 1994. "Who Committed Child Abuse at Waco?" In *From the Ashes: Making Sense of Waco*, ed. James R. Lewis. Lanham, Md.: Rowman & Littlefield, 169-73.

Lowe, Scott. 2000. "Western Millennial Ideology Goes East: The Taiping Revolution and Mao's Great Leap Forward." In *Millennialism, Persecution, and Violence: Historical Cases*, ed. Catherine Wessinger. Syracuse: Syracuse University Press, 220-40.

Lucas, Phillip. 1994. "How Future Wacos Might Be Avoided: Two Proposals." In *From the Ashes: Making Sense of Waco*, ed. James R. Lewis. Lanham, Md.: Rowman & Littlefield, 209-12.

Maaga, Mary McCormick. 1996. "Triple Erasure: Women and Power in Peoples Temple." Ph.D. diss., Drew University.

— — —. 1998. *Hearing the Voices of Jonestown: Putting a Human Face on an American Tragedy*. Syracuse: Syracuse University Press.

Macdonald, Andrew [William Pierce]. 1980. *The Turner Diaries*. 2d ed. Hillsboro, W.Va.: National Vanguard Books.

Matory, J. Lorand. 1994. *Sex and the Empire That Is No More: Gender and the Politics of Metaphor in Oyo Yoruba Religion*. Minneapolis: University of Minnesota Press.

Mayer, Jean-François. 1996. "Myths of the Solar Temple," transl. Elijah Siegler. Paper presented to the ISAR/CESNUR Symposium on "Violence and the New Religions," Nashville, Tenn., March 10.

Minges, Patrick. 1995. "Apocalypse Now! The Realized Eschatology of the 'Christian Identity' Movement." *Union Seminary Quarterly Review* 49, nos. 1–2: 83-107.

Moore, Carol. 1995. *The Davidian Massacre: Disturbing Questions about Waco Which Must Be Answered*. Franklin, Tenn., and Springfield, Va.: Legacy Communications and Gun Owners Foundation.

Moore, James. 1997. *Very Special Agents: The Inside Story of America's Most Controversial Law Enforcement Agency—The Bureau of Alcohol, Tobacco, and Firearms*. New York: Pocket Books.

Moore, Rebecca. 1985. *A Sympathetic History of Jonestown: The Moore Family Involvement in Peoples Temple*. Lewiston, N.Y.: Edwin Mellen Press.

— — —. 1986. *The Jonestown Letters: Correspondence of the Moore Family 1970-1985*. Lewiston, N.Y.: Edwin Mellen Press.

— — —. 1988. *In Defense of Peoples Temple—And Other Essays*. Lewiston, N.Y.: Edwin Mellen Press.

— — —. 2000. "'American as Cherry Pie': Peoples Temple and Violence in America." In *Millennialism, Persecution, and Violence: Historical Cases*, ed. Catherine Wessinger. Syracuse: Syracuse University Press, 121-37.

Morganthau, Tom, Michael Isikoff, and Bob Cohn. 1995. "The Echoes of Ruby Ridge." *Newsweek* (August 28): 25-28.

Mullins, Mark R. 1997. "Aum Shinrikyo as an Apocalyptic Movement." In *Millennium, Messiahs, and Mayhem: Contemporary Apocalyptic Movements*, ed. Thomas Robbins and Susan J. Palmer. New York: Routledge, 313-24.

"'The Next Level.'" 1997. *Newsweek* (April 7): 28-35.

Olds, Linda E. 1981. *Fully Human: How Everyone Can Integrate the Benefits of Masculine and Feminine Sex Roles*. Englewood Cliffs, N.J.: Prentice-Hall.

Palmer, Susan J. 1996. "Purity and Danger in the Solar Temple." *Journal of Contemporary Religion* 11, no.3 (October): 303-18.

Payne, Neill H. 1996. "Shades of Waco: CAUSE Negotiates Peaceful End to Siege of Justus Township Standoff." *The Balance: A Newsletter of Civil Rights and Current Events* 7, no.2 (Summer): 1-3.

— — —. 1996. "To Our Readers." *The Balance: A Newsletter of Civil Rights and Current Events* 7, no.2 (Summer): 4.

Pesantubbee, Michelene E. 2000. "From Vision to Violence: The Wounded Knee Massacre," in *Millennialism, Persecution, and Violence: Historical Cases*, ed. Catherine Wessinger. Syracuse: Syracuse University Press, 62-81.

Pitcavage, Mark. 1996. "Every Man a King: The Rise and Fall of the Montana Freemen." Last modified May 6. <http://www.greyware.com/authors/pitman/freemen>

Pitts, William L., Jr. 1995. "Davidians and Branch Davidians, 1929-1987." In *Armageddon in Waco: Critical Perspectives on the Branch Davidian Conflict*, ed. Stuart A. Wright. Chicago: University of Chicago Press, 20-42.

Reader, Ian. 1996. *A Poisonous Cocktail? Aum Shinrikyo's Path to Violence*. Copenhagen: Nordic Institute of Asian Studies Books.

———. 2000. "Imagined Persecution: Aum Shinrikyo, Millennialism, and the Legitimation of Violence." In *Millennialism, Persecution, and Violence: Historical Cases*, ed. Catherine Wessinger. Syracuse: Syracuse University Press, 158-82.

Reavis, Dick J. 1995. *The Ashes of Waco: An Investigation*. New York: Simon & Schuster.

Representatives from the Kingdom of Heaven. 1996. *How and When "Heaven's Gate" (The Door to the Physical Kingdom Level Above Human) May Be Entered*. New Mexico Republic, the united States of America: Heaven's Gate Representatives, Common Law Copyright.

Richardson, James T. 1985. "The 'Deformation' of New Religions: Impacts of Societal and Organizational Factors." In *Cults, Culture, and the Law: Perspectives on New Religious Movements*, ed. Thomas Robbins, William C. Shepherd, and James McBride. Chico, Calif.: Scholars Press, 163-75.

———. 1994. "Update on 'The Family': Organizational Change and Development in a Controversial New Religious Group." In *Sex, Slander, and Salvation: Investigating The Family/Children of God*, ed. James R. Lewis and J. Gordon Melton. Stanford, Calif.: Center for Academic Publications, 27-39.

———. 1995. "Manufacturing Consent about Koresh: A Structural Analysis of the Role of Media in the Waco Tragedy." In *Armageddon in Waco: Critical Perspectives on the Branch Davidian Conflict*, ed. Stuart A. Wright. Chicago: University of Chicago Press, 153-76.

Robbins, Thomas, and Dick Anthony. 1995. "Sects and Violence: Factors Enhancing the Volatility of Marginal Religious Movements." In *Armageddon in Waco: Critical Perspectives on the Branch Davidian Conflict*, ed. Stuart A. Wright. Chicago: University of Chicago Press, 236-59.

Robbins, Thomas, and Susan J. Palmer, eds. 1997. *Millennium, Messiahs, and Mayhem: Contemporary Apocalyptic Movements*. New York: Routledge.

Rosenfeld, Jean E. 1995. "Pai Marire: Peace and Violence in a New Zealand Millenarian Tradition." *Terrorism and Political Violence* (Special Issue on Millennialism and Violence, ed. Michael Barkun) 7, no.3 (Autumn): 83-108.

———. 1997. "The Importance of the Analysis of Religion in Avoiding Violent Outcomes: The Justus Freemen Crisis." *Nova Religio: The Journal of Alternative and Emergent Religions* 1, no.1 (October): 72-95.

———. 2000. "The Justus Freemen Standoff: The Importance of the Analysis of Religion in Avoiding Violent Outcomes." In *Millennialism, Persecution, and Violence: Historical Cases*, ed. Catherine Wessinger. Syracuse: Syracuse University Press, 323-44.

Salter, Richard C. 2000. "Time, Authority, and Ethics in the Khmer Rouge: Elements of the Millennial Vision in Year Zero." In *Millennialism, Persecution, and Violence: Historical Cases*, ed. Catherine Wessinger. Syracuse: Syracuse University Press, 281-98.

Sapp, Allen D. 1996. "Ideological Justification for Right Wing Extremism: An Analysis of the Nehemiah Township Charter Document." Unpublished paper. Center for Criminal Justice Research, Central Missouri State University.

Sayle, Murray. 1996. "Nerve Gas and the Four Noble Truths." *New Yorker* 72, no.6 (April 1): 56-71.

Shannan, J. Patrick. N.d. *The Montana Freemen: The Untold Story of Government Suppression and the News Media Cover-Up*. Jackson, Miss.: Center for Historical Analysis.

Shields, Steven L. 1991. "The Latter Day Saint Movement: A Study in Survival. " In *When Prophets Die: The Postcharismatic Fate of New Religious Movements*, ed. Timothy Miller. Albany: State University of New York Press, 59-77.

Shimazono, Susumu. 1995. "In the Wake of Aum: The Formation and Transformation of a Universe of Belief." *Japanese Journal of Religious Studies* 22, nos.3-4: 381-415.

Shupe, Anson, and Jeffrey K. Hadden. 1995. "Cops, News Copy, and Public Opinion: Legitimacy and the Social Construction of Evil in Waco." In *Armageddon in Waco: Critical Perspectives on the Branch Davidian Conflict*, ed. Stuart A. Wright. Chicago: University of Chicago Press, 177-202.

Sogyal Rinpoche. 1993. *The Tibetan Book of Living and Dying*, ed. Patrick Gaffney and Andrew Harvey. San Francisco: HarperSanFrancisco.

Spence, Gerry. 1993. *From Freedom to Slavery: The Rebirth of Tyranny in America*. New York: St. Martin's Press.

Steyn, Christine. 2000. "Millenarian Tragedies in South Africa: The Xhosa Cattle-Killing Movement and the Bulhoek Massacre." In *Millennialism, Persecution, and Violence: Historical Cases*, ed. Catherine Wessinger. Syracuse: Syracuse University Press, 185-202.

Stone, Jacqueline. 2000. "Japanese *Lotus* Millennialism: From Militant Japanese Nationalism to Contemporary Peace Movements." In *Millennialism, Persecution, and Violence: Historical Cases*, ed. Catherine Wessinger. Syracuse: Syracuse University Press, 261-80.

Tabor, James D. 1994. "The Waco Tragedy: An Autobiographical Account of One Attempt to Prevent Disaster." In *From the Ashes: Making Sense of Waco*, ed. James R. Lewis. Lanham, Md.: Rowman & Littlefield, 13-21.

―――. 1995. "The Events at Waco: An Interpretive Log." <http://home. maine.rr.com/waco/ww.html>.

―――. 1995. "Religious Discourse and Failed Negotiations: The Dynamics of Biblical Apocalypticism in Waco." In *Armageddon in Waco: Critical Perspectives on the Branch Davidian Conflict*, ed. Stuart A. Wright. Chicago: University of Chicago Press, 263-81.

Tabor, James D., and Eugene V. Gallagher. 1995. *Why Waco? Cults and the Battle for Religious Freedom in America*. Berkeley: University of California Press.

Thursby, Gene R. 1991. "Siddha Yoga: Swami Muktananda and the Seat of Power." In *When Prophets Die: The Postcharismatic Fate of New Religious Movements*, ed. Timothy Miller. Albany: State University of New York Press, 165-81, 232-38.

―――. 1995. "Hindu Movements Since Mid-Century: Yogis in the States." In *America's Alternative Religions*, ed. Timothy Miller. Albany: State University of New York Press, 191-213.

Underwood, Grant, 2000. "Millennialism, Persecution, and Violence: The Mormons." In *Millennialism, Persecution, and Violence: Historical Cases*, ed. Catherine Wessinger. Syracuse: Syracuse University Press, 43-61.

Walter, Jess. 1995. "'Every Knee Shall Bow': Exclusive Book Excerpt." *Newsweek* (August 28): 29-33.

―――. 1995. *Every Knee Shall Bow: The Truth and Tragedy of Ruby Ridge and the Randy Weaver Family*. New York: Harper Paperbacks.

Watanabe, Manabu. 1997. "A License to Kill: Aum Shinrikyo's Idea of Buddhist Salvation." Paper presented at the Society for the Scientific Study of Religion meeting, San Diego, November 8.

Wessinger, Catherine Lowman. 1988. *Annie Besant and Progressive Messianism*. Lewiston, N.Y.: Edwin Mellen Press.

Wessinger, Catherine. 1991. "Democracy vs. Hierarchy: The Evolution of Authority in the Theosophical Society." In *When Prophets Die: The Postcharismatic Fate of New Religious Movements*, ed. Timothy Miller. Albany: State University of New York Press, 93-106.

———. 1993. "Woman Guru, Woman Roshi: The Legitimation of Female Religious Leadership in Hindu and Buddhist Groups in America." In *Women's Leadership in Marginal Religions: Explorations Outside the Mainstream*, ed. Catherine Wessinger. Urbana: University of Illinois Press, 125-46.

———. 1997. "Review Essay: Understanding the Branch Davidian Tragedy." *Nova Religio: The Journal of Alternative and Emergent Religions* 1, no.1 (October): 122-38.

———. 1997. "Millennialism With and Without the Mayhem: Catastrophic and Progressive Expectations." In *Millennium, Messiahs, and Mayhem: Contemporary Apocalyptic Movements*, ed. Thomas Robbins and Susan J. Palmer. New York: Routledge, 47-59.

———. 1999. "Religious Studies Scholars, FBI Agents, and the Montana Freeman Standoff," *Nova Religio: The Journal of Alternative and Emergent Religions* 3, no. 1 (October): 36-44.

———, ed. 2000. *Millennialism, Persecution, and Violence: Historical Cases*, Syracuse: Syracuse University Press.

———. 2000. "The Interacting Dynamics of Millennial Beliefs, Persecution, and Violence." In *Millennialism, Persecution, and Violence: Historical Cases*, ed. Catherine Wessinger. Syracuse: Syracuse University Press.

Wojcik, Daniel. 1997. *The End of the World As We Know It: Faith, Fatalism, and Apocalypse in America*. New York: New York University Press.

Wright, Lawrence. 1993. "Orphans of Jonestown." *New Yorker* (November 22): 66-89.

Wright, Stuart A., ed. 1995. *Armageddon in Waco: Critical Perspectives on the Branch Davidian Conflict*. Chicago: University of Chicago Press.

———. 1995. "Introduction: Another View of the Mt. Carmel Standoff." In *Armageddon in Waco: Critical Perspectives on the Branch Davidian Conflict*, ed. Stuart A. Wright. Chicago: University of Chicago Press, xiii-xxvi.

———. 1995. "Construction and Escalation of a Cult Threat." In *Armageddon in Waco: Critical Perspectives on the Branch Davidian Conflict*, ed. Stuart A. Wright. Chicago: University of Chicago Press, 75-94.

Van Biema, David. 1995. "Prophet of Poison." *Time* 145, no.14 (April 3): 32.

Wallace, Anthony F. C. 1956. "Revitalization Movements," *American Anthropologist* 58, no.2 (April): 264-81.

Westrheim, Margo. 1993. *Calendars of the World: A Look at Calendars & the Ways We Celebrate*. Oxford: Oneworld Publications.

Young, Richard. 1995. "Lethal Achievements: Fragments of a Response to the Aum Shinrikyo Affair." *Japanese Religions* 20, no.2: 230-45.

Zablocki, Benjamin. 1997. "The Blacklisting of a Concept: The Strange History of the Brainwashing Conjecture in the Sociology of Religion." *Nova Religio: The Journal of Alternative and Emergent Religions* 1, no.1 (October): 96-121.

VIDEO

Gifford, Dan, William Gazecki, and Michael McNulty, producers. 1997. "Waco: The Rules of Engagement." Los Angeles: Fifth Estate Productions.

AUDIOTAPES

Koresh, David. "The Last Recorded Words of David Koresh, April 16-18, 1993," narrated by James Tabor.

Tabor, James, and J. Phillip Arnold. Discussion of the Bible on the Ron Engleman radio talk show station KGBS, April 1, 1993.

WORLD WIDE WEB

Alternative Considerations of Jonestown and Peoples Temple.
<http://www.und.nodak.edu/dept/philrel/jonestown/>

American Academy of Religion. <http://www.aar-site.org/>
CESNUR: Center for Studies of New Religions. <http://www.cesnur.org/>
Media Bypass. <http://www.4bypass.com>
New Religious Movements, Sociology 257. <http://cti.itc.virginia.edu/~jkh8x/soc257/>
Nova Religio: The Journal of Alternative and Emergent Religions.
    <http://www.novareligio.com/>
Public Good Project. <http://www.nwcitizen.com/publicgood>
Religion Religions Religious Studies. <http://www.clas.ufl.edu/users/gthursby/rel/>
Society for the Scientific Study of Religion. <http://fhss.byu.edu/soc/sssr/index.html>
Waco Never Again! The Research Center. <http://home.maine.rr.com/waco/>
Why Waco? Cults and the Battle for Religious Freedom in America by James Tabor
    and Eugene Gallagher. <http://home.maine.rr.com/waco/ww.html>

DEFUNCT WEB PAGES CITED
<http://www.alaska.net/~winter/Jefferson/>
<http://www.greyware.com/authors/pitman/freemen>
<http://www.heavensgate.com/> For mirror sites, see New Religious Movements,
    Sociology 257; and Religion Religions Religious Studies; addresses given above.
<http://www.ime.net/~mswett/>. Moved to Waco Never Again! The Research Cen-
    ter. See above for new address.
<http://www.neo.com/UCalPress/WhyWaco/>. Moved to Why Waco? See above for
    new address.
<http://www.republic.net/rot/>

Index